WELCOME TO THE BALLROOM

no.11 | TOMO TAKEUCHI

Contents

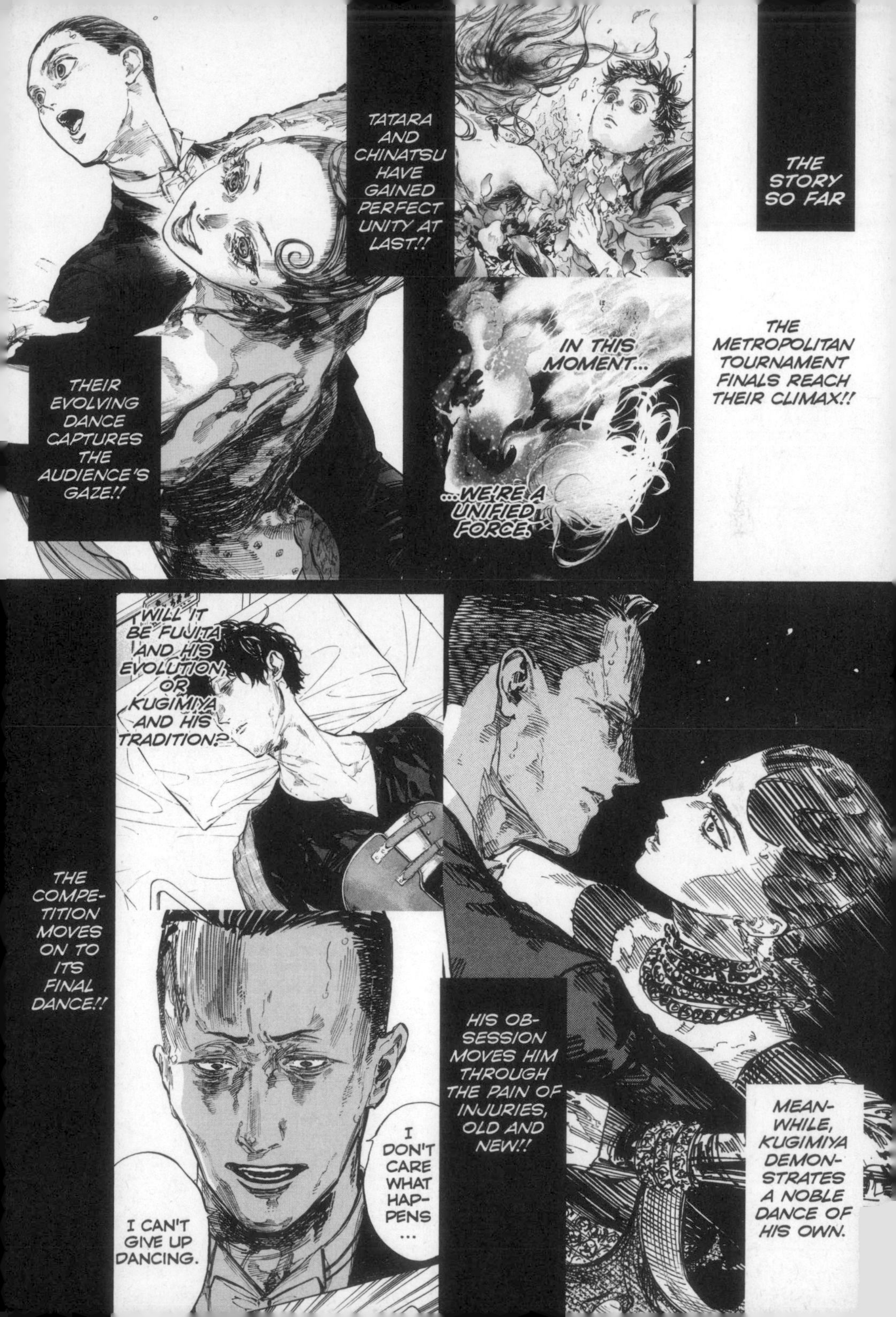
THE STORY SO FAR
THE METROPOLITAN TOURNAMENT FINALS REACH THEIR CLIMAX!!
TATARA AND CHINATSU HAVE GAINED PERFECT UNITY AT LAST!!
IN THIS MOMENT...
...WE'RE A UNIFIED FORCE.
THEIR EVOLVING DANCE CAPTURES THE AUDIENCE'S GAZE!!
MEAN-WHILE, KUGIMIYA DEMON-STRATES A NOBLE DANCE OF HIS OWN.
HIS OB-SESSION MOVES HIM THROUGH THE PAIN OF INJURIES, OLD AND NEW!!
WILL IT BE FUJITA AND HIS EVOLUTION, OR KUGIMIYA AND HIS TRADITION?
I DON'T CARE WHAT HAP-PENS ...
I CAN'T GIVE UP DANCING.
THE COMPE-TITION MOVES ON TO ITS FINAL DANCE!!

WELCOME TO THE BALLROOM

Heat 49: The Judges

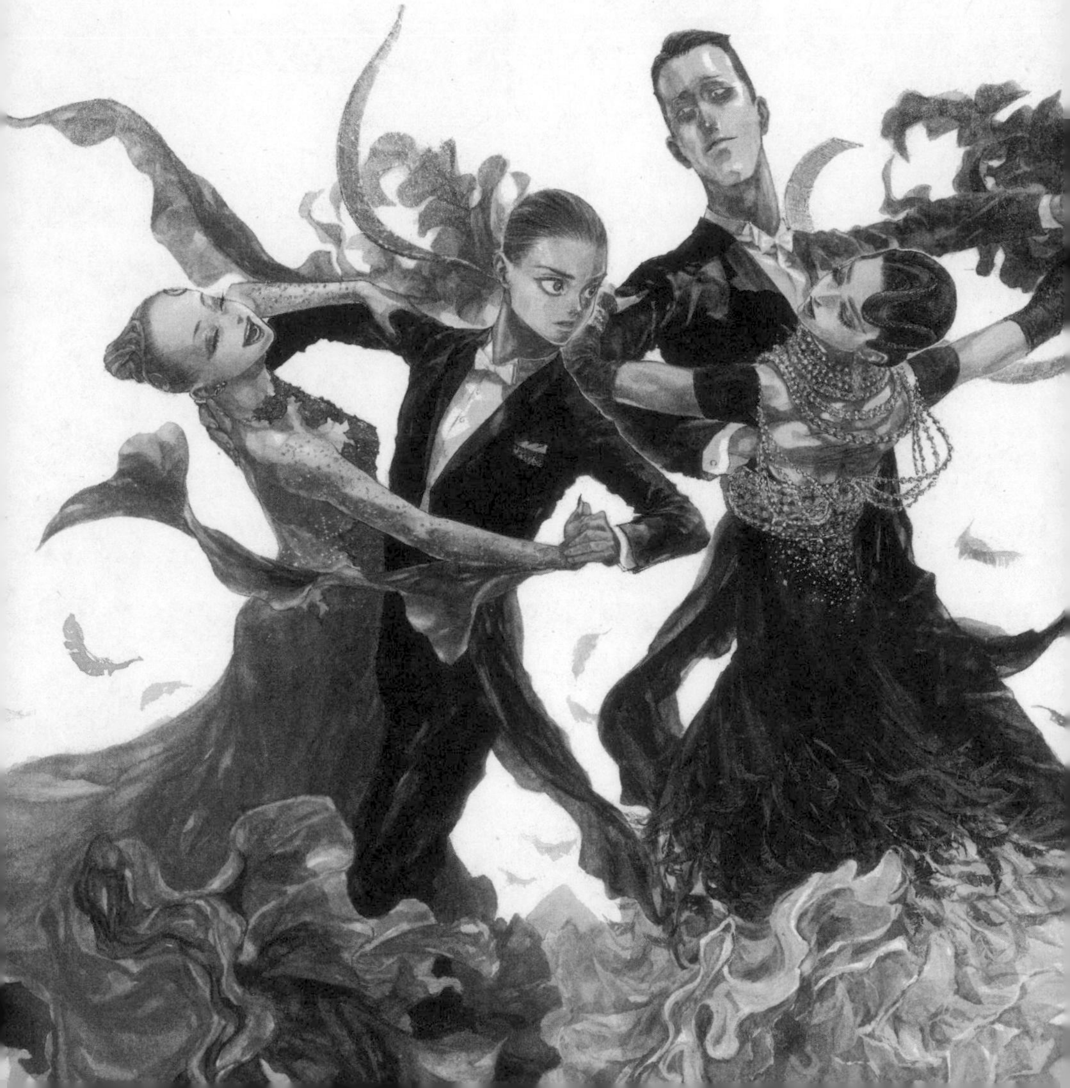

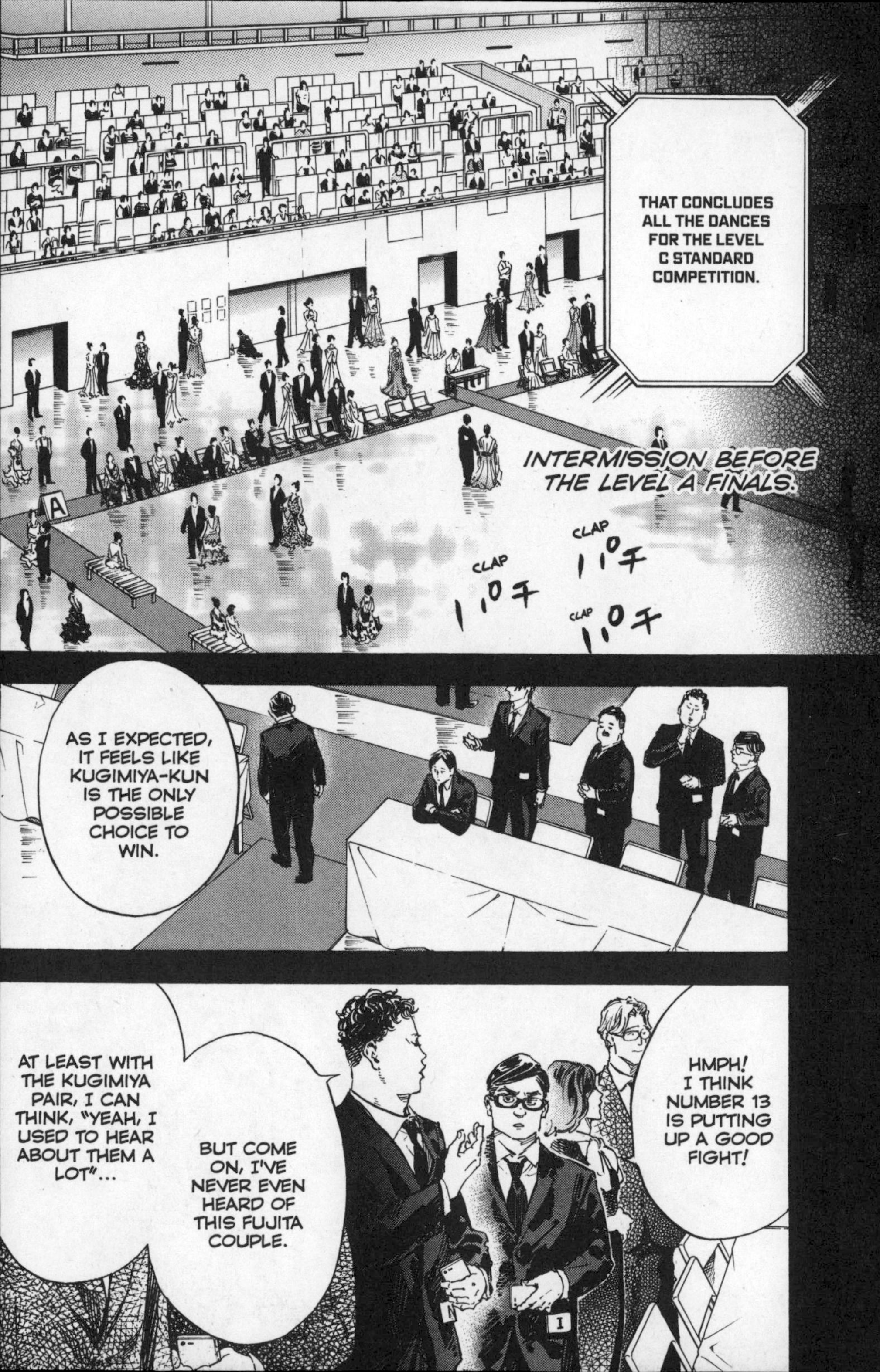
THAT CONCLUDES ALL THE DANCES FOR THE LEVEL C STANDARD COMPETITION.
INTERMISSION BEFORE THE LEVEL A FINALS.
CLAP
CLAP
CLAP
AS I EXPECTED, IT FEELS LIKE KUGIMIYA-KUN IS THE ONLY POSSIBLE CHOICE TO WIN.
HMPH! I THINK NUMBER 13 IS PUTTING UP A GOOD FIGHT!
AT LEAST WITH THE KUGIMIYA PAIR, I CAN THINK, "YEAH, I USED TO HEAR ABOUT THEM A LOT"...
BUT COME ON, I'VE NEVER EVEN HEARD OF THIS FUJITA COUPLE.

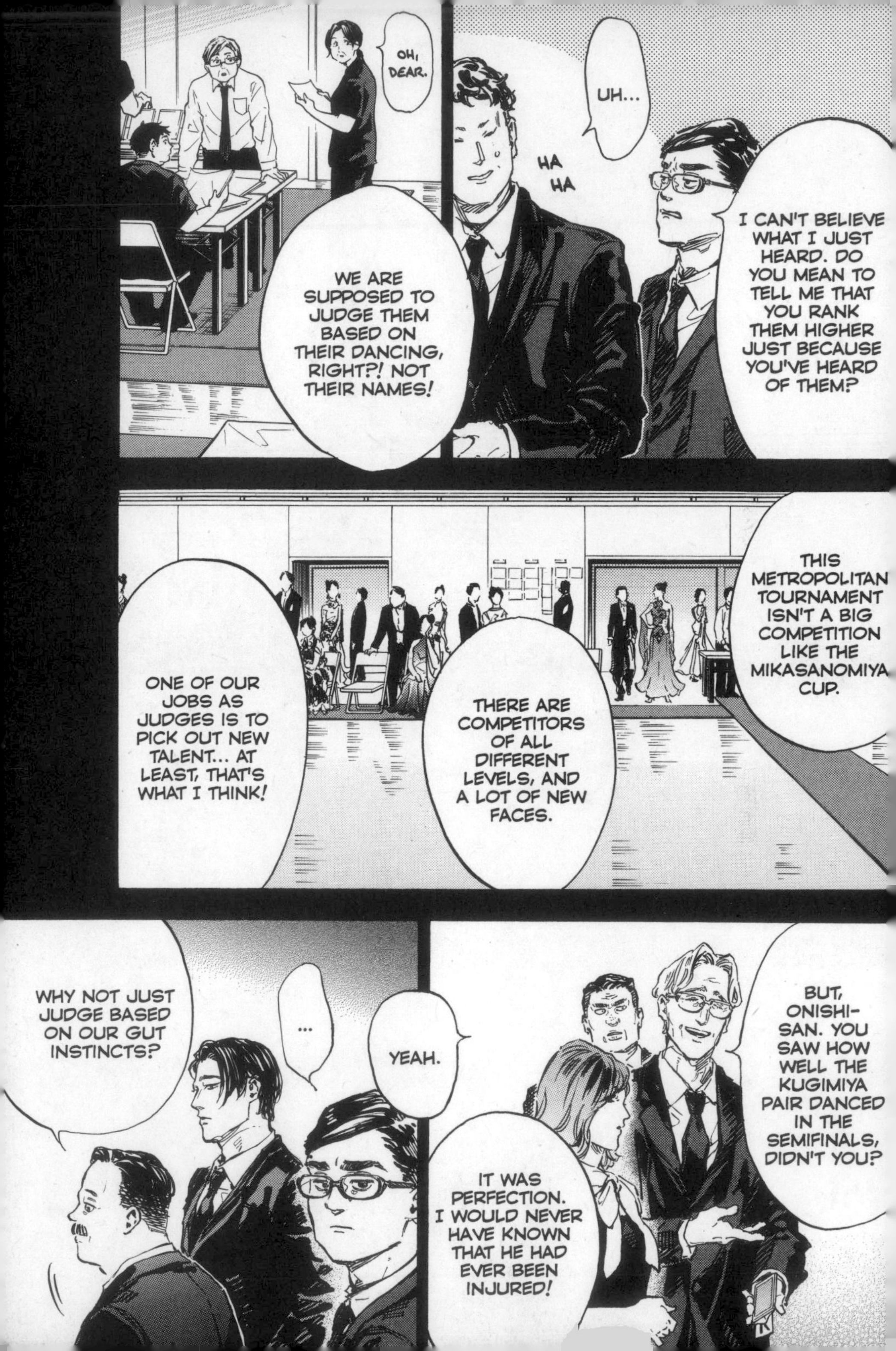
UH...
HA HA
I CAN'T BELIEVE WHAT I JUST HEARD. DO YOU MEAN TO TELL ME THAT YOU RANK THEM HIGHER JUST BECAUSE YOU'VE HEARD OF THEM?
WE ARE SUPPOSED TO JUDGE THEM BASED ON THEIR DANCING, RIGHT?! NOT THEIR NAMES!
OH, DEAR.
THIS METROPOLITAN TOURNAMENT ISN'T A BIG COMPETITION LIKE THE MIKASANOMIYA CUP.
THERE ARE COMPETITORS OF ALL DIFFERENT LEVELS, AND A LOT OF NEW FACES.
ONE OF OUR JOBS AS JUDGES IS TO PICK OUT NEW TALENT... AT LEAST, THAT'S WHAT I THINK!
BUT, ONISHI-SAN. YOU SAW HOW WELL THE KUGIMIYA PAIR DANCED IN THE SEMIFINALS, DIDN'T YOU?
IT WAS PERFECTION. I WOULD NEVER HAVE KNOWN THAT HE HAD EVER BEEN INJURED!
YEAH.
...
WHY NOT JUST JUDGE BASED ON OUR GUT INSTINCTS?

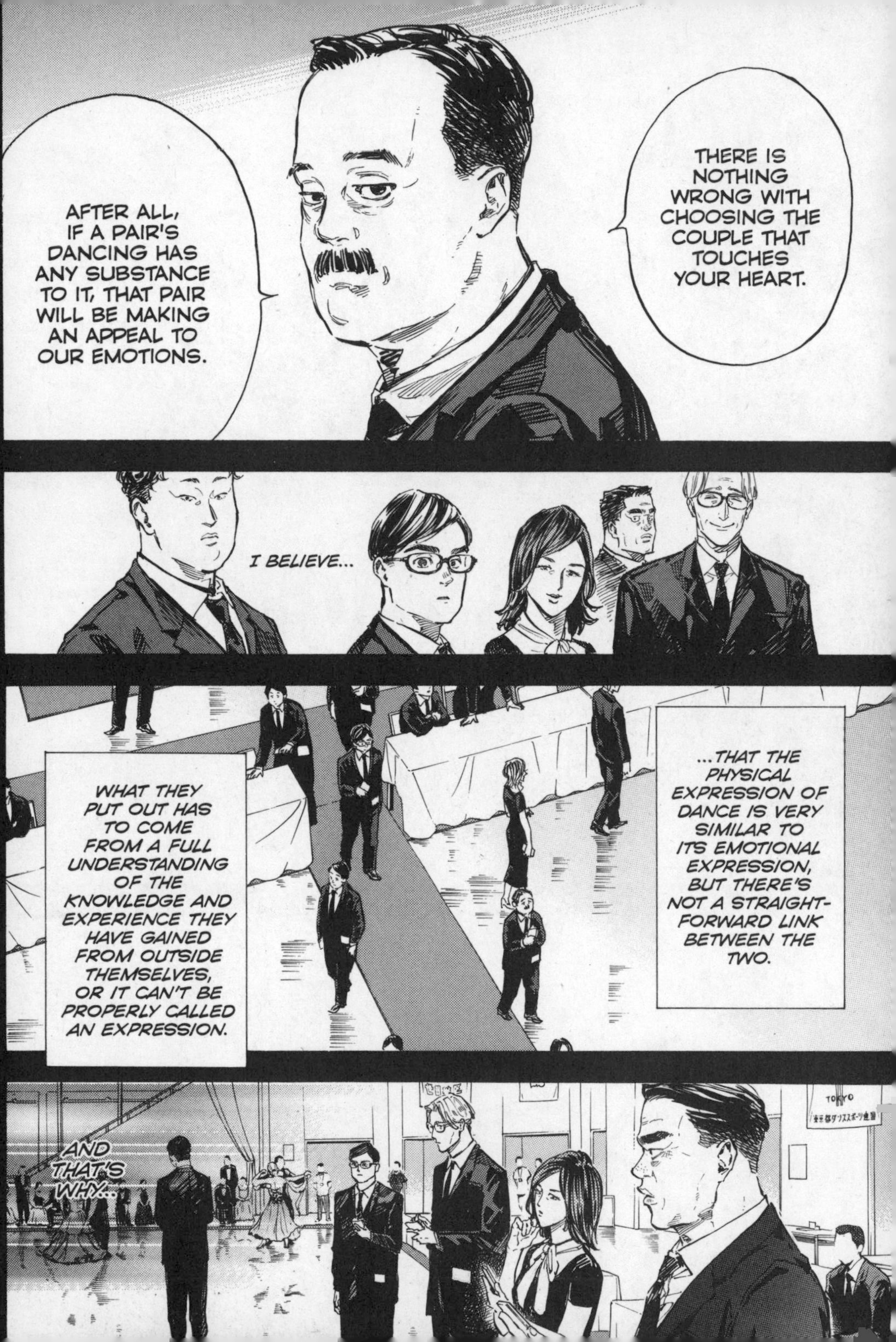
THERE IS NOTHING WRONG WITH CHOOSING THE COUPLE THAT TOUCHES YOUR HEART.
AFTER ALL, IF A PAIR'S DANCING HAS ANY SUBSTANCE TO IT, THAT PAIR WILL BE MAKING AN APPEAL TO OUR EMOTIONS.
I BELIEVE...
...THAT THE PHYSICAL EXPRESSION OF DANCE IS VERY SIMILAR TO ITS EMOTIONAL EXPRESSION, BUT THERE'S NOT A STRAIGHT-FORWARD LINK BETWEEN THE TWO.
WHAT THEY PUT OUT HAS TO COME FROM A FULL UNDERSTANDING OF THE KNOWLEDGE AND EXPERIENCE THEY HAVE GAINED FROM OUTSIDE THEMSELVES, OR IT CAN'T BE PROPERLY CALLED AN EXPRESSION.
TOKYO
AND THAT'S WHY...

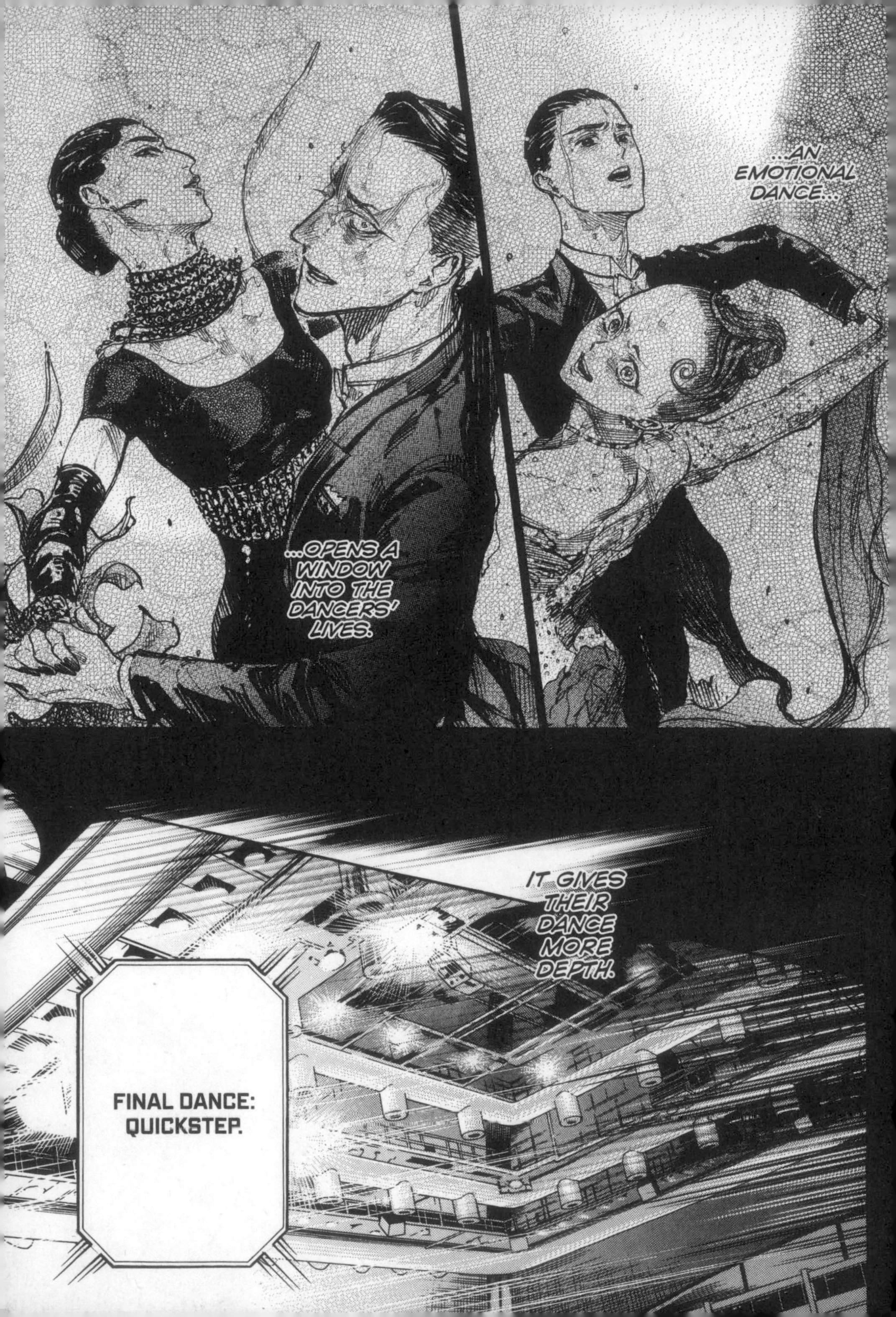
...AN EMOTIONAL DANCE...
...OPENS A WINDOW INTO THE DANCERS' LIVES.
IT GIVES THEIR DANCE MORE DEPTH.
FINAL DANCE: QUICKSTEP.

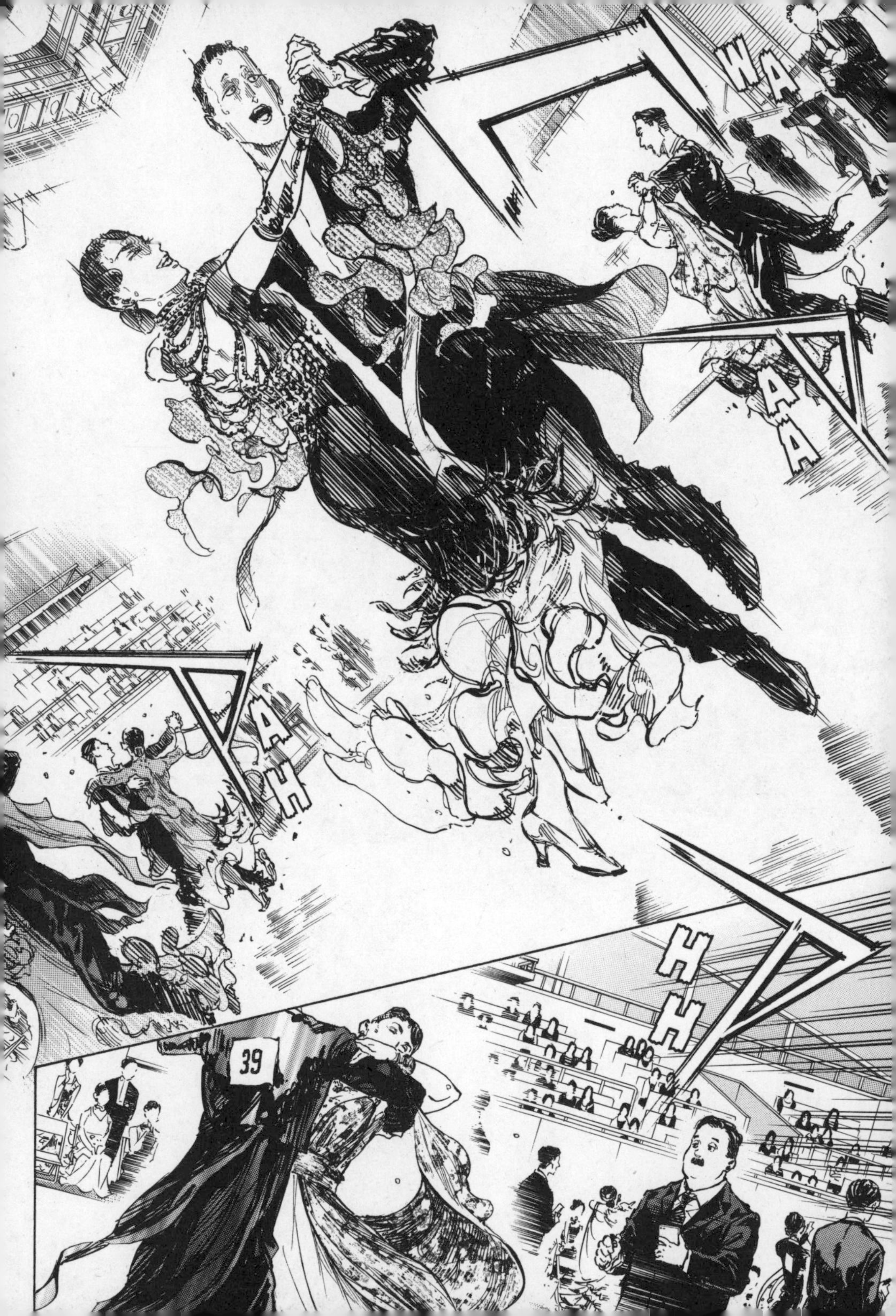
WAA
AAA
AAH
HHH
39

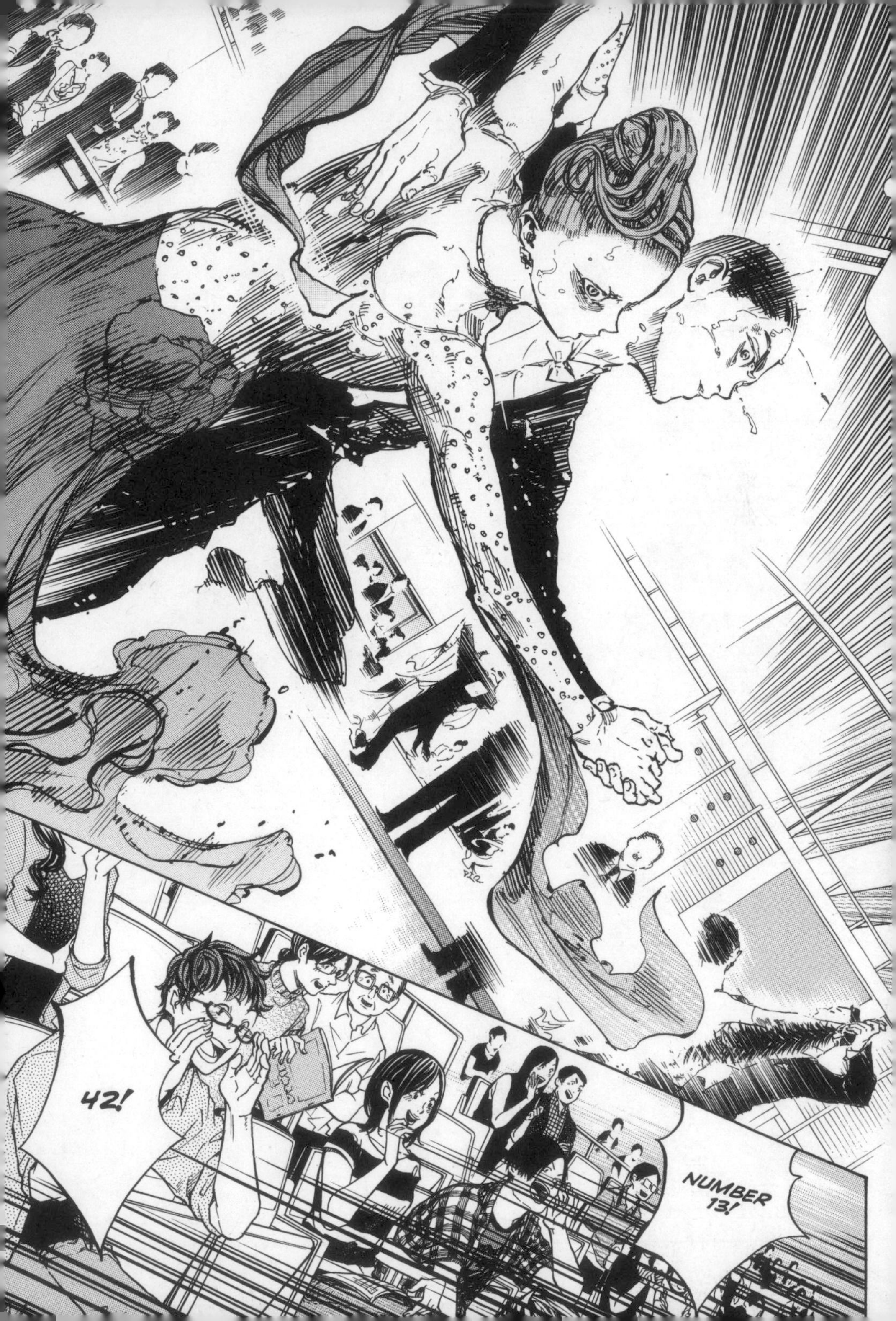
NUMBER 13!
42!

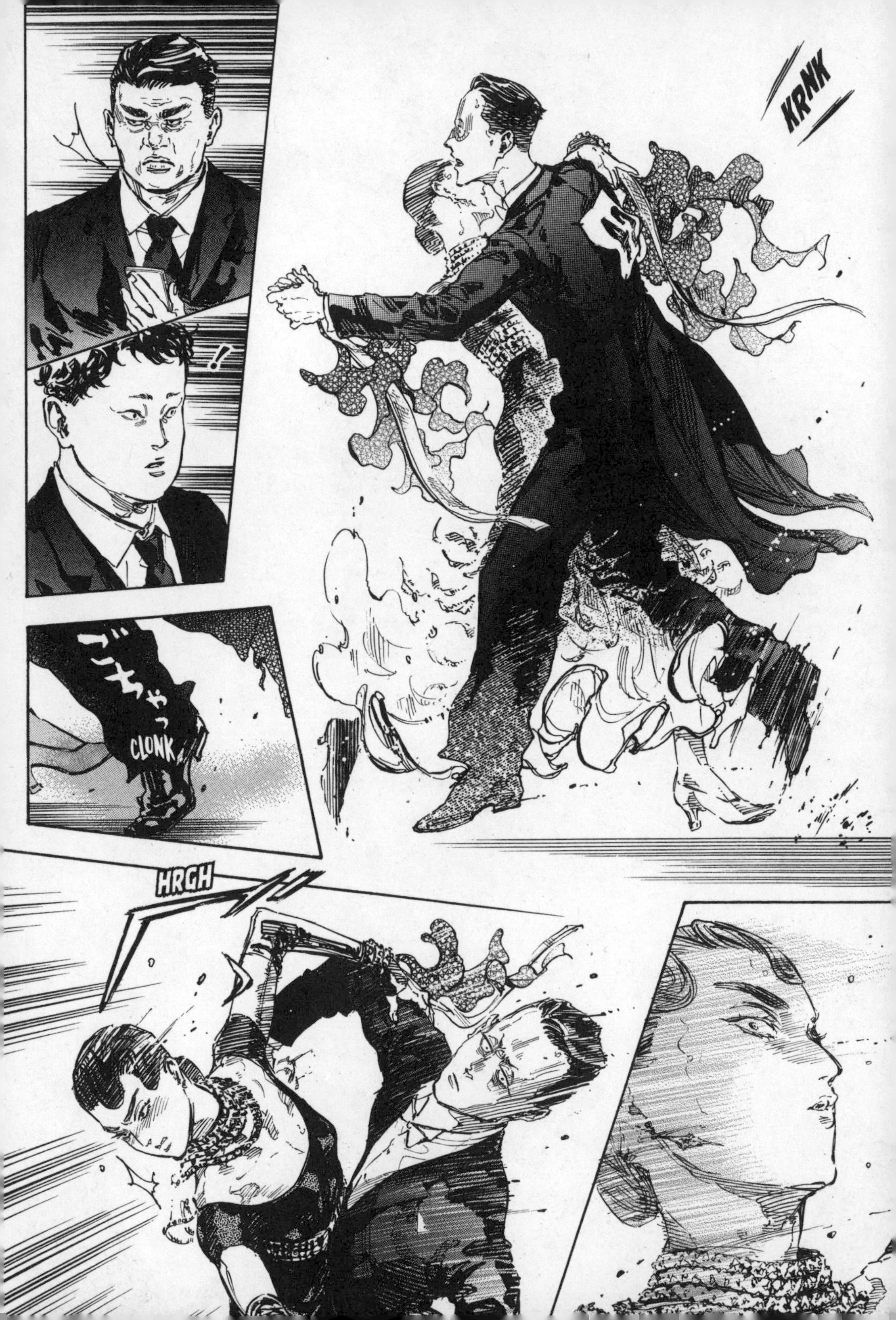
KRNK
!
ゴキャッ
CLONK
HRGH

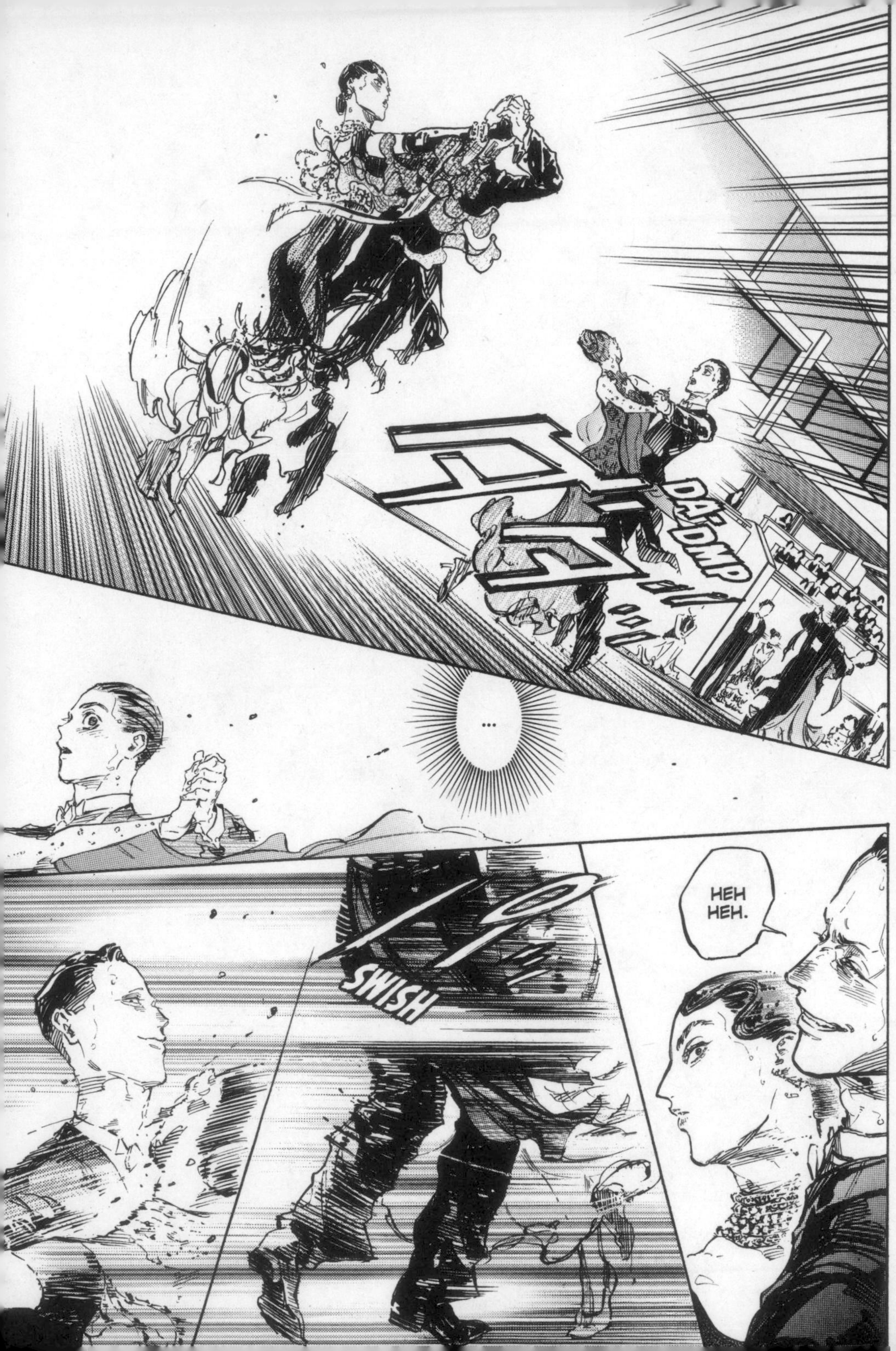
DA-DUMP
...
HEH HEH.
SWISH

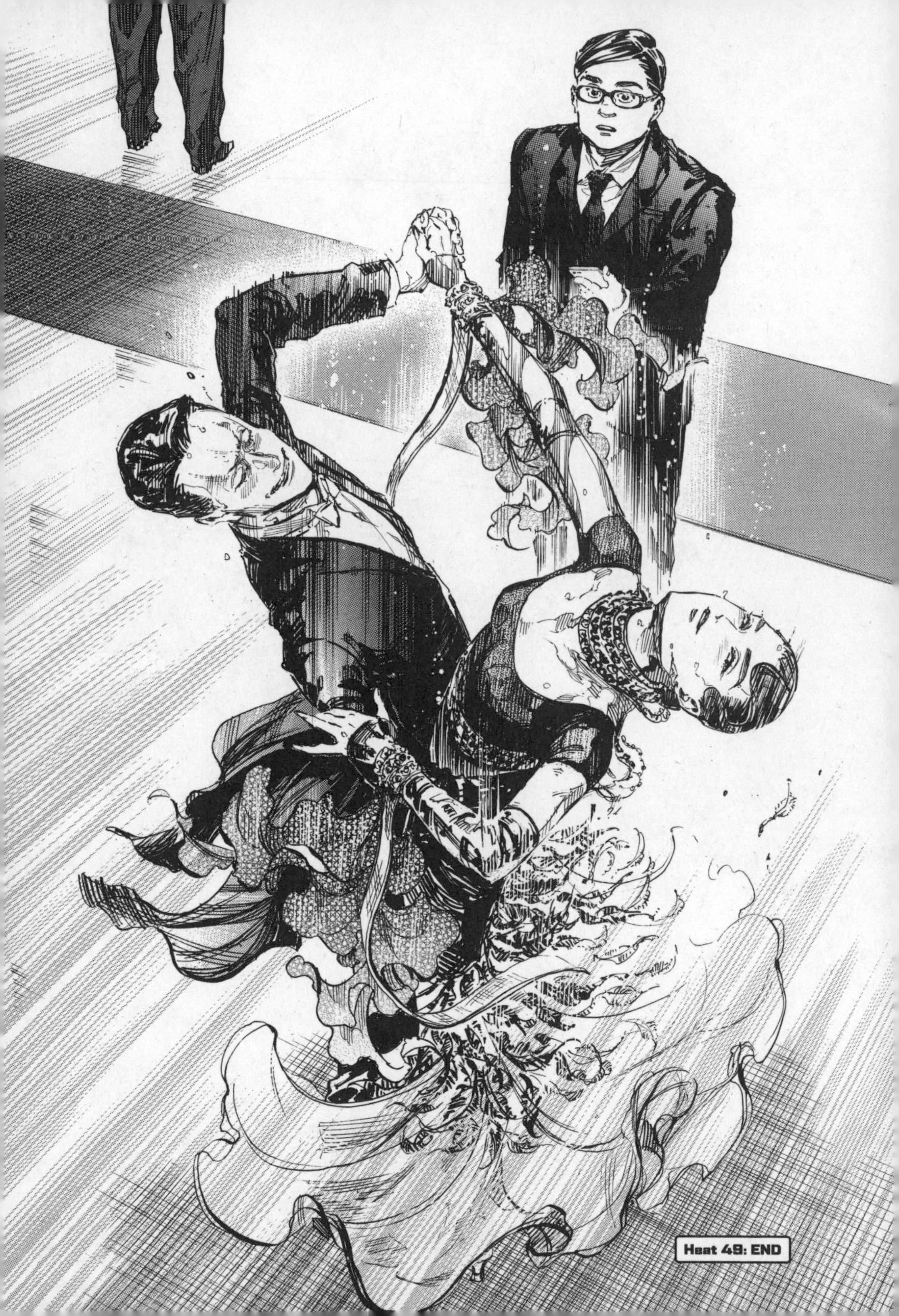
Heat 49: END

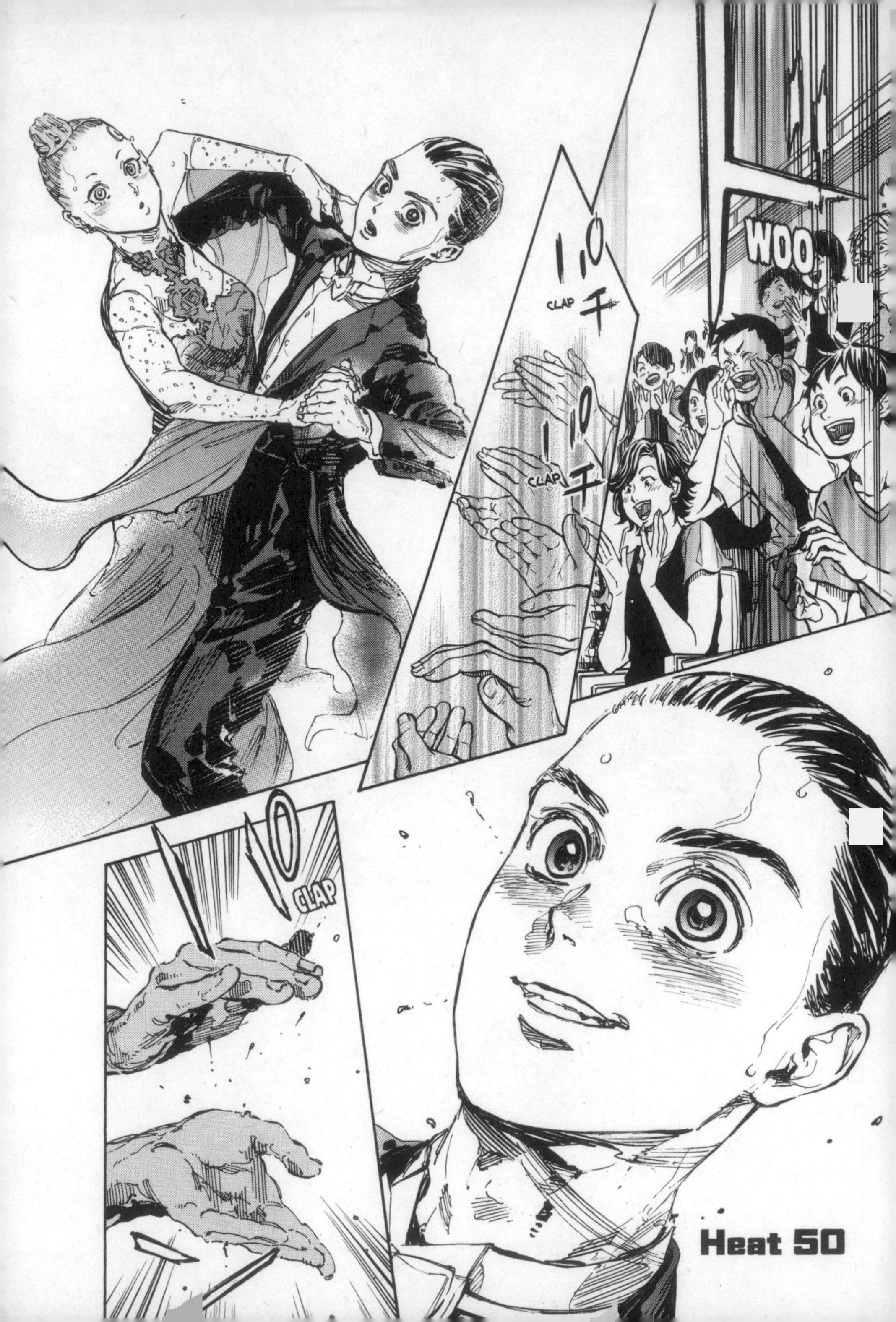
WOO
CLAP
CLAP
CLAP

Heat 50

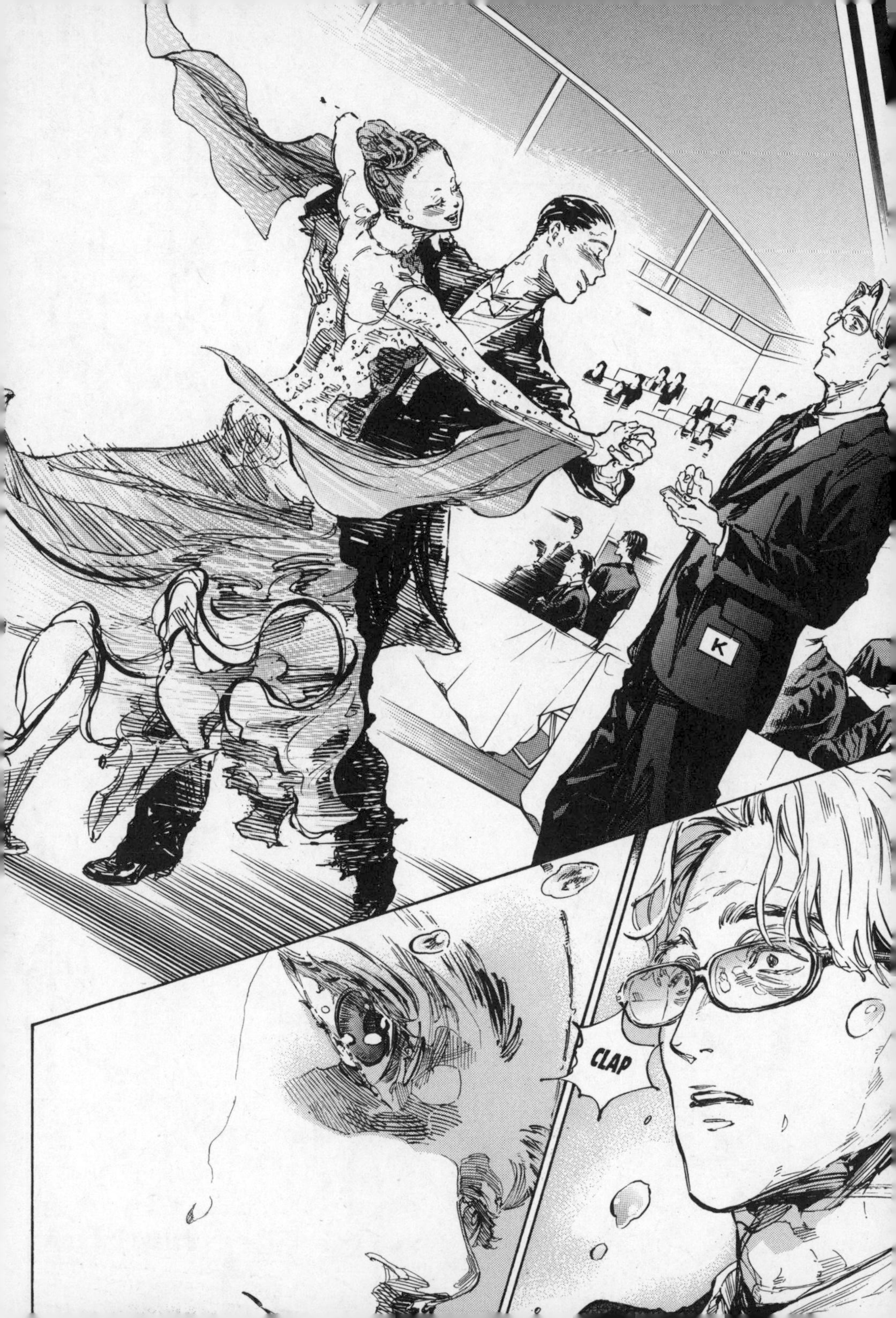
K
CLAP

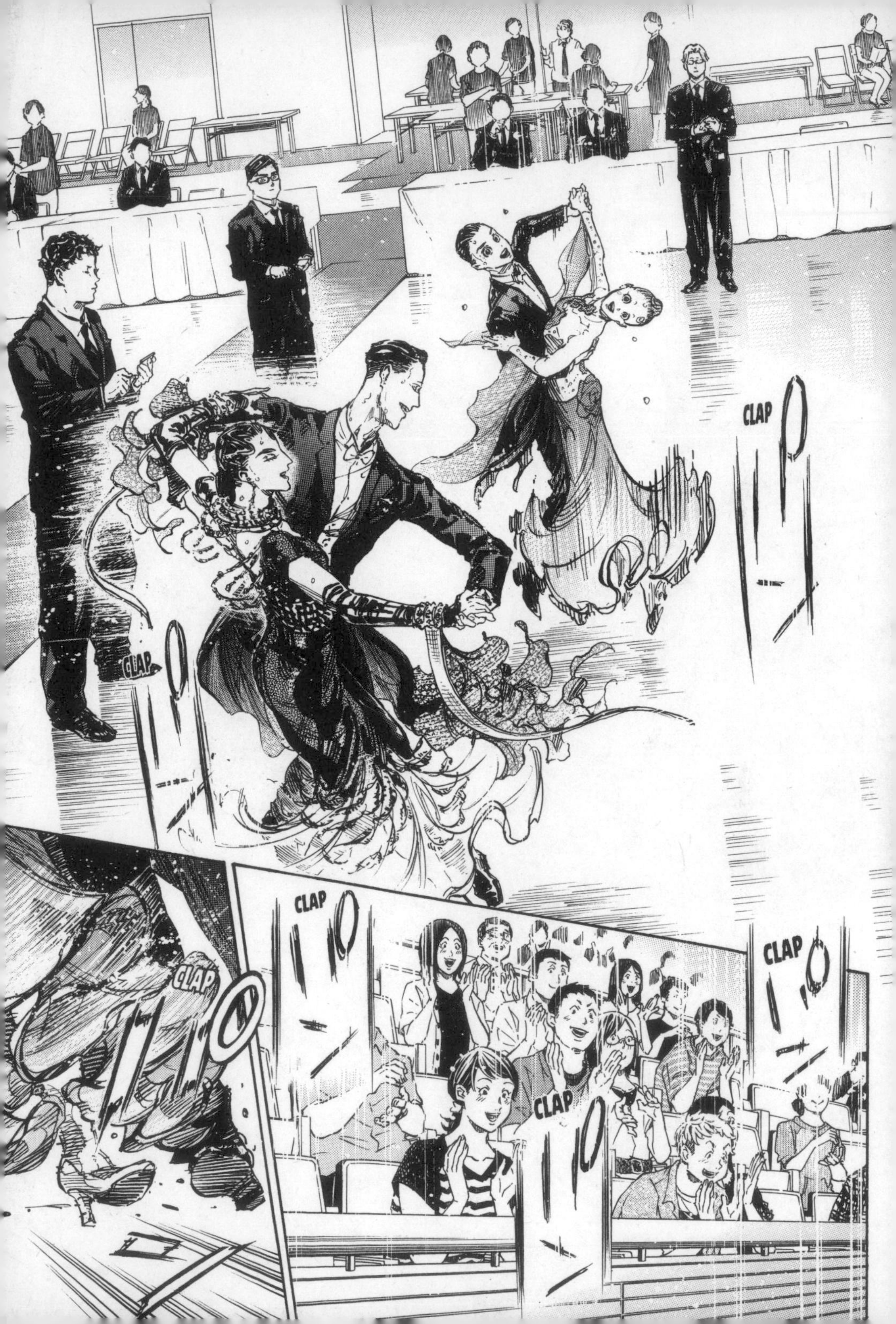
CLAP
CLAP
CLAP
CLAP
CLAP
CLAP

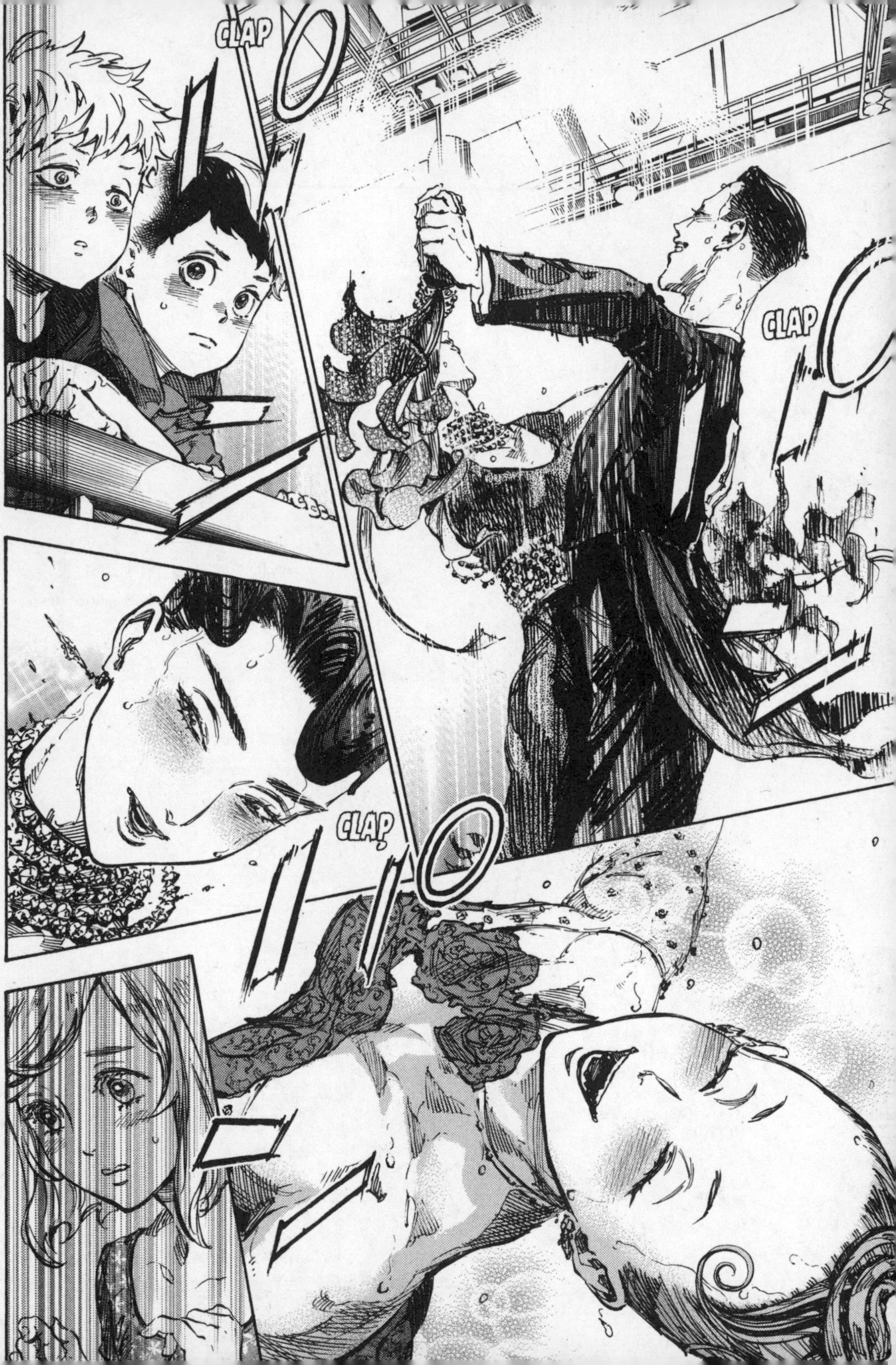
CLAP
CLAP
CLAP

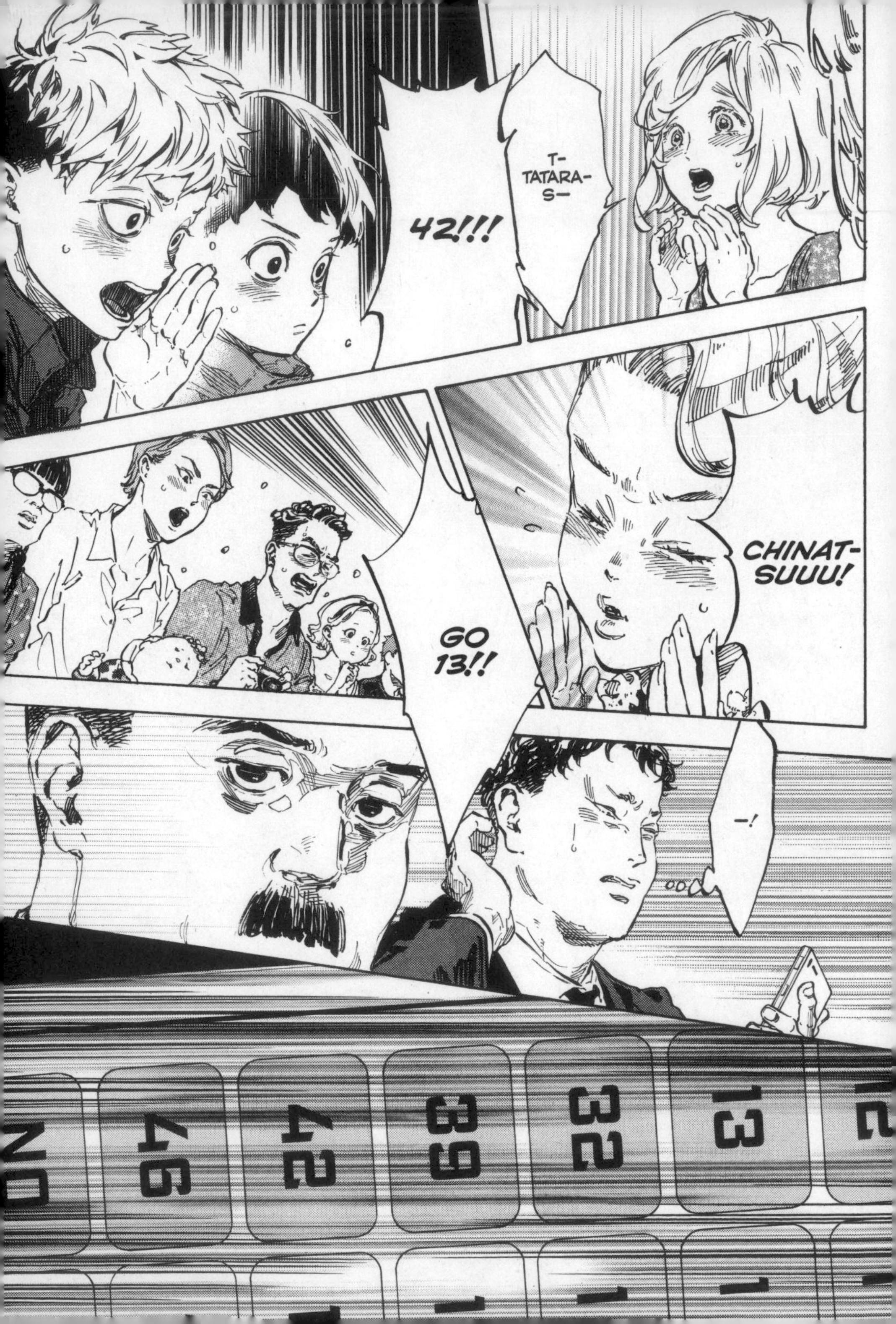
T-TATARA-S—
42!!!
CHINAT-SUUU!
GO 13!!
—!

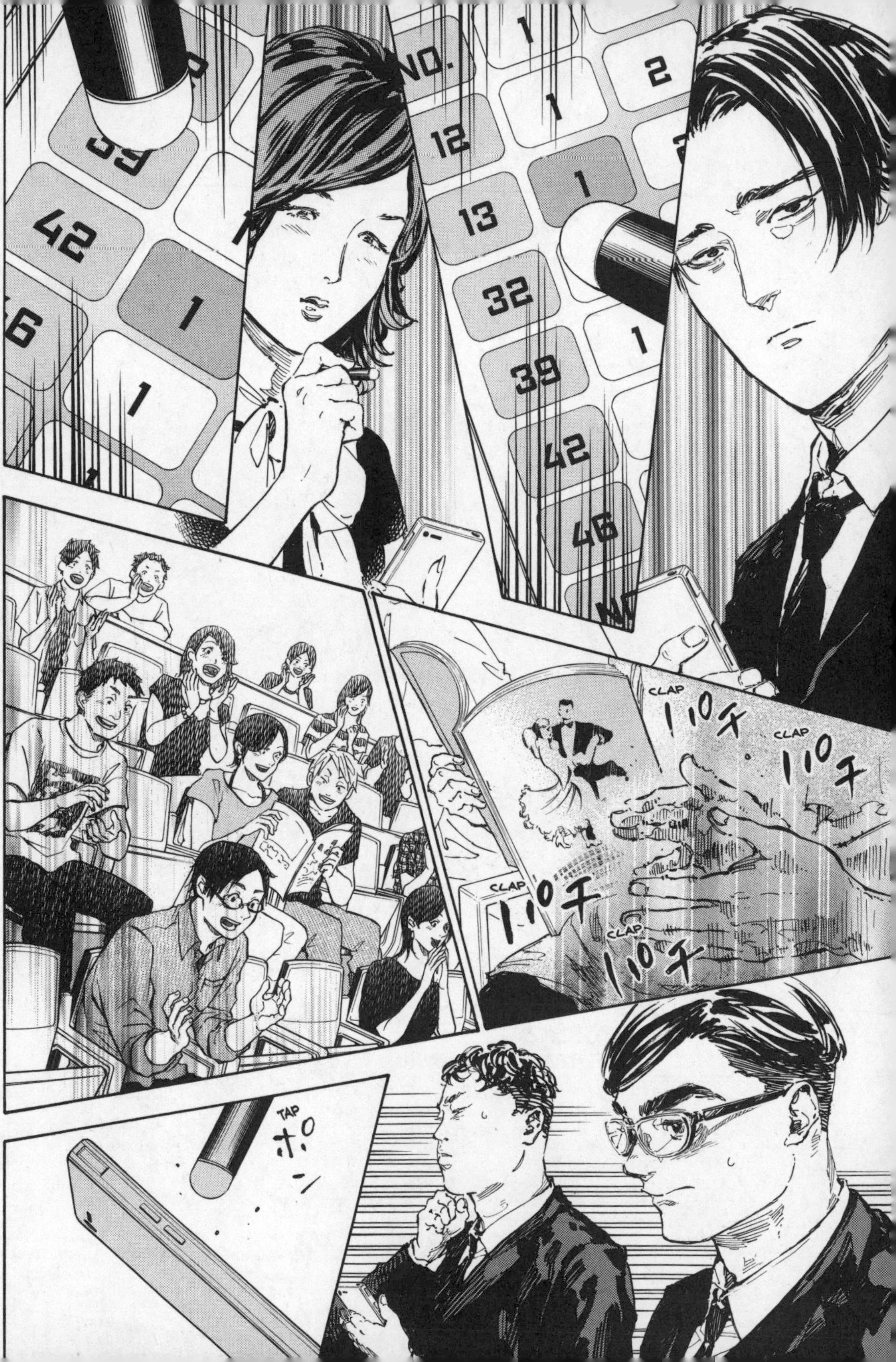
CLAP パチ
CLAP パチ
CLAP パチ
CLAP パチ
TAP ポン

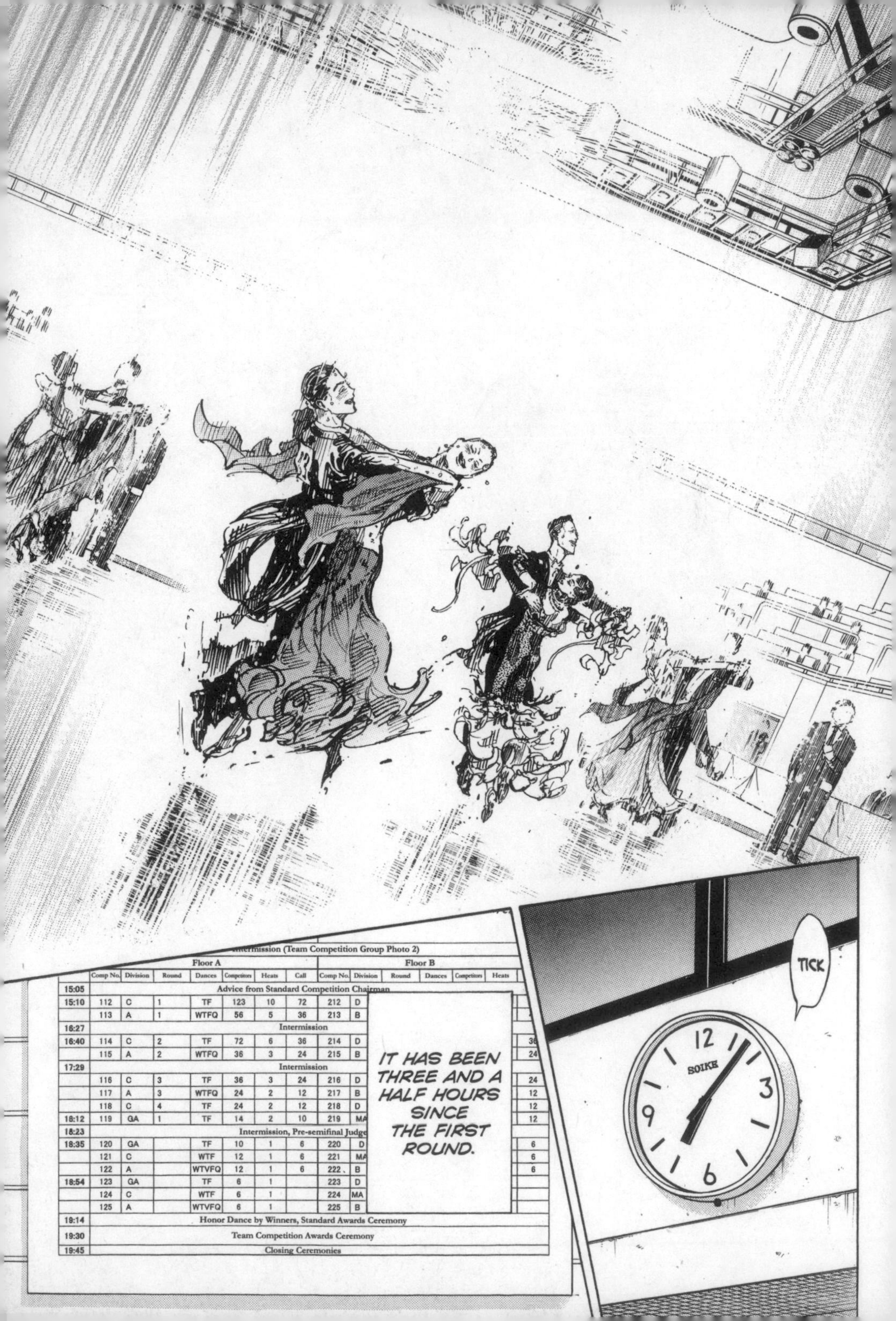
TICK
IT HAS BEEN THREE AND A HALF HOURS SINCE THE FIRST ROUND.
Floor A
Floor B
Advice from Standard Competition Chairman
Intermission
Honor Dance by Winners, Standard Awards Ceremony
Team Competition Awards Ceremony
Closing Ceremonies

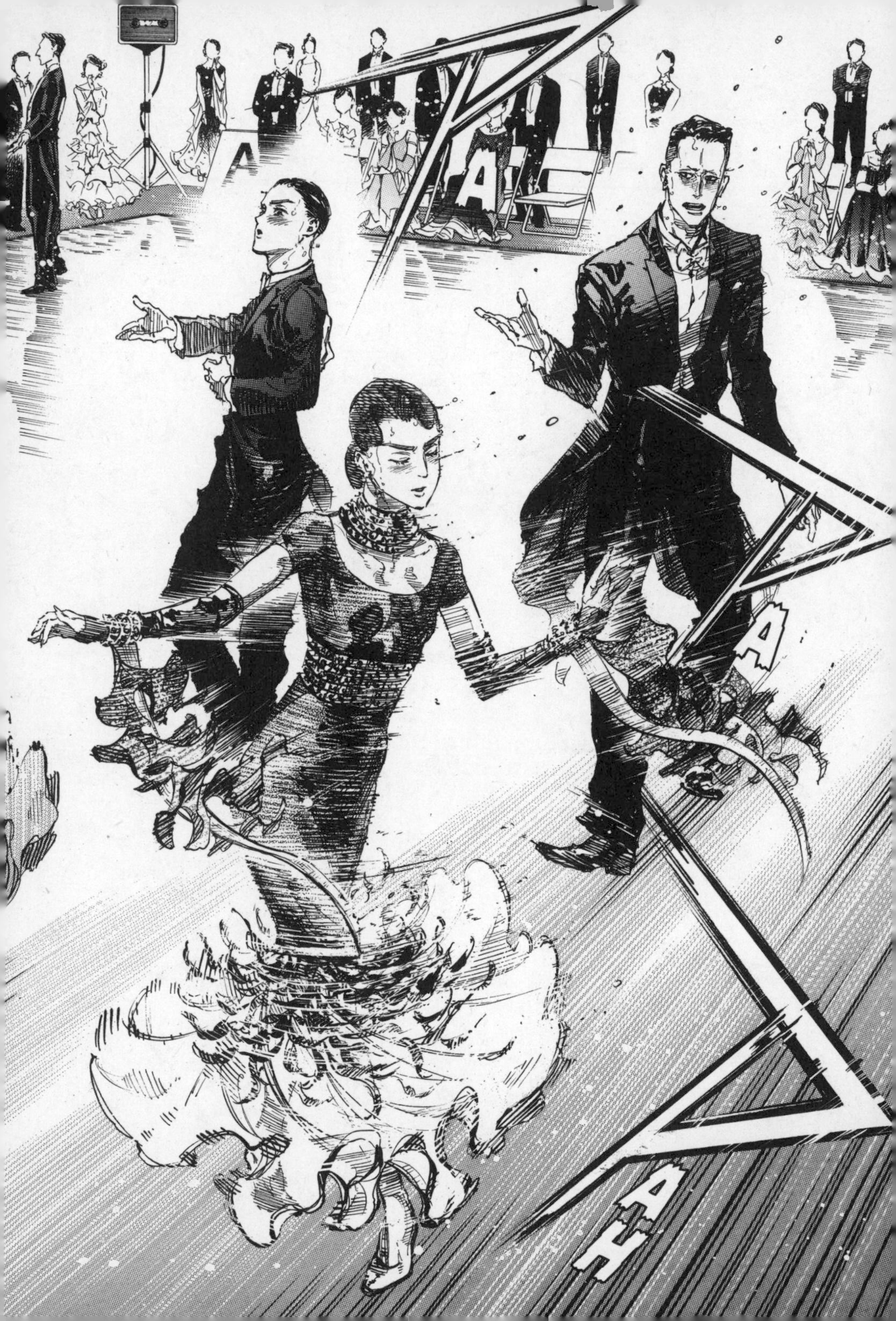
A
A
A
AH

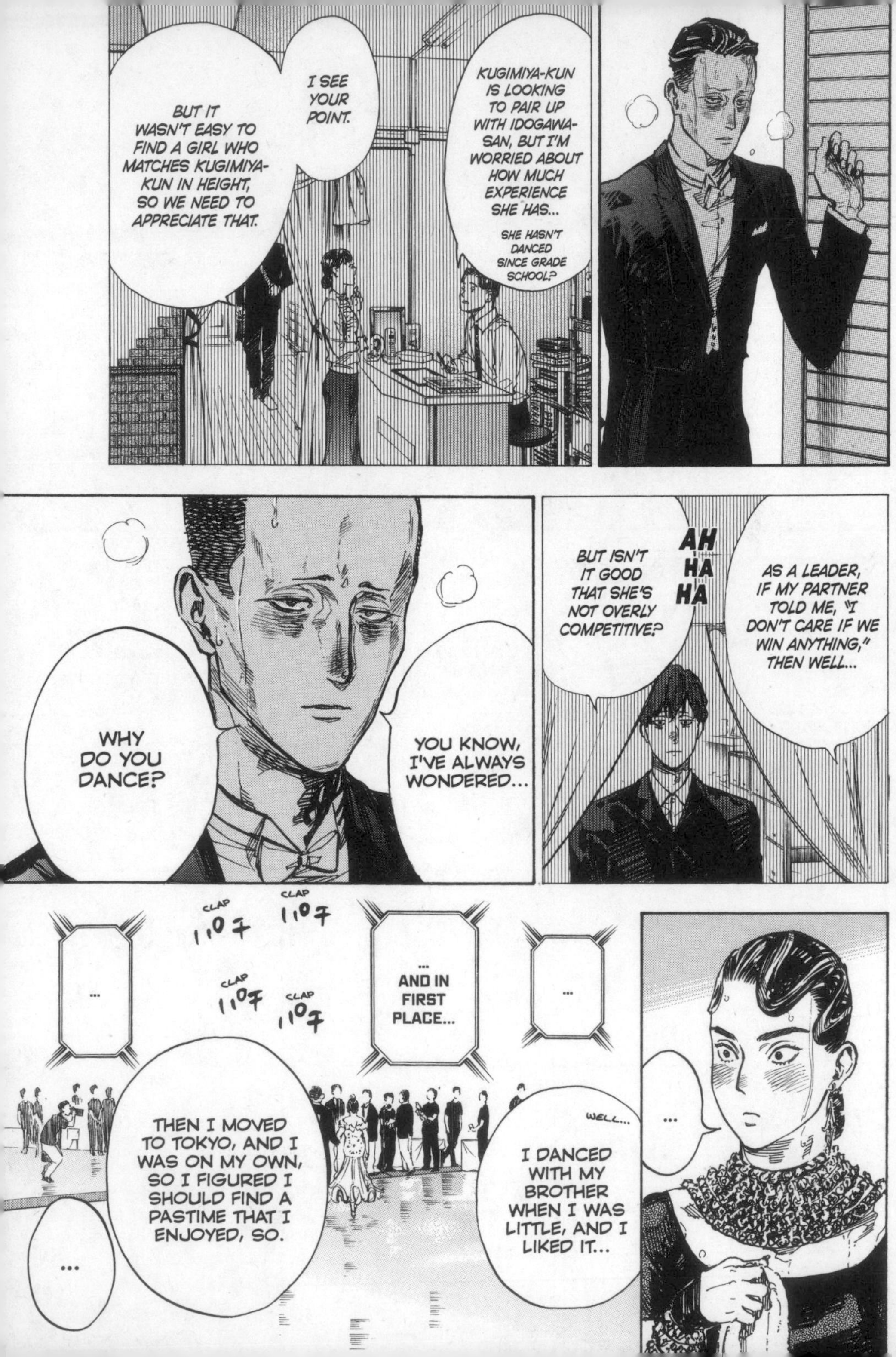
KUGIMIYA-KUN IS LOOKING TO PAIR UP WITH IDOGAWA-SAN, BUT I'M WORRIED ABOUT HOW MUCH EXPERIENCE SHE HAS...
SHE HASN'T DANCED SINCE GRADE SCHOOL?
I SEE YOUR POINT.
BUT IT WASN'T EASY TO FIND A GIRL WHO MATCHES KUGIMIYA-KUN IN HEIGHT, SO WE NEED TO APPRECIATE THAT.
AS A LEADER, IF MY PARTNER TOLD ME, "I DON'T CARE IF WE WIN ANYTHING," THEN WELL...
AH HA HA
BUT ISN'T IT GOOD THAT SHE'S NOT OVERLY COMPETITIVE?
YOU KNOW, I'VE ALWAYS WONDERED...
WHY DO YOU DANCE?
...
WELL...
I DANCED WITH MY BROTHER WHEN I WAS LITTLE, AND I LIKED IT...
...
... AND IN FIRST PLACE...
CLAP
CLAP
CLAP
CLAP
...
THEN I MOVED TO TOKYO, AND I WAS ON MY OWN, SO I FIGURED I SHOULD FIND A PASTIME THAT I ENJOYED, SO.
...

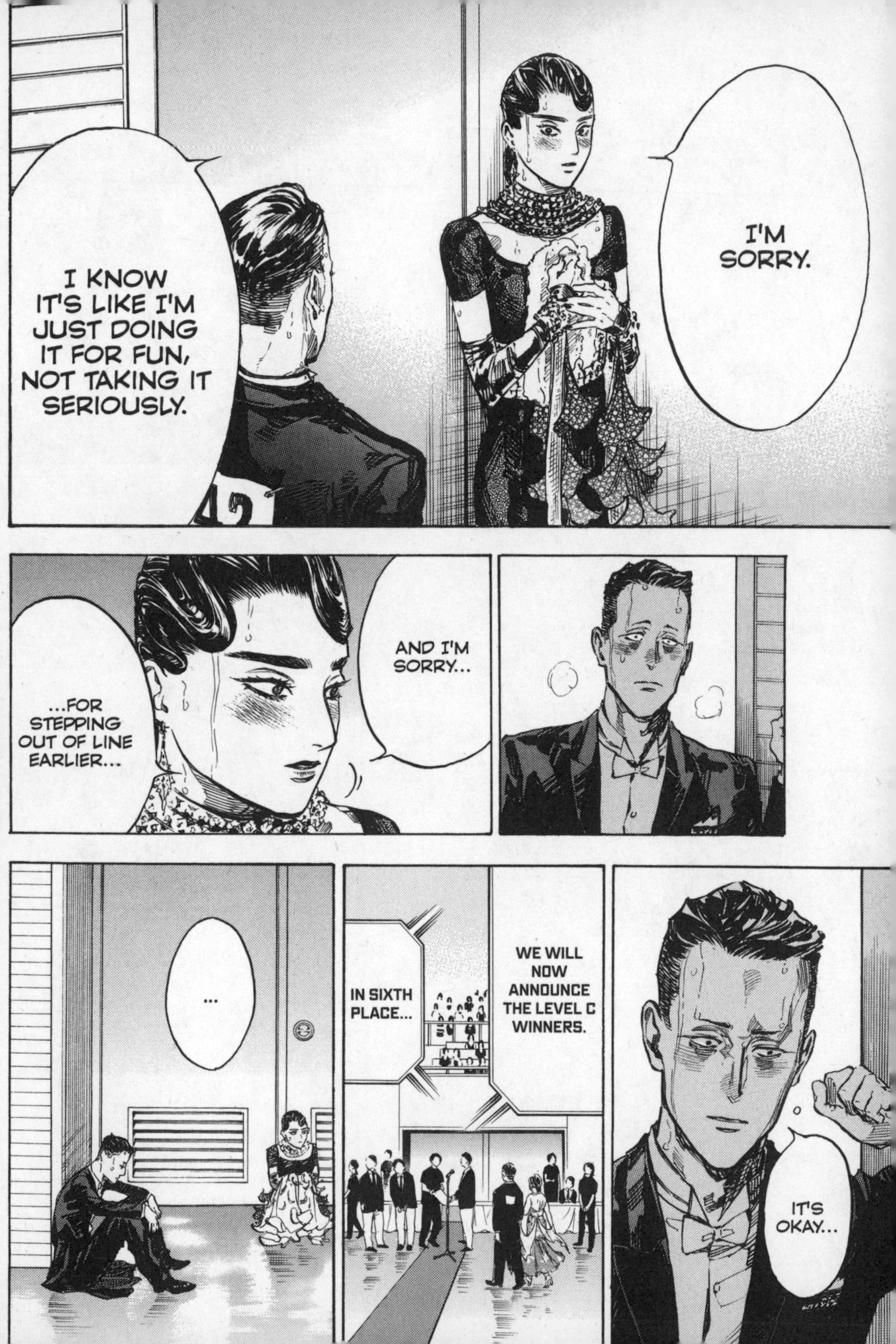
I'M SORRY.
I KNOW IT'S LIKE I'M JUST DOING IT FOR FUN, NOT TAKING IT SERIOUSLY.
AND I'M SORRY...
...FOR STEPPING OUT OF LINE EARLIER...
IT'S OKAY...
WE WILL NOW ANNOUNCE THE LEVEL C WINNERS.
IN SIXTH PLACE...
...

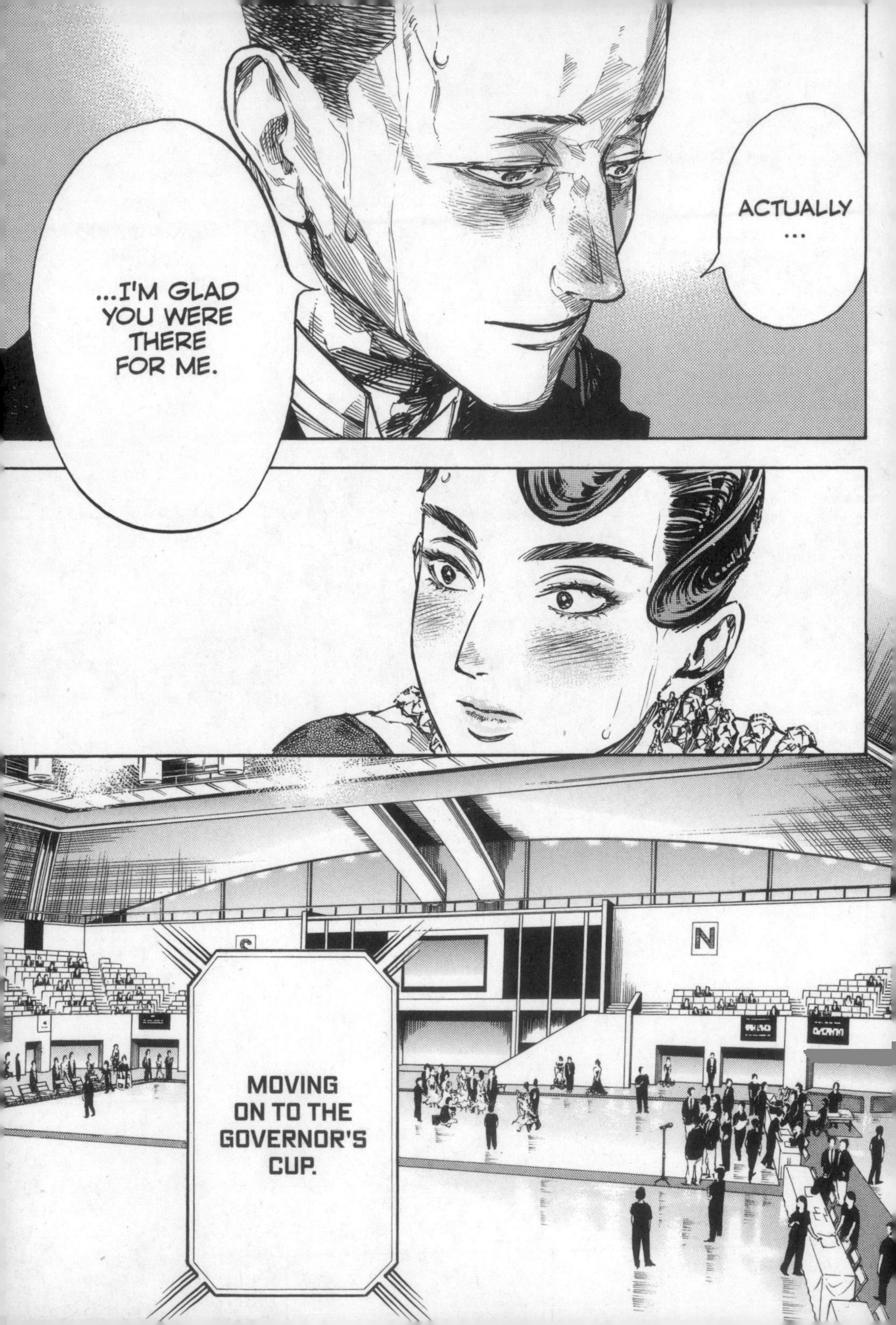
ACTUALLY ...
...I'M GLAD YOU WERE THERE FOR ME.
N
MOVING ON TO THE GOVERNOR'S CUP.

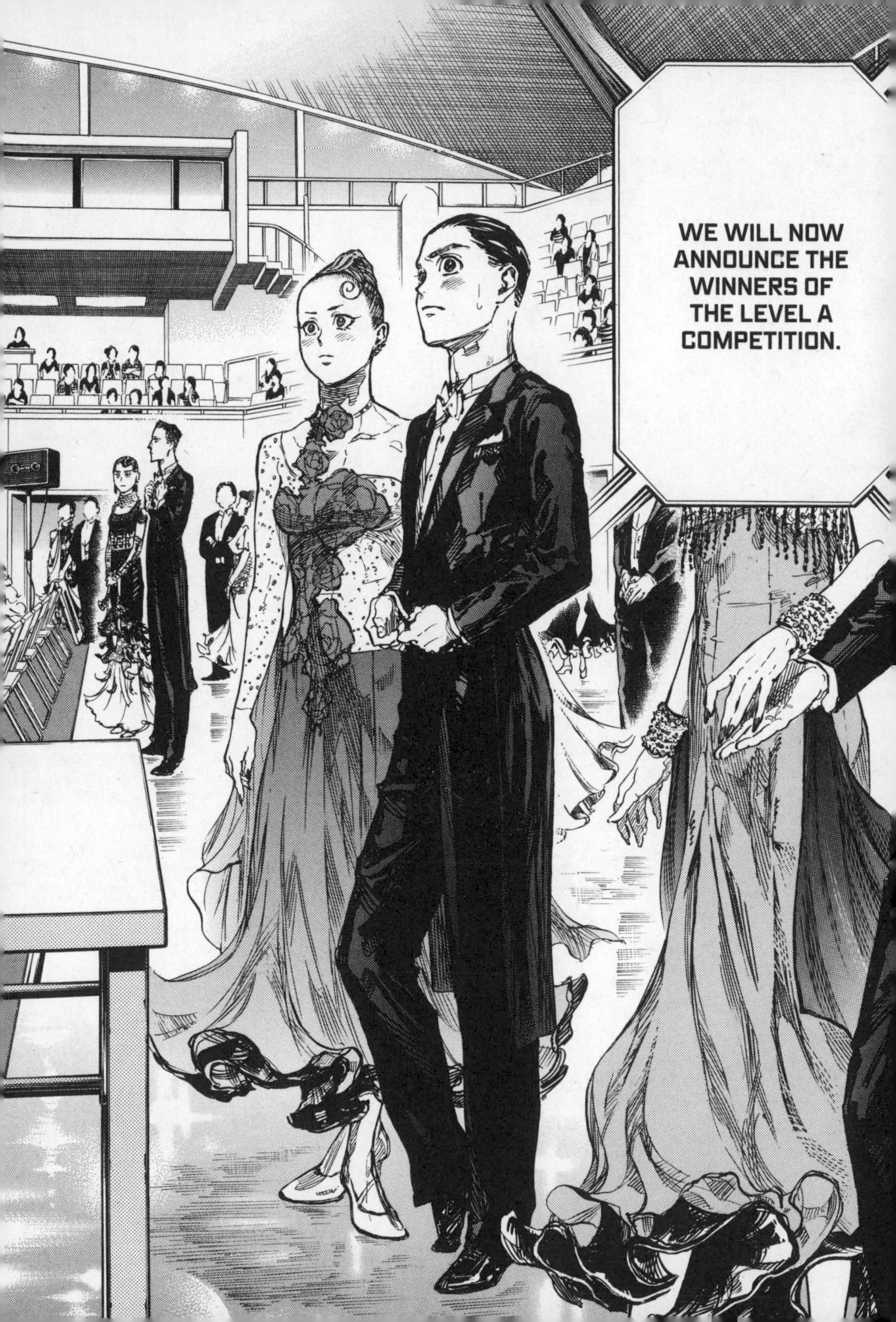
WE WILL NOW ANNOUNCE THE WINNERS OF THE LEVEL A COMPETITION.

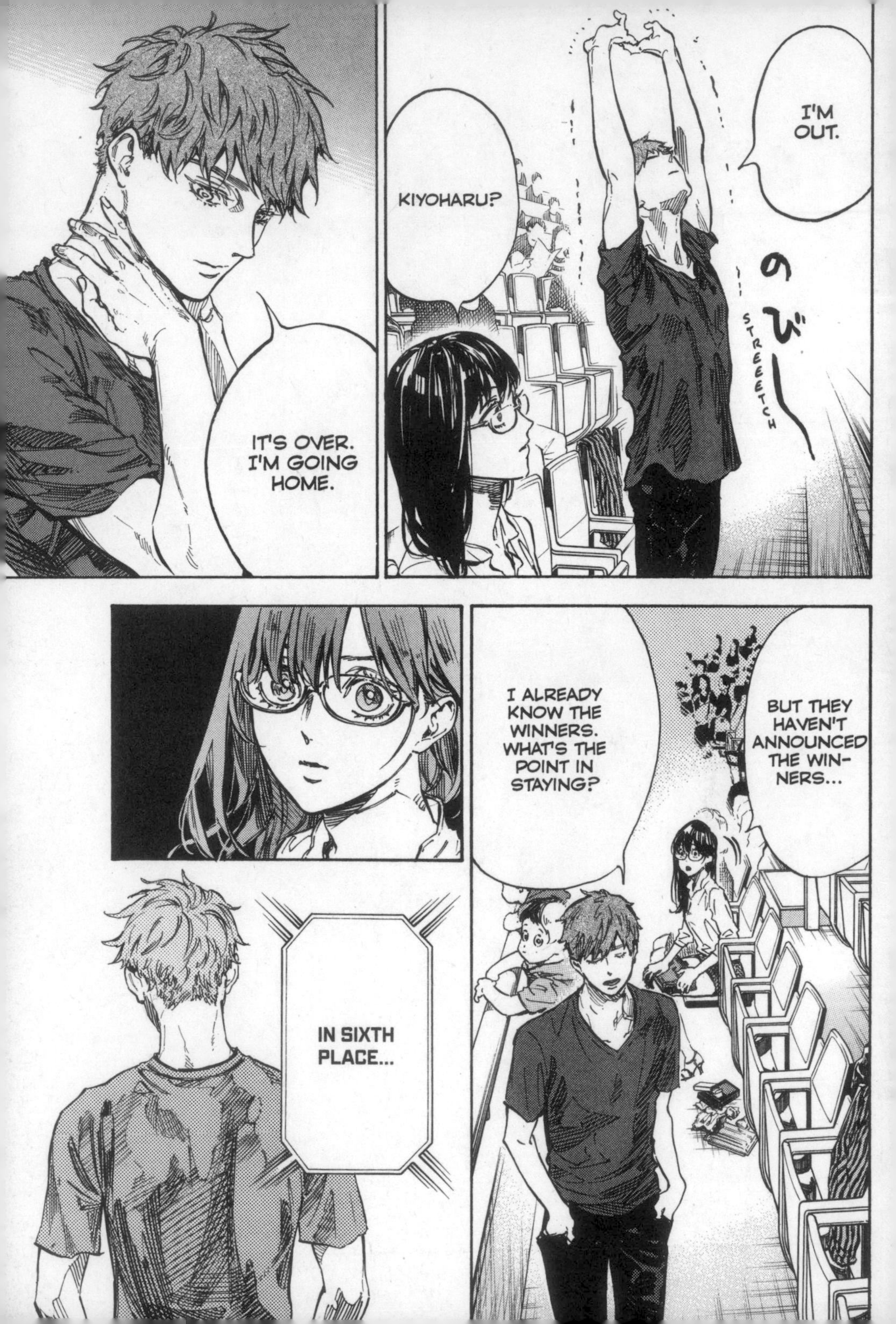
I'M OUT.
のびー
STREEETCH
KIYOHARU?
IT'S OVER. I'M GOING HOME.
BUT THEY HAVEN'T ANNOUNCED THE WIN-NERS...
I ALREADY KNOW THE WINNERS. WHAT'S THE POINT IN STAYING?
IN SIXTH PLACE...

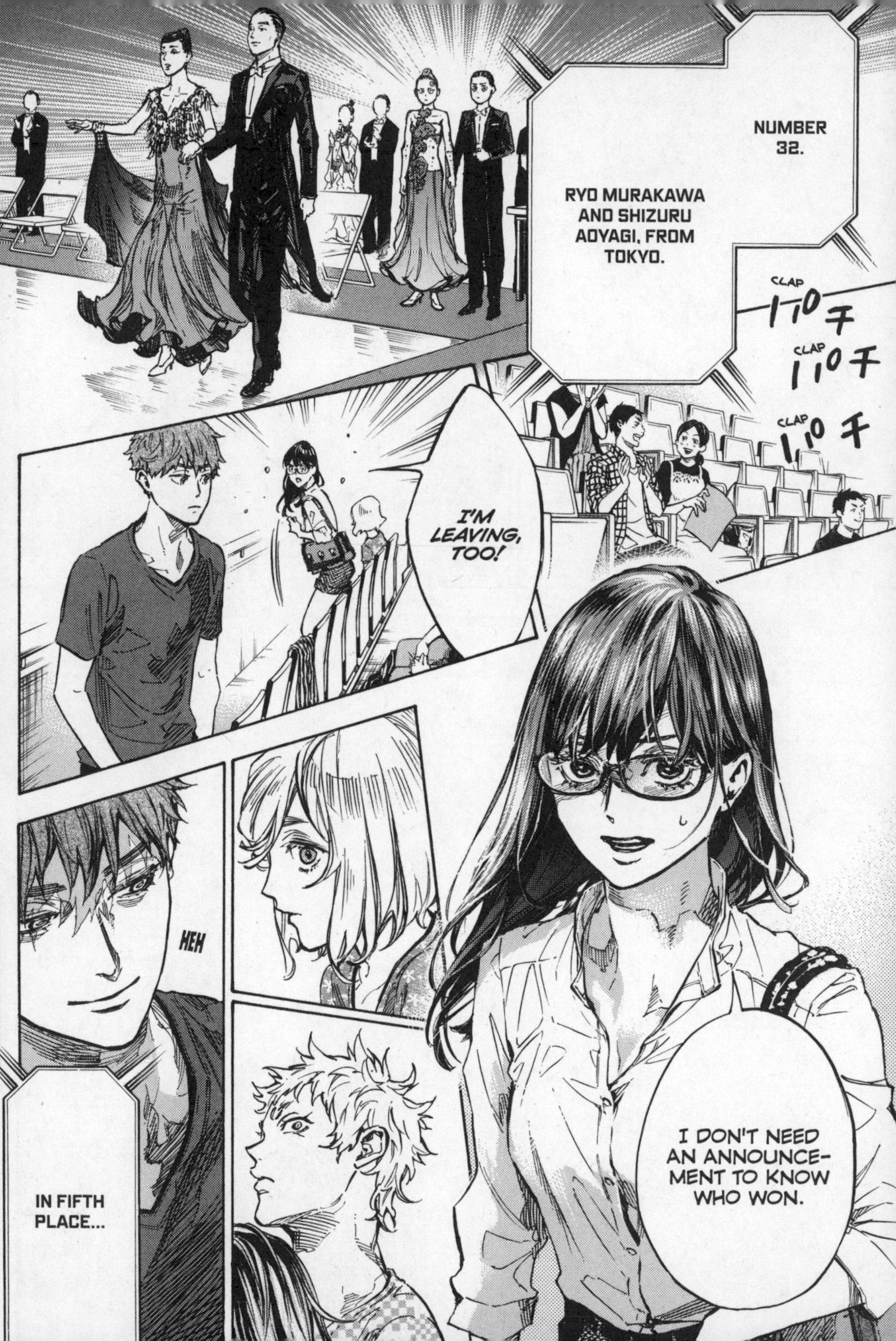
NUMBER 32.
RYO MURAKAWA AND SHIZURU AOYAGI, FROM TOKYO.
CLAP
CLAP
CLAP
I'M LEAVING, TOO!
I DON'T NEED AN ANNOUNCEMENT TO KNOW WHO WON.
HEH
IN FIFTH PLACE...

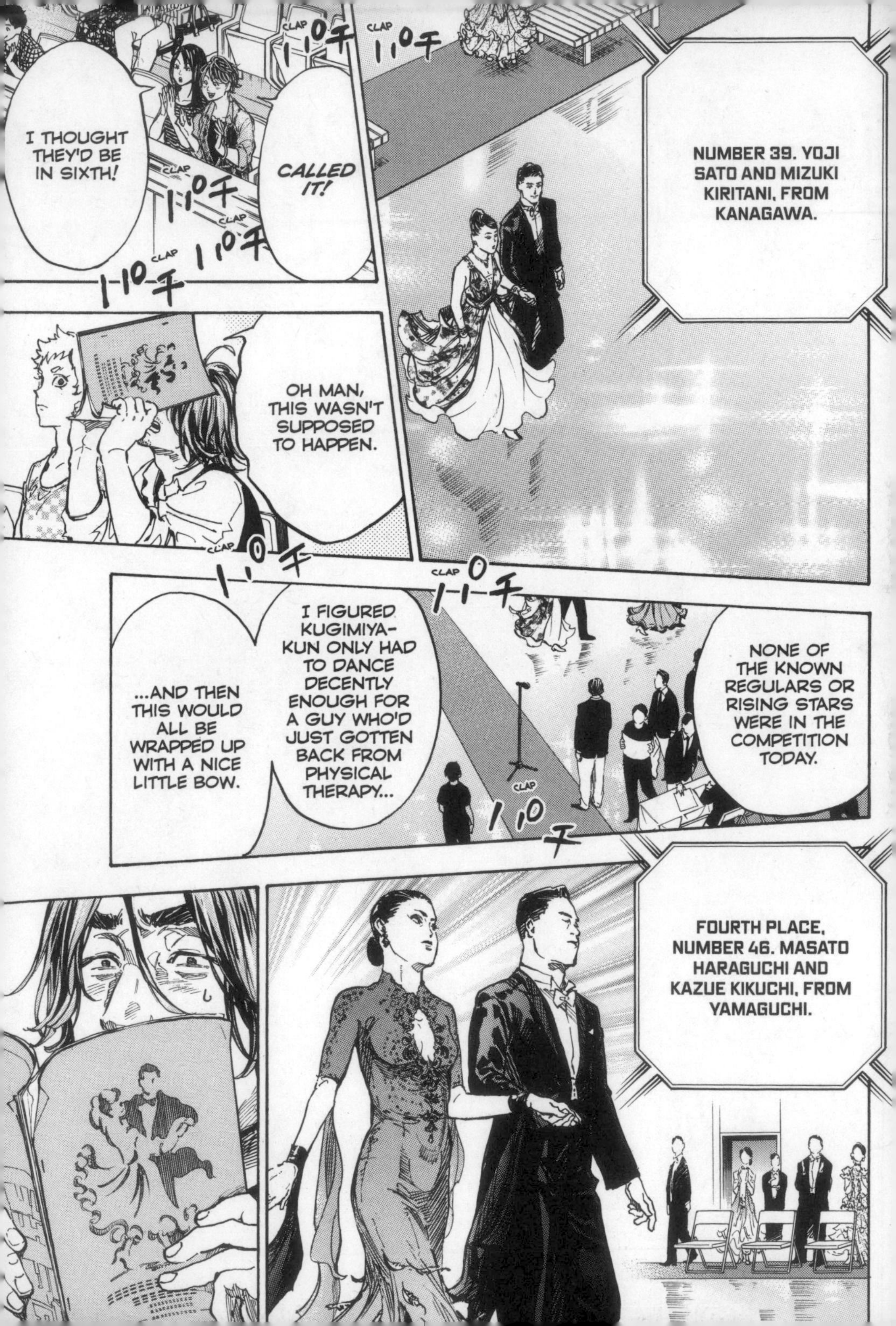
NUMBER 39. YOJI SATO AND MIZUKI KIRITANI, FROM KANAGAWA.
CLAP
CLAP
CALLED IT!
I THOUGHT THEY'D BE IN SIXTH!
CLAP
CLAP
CLAP
OH MAN, THIS WASN'T SUPPOSED TO HAPPEN.
CLAP
CLAP
NONE OF THE KNOWN REGULARS OR RISING STARS WERE IN THE COMPETITION TODAY.
I FIGURED KUGIMIYA-KUN ONLY HAD TO DANCE DECENTLY ENOUGH FOR A GUY WHO'D JUST GOTTEN BACK FROM PHYSICAL THERAPY...
...AND THEN THIS WOULD ALL BE WRAPPED UP WITH A NICE LITTLE BOW.
CLAP
FOURTH PLACE, NUMBER 46. MASATO HARAGUCHI AND KAZUE KIKUCHI, FROM YAMAGUCHI.

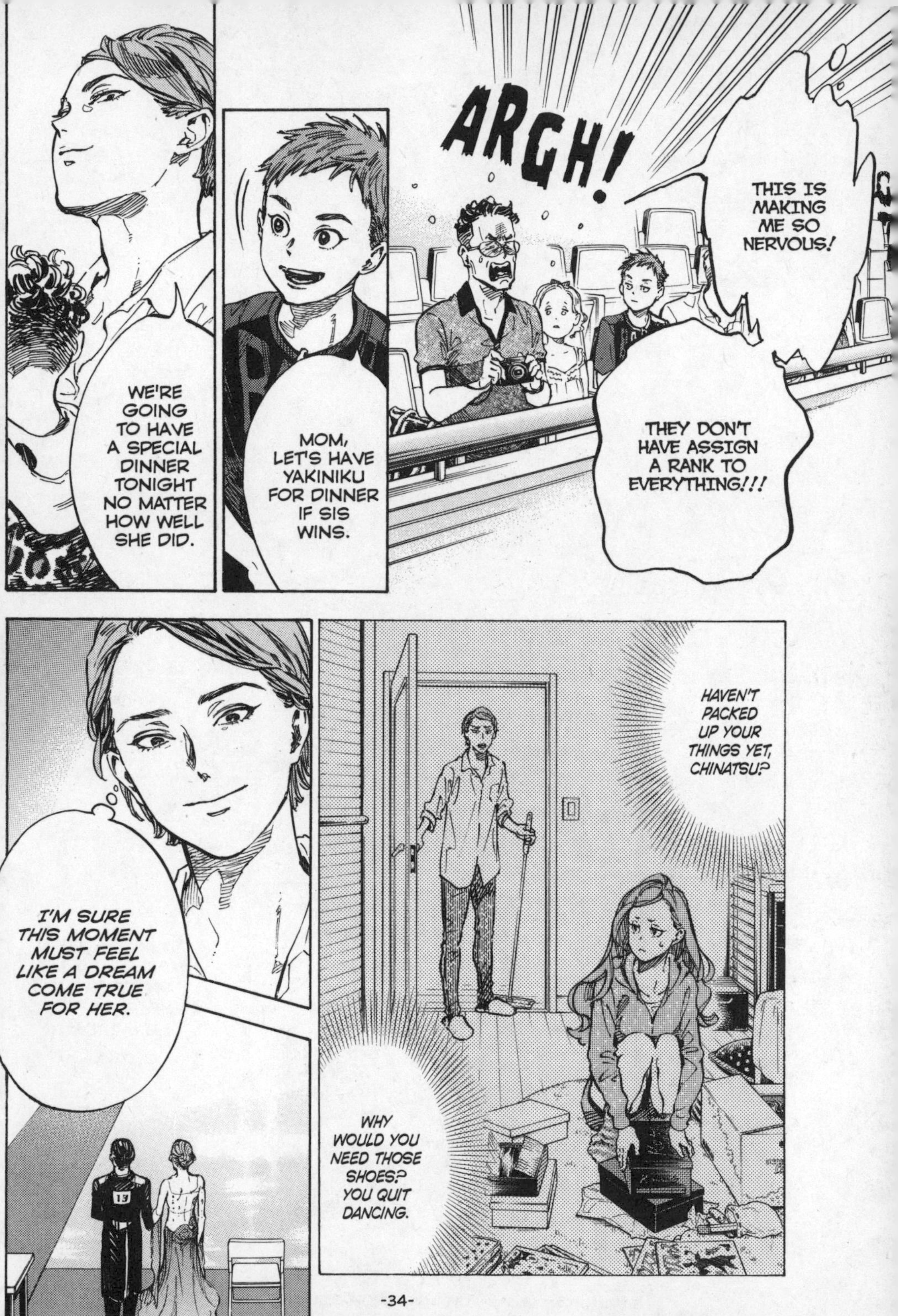
ARGH!
THIS IS MAKING ME SO NERVOUS!
THEY DON'T HAVE ASSIGN A RANK TO EVERYTHING!!!
MOM, LET'S HAVE YAKINIKU FOR DINNER IF SIS WINS.
WE'RE GOING TO HAVE A SPECIAL DINNER TONIGHT NO MATTER HOW WELL SHE DID.
HAVEN'T PACKED UP YOUR THINGS YET, CHINATSU?
WHY WOULD YOU NEED THOSE SHOES? YOU QUIT DANCING.
I'M SURE THIS MOMENT MUST FEEL LIKE A DREAM COME TRUE FOR HER.

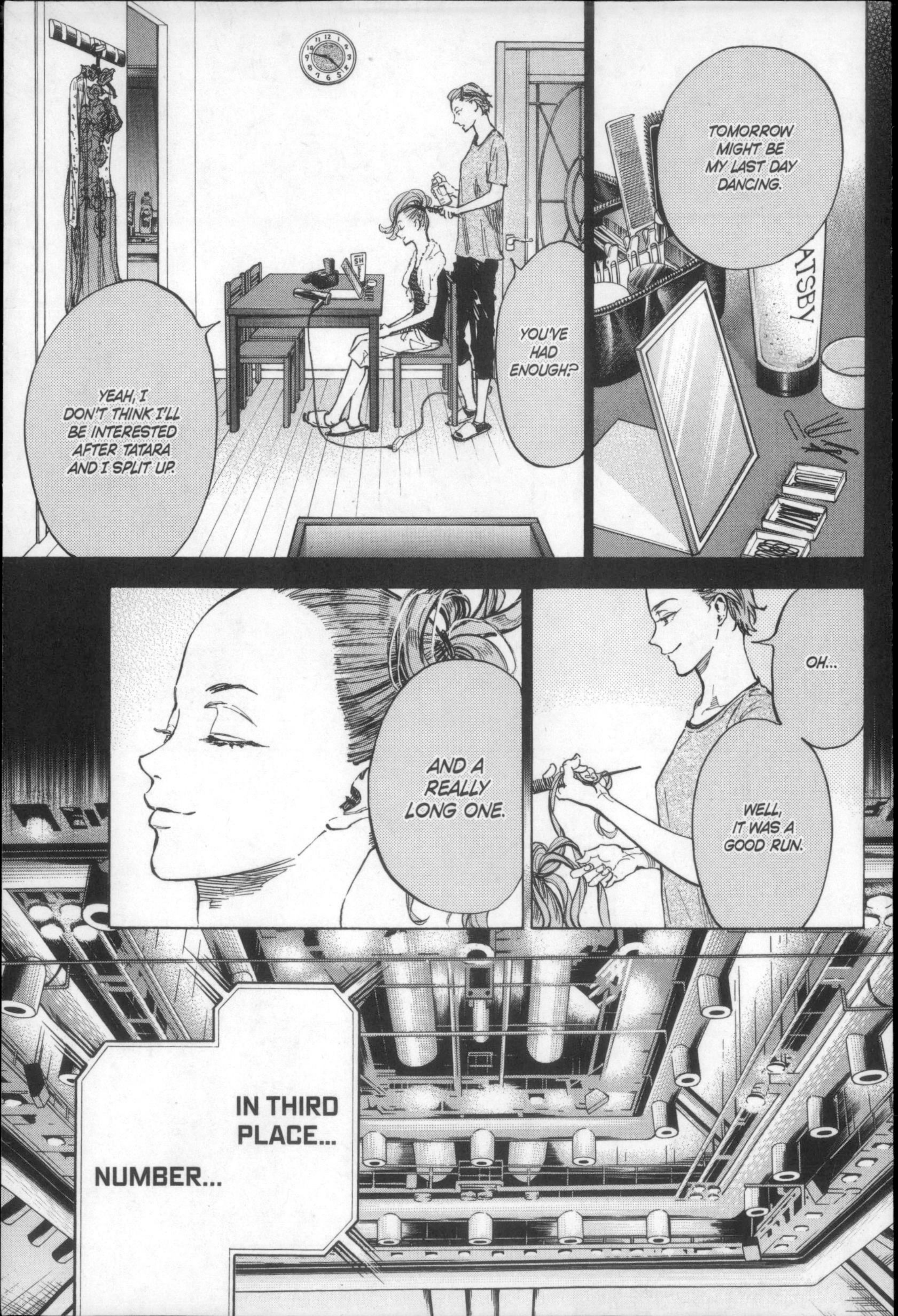
TOMORROW MIGHT BE MY LAST DAY DANCING.
YOU'VE HAD ENOUGH?
YEAH, I DON'T THINK I'LL BE INTERESTED AFTER TATARA AND I SPLIT UP.
OH...
WELL, IT WAS A GOOD RUN.
AND A REALLY LONG ONE.
IN THIRD PLACE...
NUMBER...

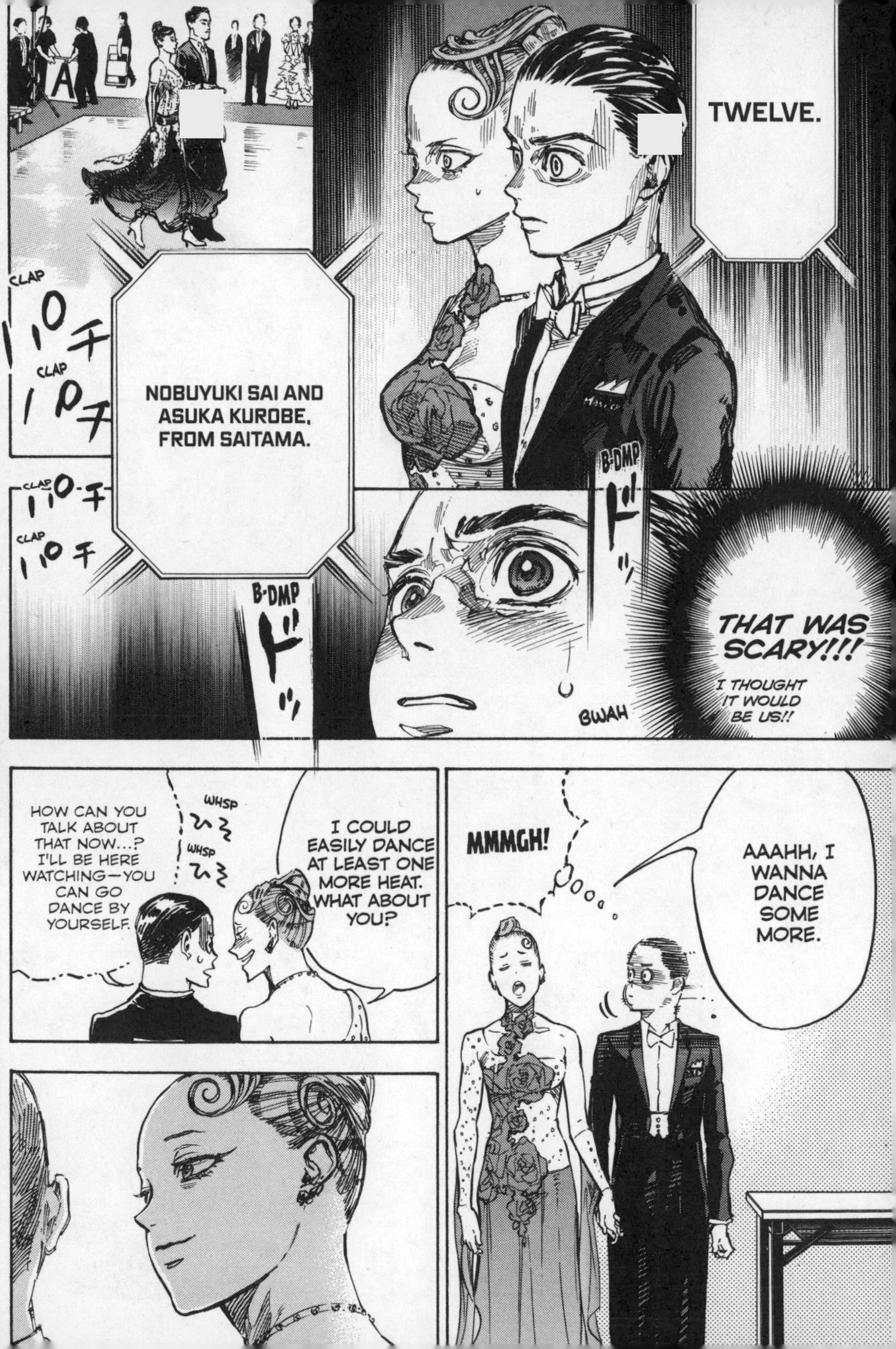
TWELVE.
CLAP パチ
CLAP パチ
NOBUYUKI SAI AND ASUKA KUROBE, FROM SAITAMA.
CLAP パチ
CLAP パチ
B-DMP ド
B-DMP ド
THAT WAS SCARY!!!
I THOUGHT IT WOULD BE US!!
BWAH
AAAHH, I WANNA DANCE SOME MORE.
MMMGH!
I COULD EASILY DANCE AT LEAST ONE MORE HEAT. WHAT ABOUT YOU?
WHSP ひそ
WHSP ひそ
HOW CAN YOU TALK ABOUT THAT NOW...? I'LL BE HERE WATCHING—YOU CAN GO DANCE BY YOURSELF.

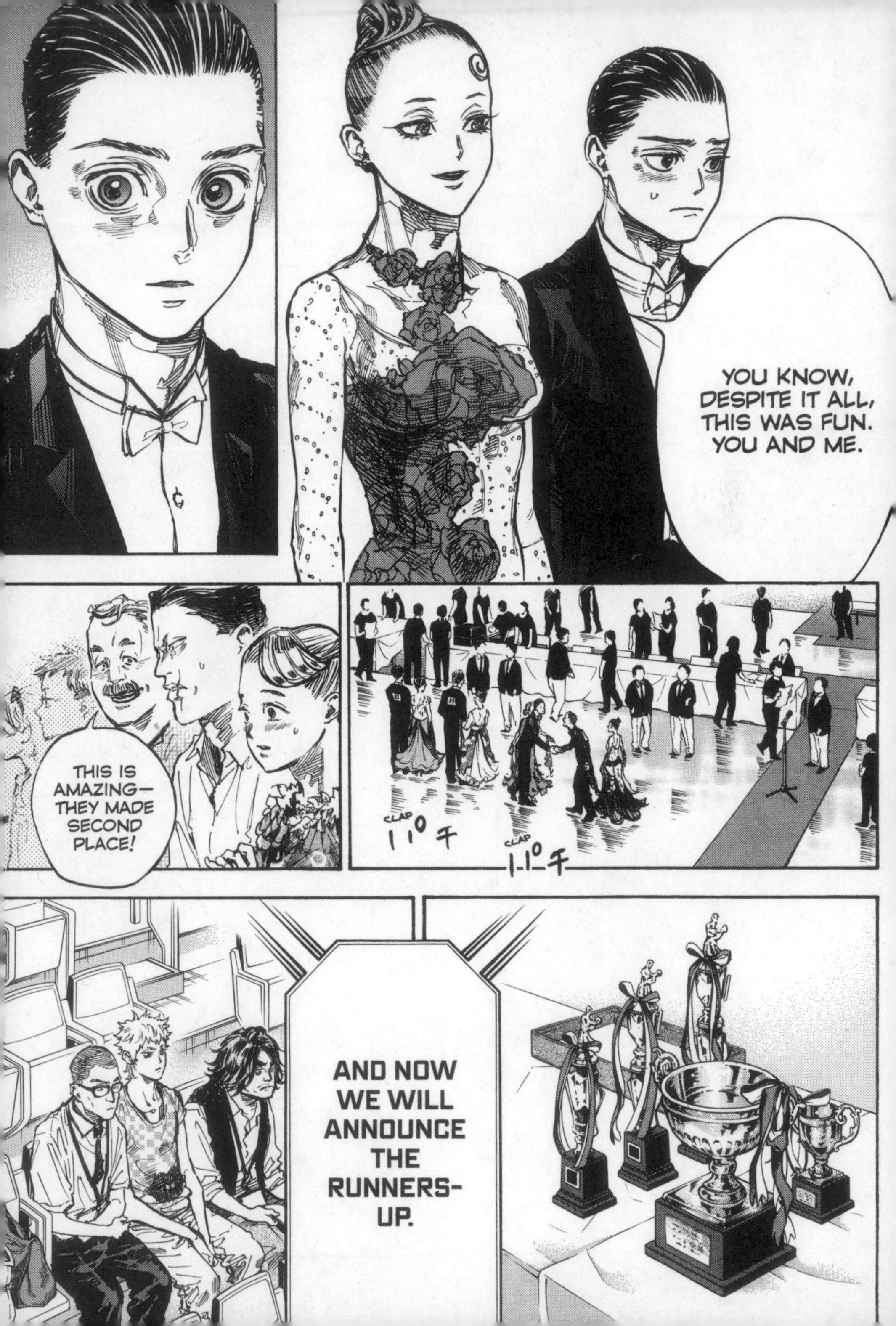
YOU KNOW, DESPITE IT ALL, THIS WAS FUN. YOU AND ME.
CLAP
CLAP
THIS IS AMAZING—THEY MADE SECOND PLACE!
AND NOW WE WILL ANNOUNCE THE RUNNERS-UP.

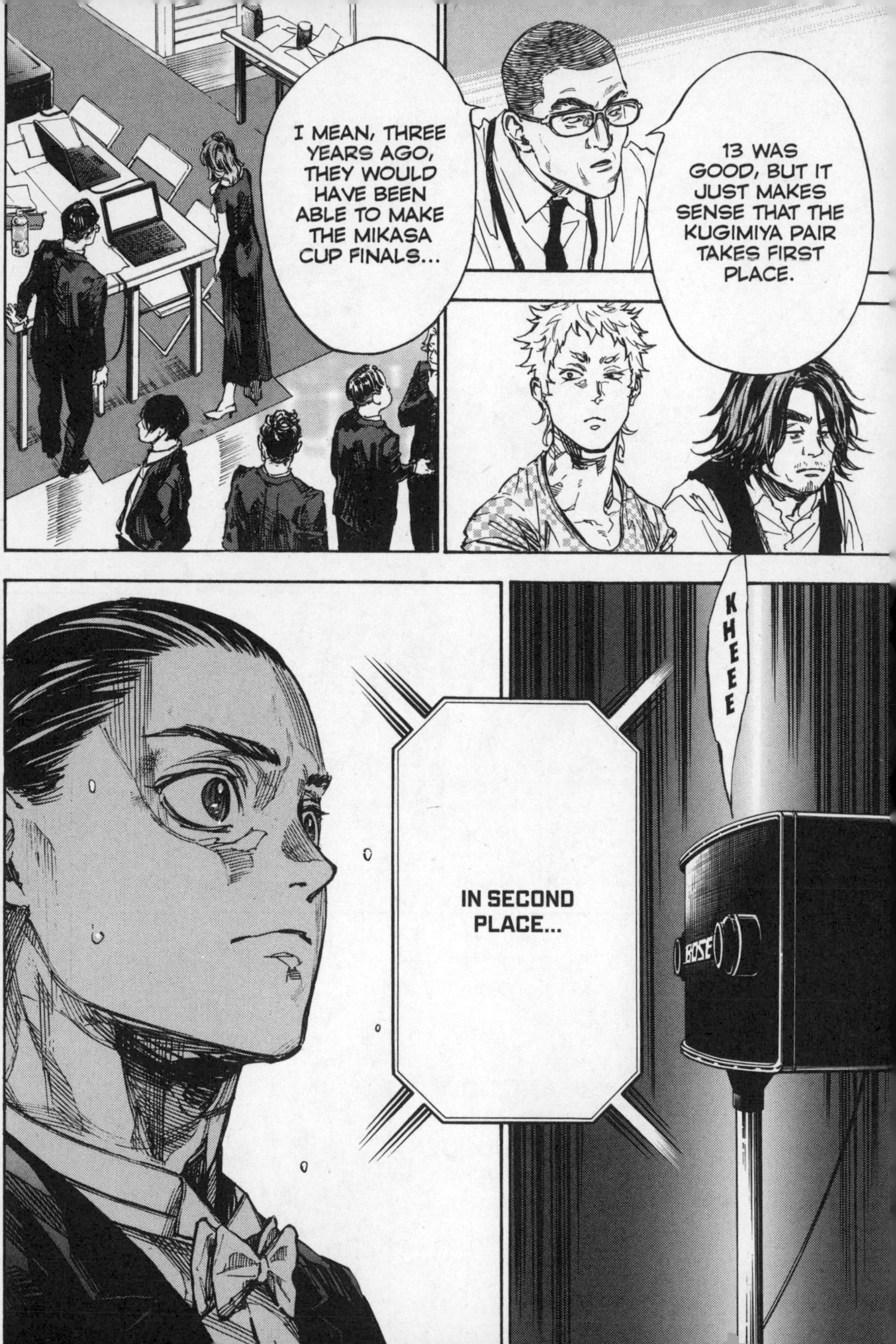
13 WAS GOOD, BUT IT JUST MAKES SENSE THAT THE KUGIMIYA PAIR TAKES FIRST PLACE.
I MEAN, THREE YEARS AGO, THEY WOULD HAVE BEEN ABLE TO MAKE THE MIKASA CUP FINALS...
KHEEE
IN SECOND PLACE...
BOSE

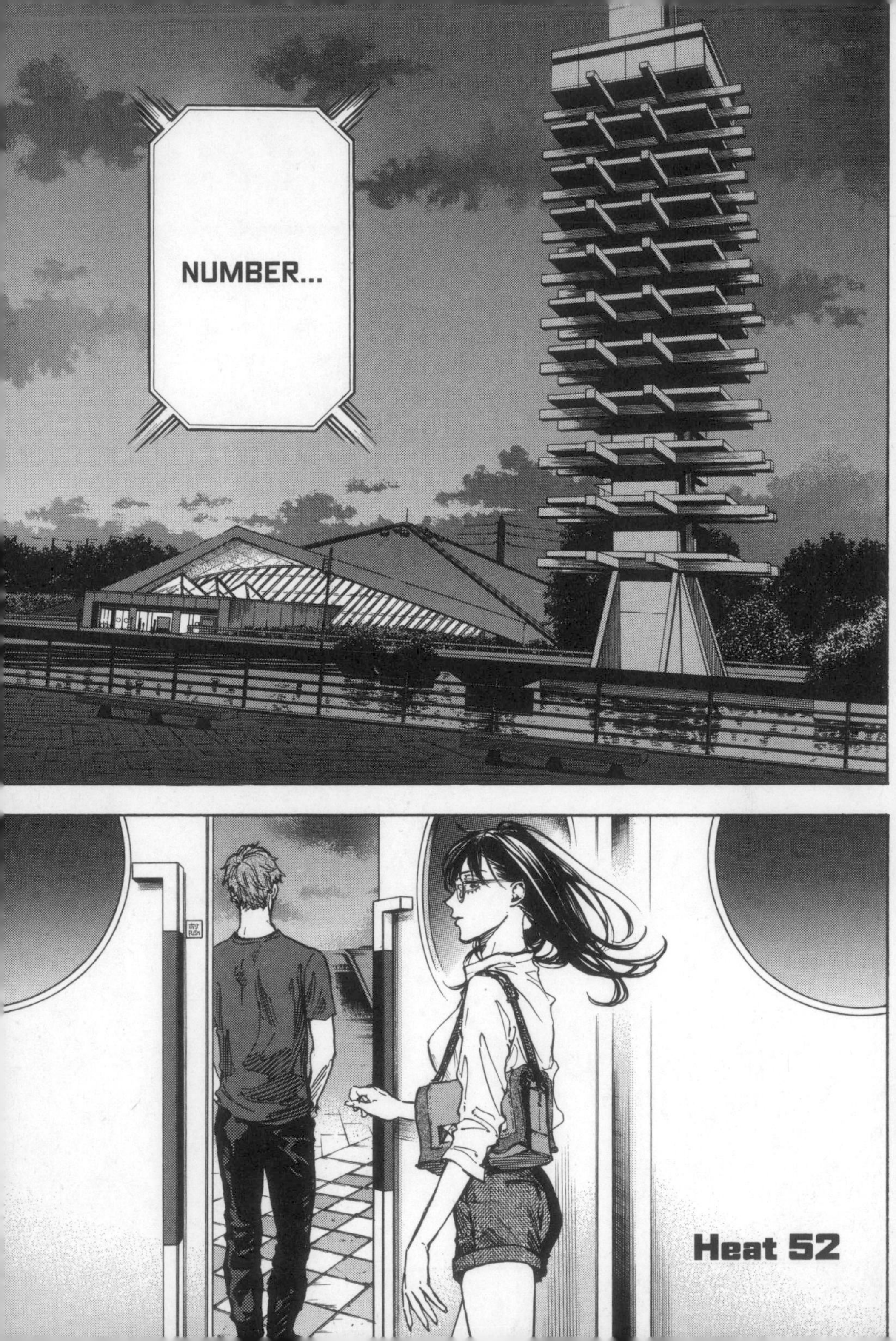
NUMBER...
Heat 52

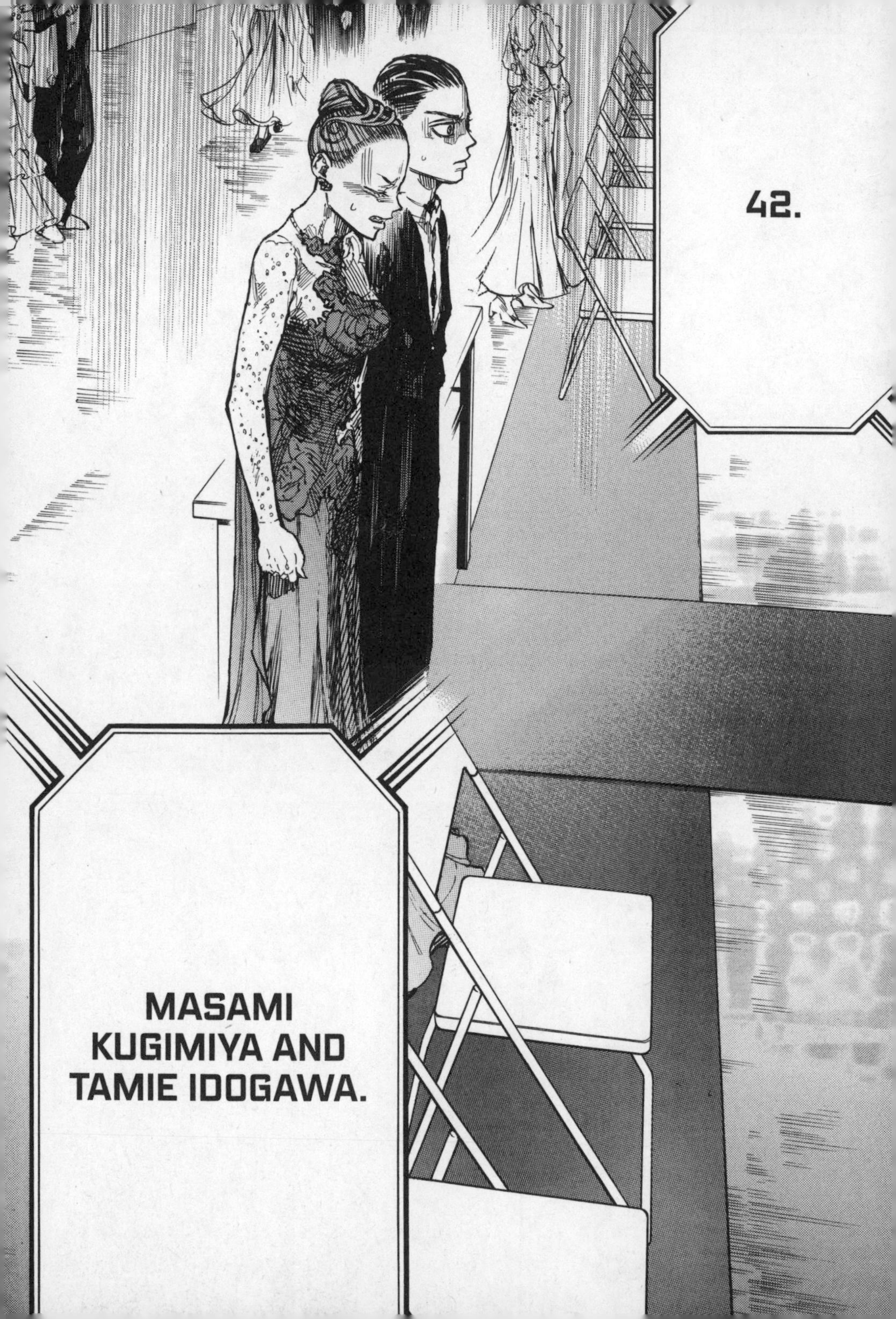
42.
MASAMI KUGIMIYA AND TAMIE IDOGAWA.

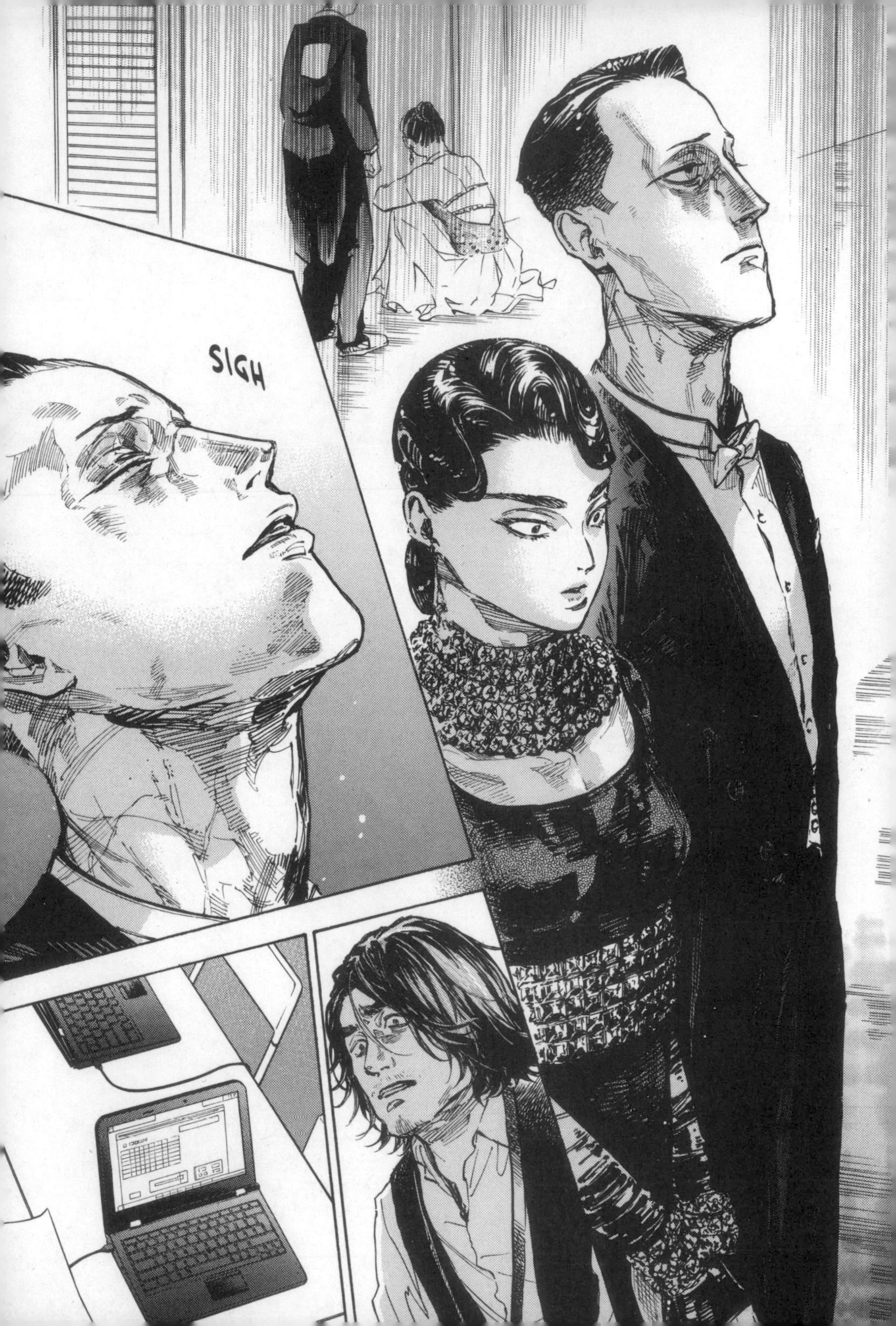
SIGH

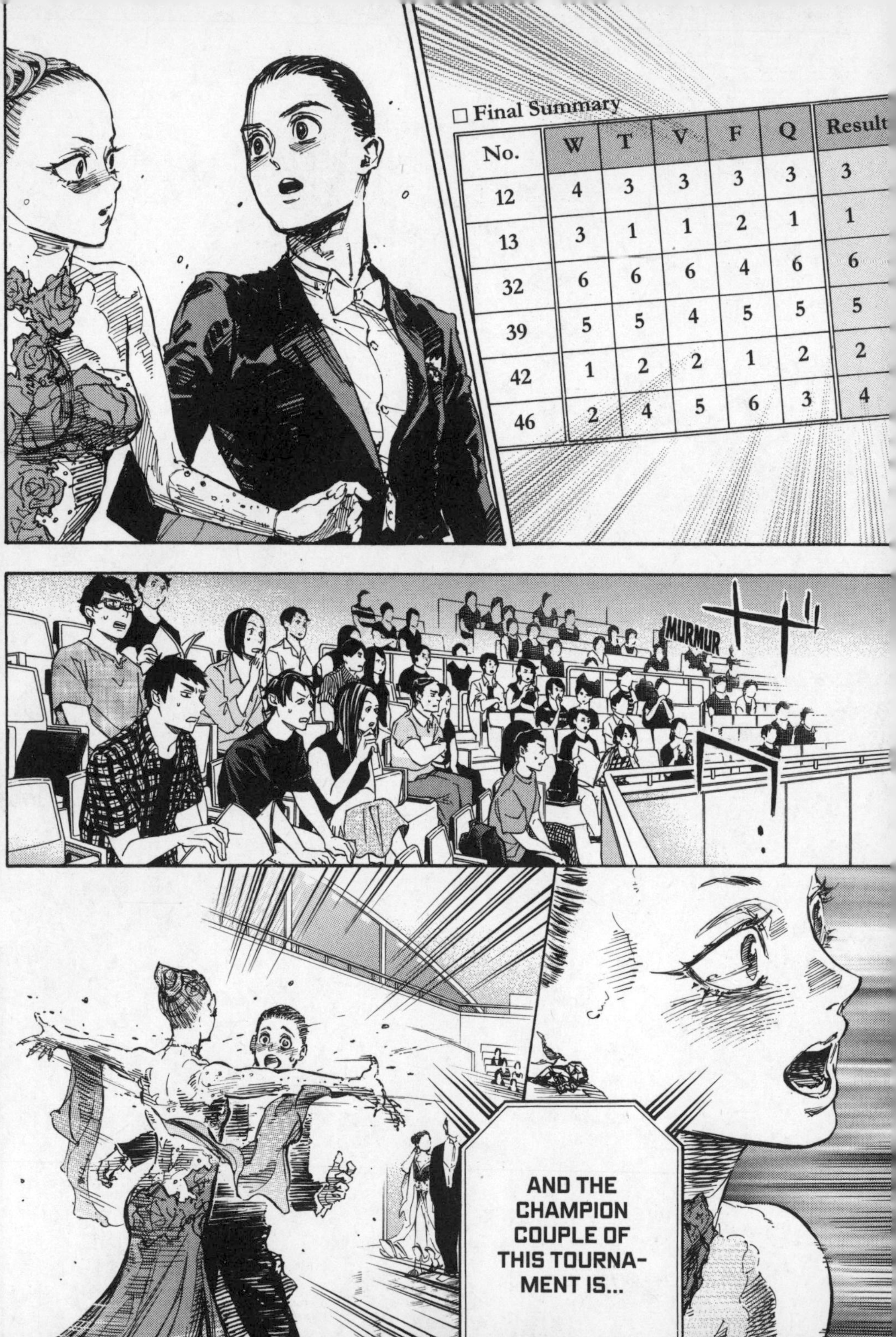

□ Final Summary
No. | W | T | V | F | Q | Result
12 | 4 | 3 | 3 | 3 | 3 | 3
13 | 3 | 1 | 1 | 2 | 1 | 1
32 | 6 | 6 | 6 | 4 | 6 | 6
39 | 5 | 5 | 4 | 5 | 5 | 5
42 | 1 | 2 | 2 | 1 | 2 | 2
46 | 2 | 4 | 5 | 6 | 3 | 4
MURMUR
AND THE CHAMPION COUPLE OF THIS TOURNA-MENT IS...

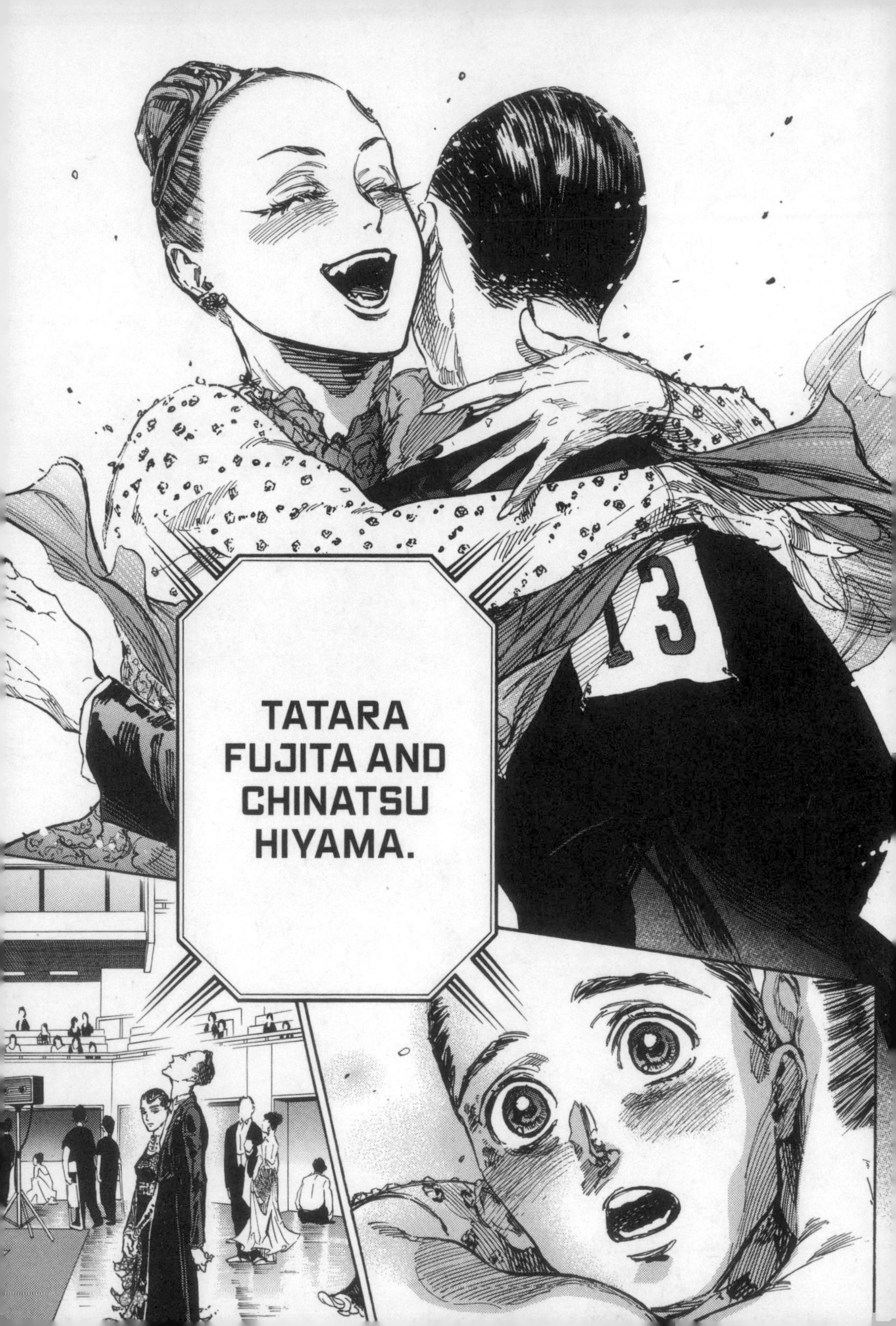
TATARA FUJITA AND CHINATSU HIYAMA.
13

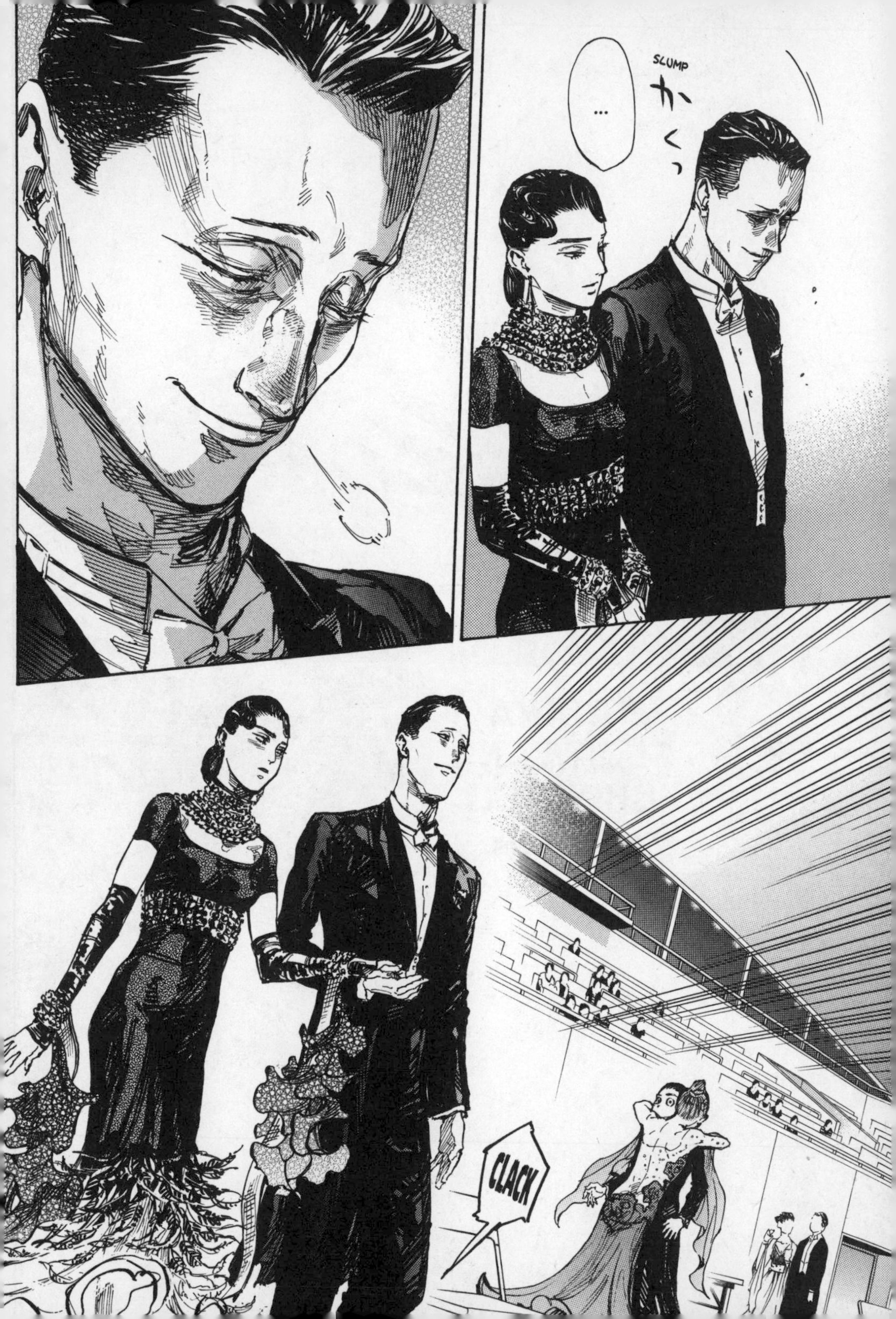
...
SLUMP
かくっ
CLACK

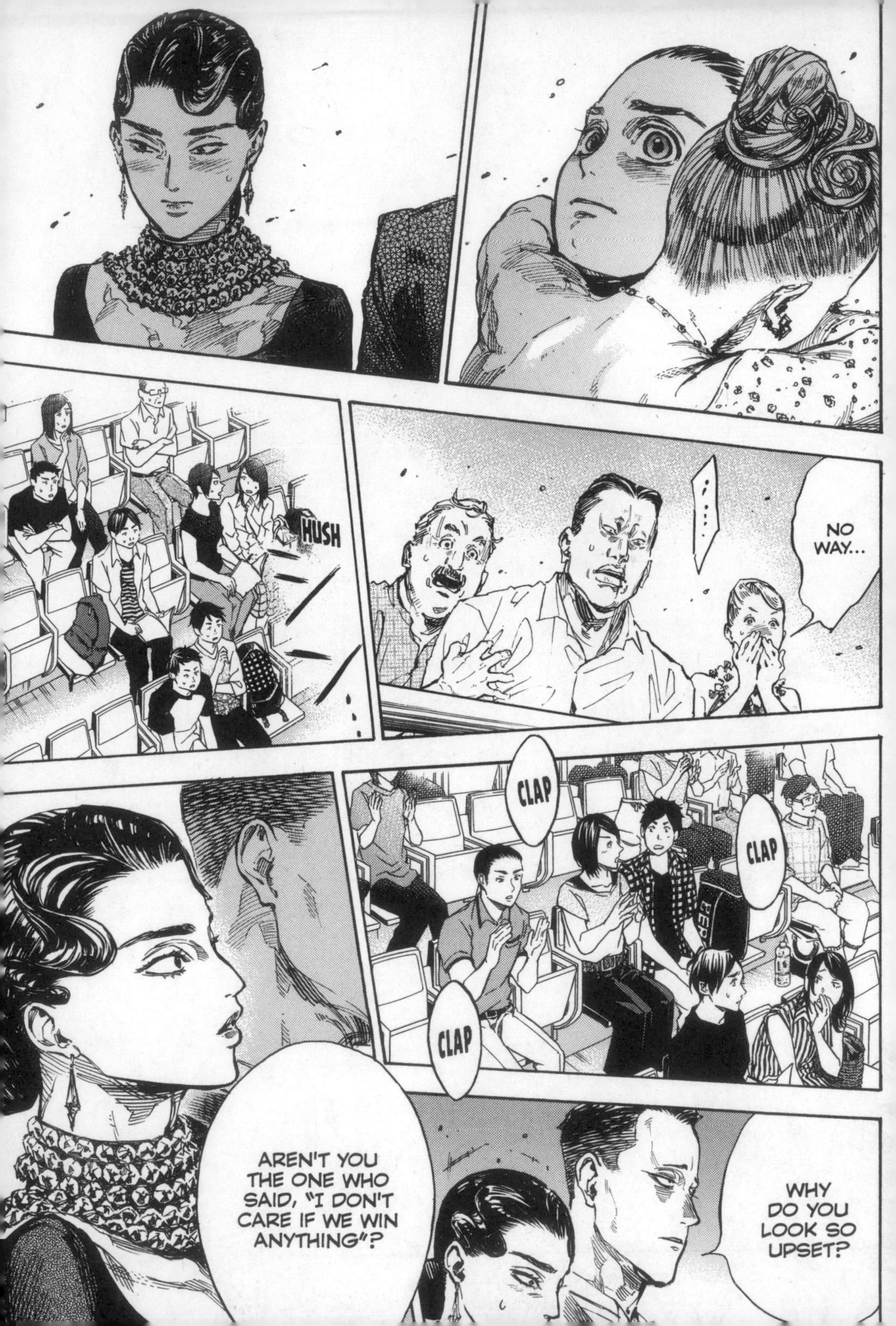
...!
NO WAY...
HUSH
CLAP
CLAP
CLAP
WHY DO YOU LOOK SO UPSET?
AREN'T YOU THE ONE WHO SAID, "I DON'T CARE IF WE WIN ANYTHING"?

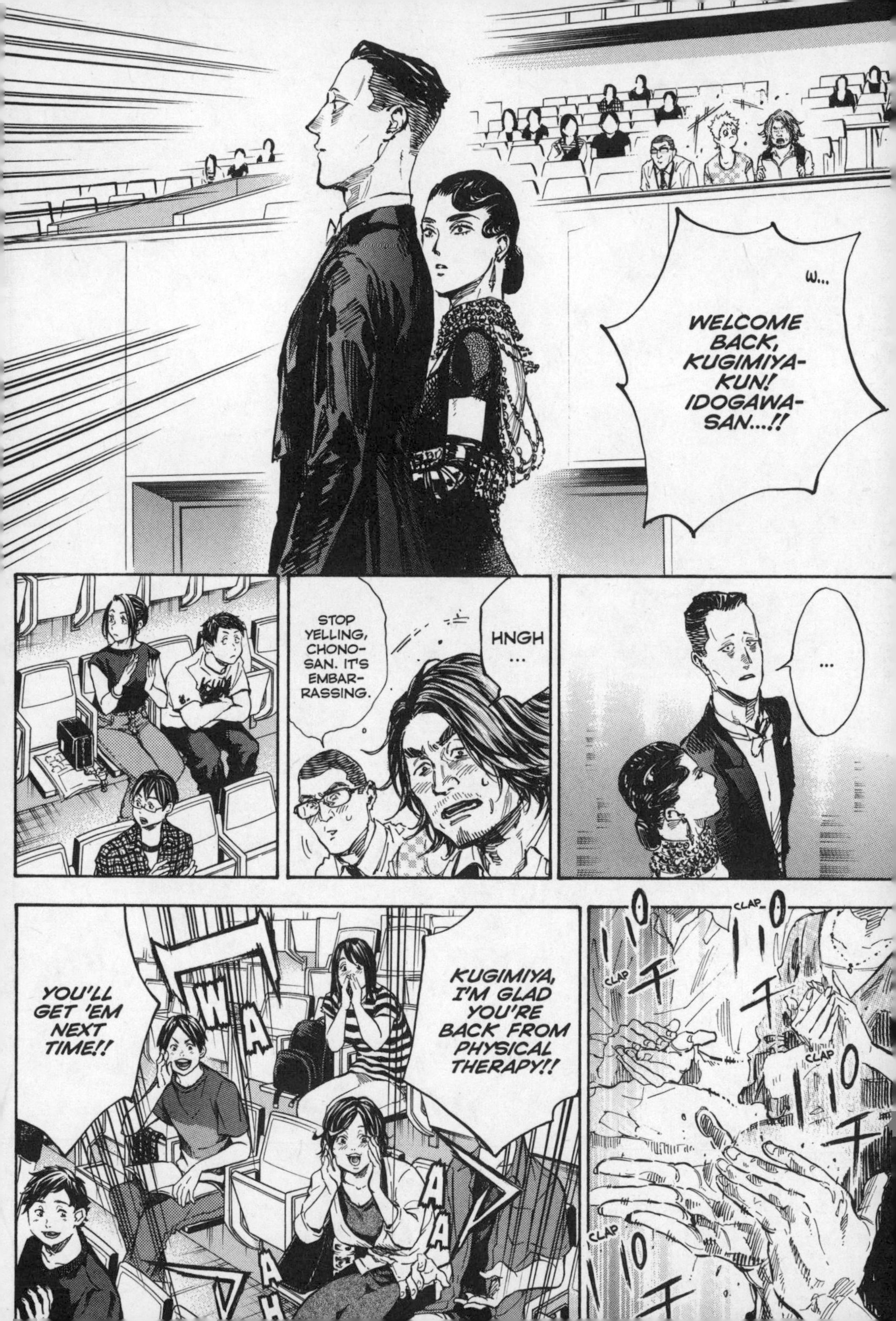
W...
WELCOME BACK, KUGIMIYA-KUN! IDOGAWA-SAN...!!
...
HNGH ...
STOP YELLING, CHONO-SAN. IT'S EMBAR-RASSING.
CLAP
CLAP
CLAP
CLAP
KUGIMIYA, I'M GLAD YOU'RE BACK FROM PHYSICAL THERAPY!!
YOU'LL GET 'EM NEXT TIME!!

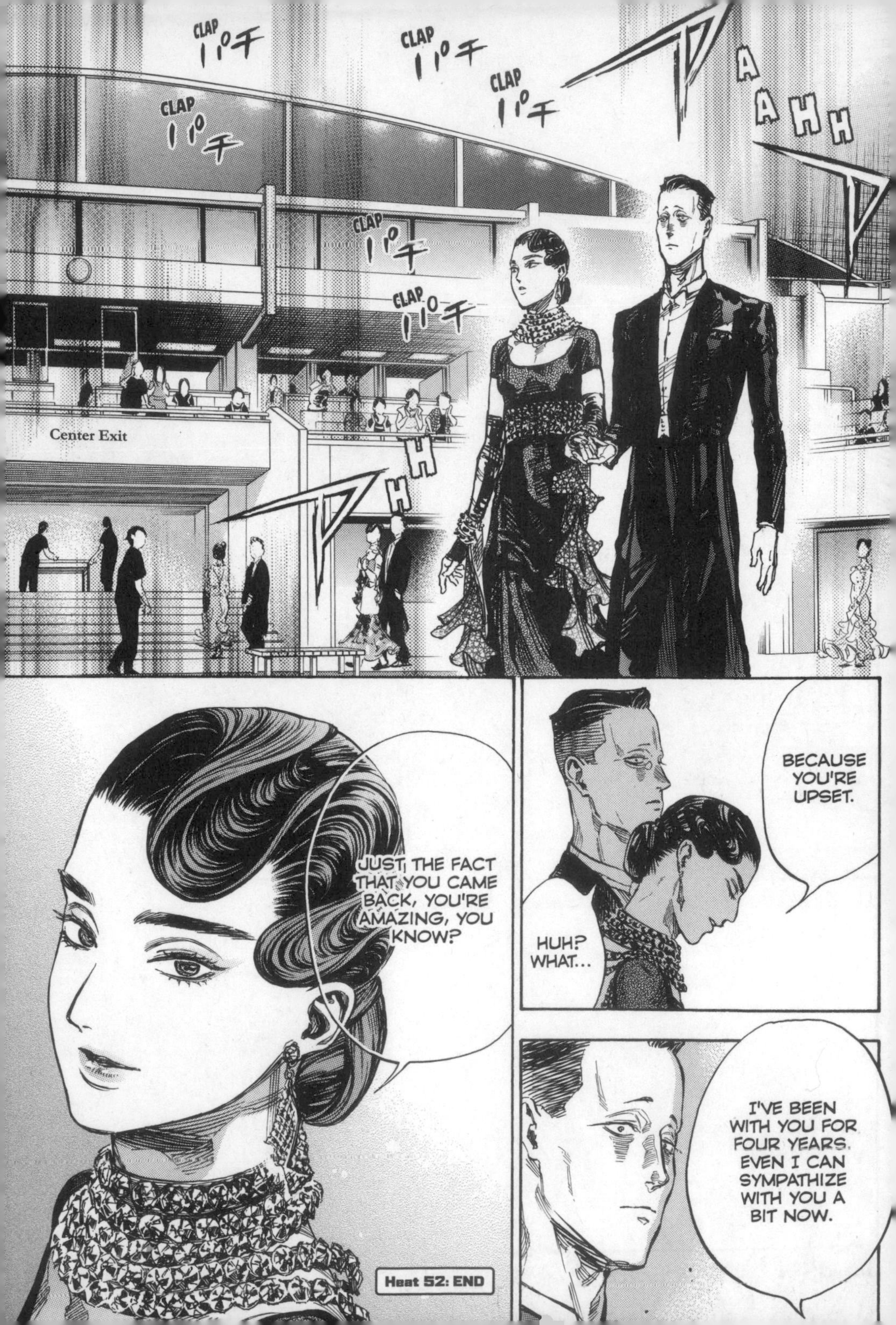
AAHHH
CLAP パチ
CLAP パチ
CLAP パチ
CLAP パチ
CLAP パチ
CLAP パチ
HH
Center Exit
BECAUSE YOU'RE UPSET.
HUH? WHAT...
I'VE BEEN WITH YOU FOR FOUR YEARS. EVEN I CAN SYMPATHIZE WITH YOU A BIT NOW.
JUST THE FACT THAT YOU CAME BACK, YOU'RE AMAZING, YOU KNOW?
Heat 52: END

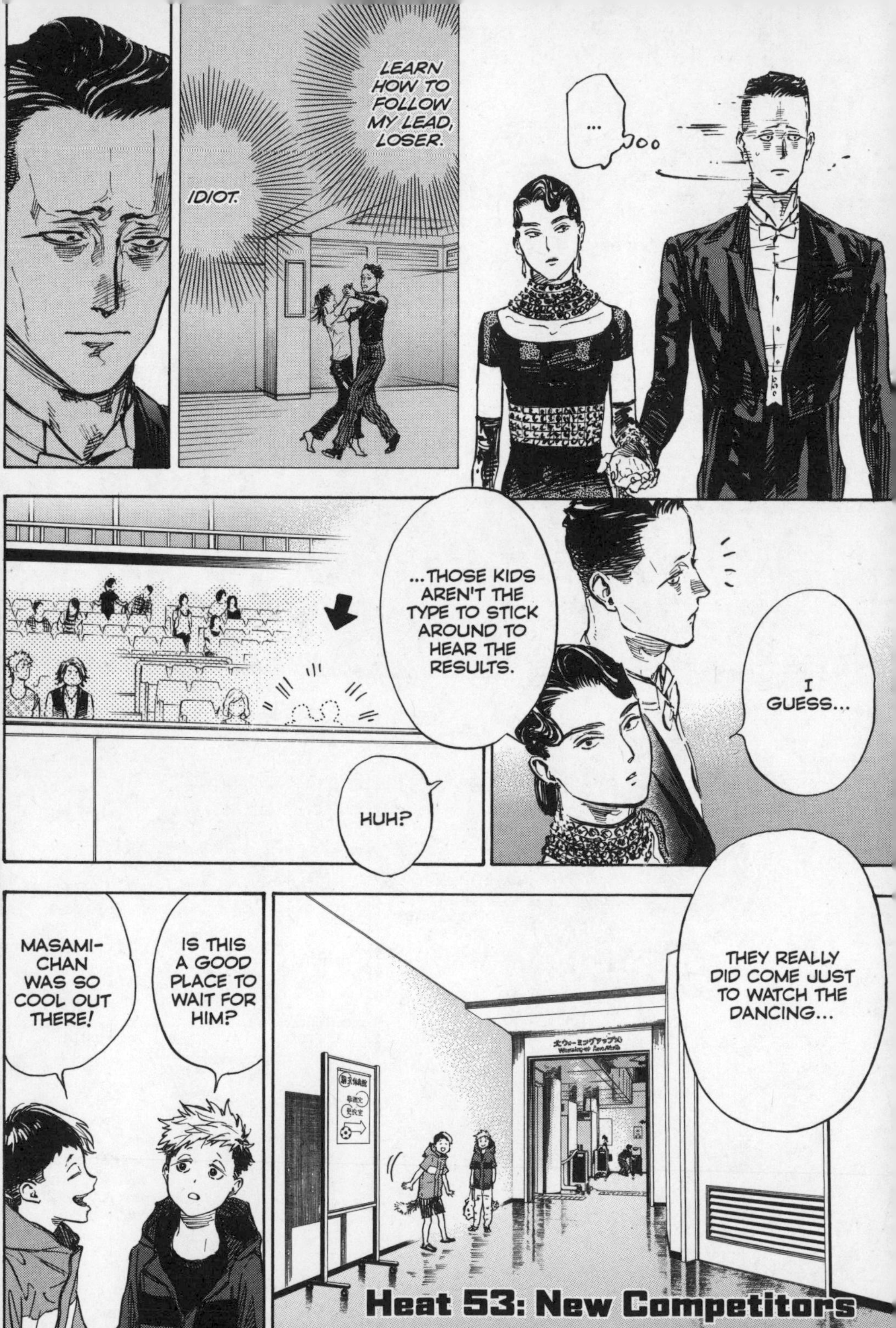
...
Ooo
LEARN HOW TO FOLLOW MY LEAD, LOSER.
IDIOT.
...THOSE KIDS AREN'T THE TYPE TO STICK AROUND TO HEAR THE RESULTS.
I GUESS...
HUH?
THEY REALLY DID COME JUST TO WATCH THE DANCING...
IS THIS A GOOD PLACE TO WAIT FOR HIM?
MASAMI-CHAN WAS SO COOL OUT THERE!

Heat 53: New Competitors

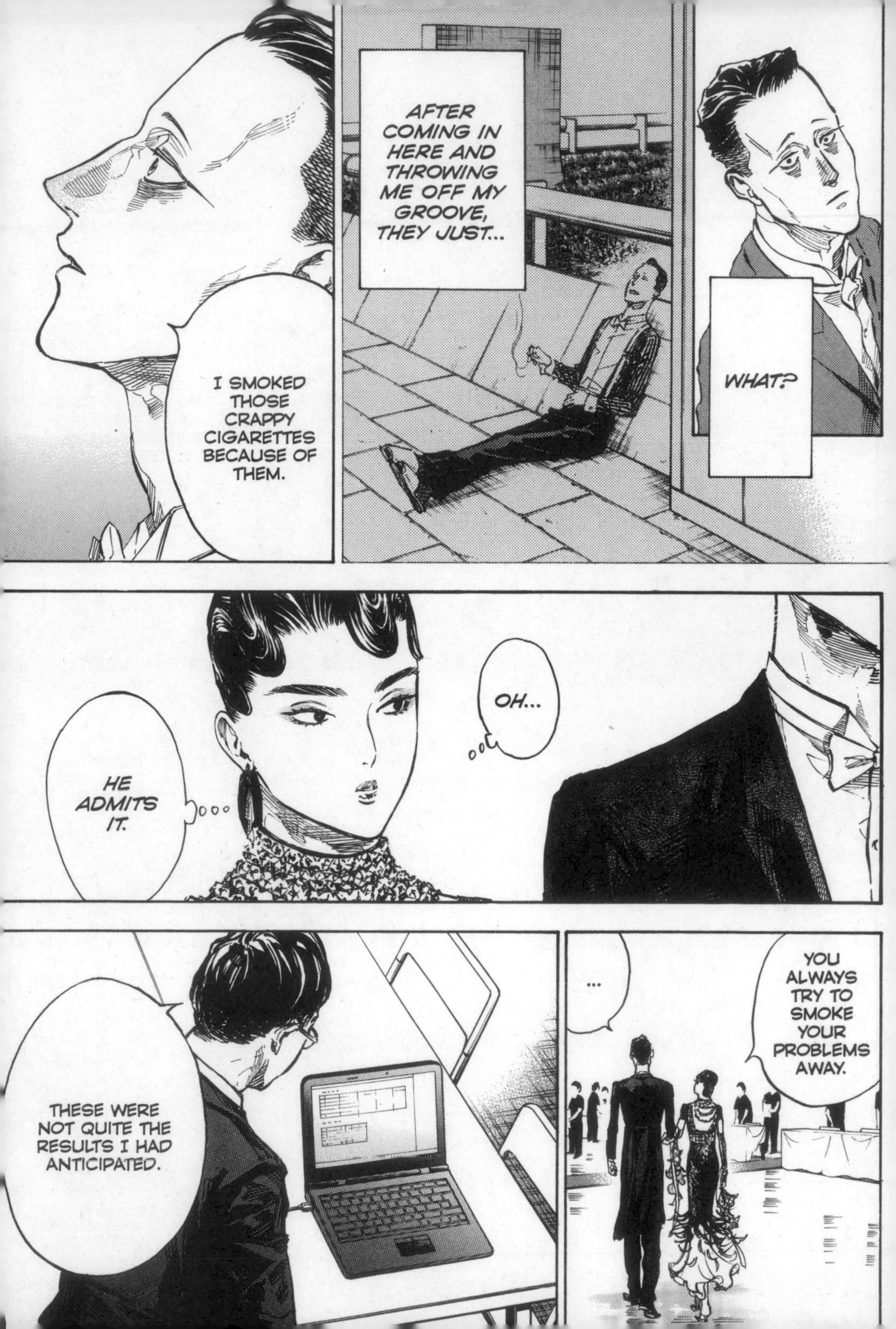
WHAT?
AFTER COMING IN HERE AND THROWING ME OFF MY GROOVE, THEY JUST...
I SMOKED THOSE CRAPPY CIGARETTES BECAUSE OF THEM.
OH...
HE ADMITS IT.
YOU ALWAYS TRY TO SMOKE YOUR PROBLEMS AWAY.
...
THESE WERE NOT QUITE THE RESULTS I HAD ANTICIPATED.

No.	W							
	H	I	J	K	L	M	N	Total
12	4	4	3	4	4	4	2	4
13	3	2	4	3	2	3	4	3
32	6	6	6	6	6	6	5	6
39	5	5	5	5	5	5	6	5
42	1	1	1	1	1	1	1	1
46	2	3	2	2	3	2	3	2

No.	T							
	H	I	J	K	L	M	N	Total
12	3	2	4	3	2	4	3	3
13	1	1	2	2	1	2	1	1
32	6	6	5	6	6	6	5	6
39	5	5	6	5	5	5	6	5
42	2	3	1	1	3	1	2	2
46	4	4	3	4	4	3	4	4

No.	V							
	H	I	J	K	L	M	N	Total
12	4	2	3	3	2	5	3	3
13	1	1	2	2	1	1	1	1
32	6	6	4	6	6	6	5	6
39	3	4	5	4	4	3	4	4
42	2	3	1	1	3	2	2	2
46	5	5	6	5	5	4	6	5

No.	F							
	H	I	J	K	L	M	N	Total
12	5	4	4	3	3	3	3	3
13	2	1	2	2	2	2	2	2
32	3	3	3	5	4	4	4	4
39	4	5	5	6	6	6	5	5
42	1	2	1	1	1	1	1	1
46	6	6	6	4	5	5	6	6

No.	Q							
	H	I	J	K	L	M	N	Total
12	5	3	4	4	4	5	3	4
13	1	1	2	1	1	2	2	1
32	6	6	5	6	6	6	5	6
39	4	5	6	5	5	4	6	5
42	2	2	1	2	2	1	1	2
46	3	4	3	3	3	3	4	3

□Final Summary

No.	W	T	V	F	Q	Result	Totals	Verdict

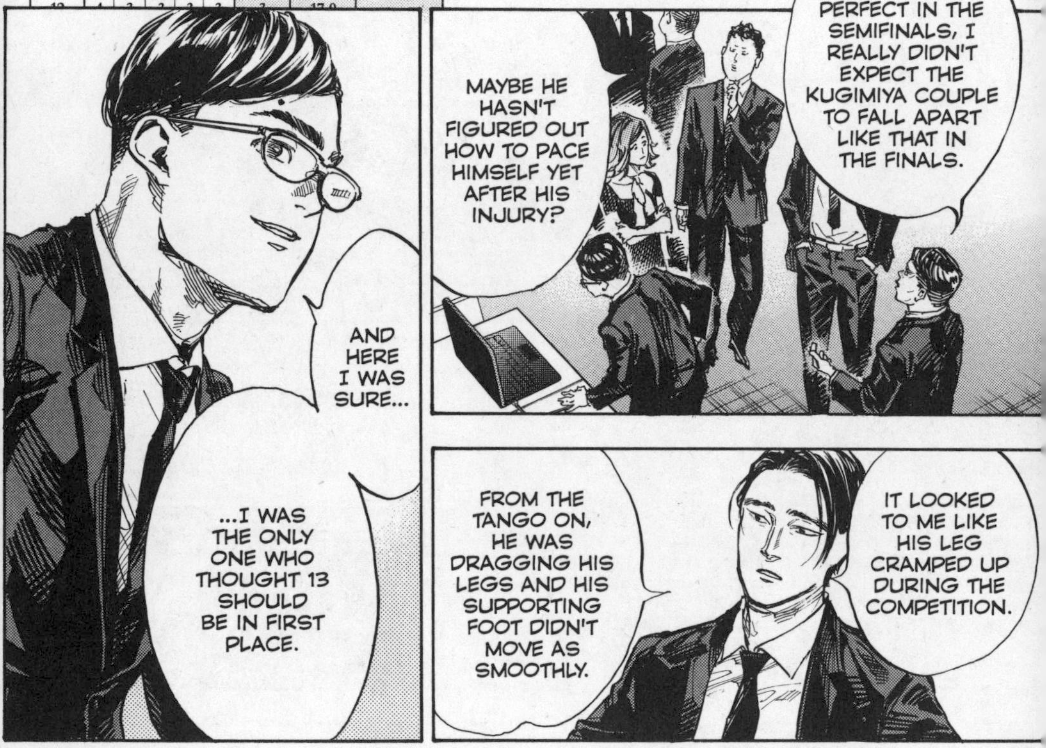
AFTER THEY WERE SO PERFECT IN THE SEMIFINALS, I REALLY DIDN'T EXPECT THE KUGIMIYA COUPLE TO FALL APART LIKE THAT IN THE FINALS.
MAYBE HE HASN'T FIGURED OUT HOW TO PACE HIMSELF YET AFTER HIS INJURY?
IT LOOKED TO ME LIKE HIS LEG CRAMPED UP DURING THE COMPETITION.
FROM THE TANGO ON, HE WAS DRAGGING HIS LEGS AND HIS SUPPORTING FOOT DIDN'T MOVE AS SMOOTHLY.
AND HERE I WAS SURE...
...I WAS THE ONLY ONE WHO THOUGHT 13 SHOULD BE IN FIRST PLACE.

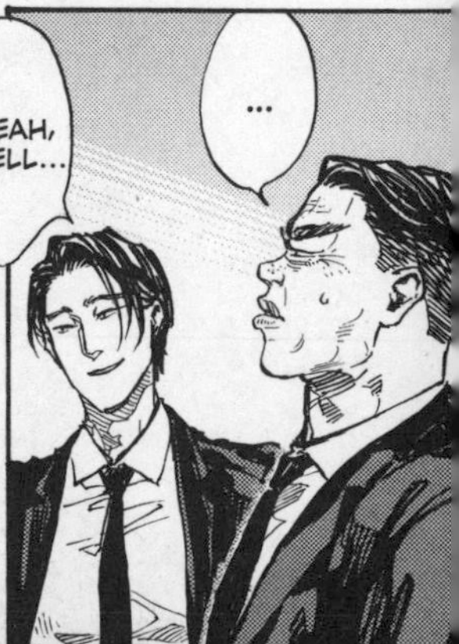
...
YEAH, WELL...

□Final Summary

No.	W	T	V	F	Q	Result	Totals	Verdict
12	4	3	3	3	3	3	17.0	
13	3	1	1	2	1	1	8.0	Majority
32	6	6	6	4	6	6	28.0	
39	5	5	4	5	5	5	24.0	
42	1	2	2	1	2	2	8.0	Majority
46	2	4	5	6	3	4	20.0	

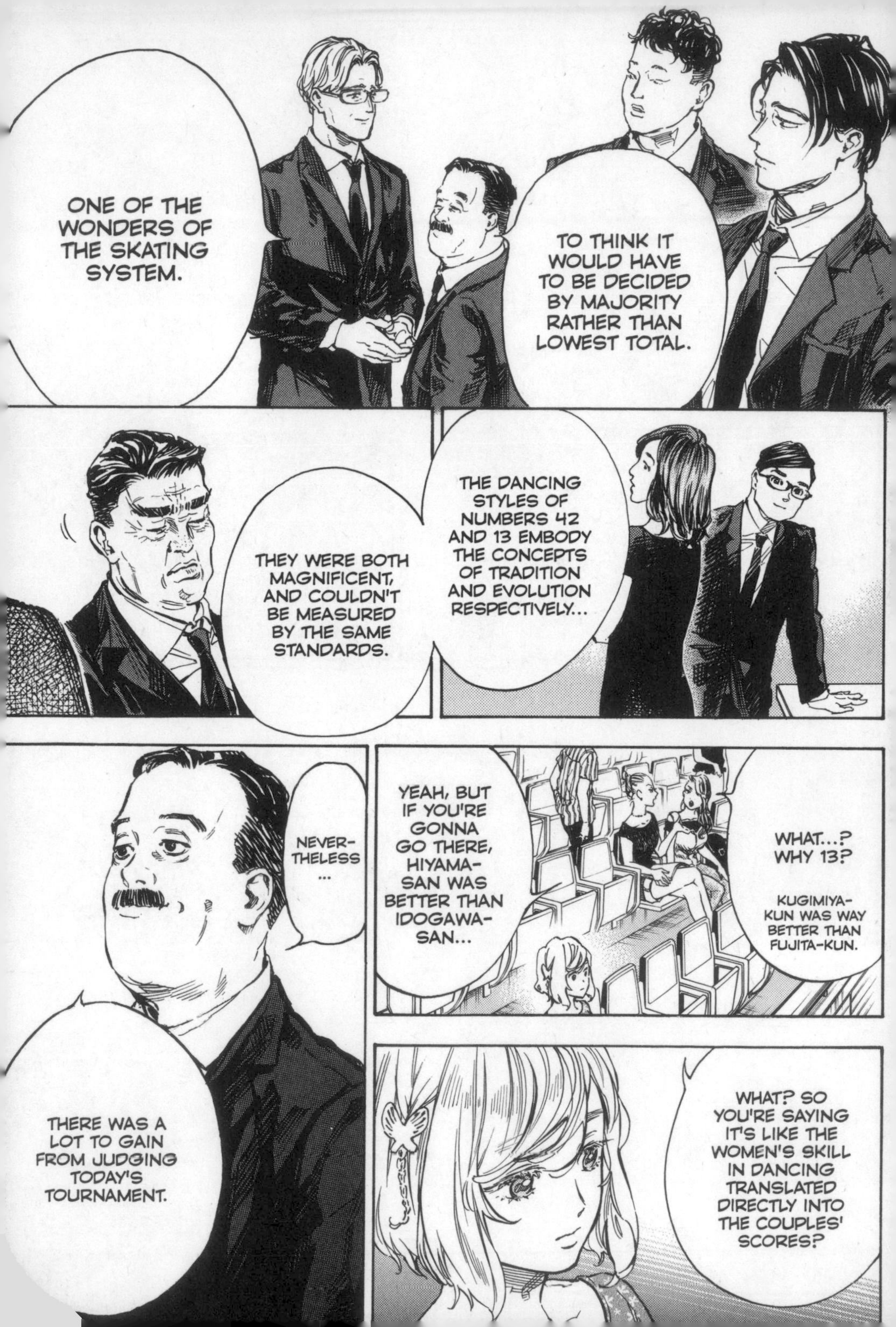
TO THINK IT WOULD HAVE TO BE DECIDED BY MAJORITY RATHER THAN LOWEST TOTAL.
ONE OF THE WONDERS OF THE SKATING SYSTEM.
THE DANCING STYLES OF NUMBERS 42 AND 13 EMBODY THE CONCEPTS OF TRADITION AND EVOLUTION RESPECTIVELY...
THEY WERE BOTH MAGNIFICENT, AND COULDN'T BE MEASURED BY THE SAME STANDARDS.
WHAT...? WHY 13?
KUGIMIYA-KUN WAS WAY BETTER THAN FUJITA-KUN.
YEAH, BUT IF YOU'RE GONNA GO THERE, HIYAMA-SAN WAS BETTER THAN IDOGAWA-SAN...
WHAT? SO YOU'RE SAYING IT'S LIKE THE WOMEN'S SKILL IN DANCING TRANSLATED DIRECTLY INTO THE COUPLES' SCORES?
NEVER-THELESS...
THERE WAS A LOT TO GAIN FROM JUDGING TODAY'S TOURNAMENT.

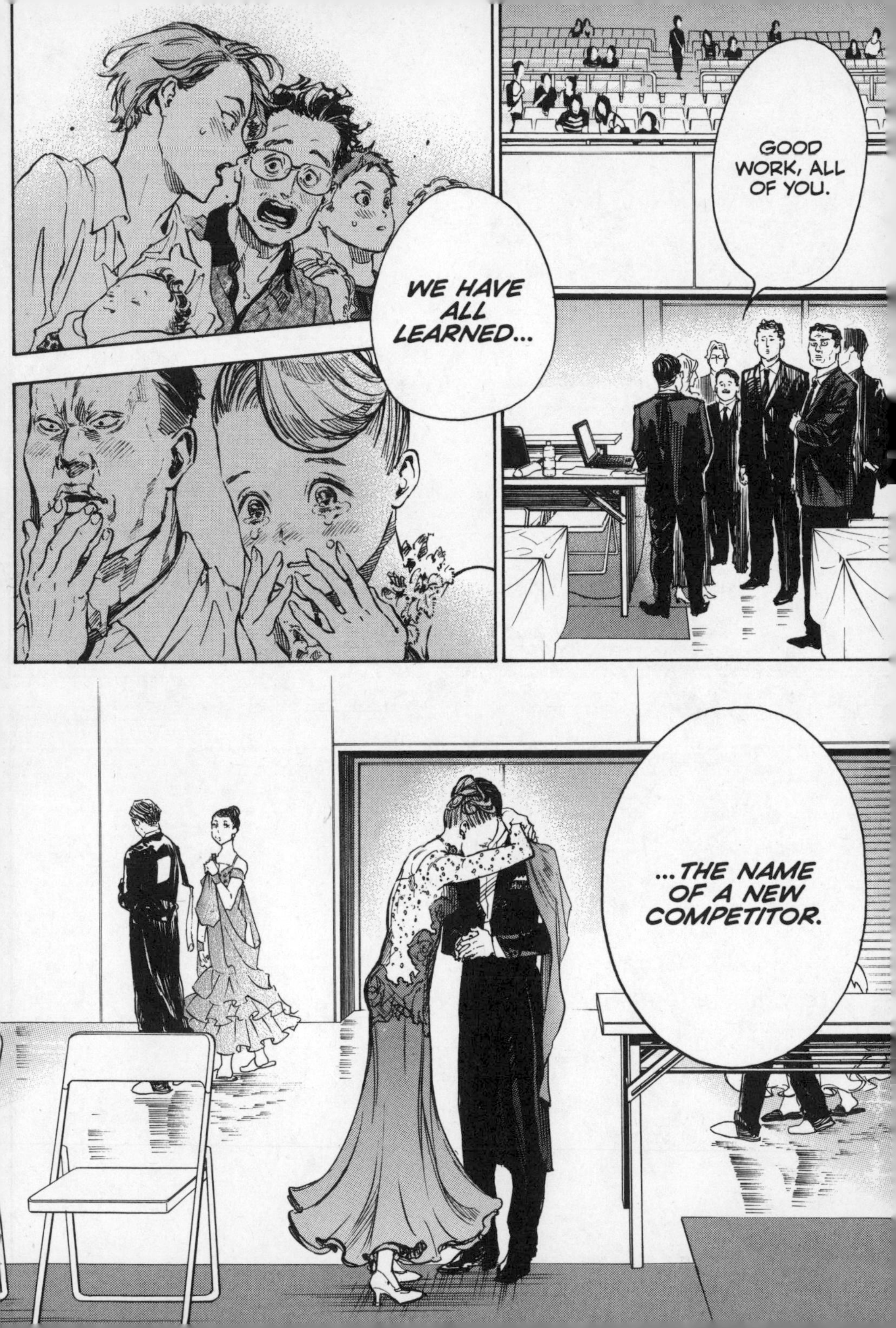
GOOD WORK, ALL OF YOU.
WE HAVE ALL LEARNED...
...THE NAME OF A NEW COMPETITOR.

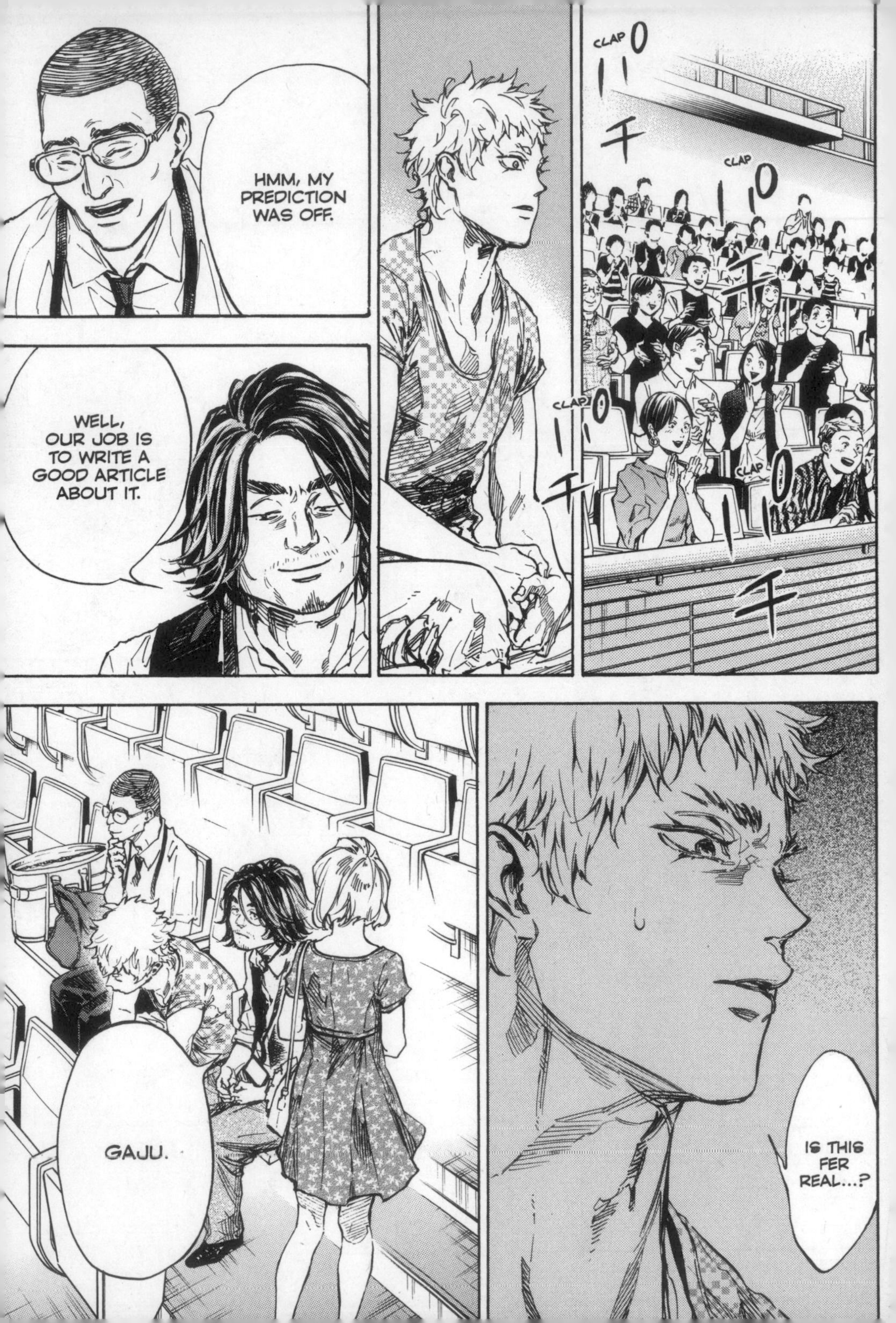
CLAP
パチ
CLAP
パチ
CLAP
パチ
CLAP
パチ
HMM, MY PREDICTION WAS OFF.
WELL, OUR JOB IS TO WRITE A GOOD ARTICLE ABOUT IT.
IS THIS FER REAL...?
GAJU.

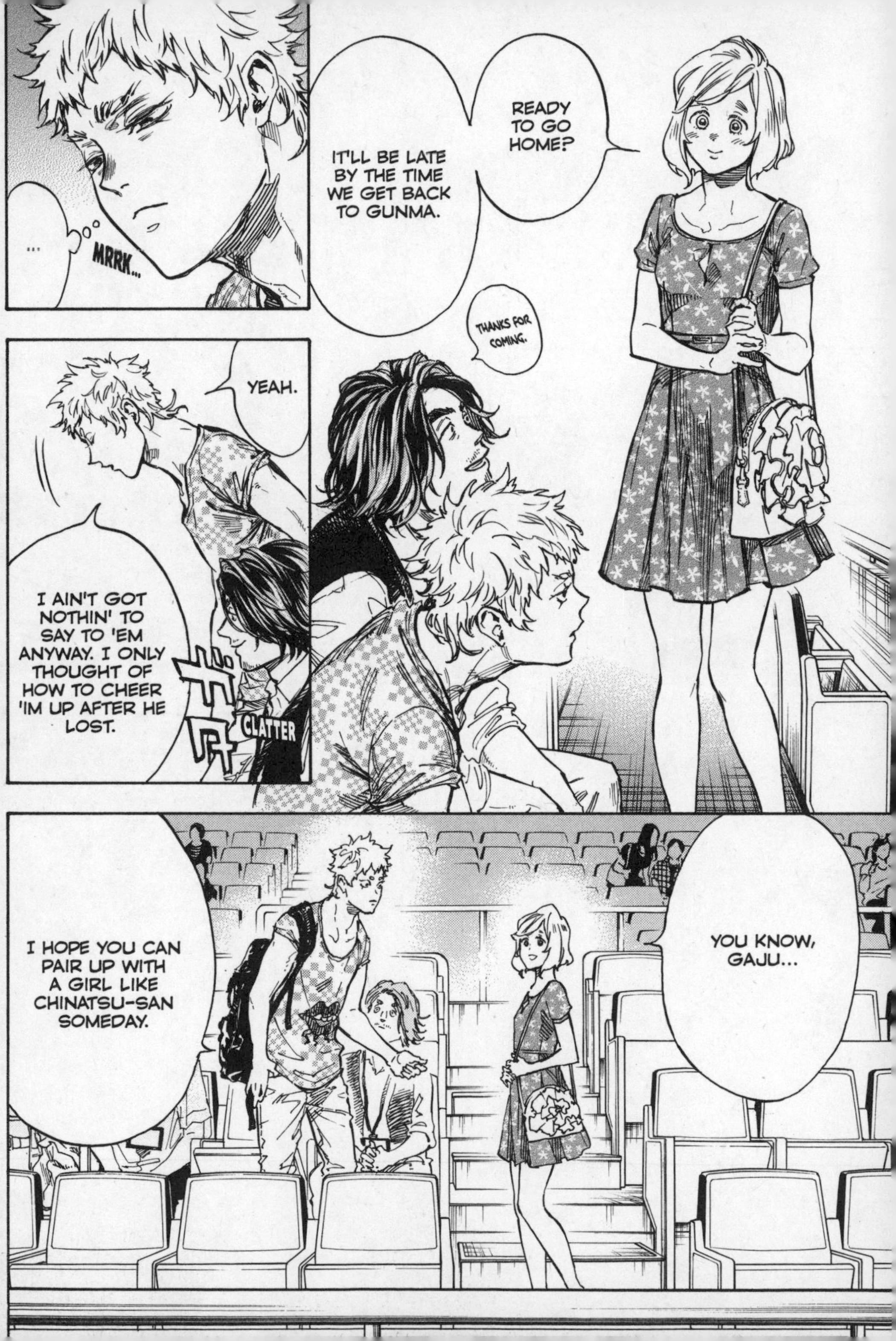
READY TO GO HOME?
IT'LL BE LATE BY THE TIME WE GET BACK TO GUNMA.
THANKS FOR COMING.
...
MRRK...
YEAH.
I AIN'T GOT NOTHIN' TO SAY TO 'EM ANYWAY. I ONLY THOUGHT OF HOW TO CHEER 'IM UP AFTER HE LOST.
CLATTER
YOU KNOW, GAJU...
I HOPE YOU CAN PAIR UP WITH A GIRL LIKE CHINATSU-SAN SOMEDAY.

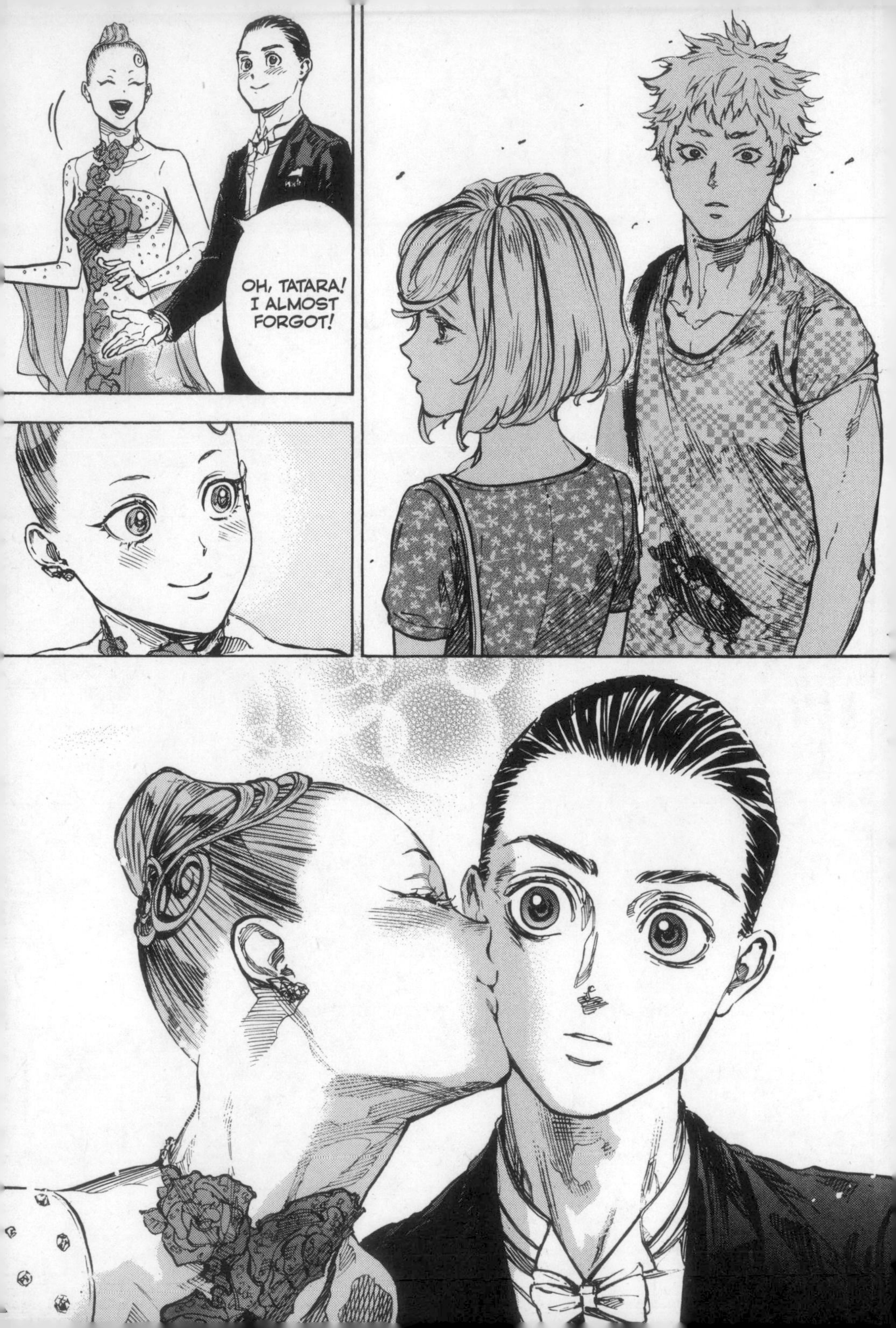
OH, TATARA! I ALMOST FORGOT!

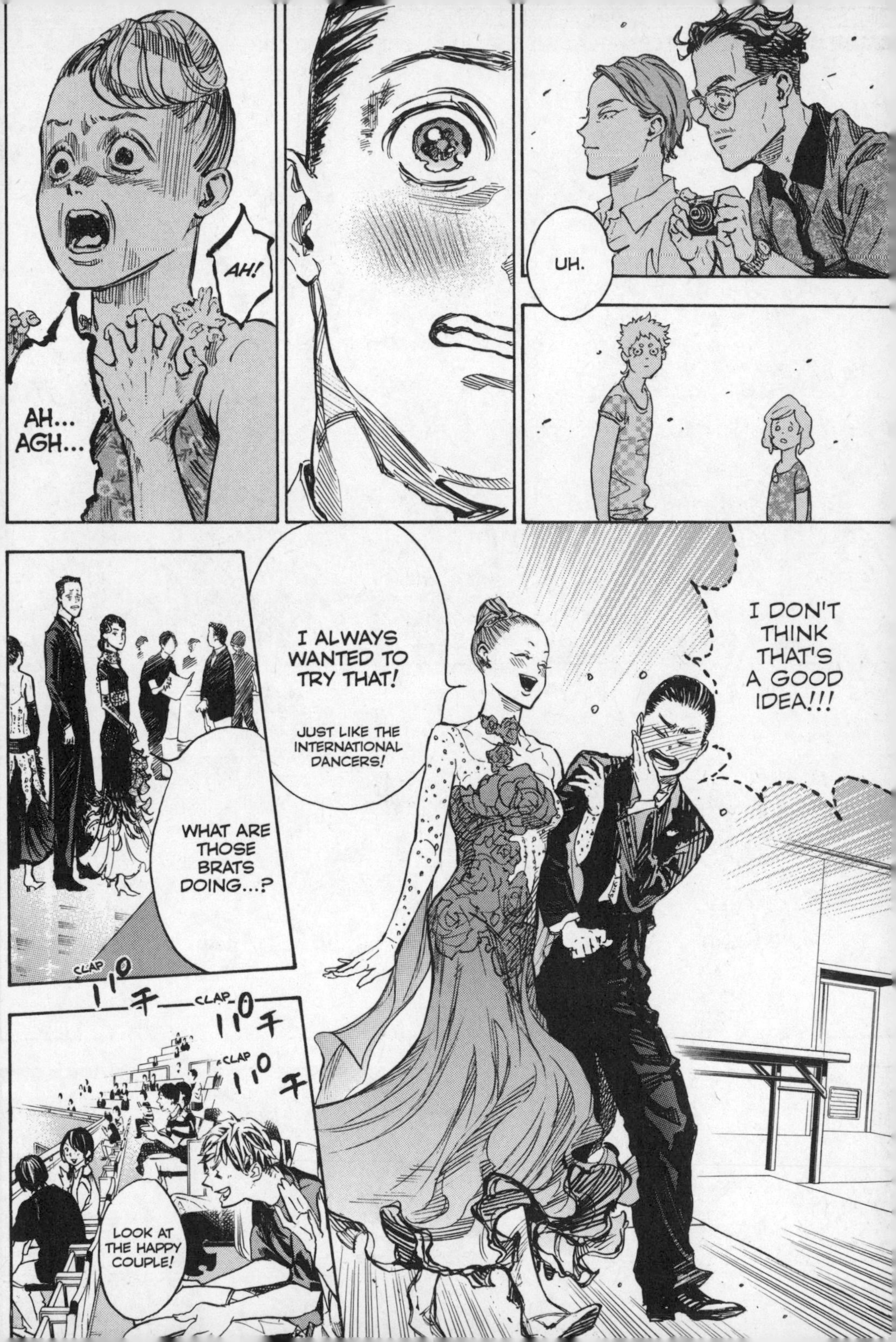
UH.
AH!
AH... AGH...
I DON'T THINK THAT'S A GOOD IDEA!!!
I ALWAYS WANTED TO TRY THAT!
JUST LIKE THE INTERNATIONAL DANCERS!
WHAT ARE THOSE BRATS DOING...?
CLAP
CLAP
CLAP
LOOK AT THE HAPPY COUPLE!

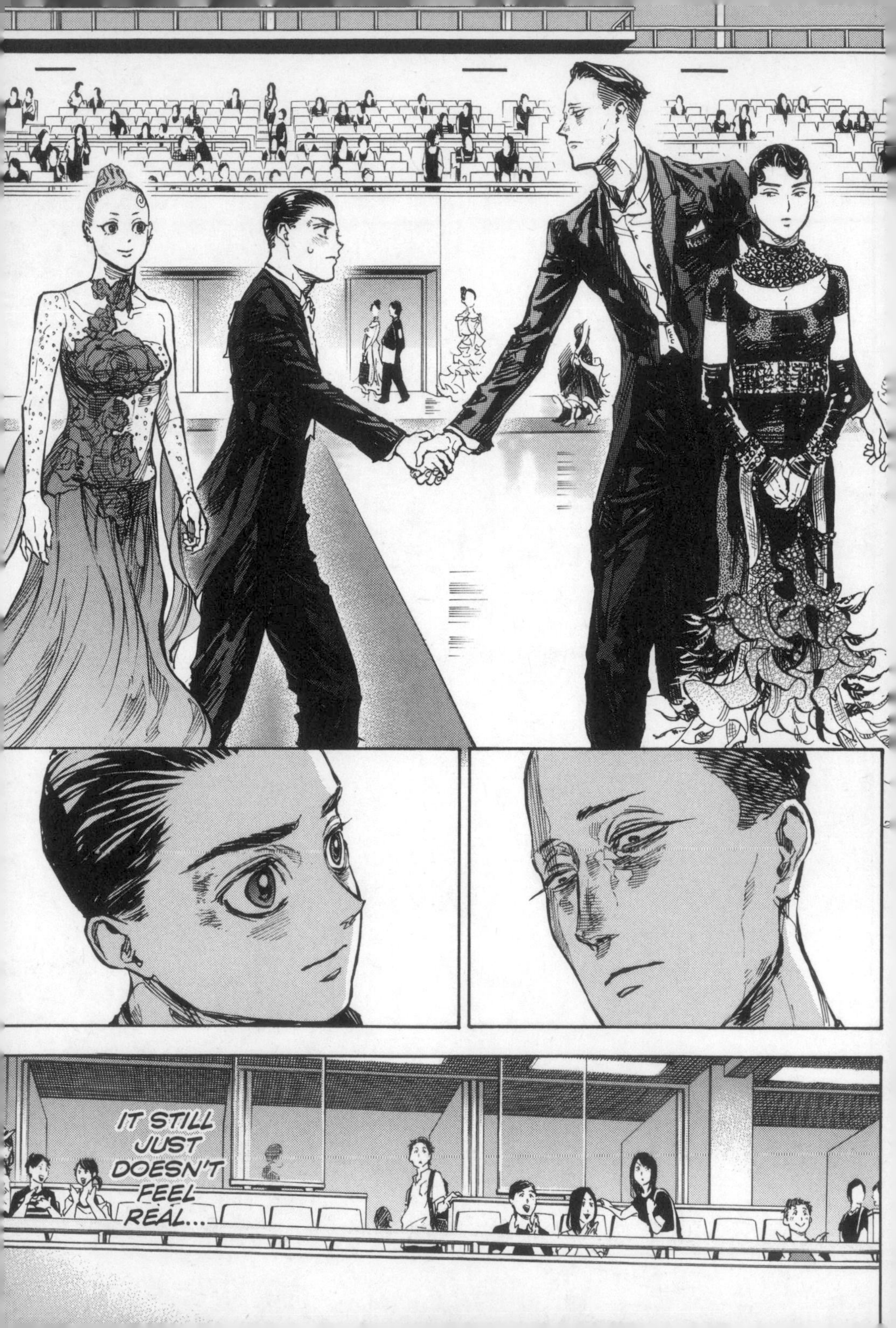
IT STILL JUST DOESN'T FEEL REAL...

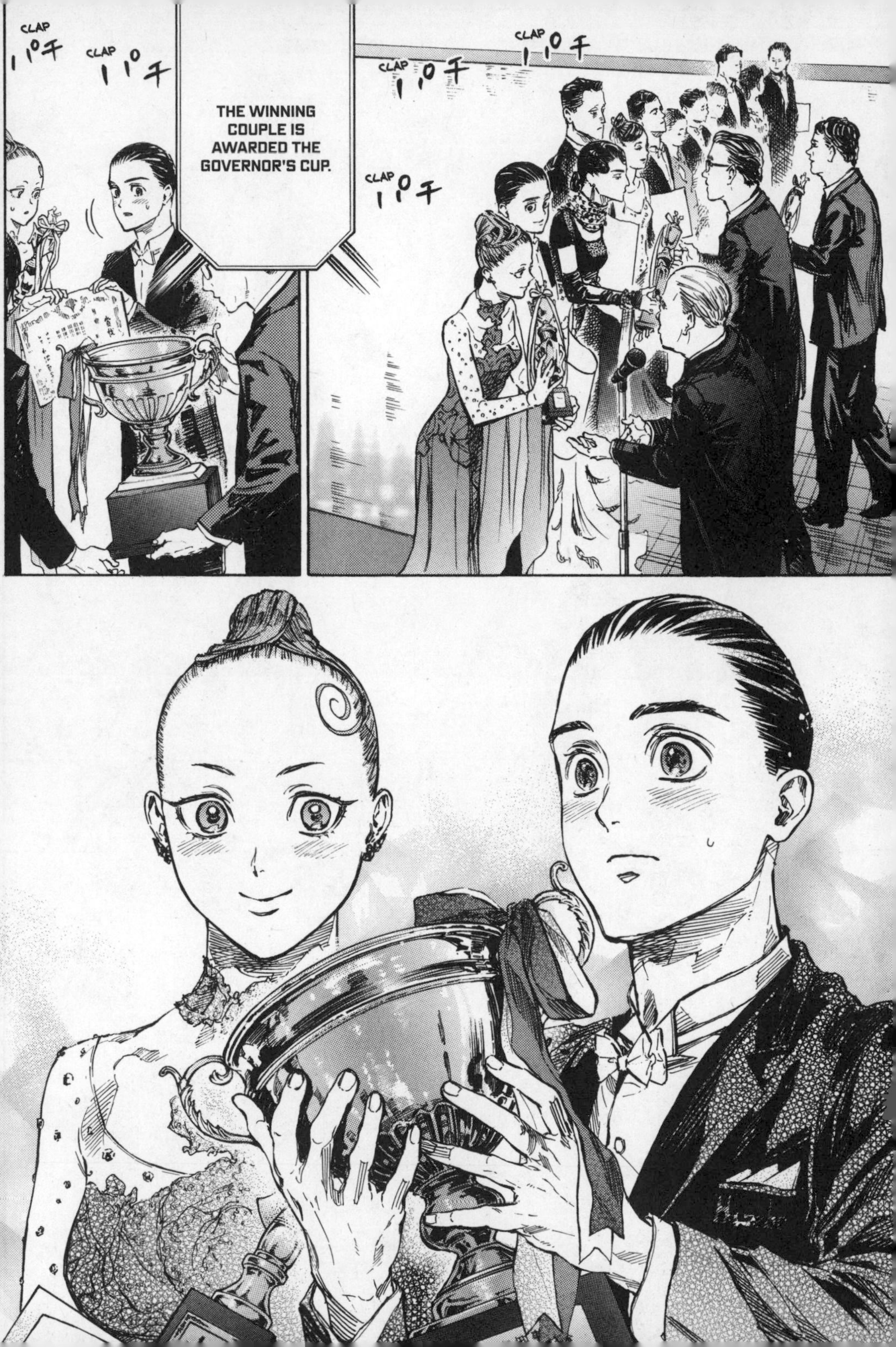
CLAP パチ
CLAP パチ
CLAP パチ
CLAP パチ
CLAP パチ
THE WINNING COUPLE IS AWARDED THE GOVERNOR'S CUP.

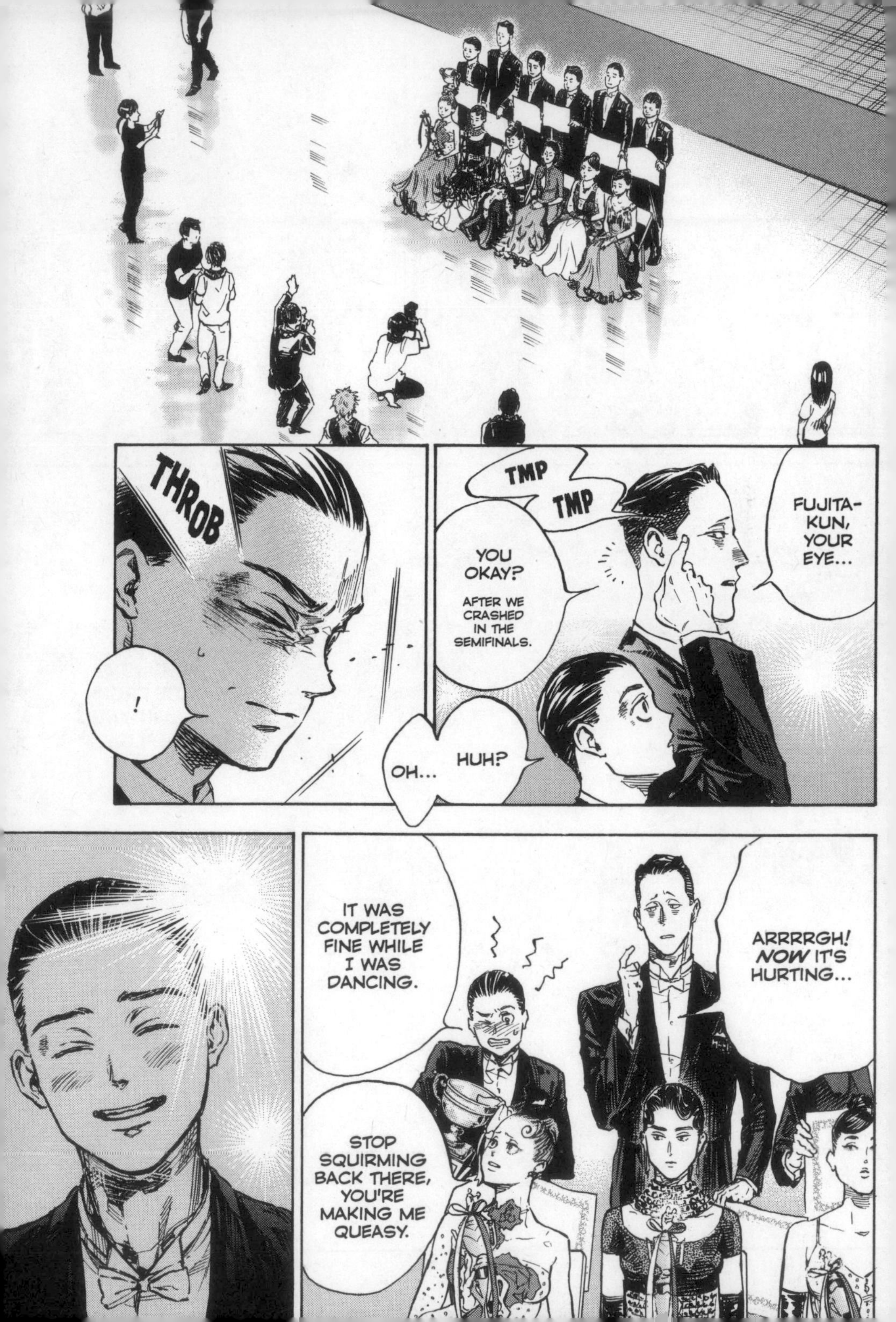
FUJITA-KUN, YOUR EYE...
TMP
TMP
YOU OKAY?
AFTER WE CRASHED IN THE SEMIFINALS.
HUH?
OH...
THROB
...
!
ARRRRGH! *NOW* IT'S HURTING...
IT WAS COMPLETELY FINE WHILE I WAS DANCING.
STOP SQUIRMING BACK THERE, YOU'RE MAKING ME QUEASY.

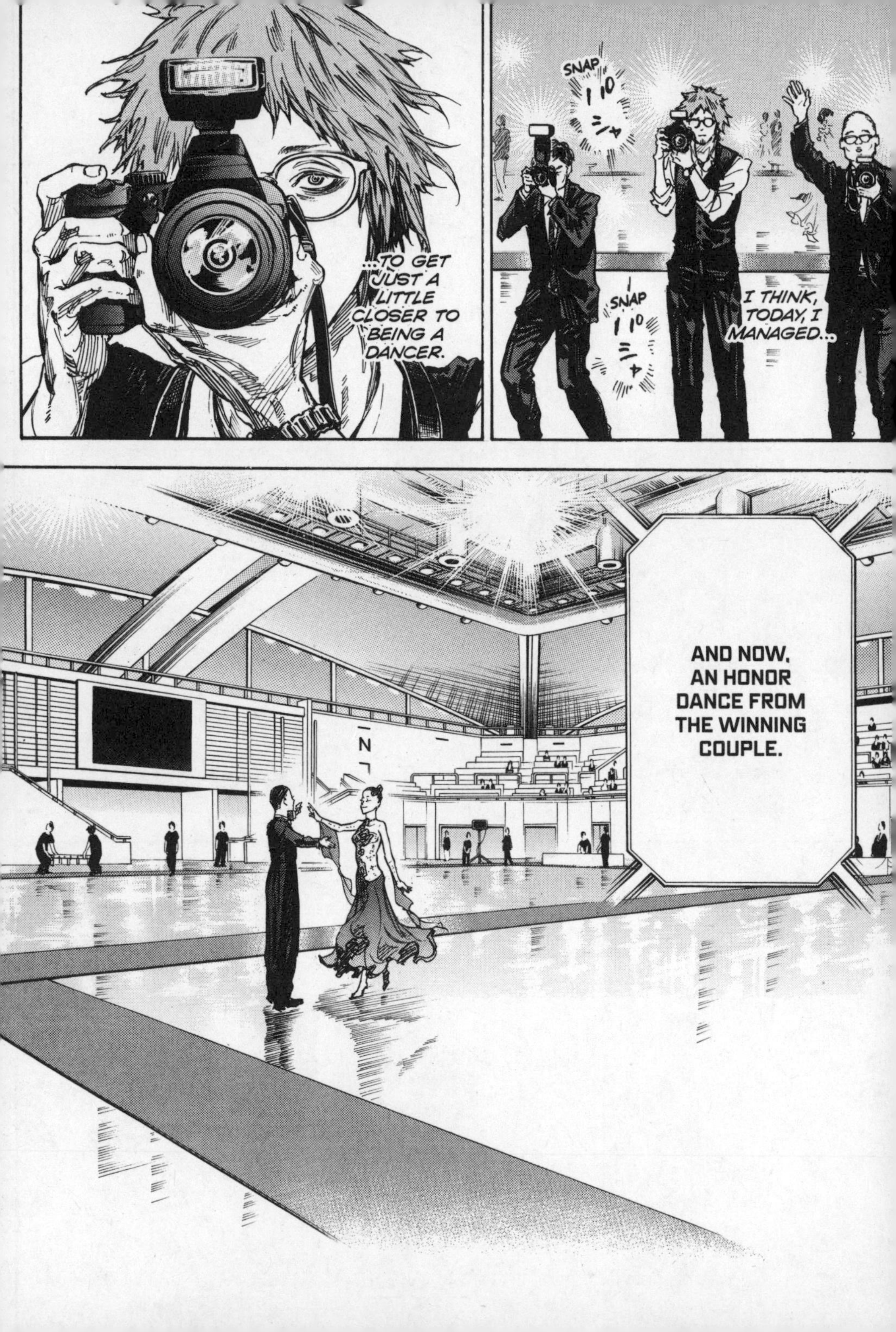
SNAP
パシャ
SNAP
パシャ
I THINK, TODAY, I MANAGED...
...TO GET JUST A LITTLE CLOSER TO BEING A DANCER.
AND NOW, AN HONOR DANCE FROM THE WINNING COUPLE.

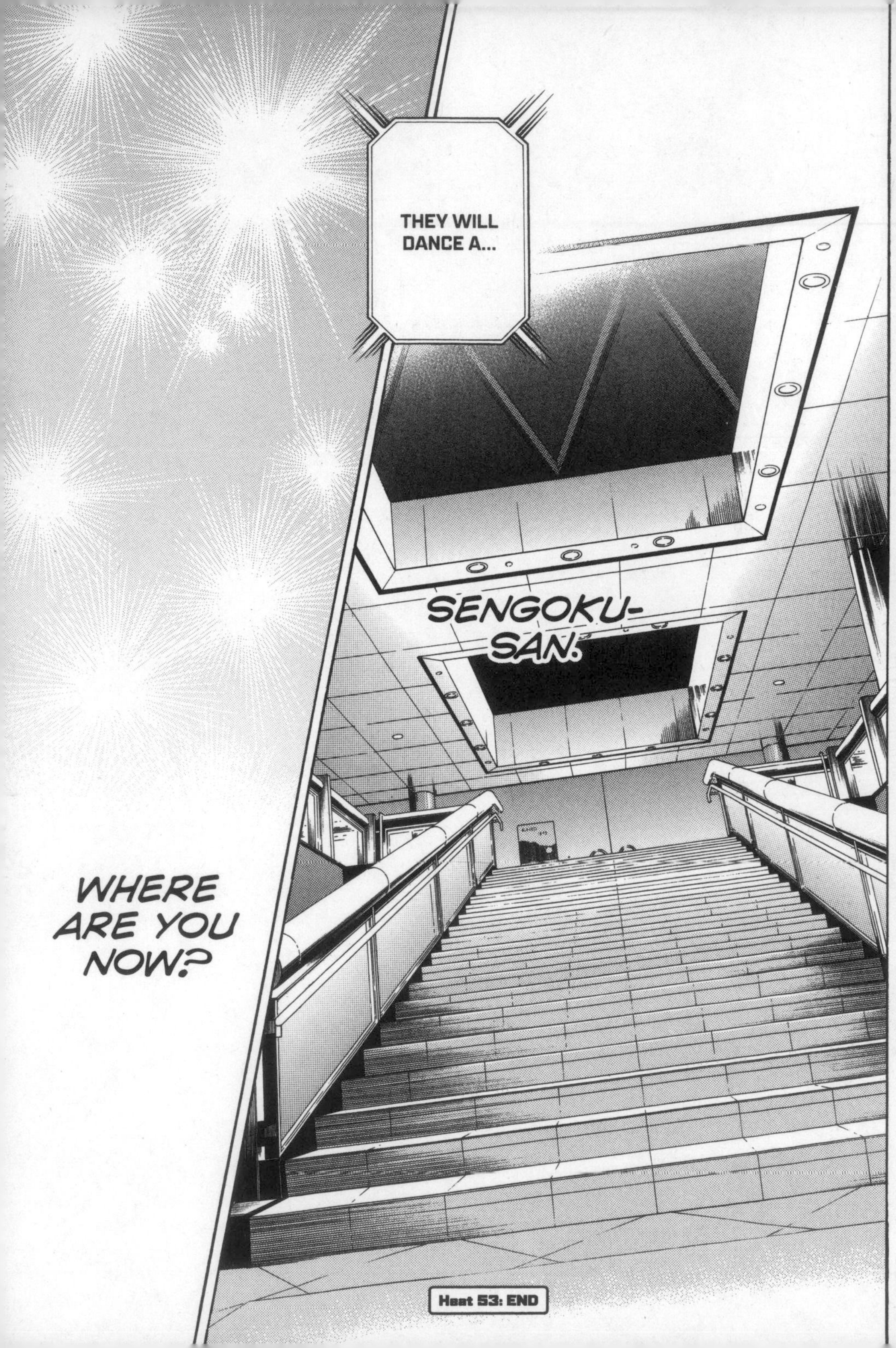
THEY WILL DANCE A...
SENGOKU-SAN.
WHERE ARE YOU NOW?
Heat 53: END

Special Thanks!

For providing reference material

Japan DanceSports Federation

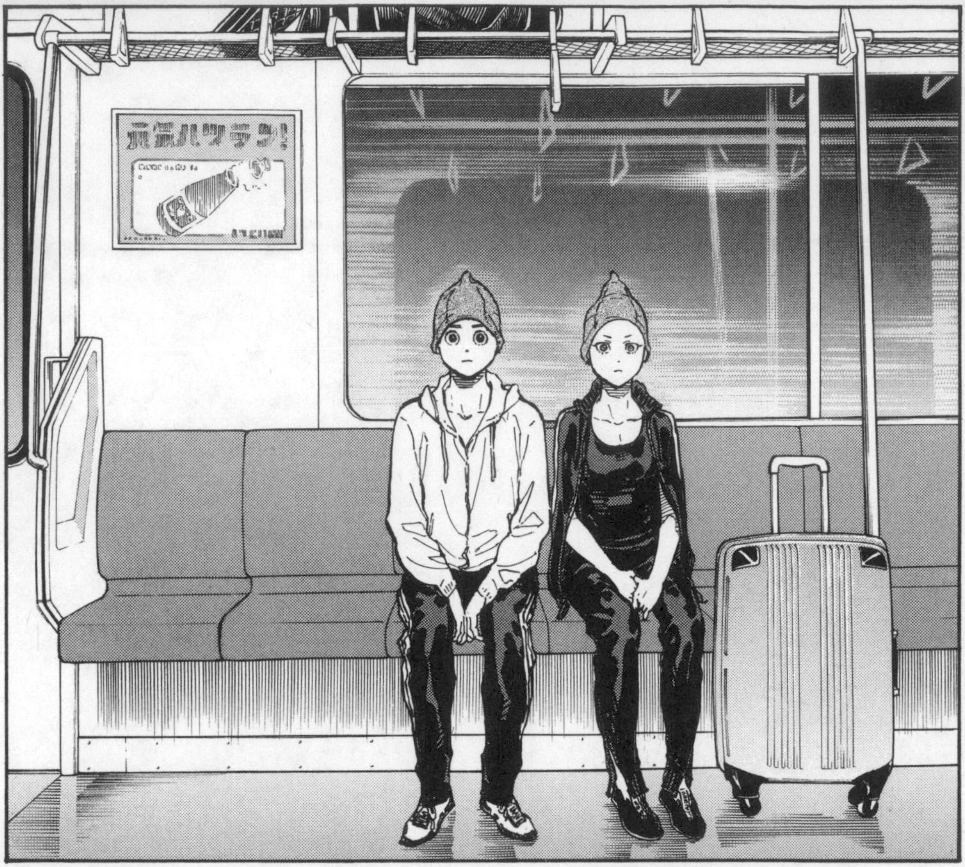

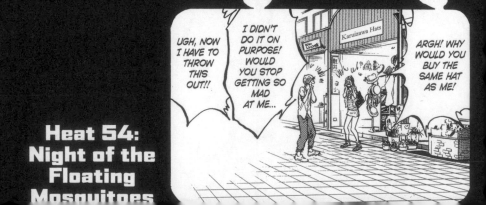

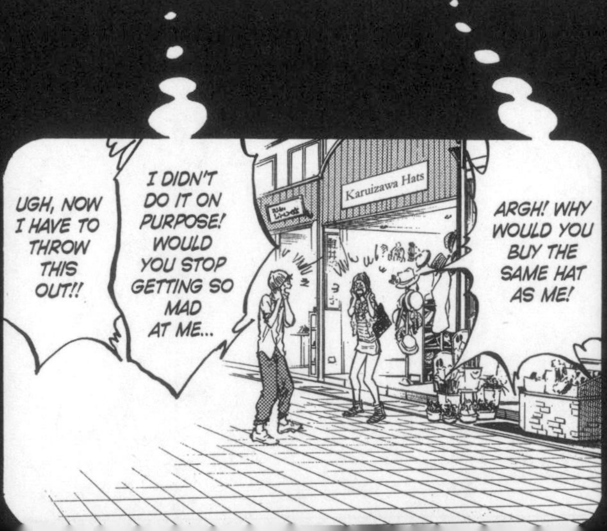
ARGH! WHY WOULD YOU BUY THE SAME HAT AS ME!
Karuizawa Hats
I DIDN'T DO IT ON PURPOSE! WOULD YOU STOP GETTING SO MAD AT ME...
UGH, NOW I HAVE TO THROW THIS OUT!!

Heat 54: Night of the Floating Mosquitoes

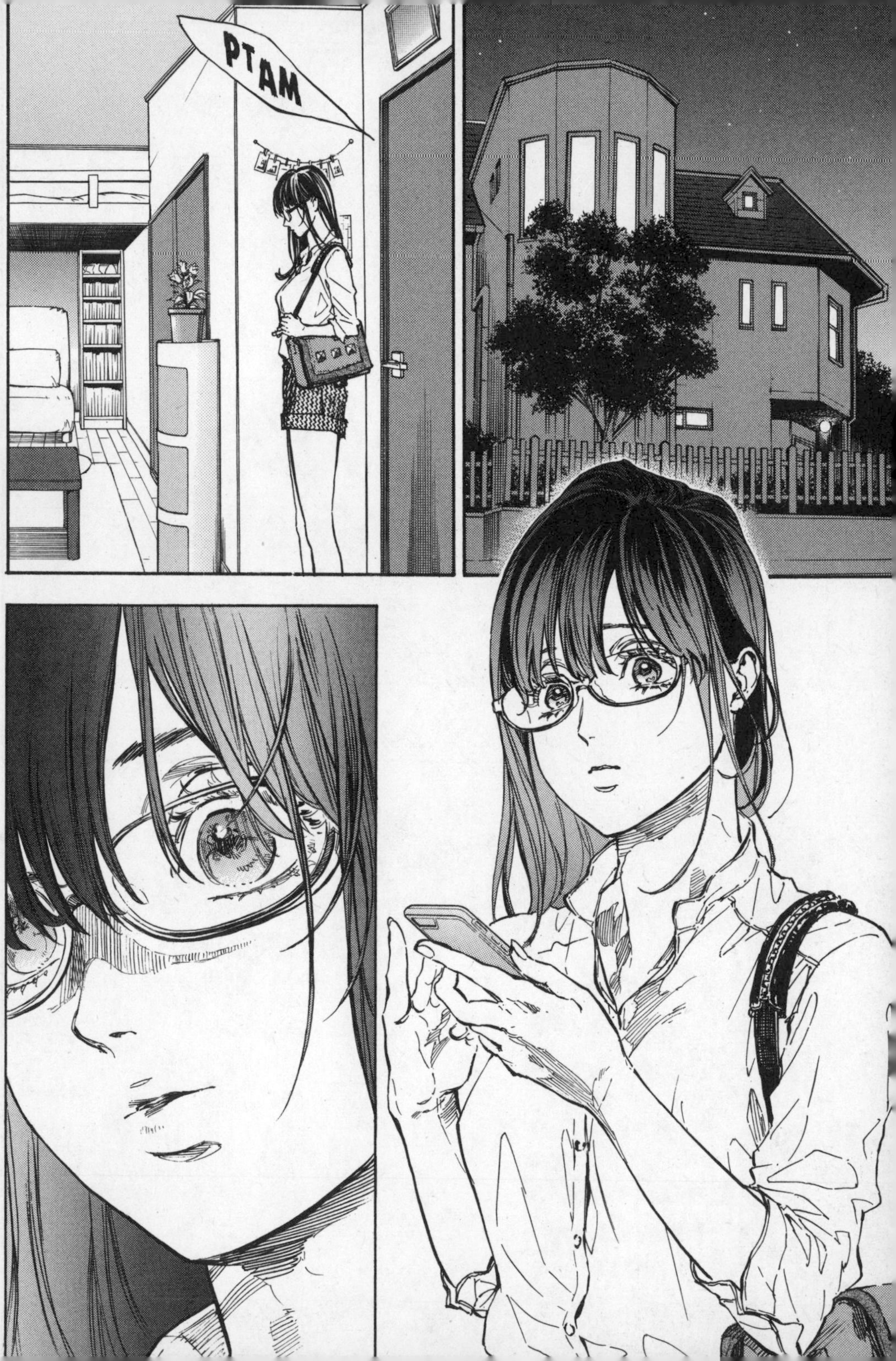
PTAM

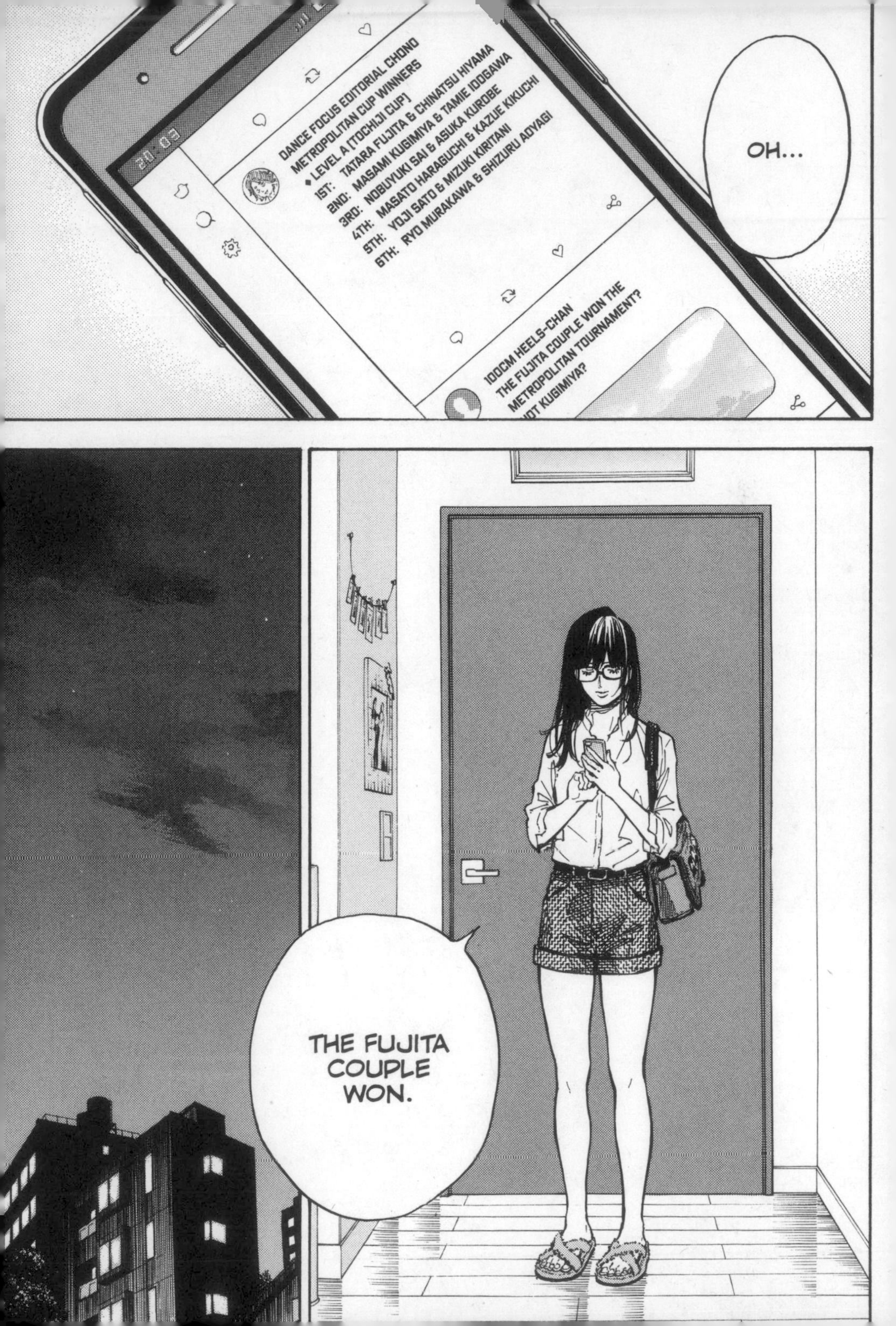
OH...
DANCE FOCUS EDITORIAL CHONO
METROPOLITAN CUP WINNERS
◆ LEVEL A [TOCHIJI CUP]
1ST: TATARA FUJITA & CHINATSU HIYAMA
2ND: MASAMI KUGIMIYA & TAMIE IDOGAWA
3RD: NOBUYUKI SAI & ASUKA KUROBE
4TH: MASATO HARAGUCHI & KAZUE KIKUCHI
5TH: YOJI SATO & MIZUKI KIRITANI
6TH: RYO MURAKAWA & SHIZURU AOYAGI
100CM HEELS-CHAN
THE FUJITA COUPLE WON THE
METROPOLITAN TOURNAMENT?
KUGIMIYA?
THE FUJITA COUPLE WON.

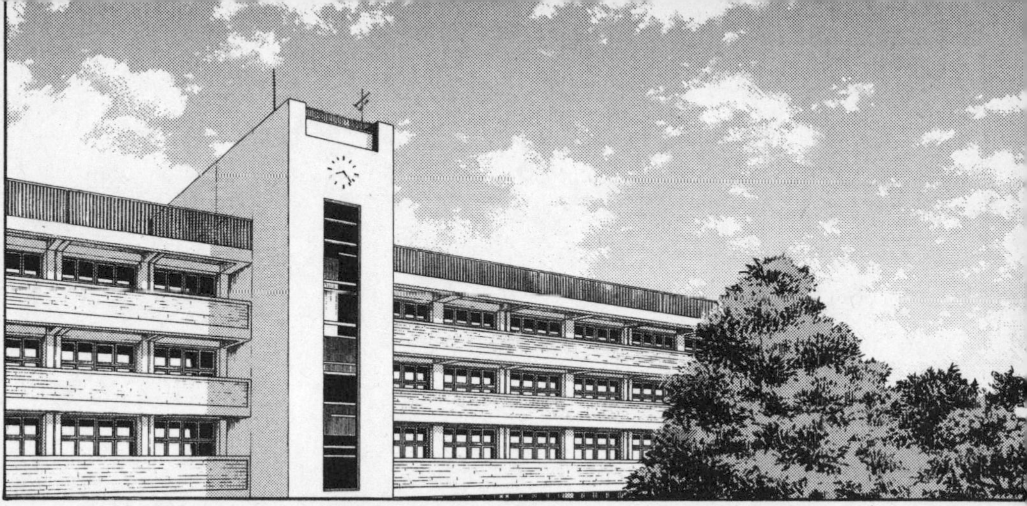

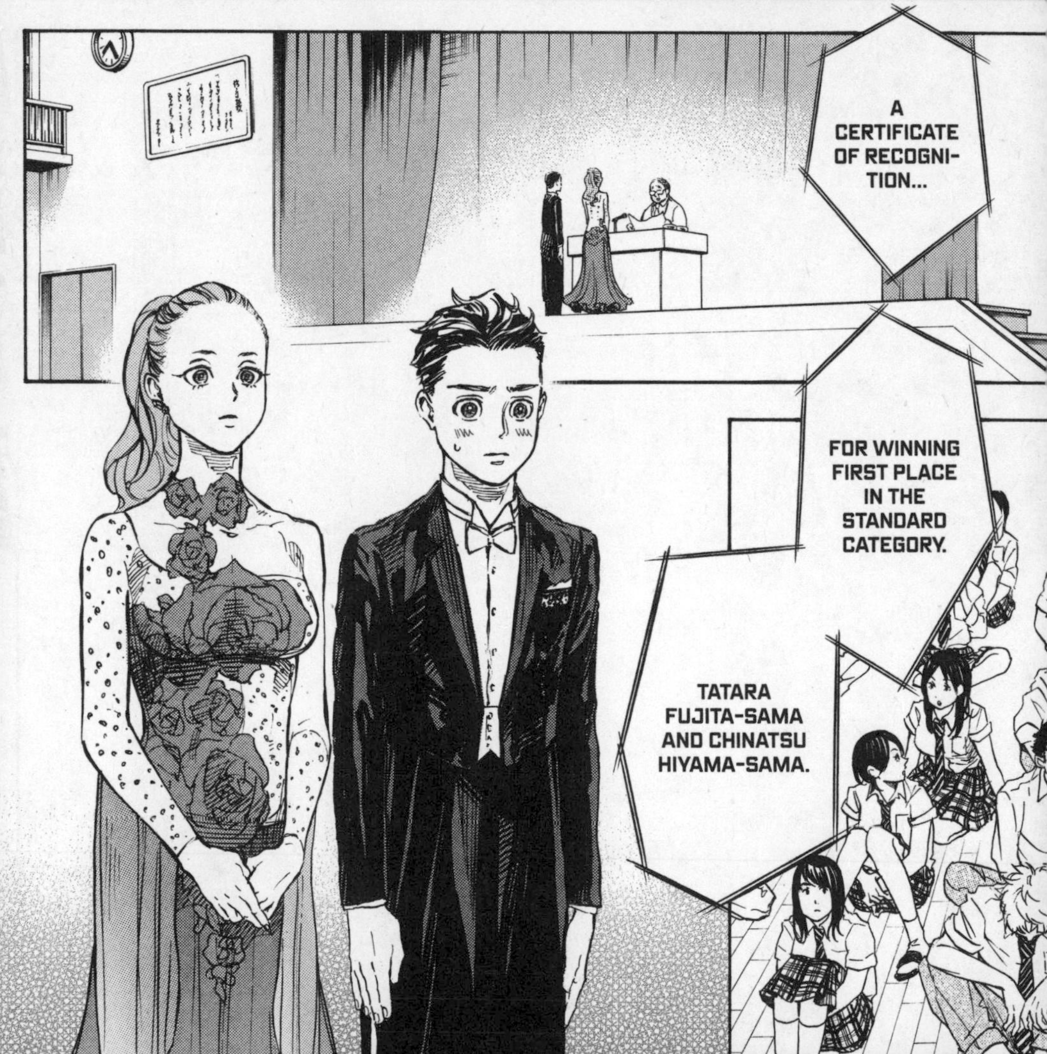
A CERTIFICATE OF RECOGNITION...
FOR WINNING FIRST PLACE IN THE STANDARD CATEGORY.
TATARA FUJITA-SAMA AND CHINATSU HIYAMA-SAMA.

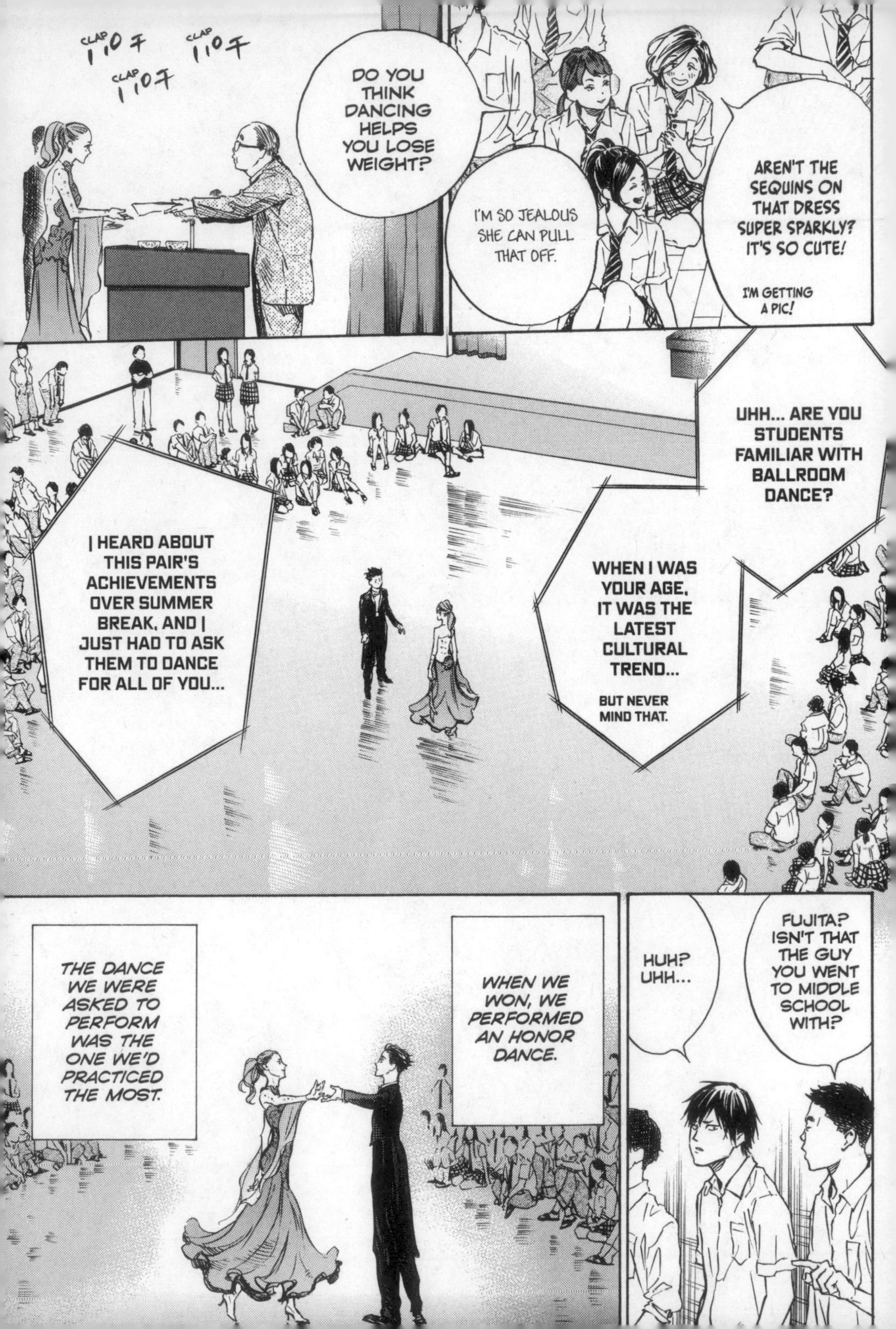
AREN'T THE SEQUINS ON THAT DRESS SUPER SPARKLY? IT'S SO CUTE!
I'M GETTING A PIC!
I'M SO JEALOUS SHE CAN PULL THAT OFF.
DO YOU THINK DANCING HELPS YOU LOSE WEIGHT?
CLAP
CLAP
CLAP
UHH... ARE YOU STUDENTS FAMILIAR WITH BALLROOM DANCE?
WHEN I WAS YOUR AGE, IT WAS THE LATEST CULTURAL TREND...
BUT NEVER MIND THAT.
I HEARD ABOUT THIS PAIR'S ACHIEVEMENTS OVER SUMMER BREAK, AND I JUST HAD TO ASK THEM TO DANCE FOR ALL OF YOU...
FUJITA? ISN'T THAT THE GUY YOU WENT TO MIDDLE SCHOOL WITH?
HUH? UHH...
WHEN WE WON, WE PERFORMED AN HONOR DANCE.
THE DANCE WE WERE ASKED TO PERFORM WAS THE ONE WE'D PRACTICED THE MOST.

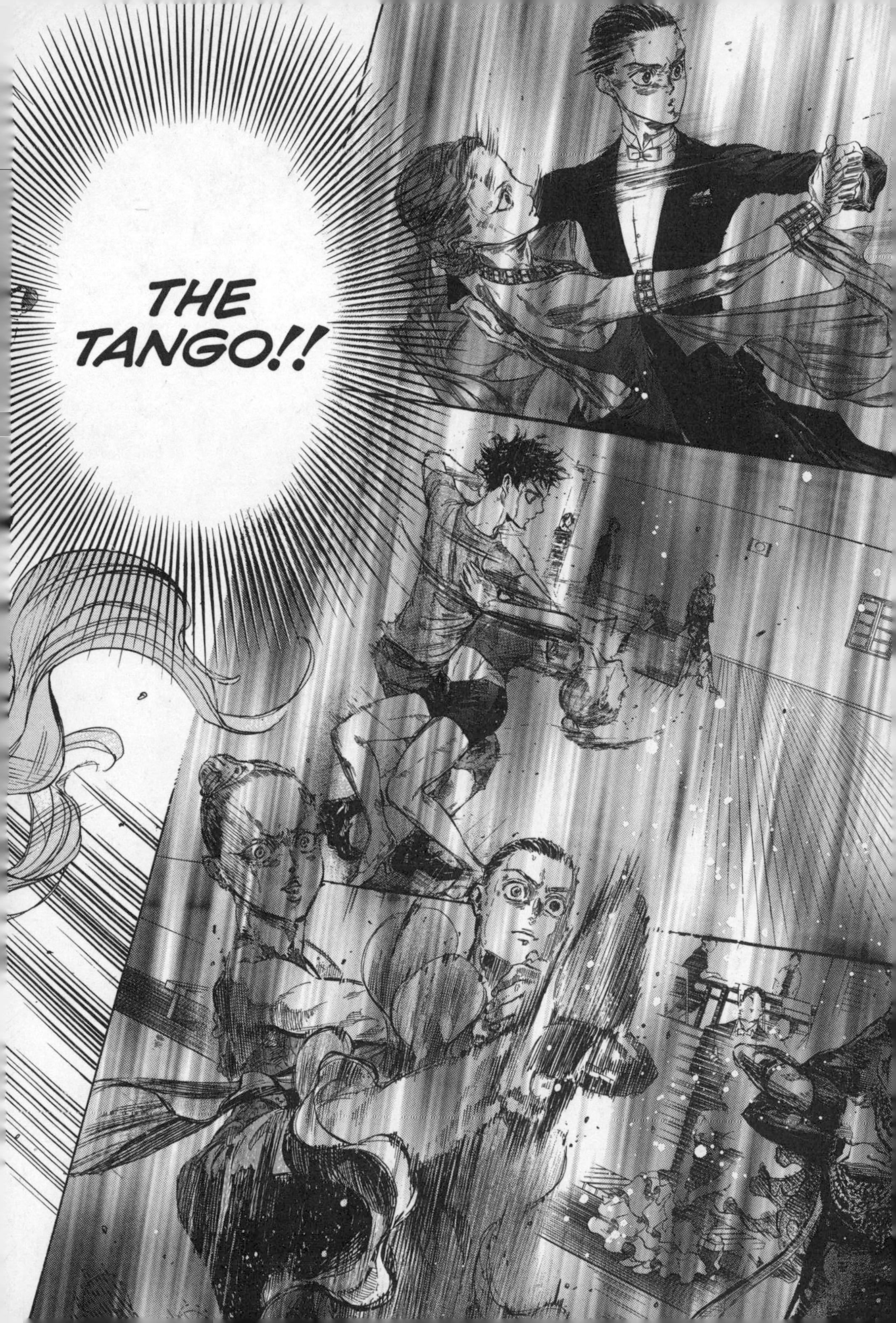
THE TANGO!!

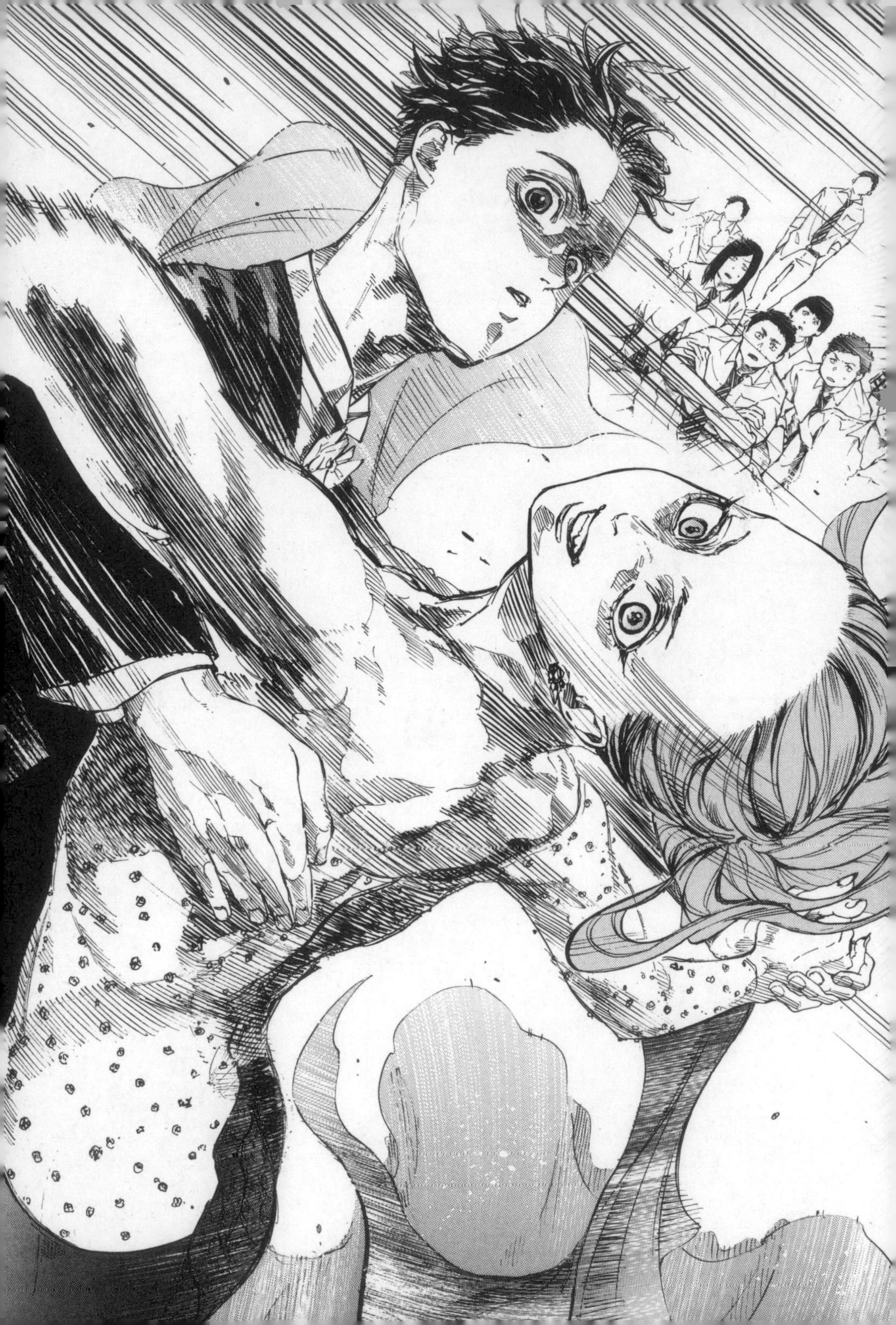

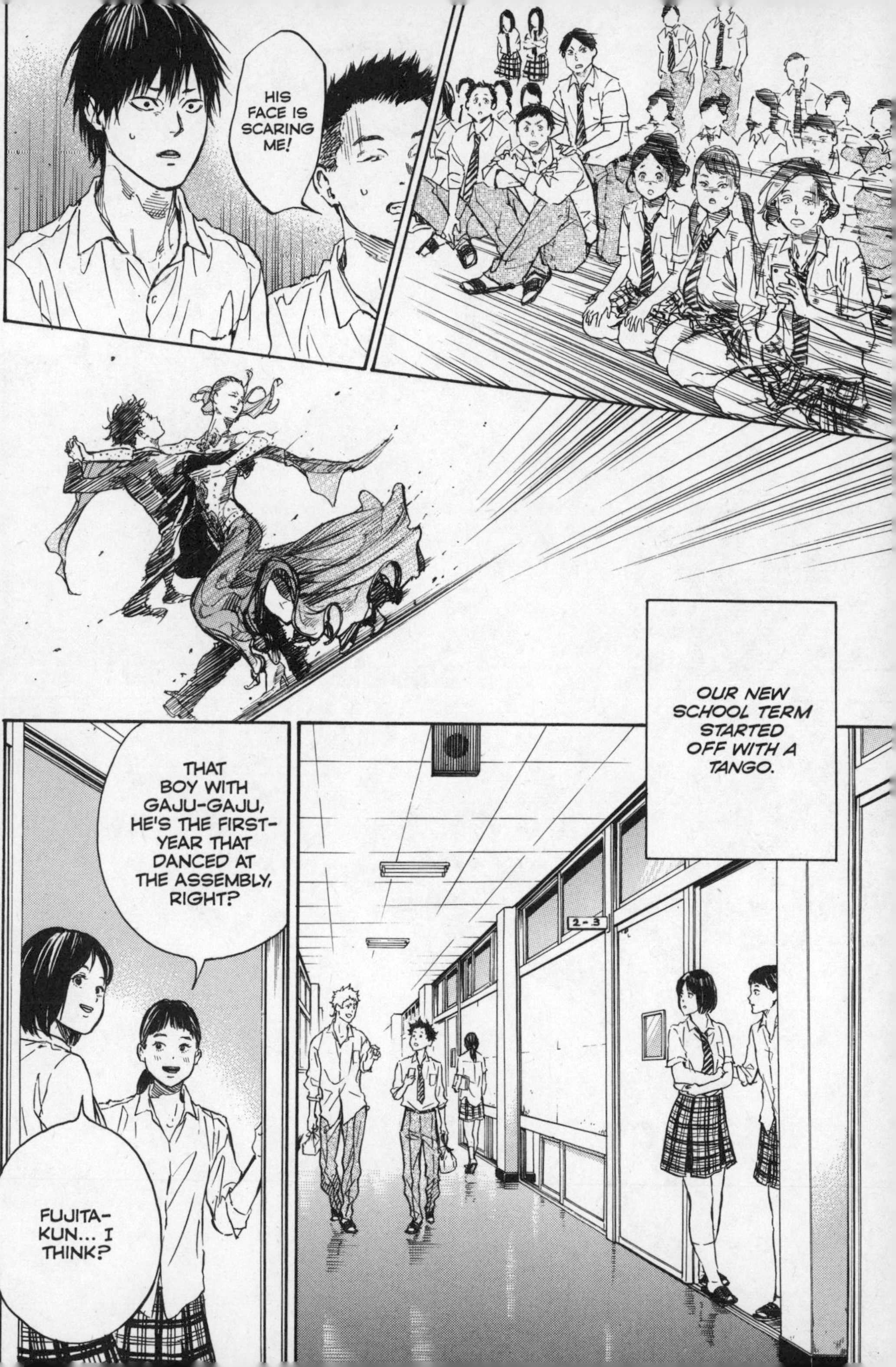
HIS FACE IS SCARING ME!
OUR NEW SCHOOL TERM STARTED OFF WITH A TANGO.
THAT BOY WITH GAJU-GAJU, HE'S THE FIRST-YEAR THAT DANCED AT THE ASSEMBLY, RIGHT?
FUJITA-KUN... I THINK?
2-3

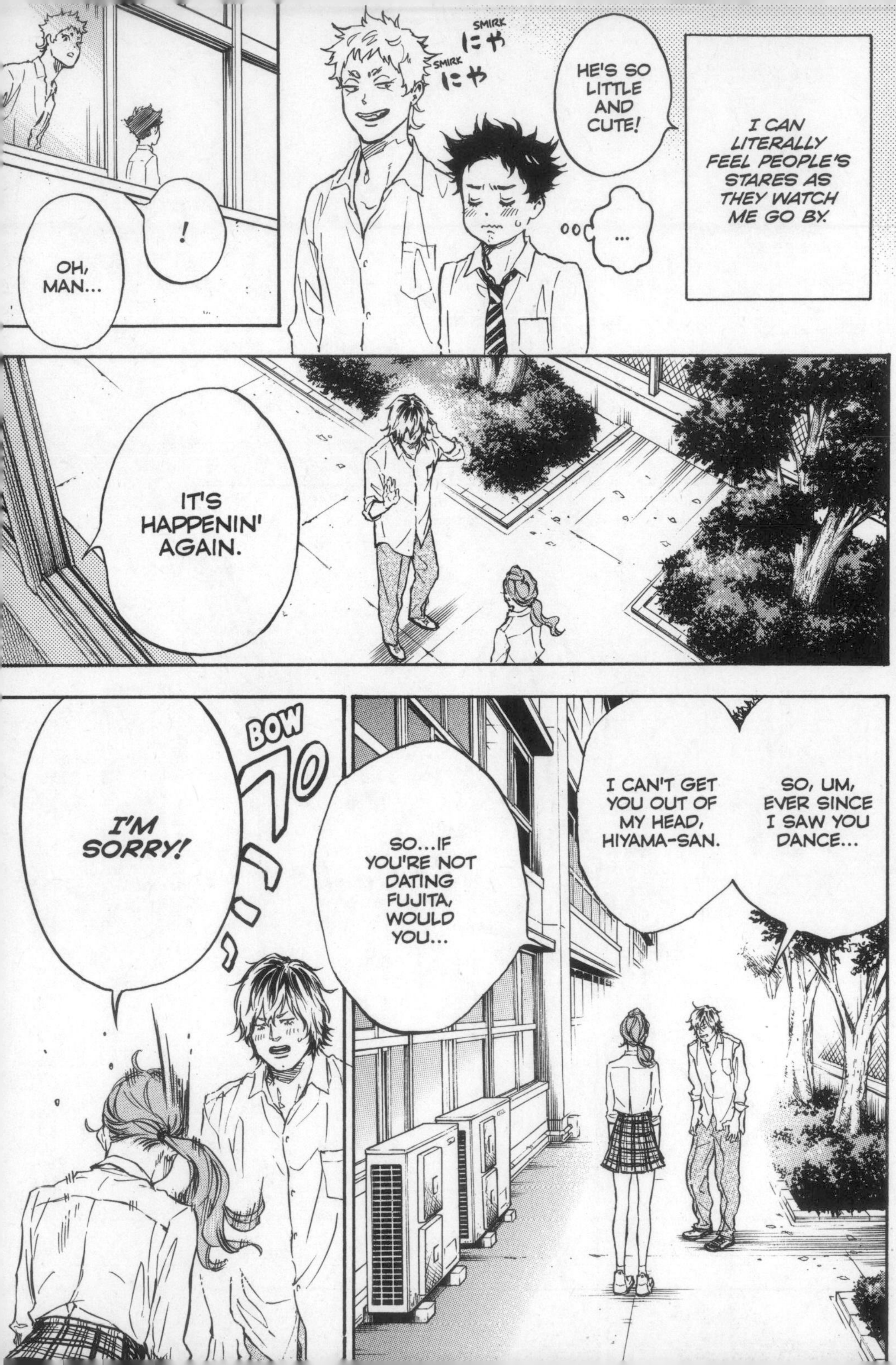
I CAN LITERALLY FEEL PEOPLE'S STARES AS THEY WATCH ME GO BY.
HE'S SO LITTLE AND CUTE!
SMIRK にや
SMIRK にや
...
!
OH, MAN...
IT'S HAPPENIN' AGAIN.
SO, UM, EVER SINCE I SAW YOU DANCE...
I CAN'T GET YOU OUT OF MY HEAD, HIYAMA-SAN.
SO...IF YOU'RE NOT DATING FUJITA, WOULD YOU...
BOW
I'M SORRY!

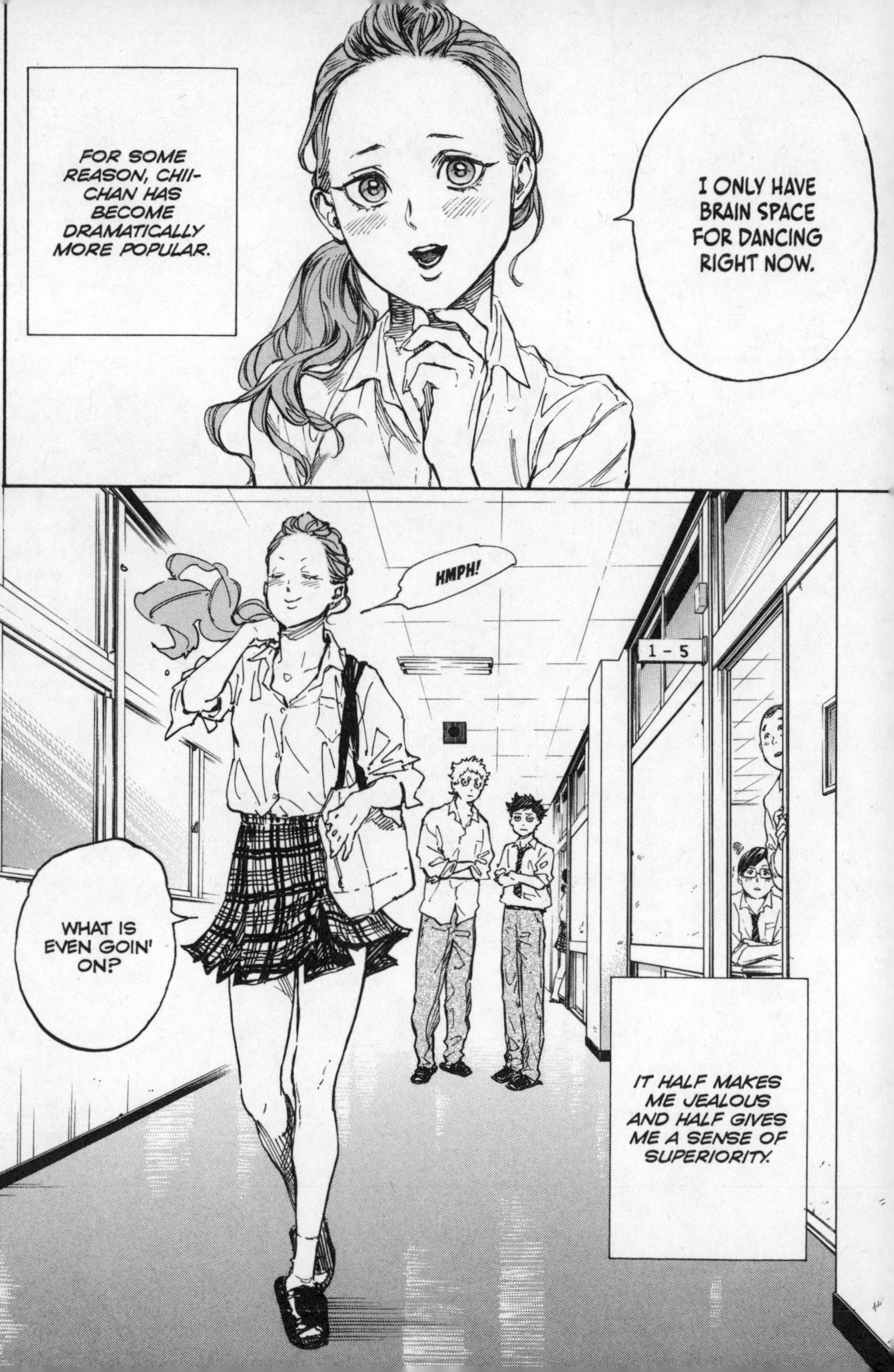
I ONLY HAVE BRAIN SPACE FOR DANCING RIGHT NOW.
FOR SOME REASON, CHII-CHAN HAS BECOME DRAMATICALLY MORE POPULAR.
HMPH!
1 - 5
IT HALF MAKES ME JEALOUS AND HALF GIVES ME A SENSE OF SUPERIORITY.
WHAT IS EVEN GOIN' ON?

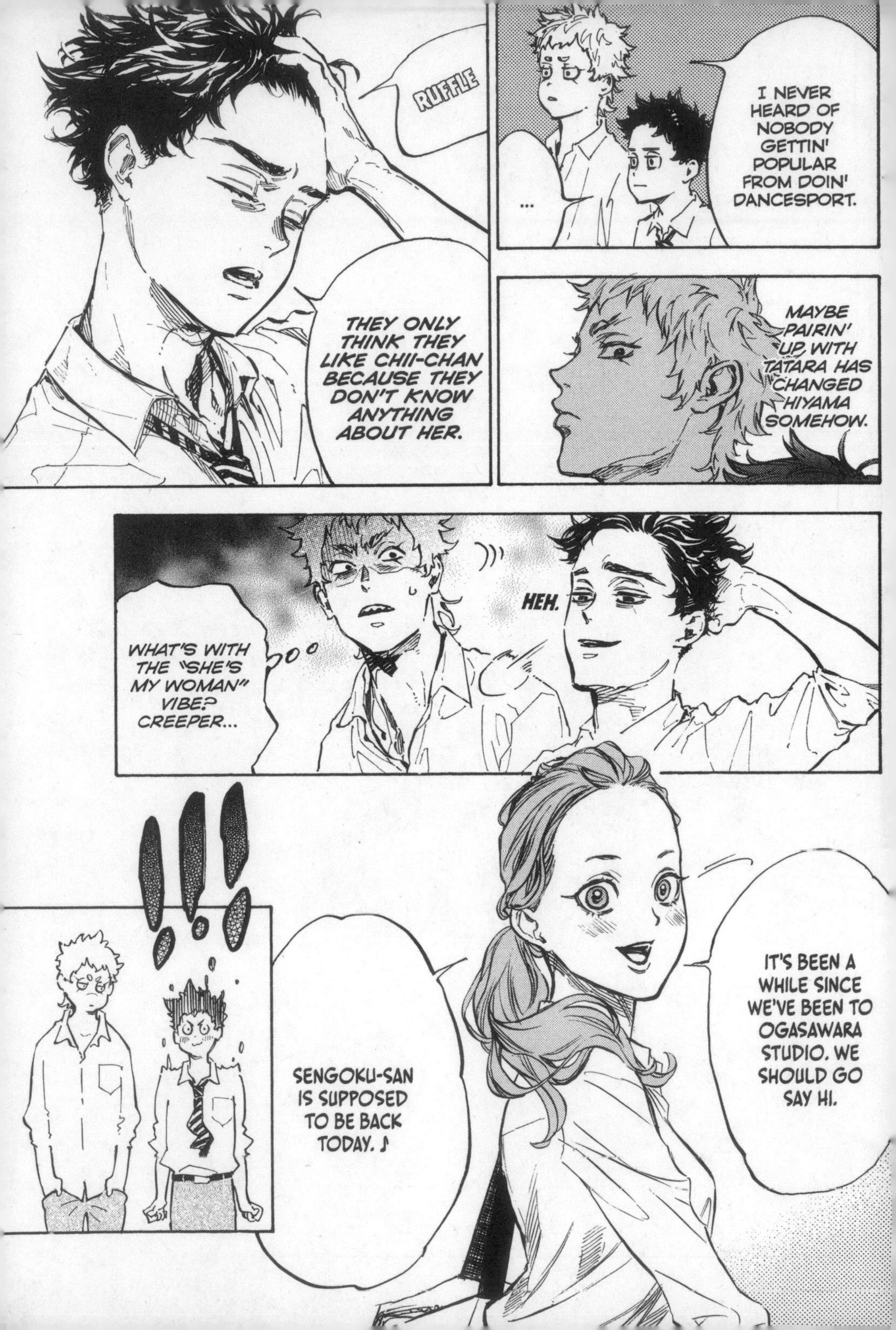
I NEVER HEARD OF NOBODY GETTIN' POPULAR FROM DOIN' DANCESPORT.
...
MAYBE PAIRIN' UP WITH TATARA HAS CHANGED HIYAMA SOMEHOW.
RUFFLE
THEY ONLY THINK THEY LIKE CHII-CHAN BECAUSE THEY DON'T KNOW ANYTHING ABOUT HER.
HEH.
WHAT'S WITH THE "SHE'S MY WOMAN" VIBE? CREEPER...
IT'S BEEN A WHILE SINCE WE'VE BEEN TO OGASAWARA STUDIO. WE SHOULD GO SAY HI.
SENGOKU-SAN IS SUPPOSED TO BE BACK TODAY. ♪

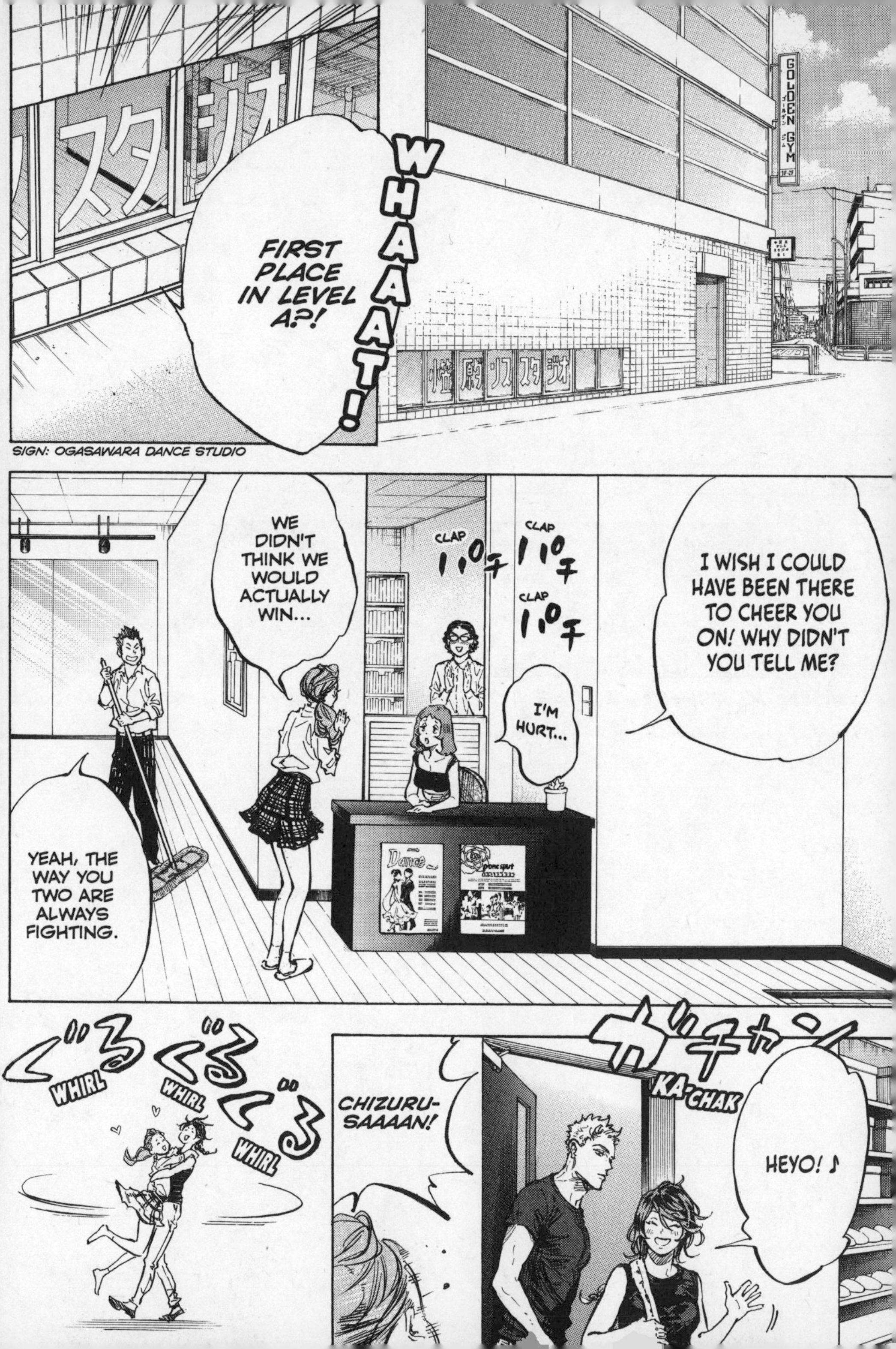
GOLDEN GYM
WHAAAAT!
FIRST PLACE IN LEVEL A?!
SIGN: OGASAWARA DANCE STUDIO
I WISH I COULD HAVE BEEN THERE TO CHEER YOU ON! WHY DIDN'T YOU TELL ME?
I'M HURT...
CLAP
CLAP
CLAP
WE DIDN'T THINK WE WOULD ACTUALLY WIN...
YEAH, THE WAY YOU TWO ARE ALWAYS FIGHTING.
KA-CHAK
HEYO! ♪
CHIZURU-SAAAAN!
WHIRL
WHIRL
WHIRL

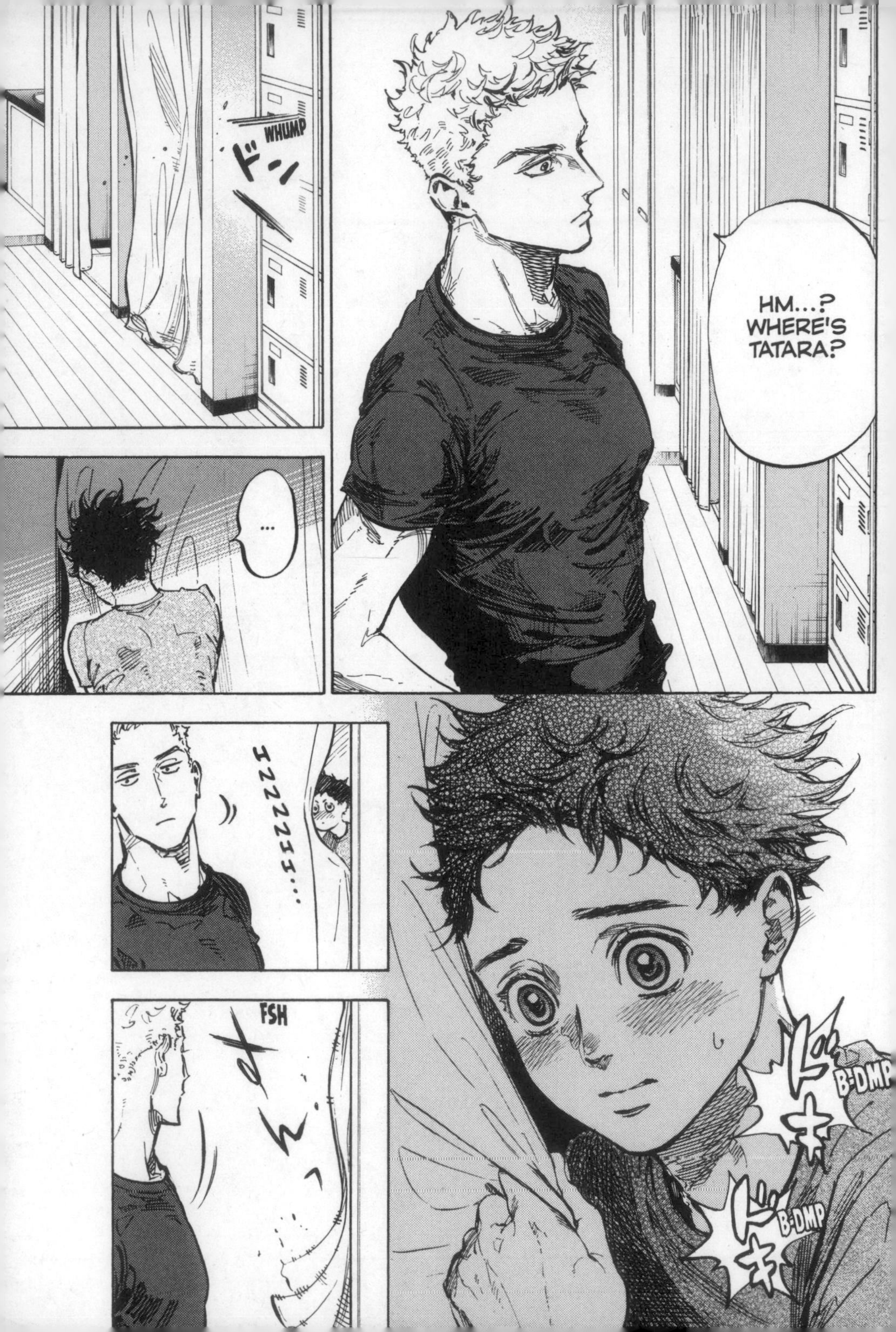
HM...? WHERE'S TATARA?
WHUMP
ドン
...
ドキ
B-DMP
ドキ
B-DMP
FSH

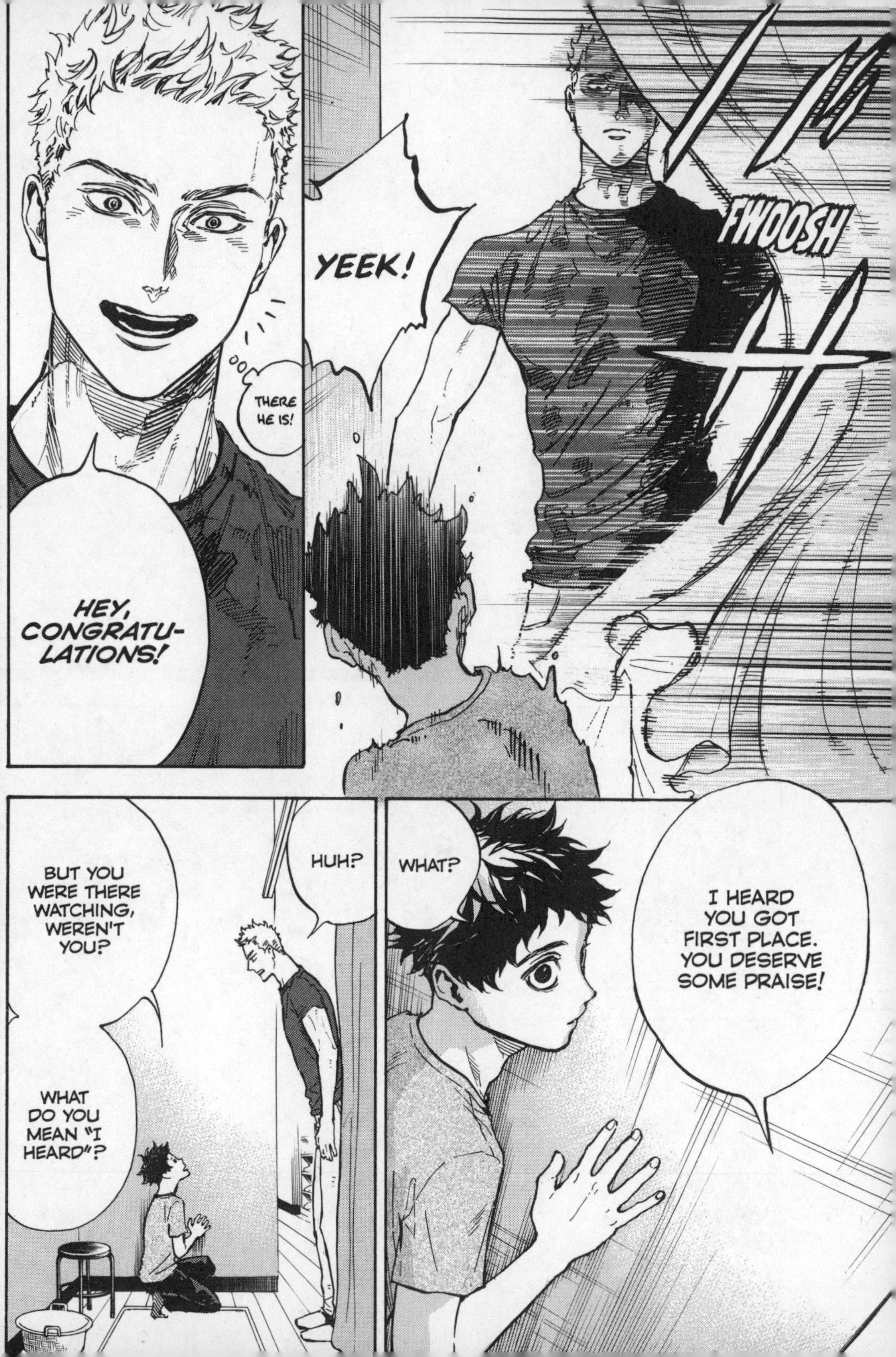
FWOOSH
YEEK!
THERE HE IS!
HEY, CONGRATULATIONS!
I HEARD YOU GOT FIRST PLACE. YOU DESERVE SOME PRAISE!
WHAT?
HUH?
BUT YOU WERE THERE WATCHING, WEREN'T YOU?
WHAT DO YOU MEAN "I HEARD"?

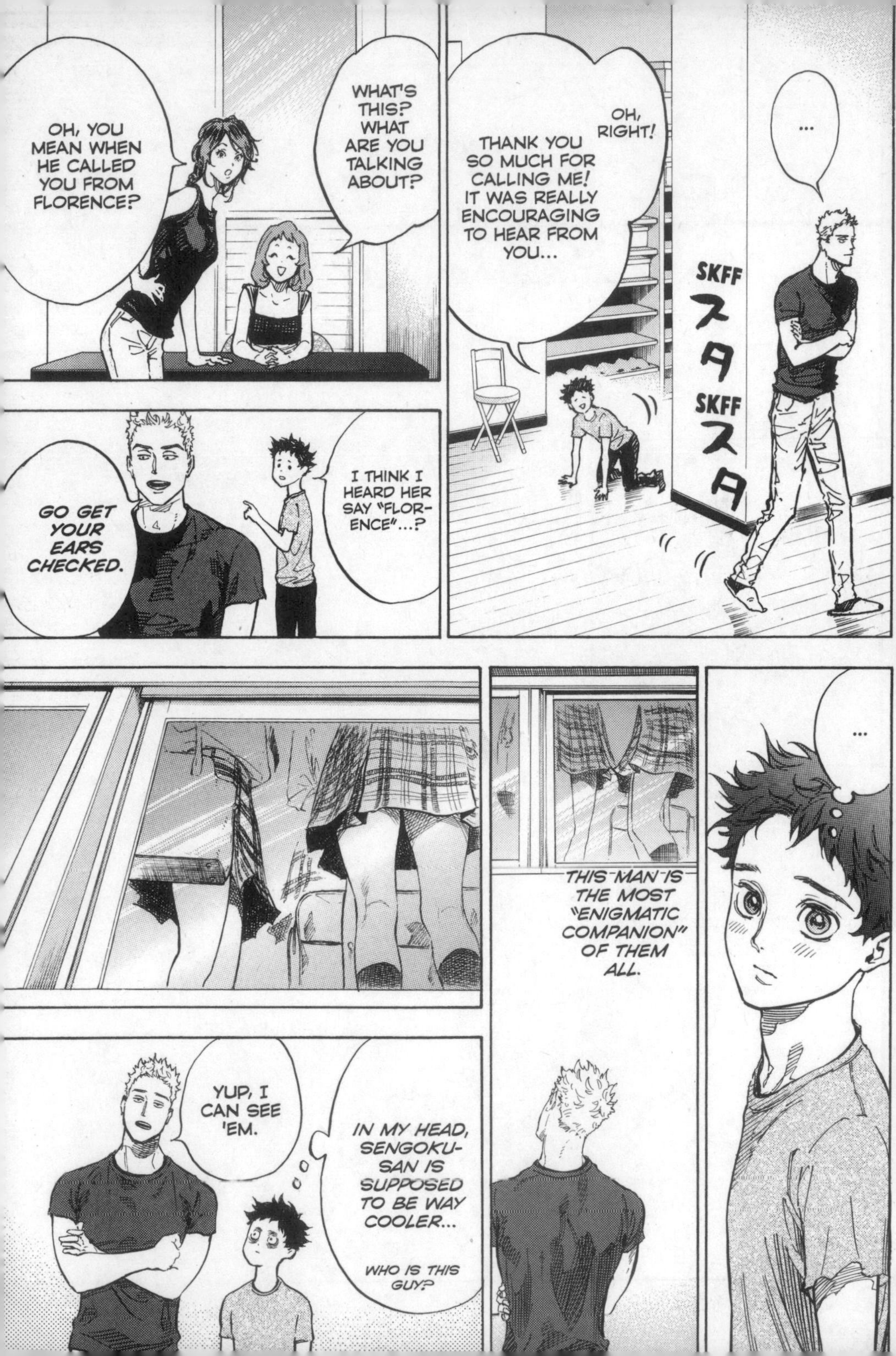
...
OH, RIGHT!
THANK YOU SO MUCH FOR CALLING ME! IT WAS REALLY ENCOURAGING TO HEAR FROM YOU...
SKFF スタ
SKFF スタ
WHAT'S THIS? WHAT ARE YOU TALKING ABOUT?
OH, YOU MEAN WHEN HE CALLED YOU FROM FLORENCE?
I THINK I HEARD HER SAY "FLOR-ENCE"...?
GO GET YOUR EARS CHECKED.
...
THIS MAN IS THE MOST "ENIGMATIC COMPANION" OF THEM ALL.
YUP, I CAN SEE 'EM.
IN MY HEAD, SENGOKU-SAN IS SUPPOSED TO BE WAY COOLER...
WHO IS THIS GUY?

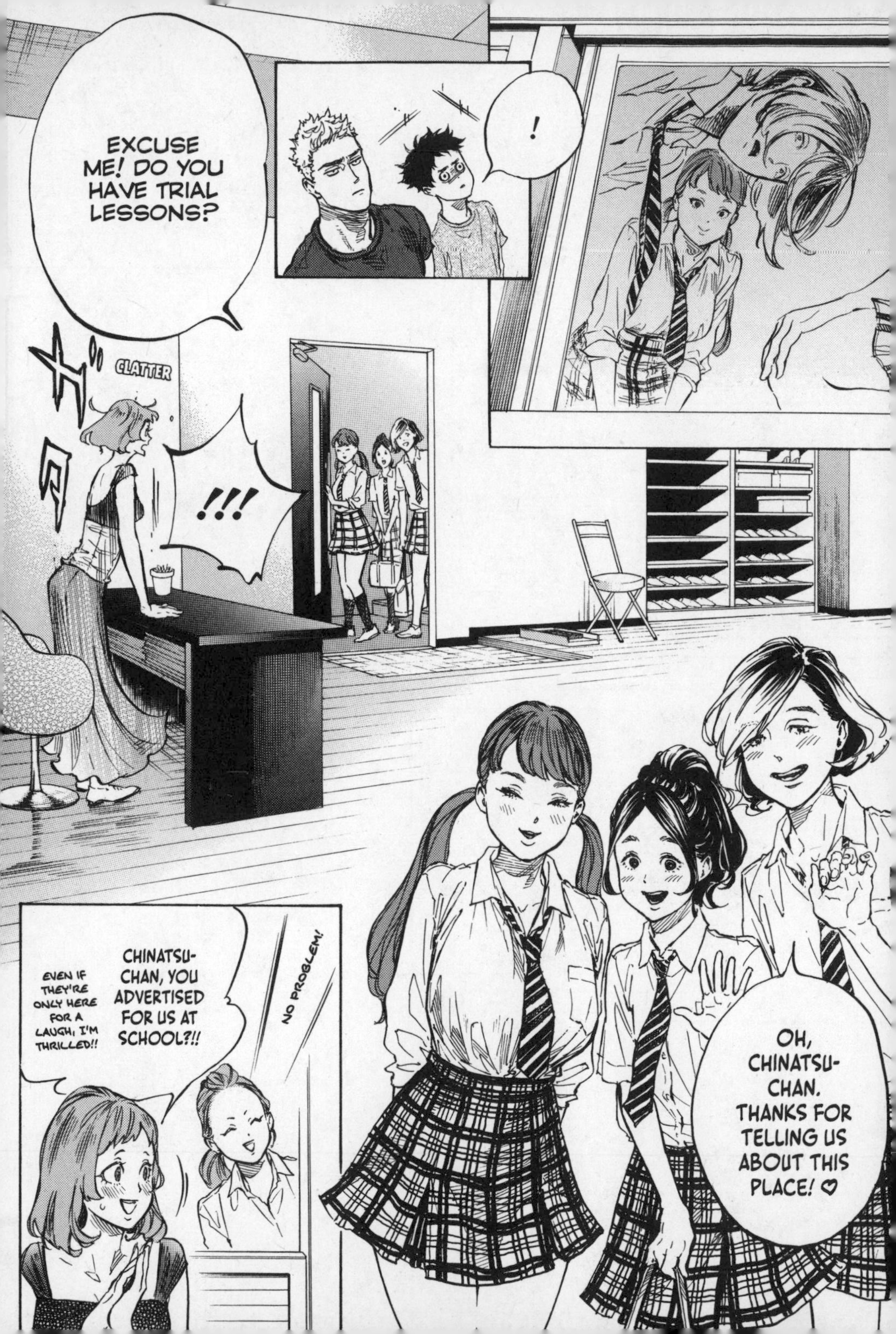
!
EXCUSE ME! DO YOU HAVE TRIAL LESSONS?
CLATTER
!!!
OH, CHINATSU-CHAN. THANKS FOR TELLING US ABOUT THIS PLACE! ♡
NO PROBLEM!
CHINATSU-CHAN, YOU ADVERTISED FOR US AT SCHOOL?!!
EVEN IF THEY'RE ONLY HERE FOR A LAUGH, I'M THRILLED!!

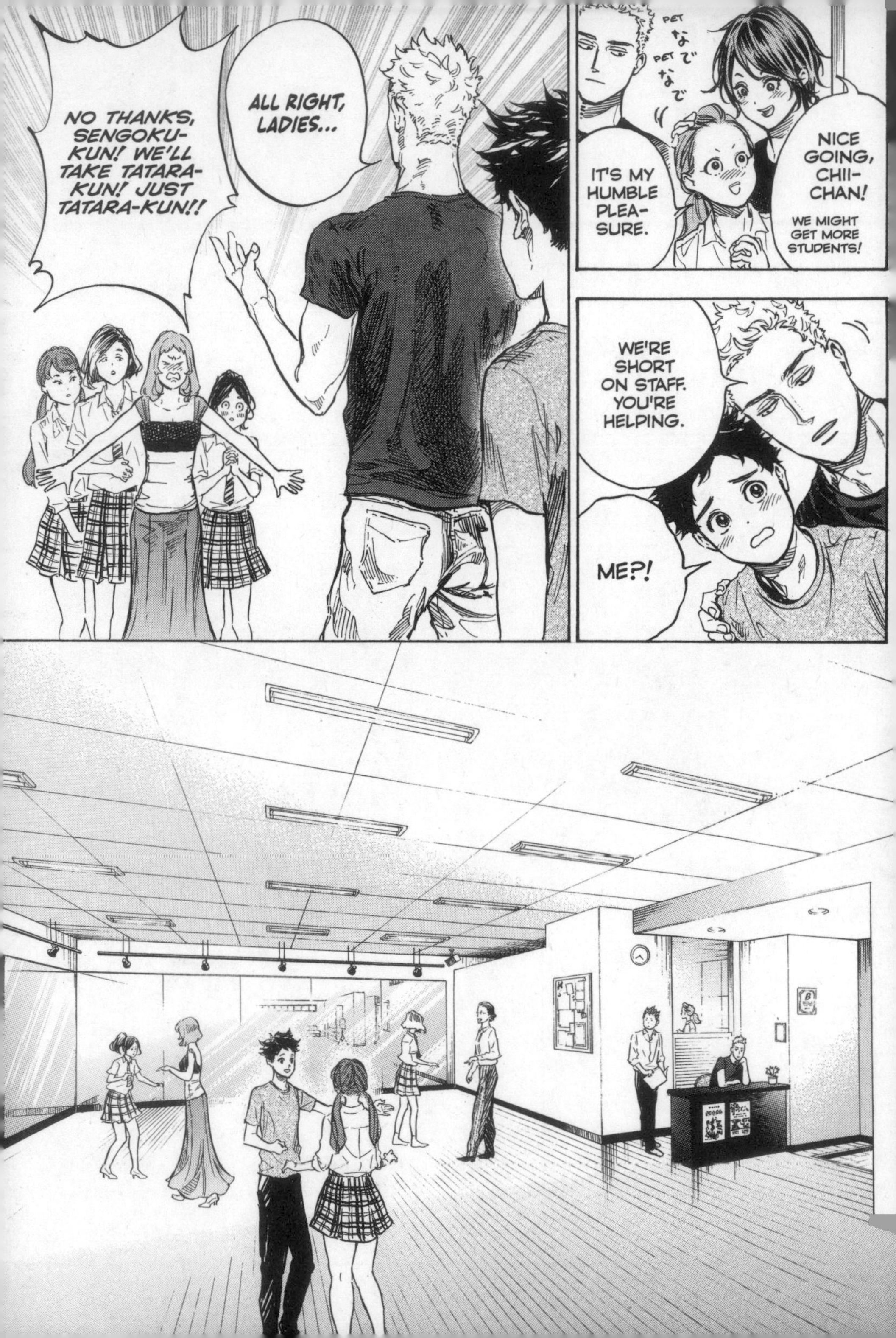
NICE GOING, CHII-CHAN!
WE MIGHT GET MORE STUDENTS!
PET なで PET なで
IT'S MY HUMBLE PLEASURE.
WE'RE SHORT ON STAFF. YOU'RE HELPING.
ME?!
ALL RIGHT, LADIES...
NO THANKS, SENGOKU-KUN! WE'LL TAKE TATARA-KUN! JUST TATARA-KUN!!

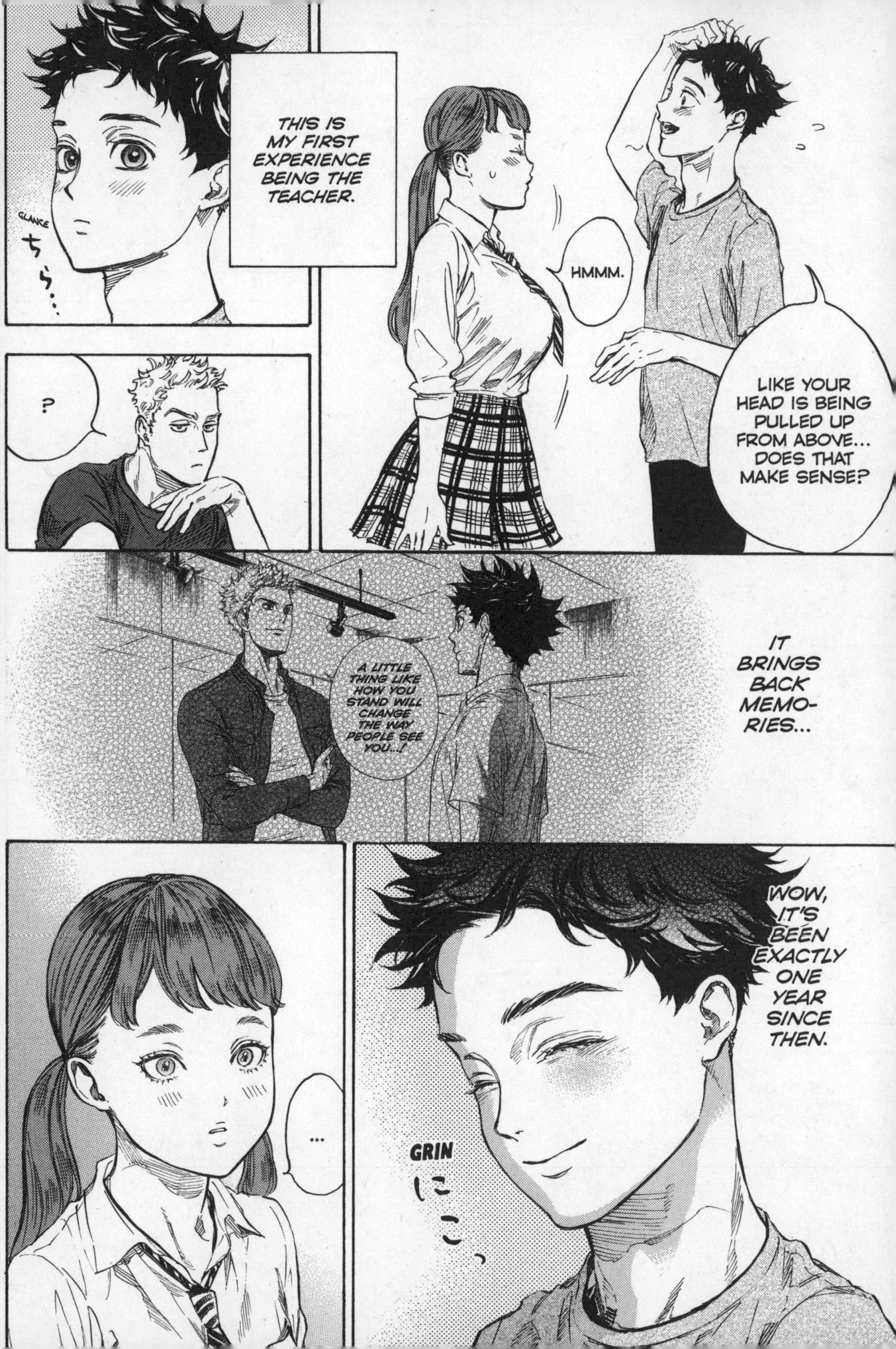
LIKE YOUR HEAD IS BEING PULLED UP FROM ABOVE... DOES THAT MAKE SENSE?
HMMM.
THIS IS MY FIRST EXPERIENCE BEING THE TEACHER.
GLANCE
ちら…
?
IT BRINGS BACK MEMORIES...
A LITTLE THING LIKE HOW YOU STAND WILL CHANGE THE WAY PEOPLE SEE YOU...!
WOW, IT'S BEEN EXACTLY ONE YEAR SINCE THEN.
GRIN
にこっ
...

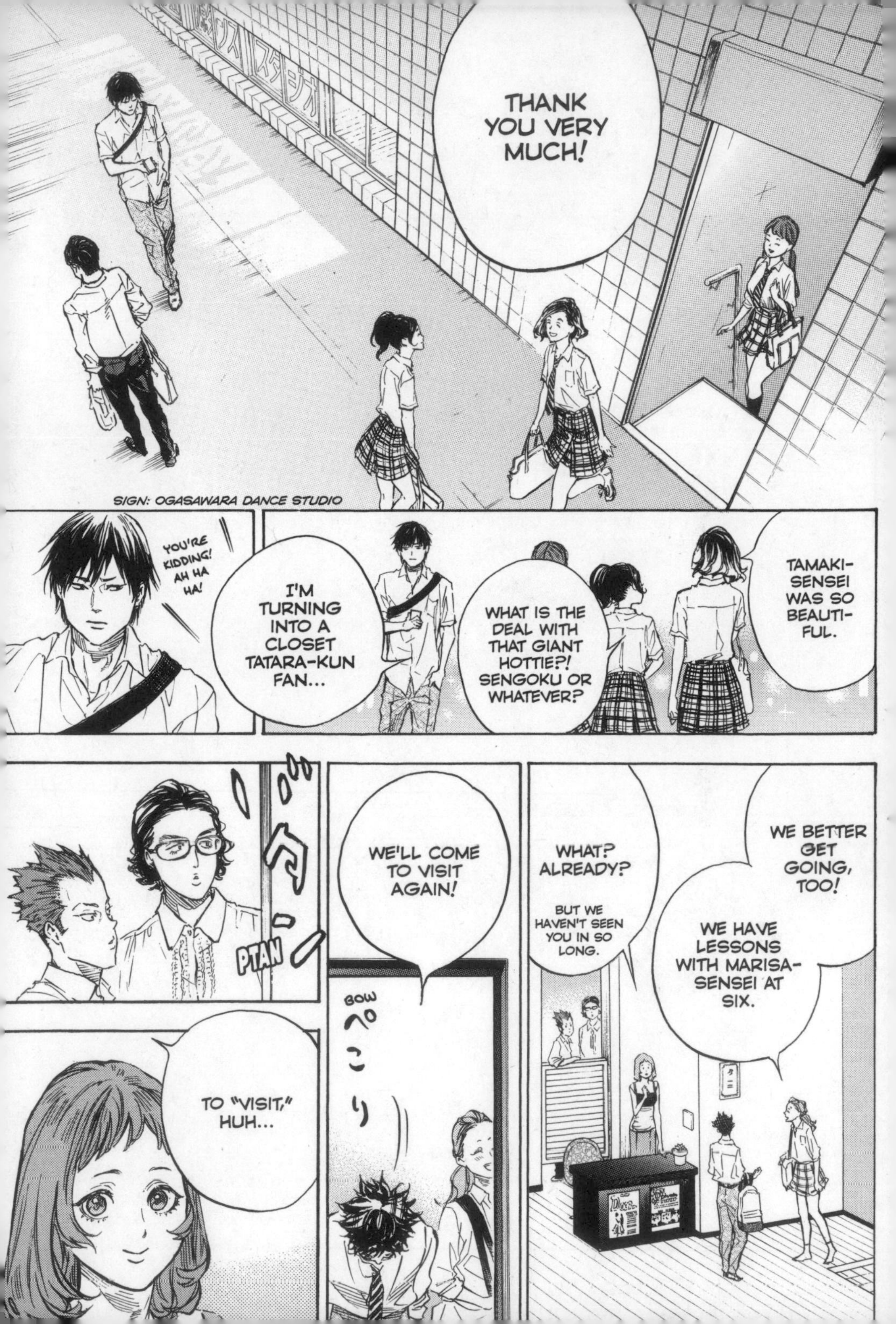
THANK YOU VERY MUCH!
SIGN: OGASAWARA DANCE STUDIO
TAMAKI-SENSEI WAS SO BEAUTIFUL.
WHAT IS THE DEAL WITH THAT GIANT HOTTIE?! SENGOKU OR WHATEVER?
I'M TURNING INTO A CLOSET TATARA-KUN FAN...
YOU'RE KIDDING! AH HA HA!
WE BETTER GET GOING, TOO!
WE HAVE LESSONS WITH MARISA-SENSEI AT SIX.
WHAT? ALREADY?
BUT WE HAVEN'T SEEN YOU IN SO LONG.
WE'LL COME TO VISIT AGAIN!
BOW
PTAN
TO "VISIT," HUH...

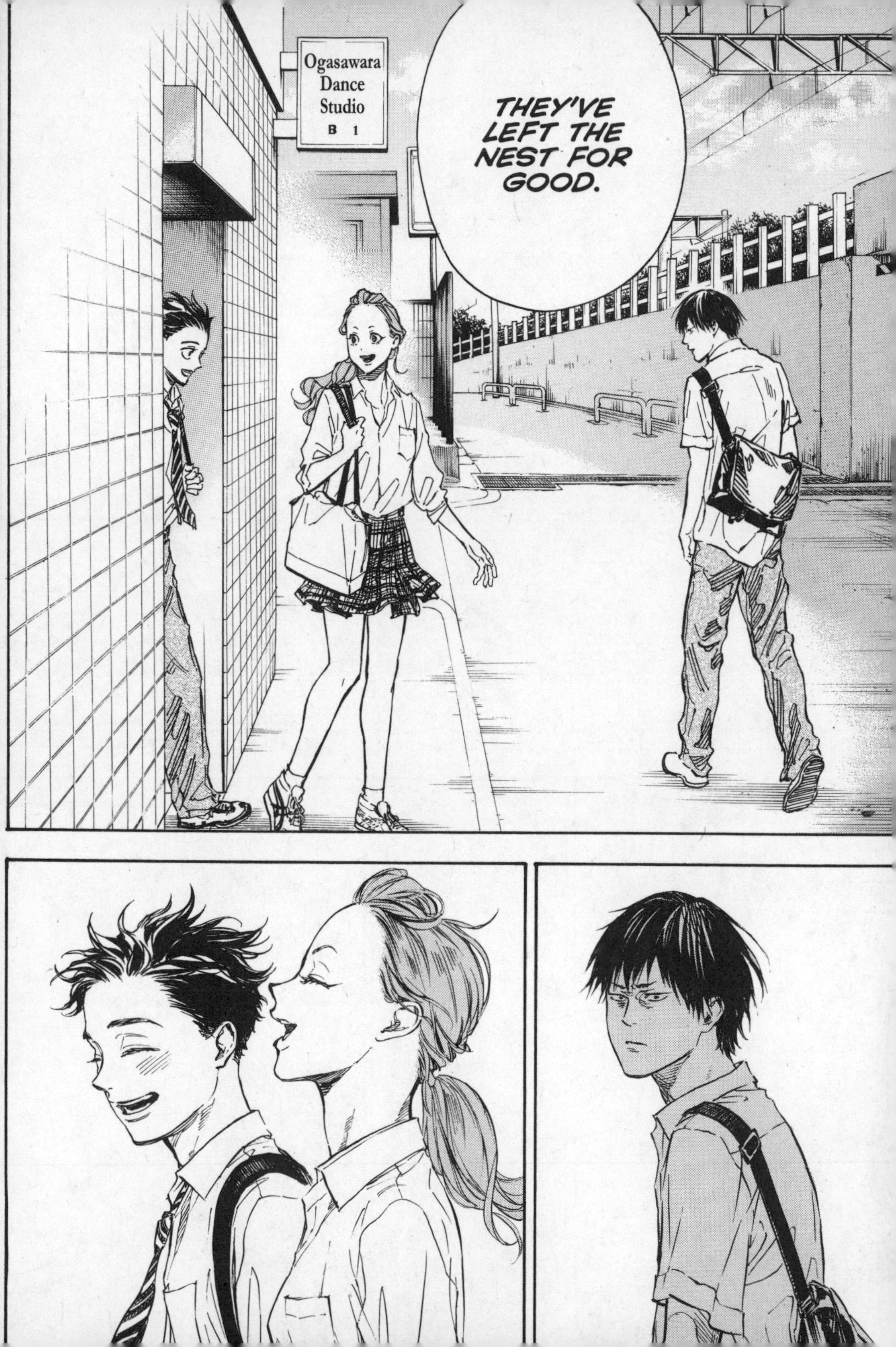
THEY'VE LEFT THE NEST FOR GOOD.
Ogasawara Dance Studio B 1

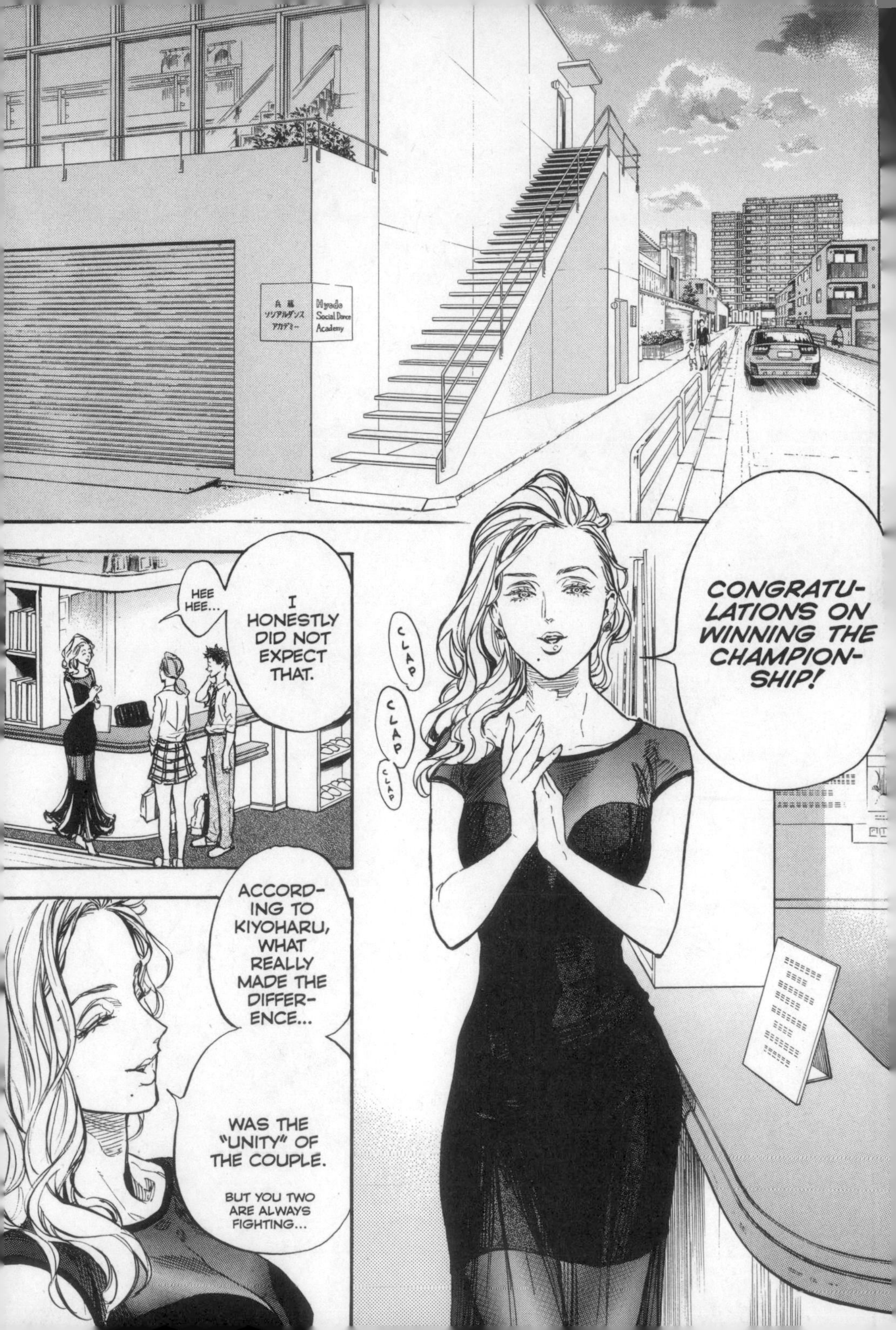

兵藤 ソシアルダンス アカデミー
Hyodo Social Dance Academy
CONGRATULATIONS ON WINNING THE CHAMPIONSHIP!
CLAP
CLAP
CLAP
HEE HEE...
I HONESTLY DID NOT EXPECT THAT.
ACCORDING TO KIYOHARU, WHAT REALLY MADE THE DIFFERENCE...
WAS THE "UNITY" OF THE COUPLE.
BUT YOU TWO ARE ALWAYS FIGHTING...

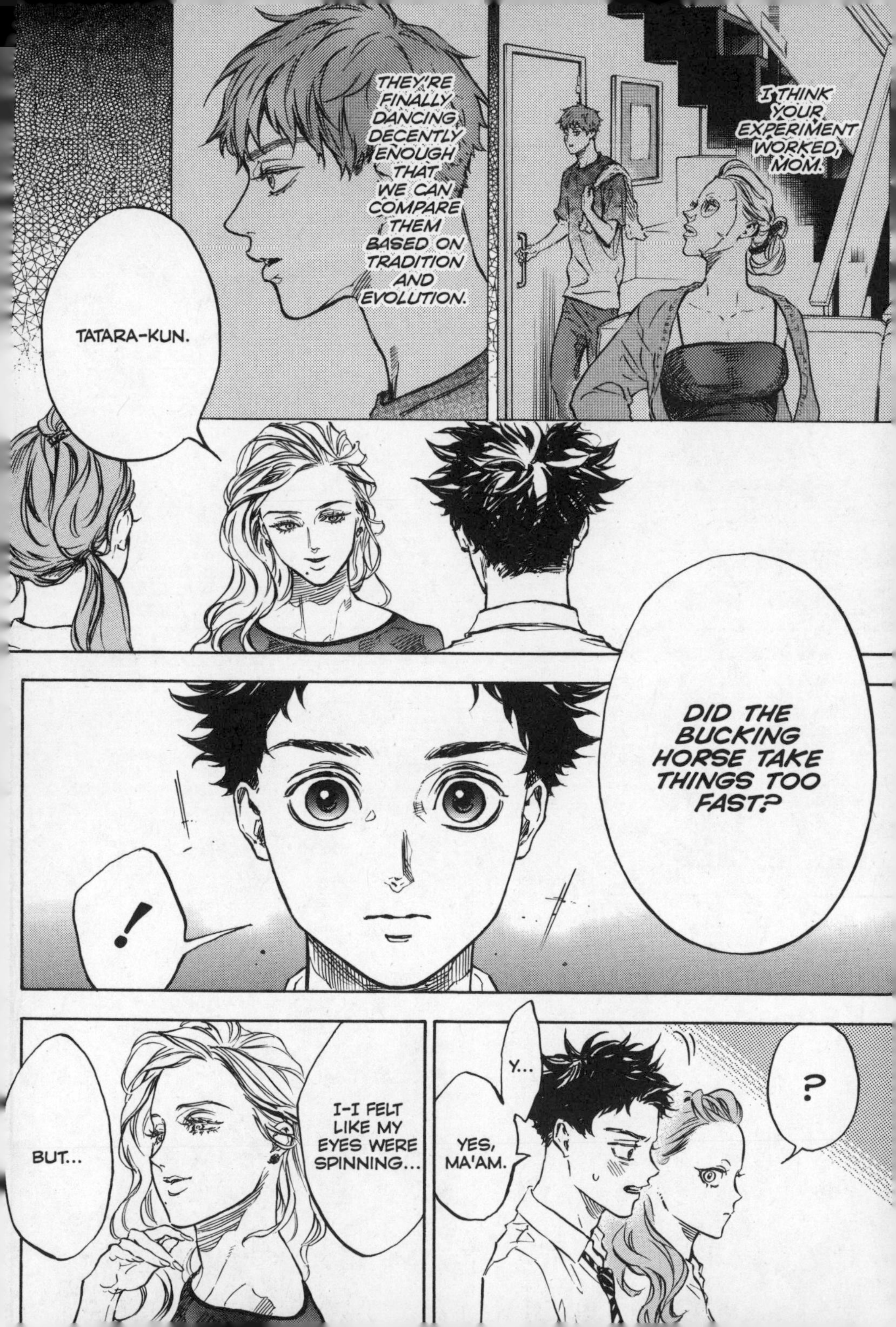
I THINK YOUR EXPERIMENT WORKED, MOM.
THEY'RE FINALLY DANCING DECENTLY ENOUGH THAT WE CAN COMPARE THEM BASED ON TRADITION AND EVOLUTION.
TATARA-KUN.
DID THE BUCKING HORSE TAKE THINGS TOO FAST?
!
?
Y...
YES, MA'AM.
I-I FELT LIKE MY EYES WERE SPINNING...
BUT...

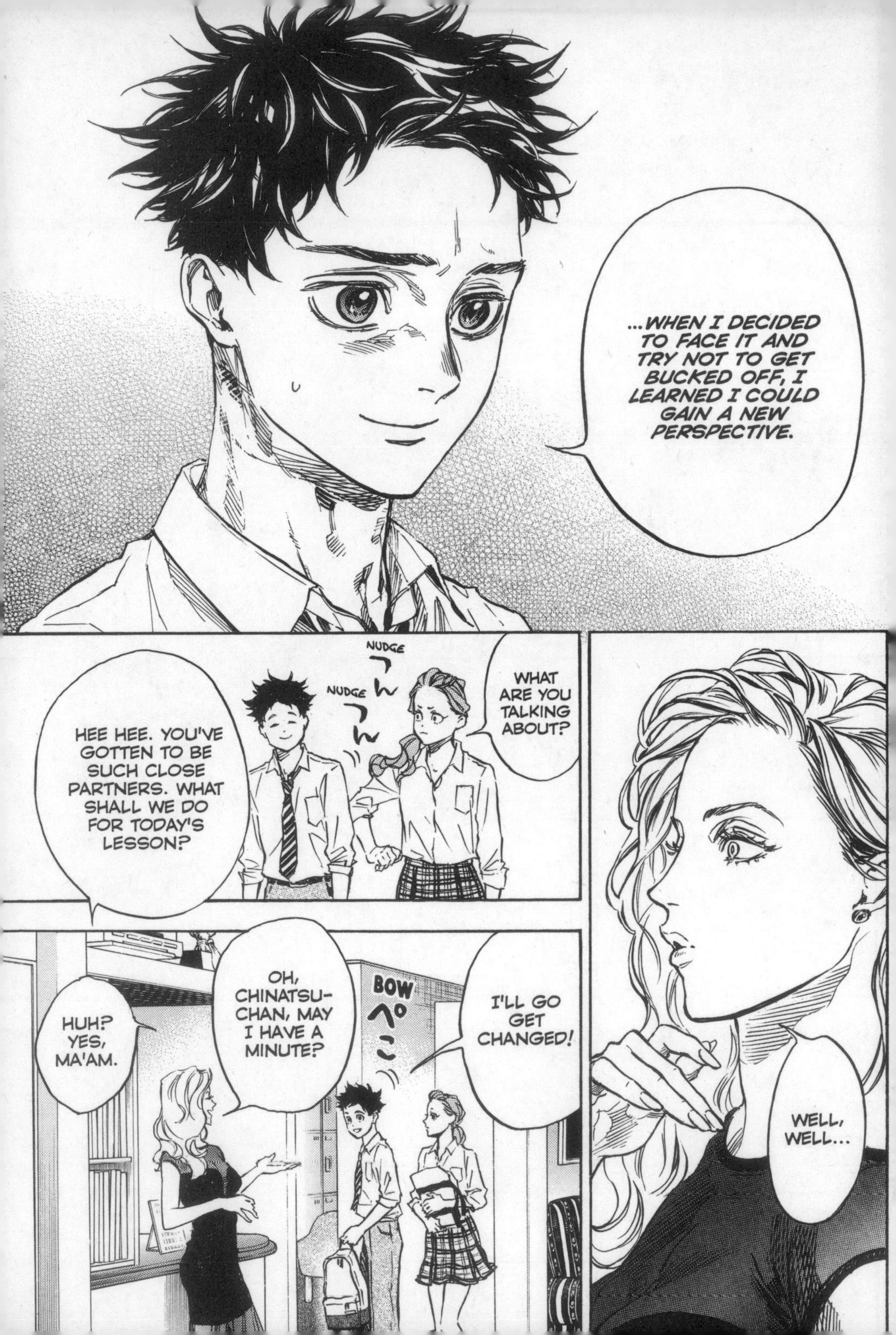
...WHEN I DECIDED TO FACE IT AND TRY NOT TO GET BUCKED OFF, I LEARNED I COULD GAIN A NEW PERSPECTIVE.
WELL, WELL...
NUDGE
NUDGE
WHAT ARE YOU TALKING ABOUT?
HEE HEE. YOU'VE GOTTEN TO BE SUCH CLOSE PARTNERS. WHAT SHALL WE DO FOR TODAY'S LESSON?
I'LL GO GET CHANGED!
BOW
OH, CHINATSU-CHAN, MAY I HAVE A MINUTE?
HUH? YES, MA'AM.

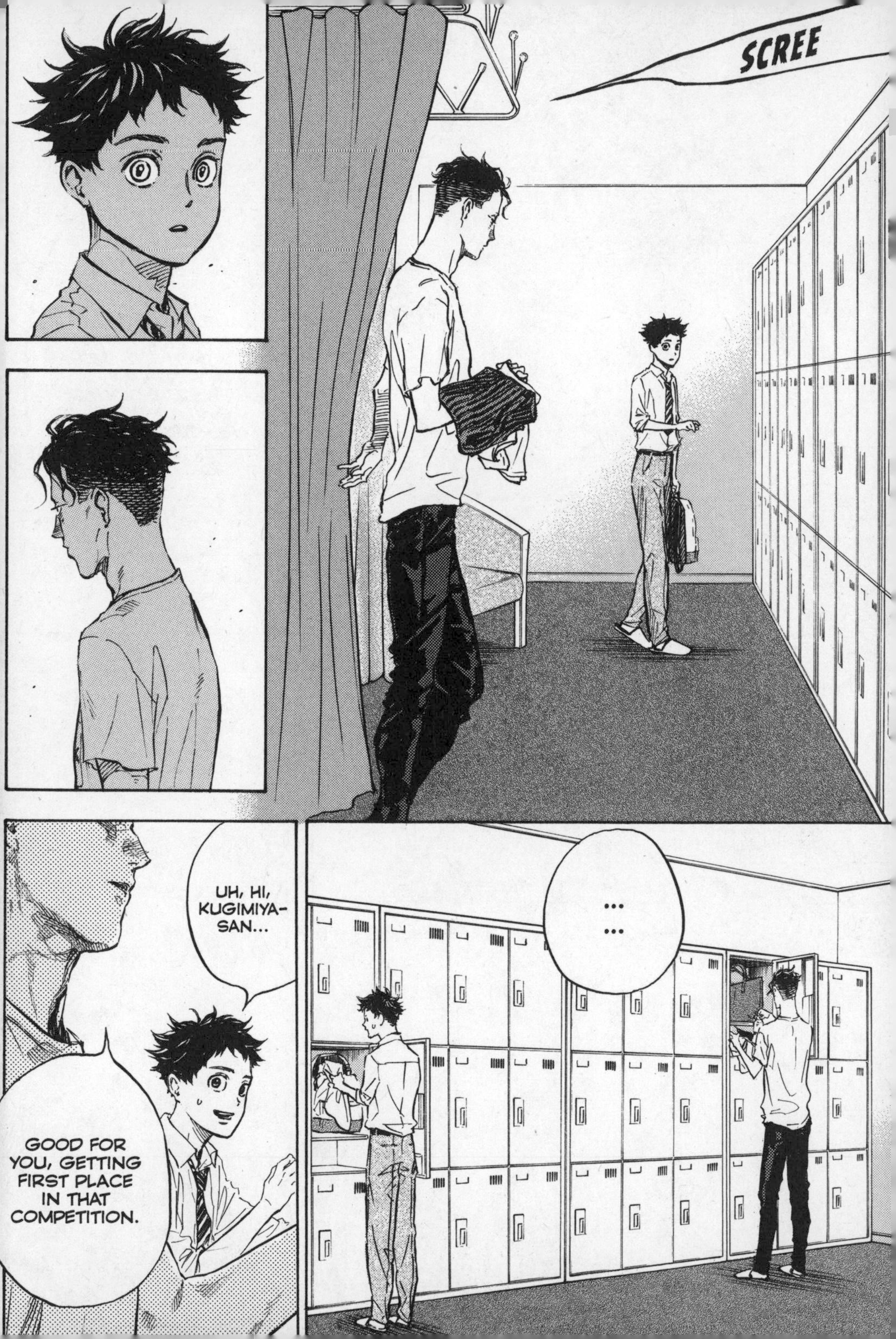
SCREE
...
...
UH, HI, KUGIMIYA-SAN...
GOOD FOR YOU, GETTING FIRST PLACE IN THAT COMPETITION.

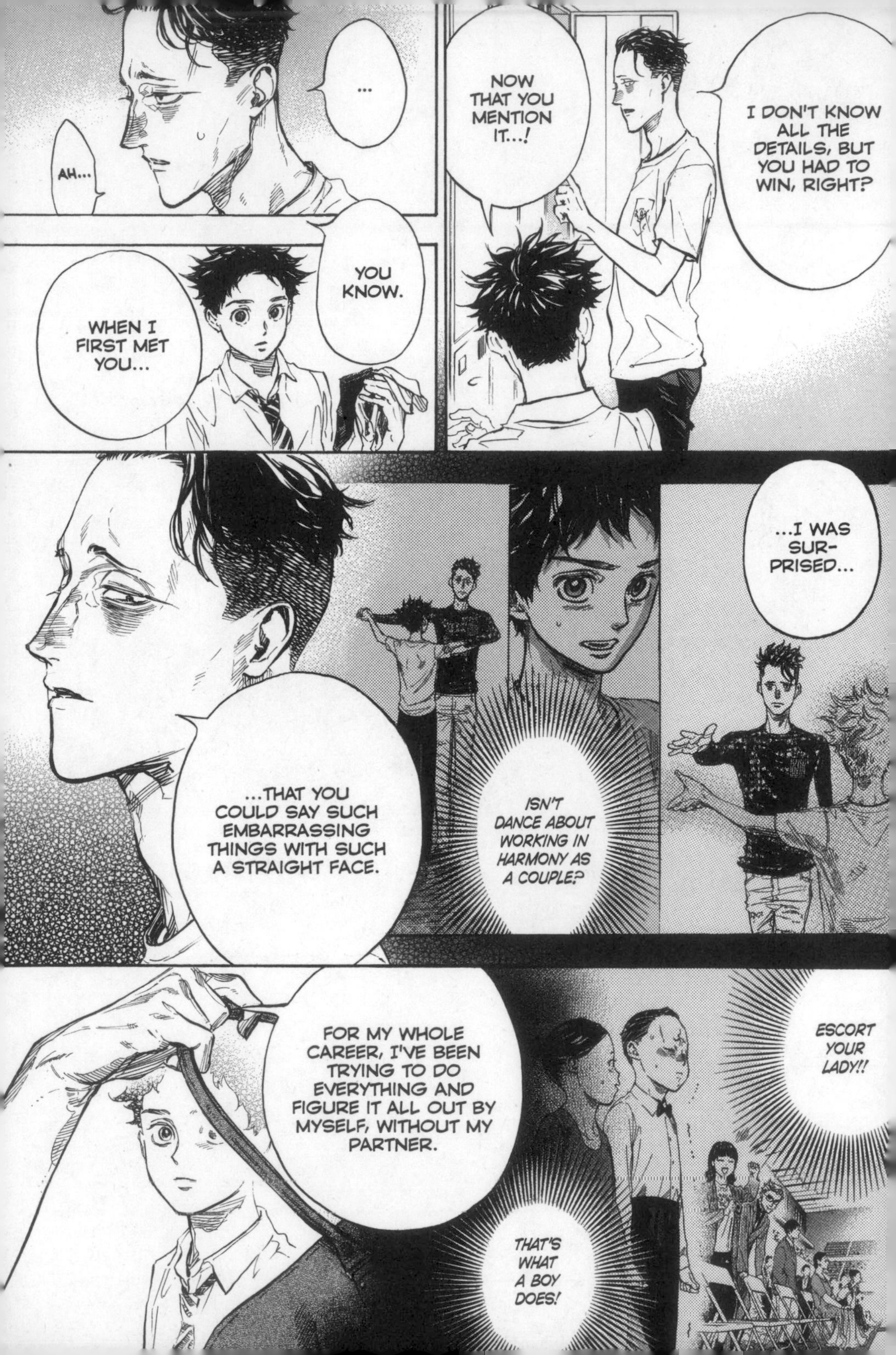
I DON'T KNOW ALL THE DETAILS, BUT YOU HAD TO WIN, RIGHT?
NOW THAT YOU MENTION IT...!
...
AH...
YOU KNOW.
WHEN I FIRST MET YOU...
...I WAS SUR-PRISED...
ISN'T DANCE ABOUT WORKING IN HARMONY AS A COUPLE?
...THAT YOU COULD SAY SUCH EMBARRASSING THINGS WITH SUCH A STRAIGHT FACE.
ESCORT YOUR LADY!!
THAT'S WHAT A BOY DOES!
FOR MY WHOLE CAREER, I'VE BEEN TRYING TO DO EVERYTHING AND FIGURE IT ALL OUT BY MYSELF, WITHOUT MY PARTNER.

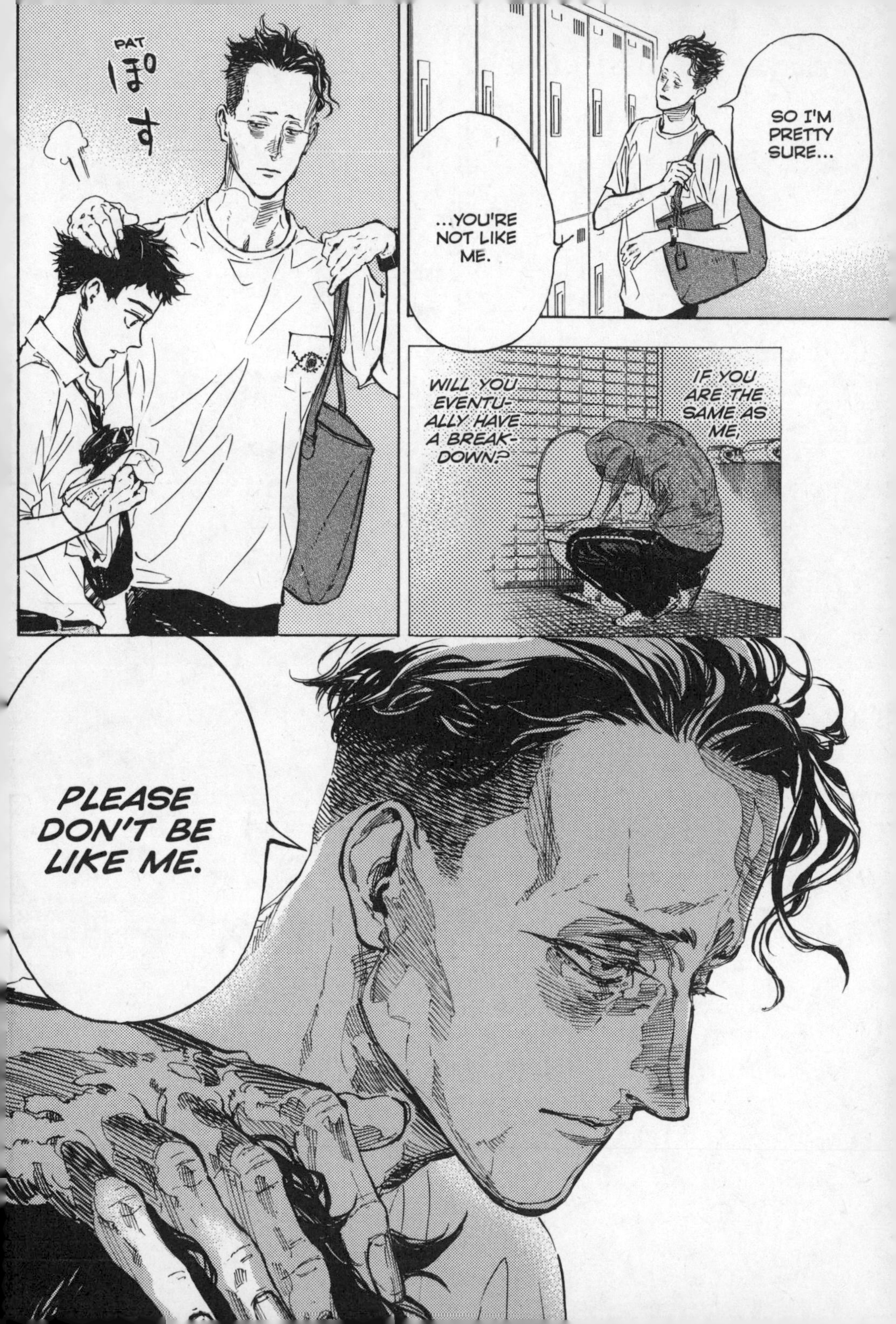
SO I'M PRETTY SURE...
...YOU'RE NOT LIKE ME.
IF YOU ARE THE SAME AS ME,
WILL YOU EVENTUALLY HAVE A BREAKDOWN?
PAT
ぽす
PLEASE DON'T BE LIKE ME.

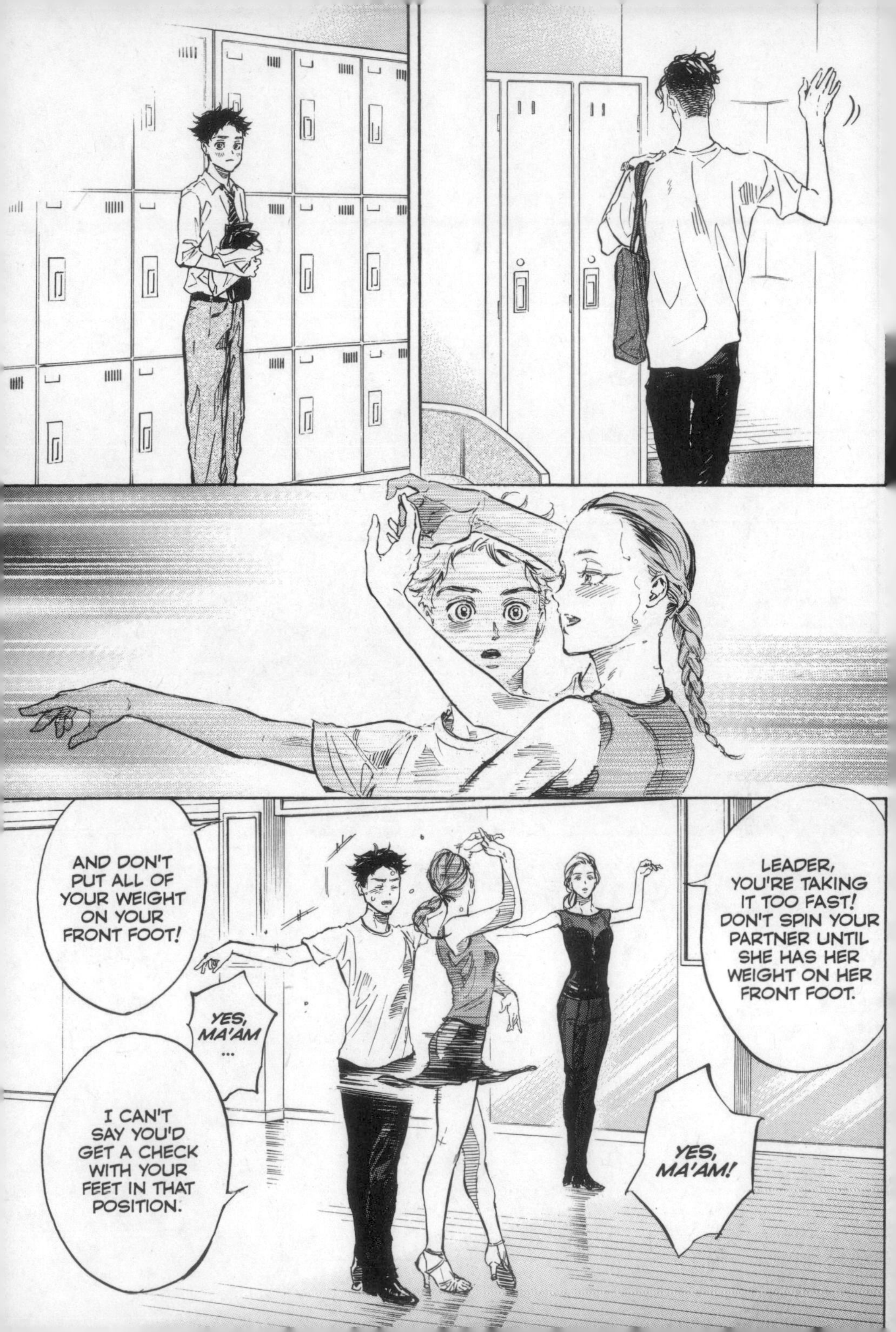
LEADER, YOU'RE TAKING IT TOO FAST! DON'T SPIN YOUR PARTNER UNTIL SHE HAS HER WEIGHT ON HER FRONT FOOT.
YES, MA'AM!
AND DON'T PUT ALL OF YOUR WEIGHT ON YOUR FRONT FOOT!
YES, MA'AM ...
I CAN'T SAY YOU'D GET A CHECK WITH YOUR FEET IN THAT POSITION.

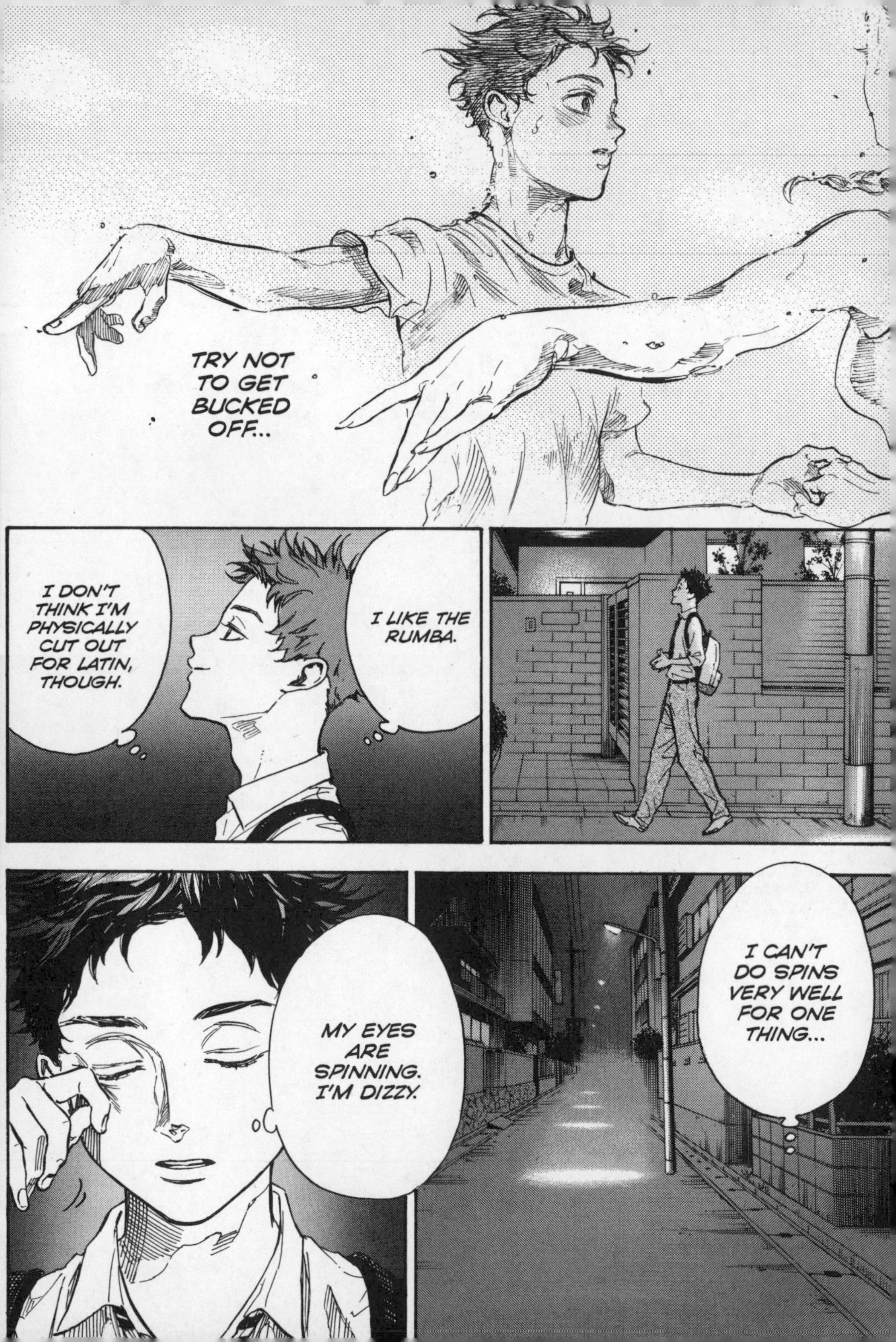
TRY NOT TO GET BUCKED OFF...
I LIKE THE RUMBA.
I DON'T THINK I'M PHYSICALLY CUT OUT FOR LATIN, THOUGH.
I CAN'T DO SPINS VERY WELL FOR ONE THING...
MY EYES ARE SPINNING. I'M DIZZY.

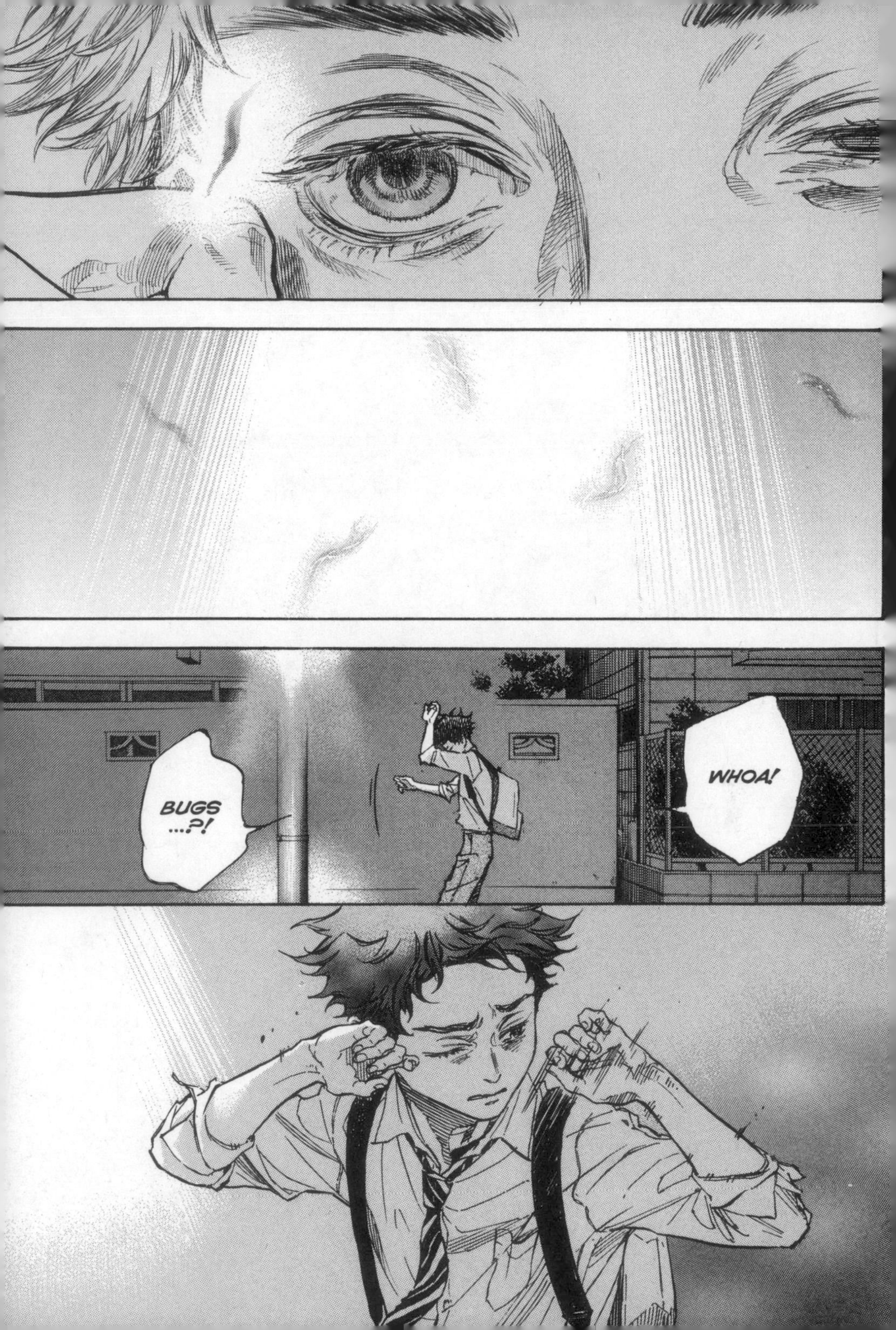
WHOA!
BUGS ...?!

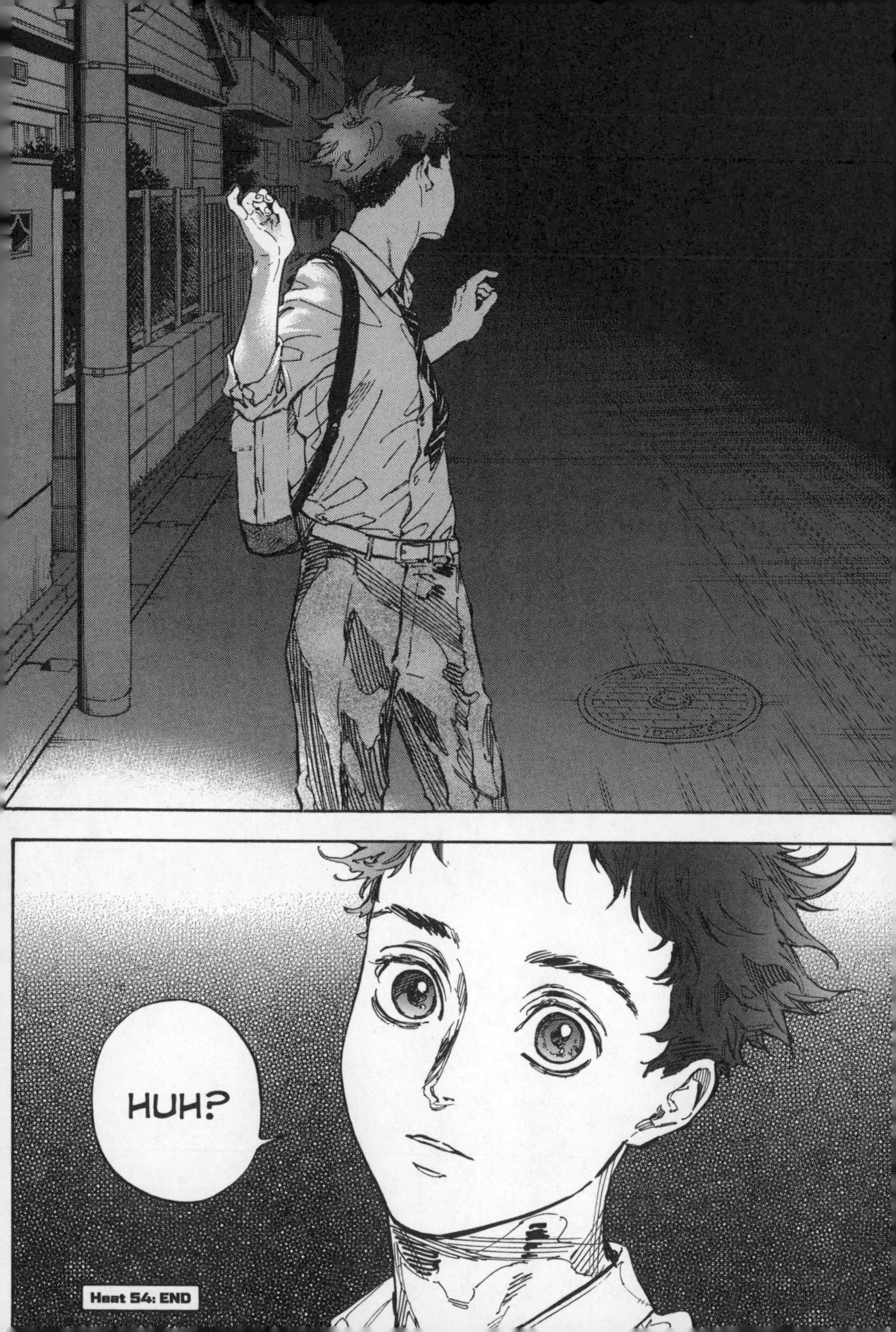
HUH?
Heat 54: END

WELCOME TO THE BALLROOM

Heat 49 Front Page Illustration from Monthly Shonen Magazine

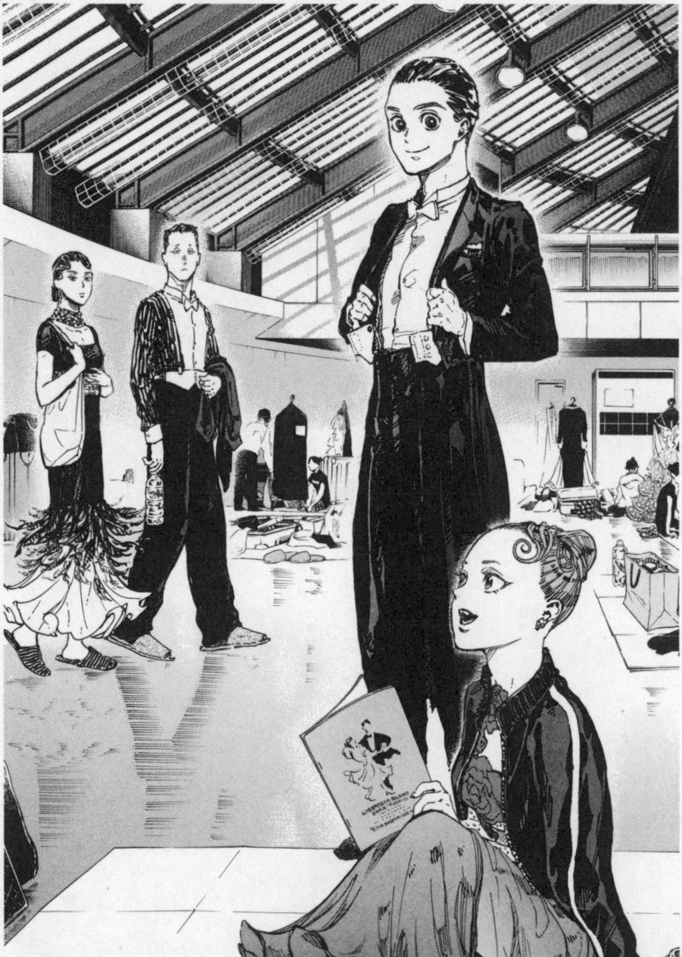

Heat 55: Lookers On

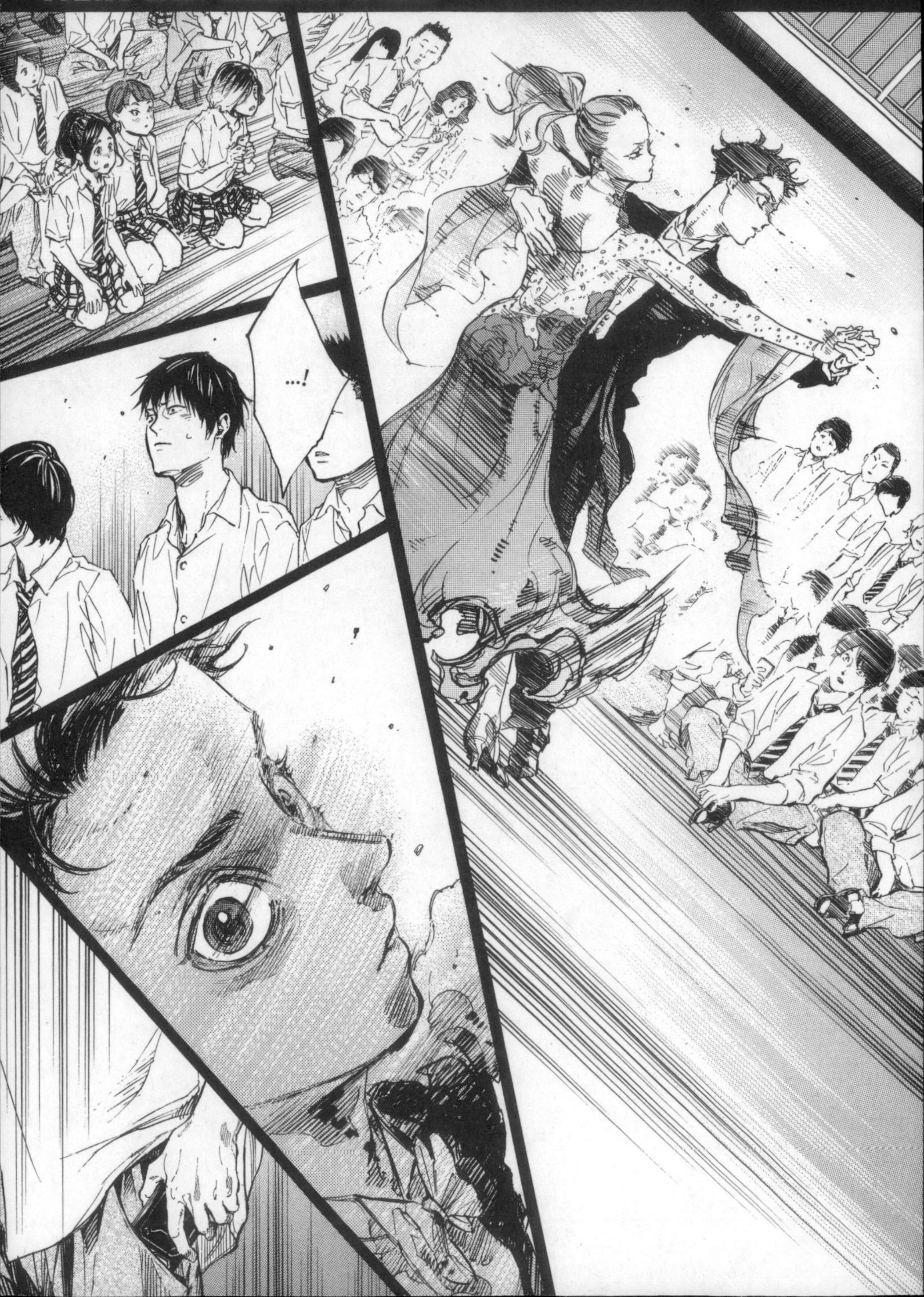
...!

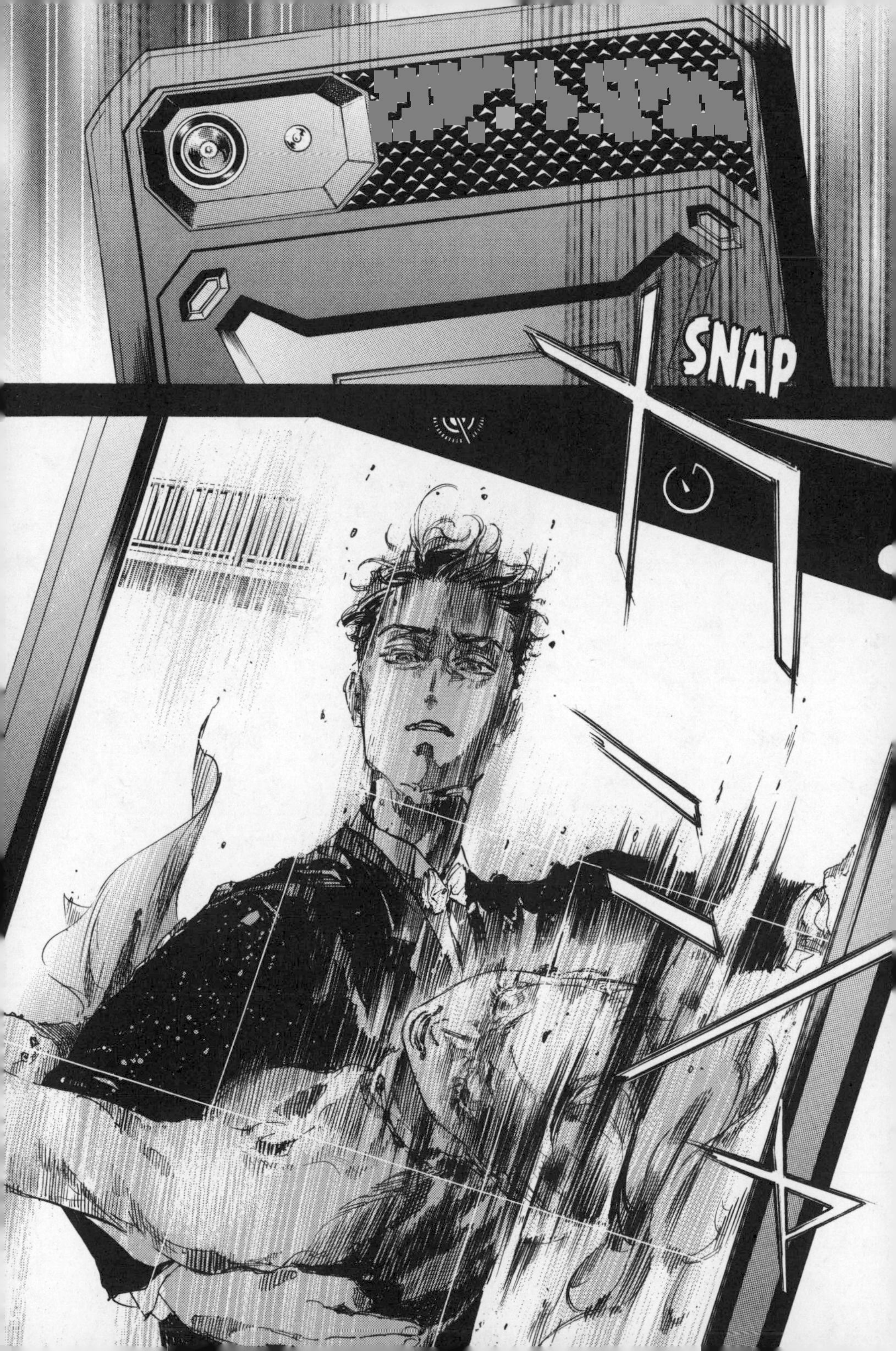
SNAP

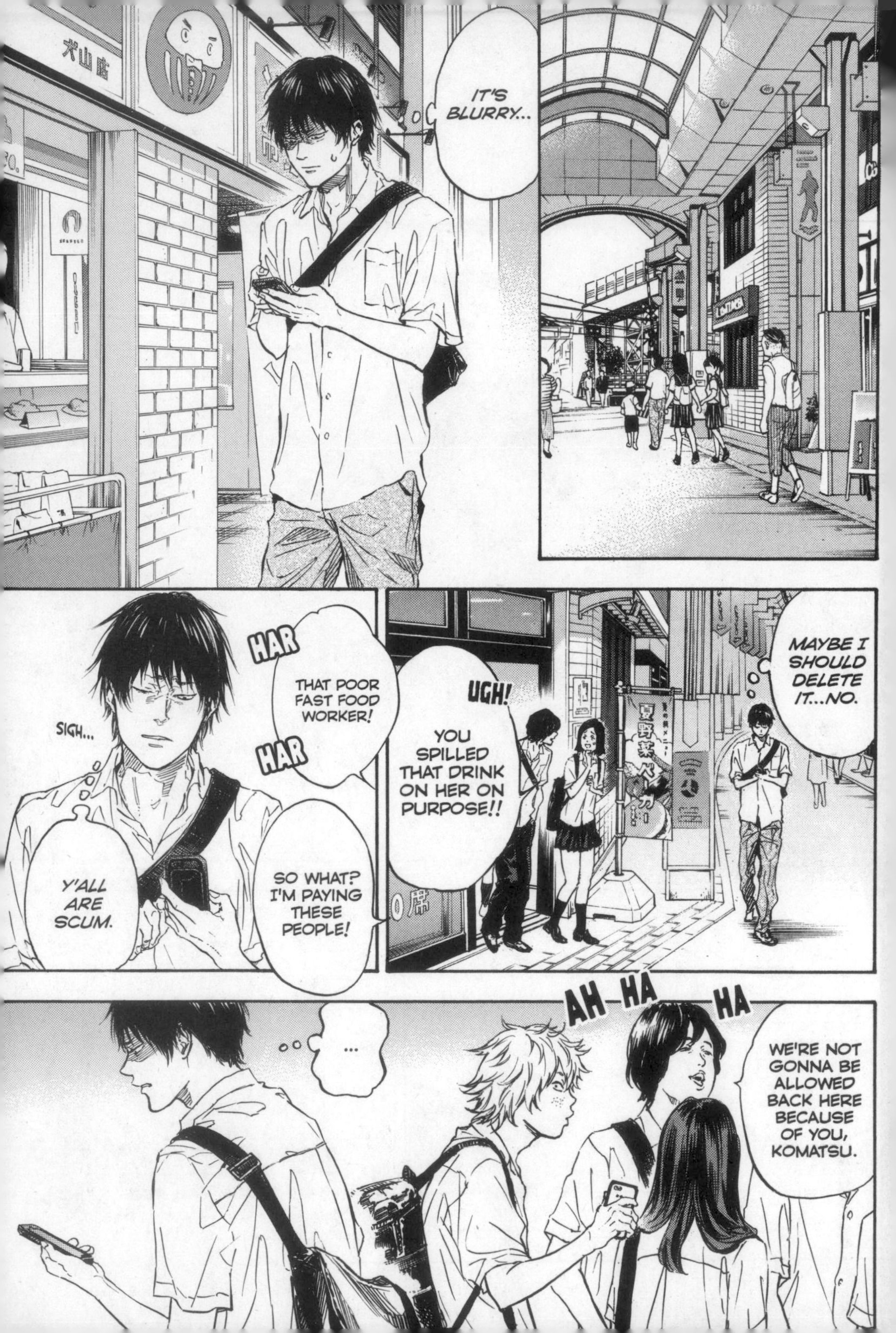
IT'S BLURRY...
MAYBE I SHOULD DELETE IT...NO.
UGH!
YOU SPILLED THAT DRINK ON HER ON PURPOSE!!
HAR
THAT POOR FAST FOOD WORKER!
HAR
SO WHAT? I'M PAYING THESE PEOPLE!
SIGH...
Y'ALL ARE SCUM.
AH HA HA
WE'RE NOT GONNA BE ALLOWED BACK HERE BECAUSE OF YOU, KOMATSU.
...

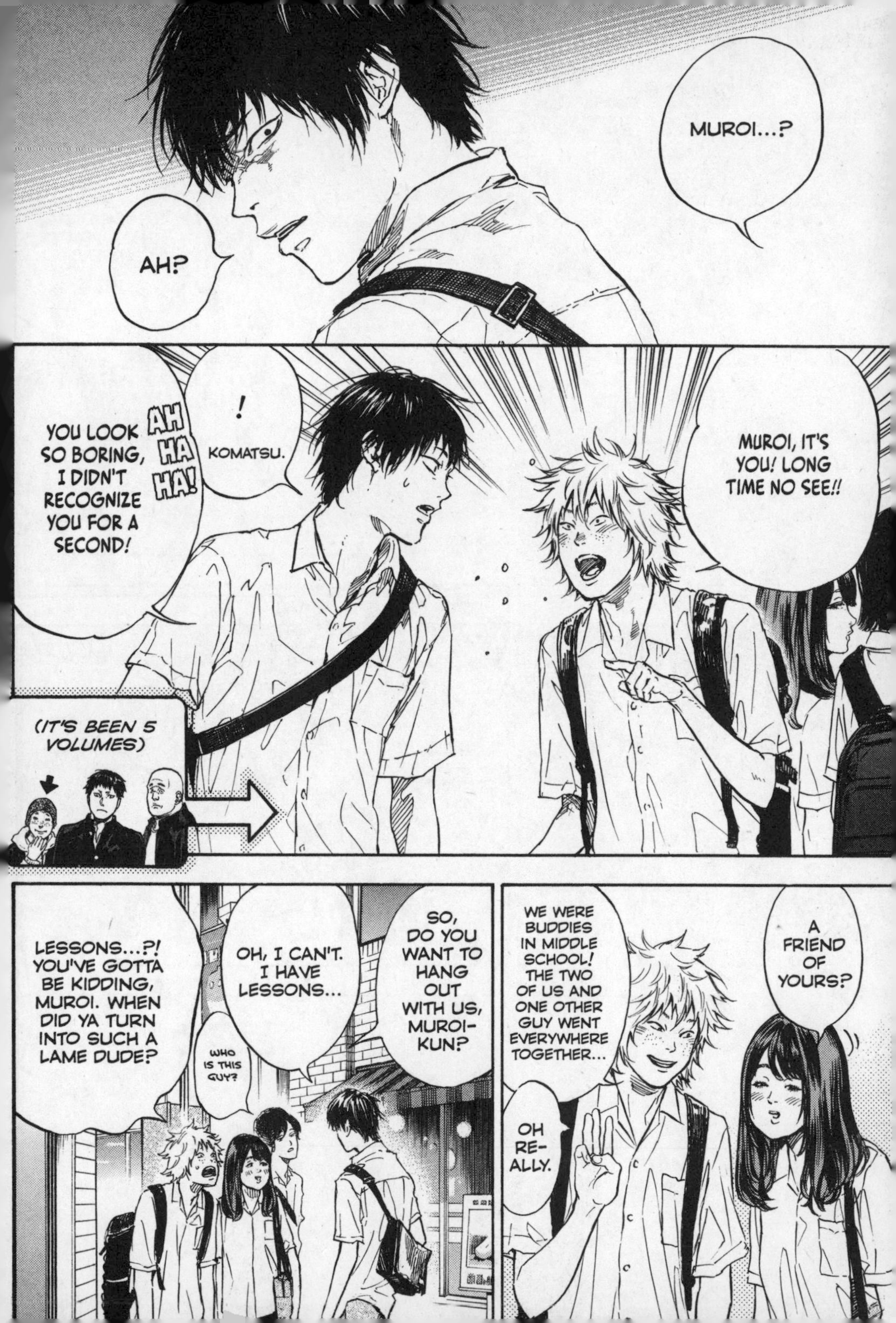
MUROI...?
AH?
MUROI, IT'S YOU! LONG TIME NO SEE!!
!
KOMATSU.
AH HA HA!
YOU LOOK SO BORING, I DIDN'T RECOGNIZE YOU FOR A SECOND!
(IT'S BEEN 5 VOLUMES)
A FRIEND OF YOURS?
WE WERE BUDDIES IN MIDDLE SCHOOL! THE TWO OF US AND ONE OTHER GUY WENT EVERYWHERE TOGETHER...
OH REALLY.
SO, DO YOU WANT TO HANG OUT WITH US, MUROI-KUN?
OH, I CAN'T. I HAVE LESSONS...
WHO IS THIS GUY?
LESSONS...?! YOU'VE GOTTA BE KIDDING, MUROI. WHEN DID YA TURN INTO SUCH A LAME DUDE?

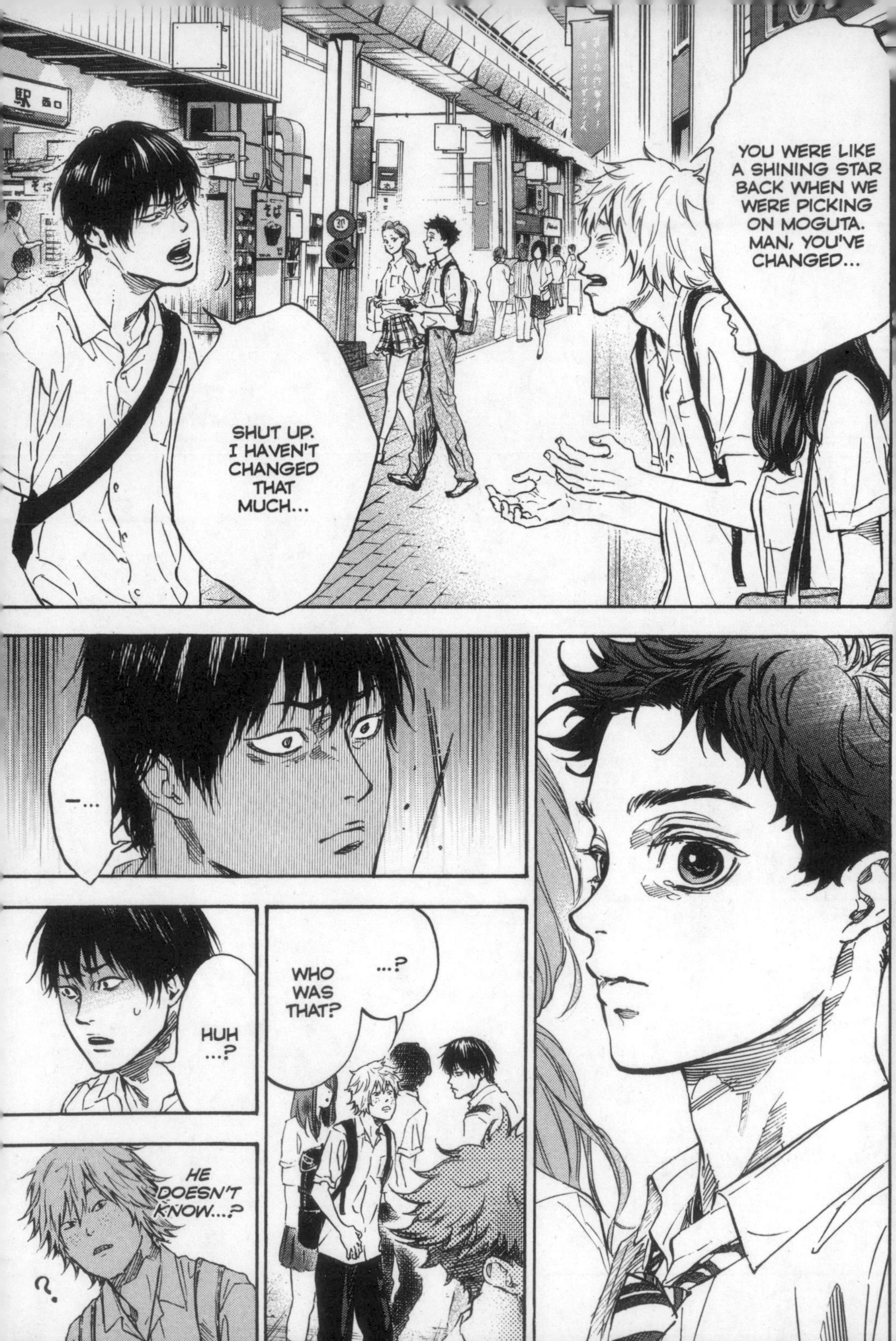
YOU WERE LIKE A SHINING STAR BACK WHEN WE WERE PICKING ON MOGUTA. MAN, YOU'VE CHANGED...
SHUT UP. I HAVEN'T CHANGED THAT MUCH...
—...
...?
WHO WAS THAT?
HUH ...?
HE DOESN'T KNOW...?
?

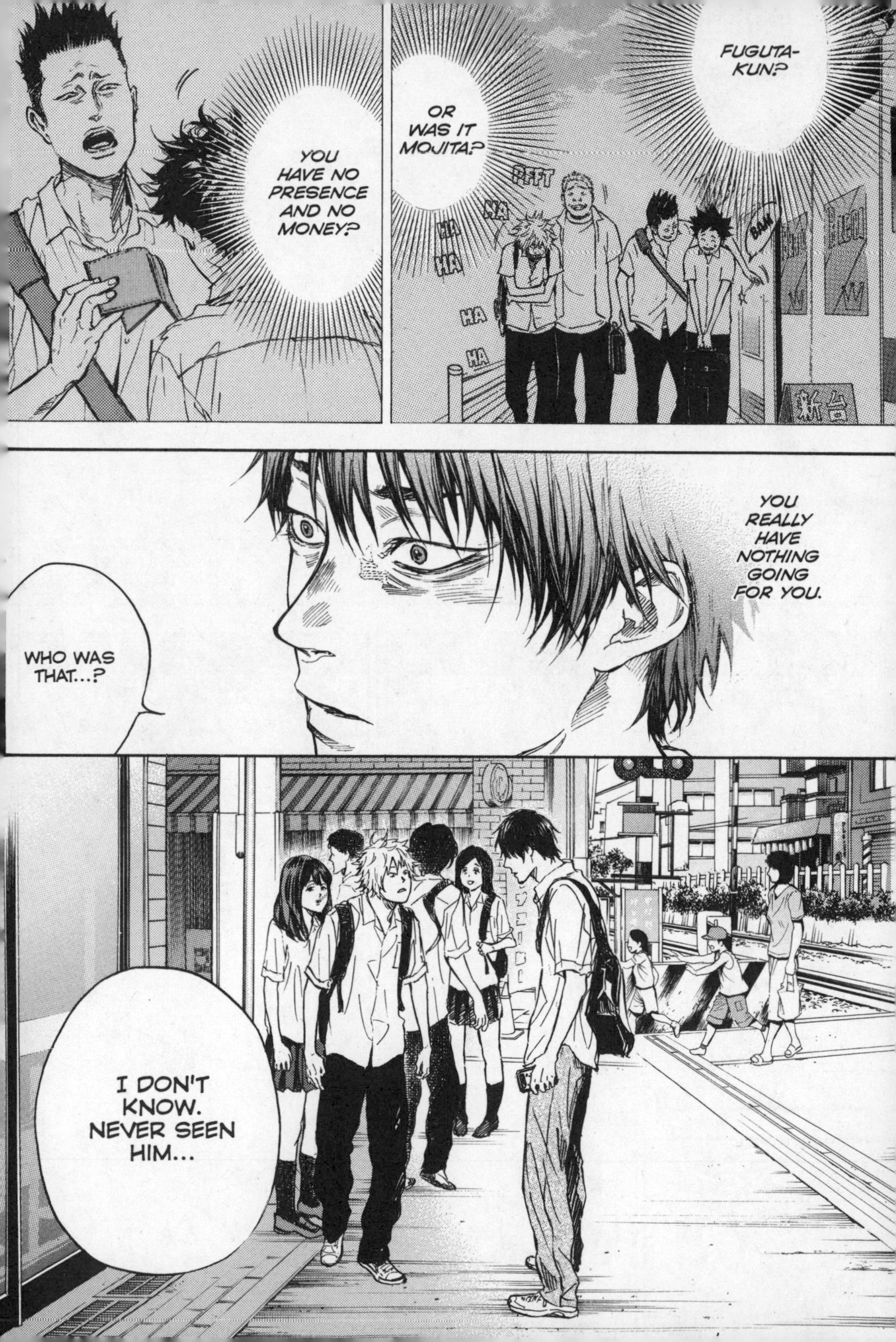
FUGUTA-KUN?
OR WAS IT MOJITA?
PFFT
HA
HA
HA
HA
HA
BAN
YOU HAVE NO PRESENCE AND NO MONEY?
YOU REALLY HAVE NOTHING GOING FOR YOU.
WHO WAS THAT...?
I DON'T KNOW. NEVER SEEN HIM...

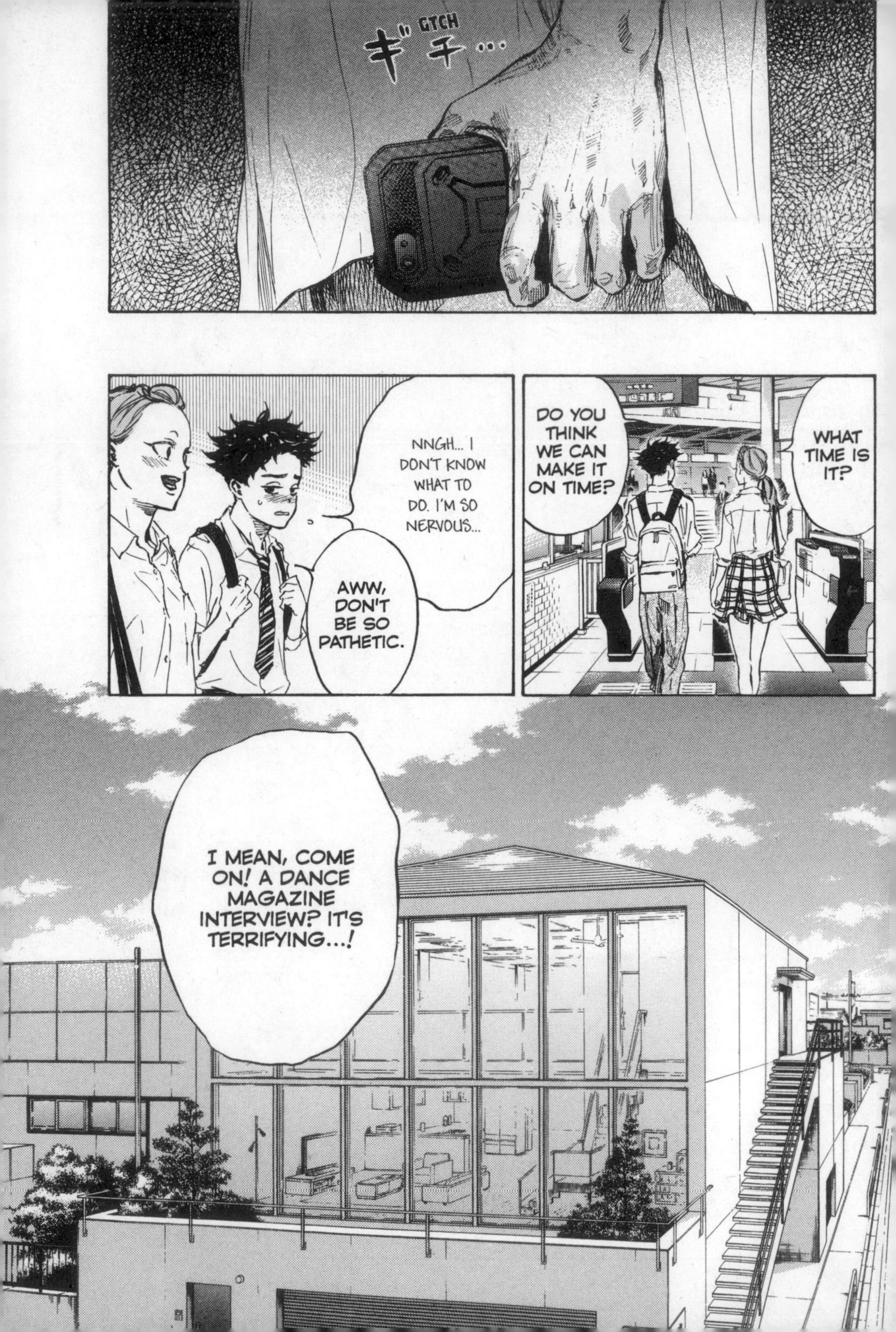
ギチ... GTCH
WHAT TIME IS IT?
DO YOU THINK WE CAN MAKE IT ON TIME?
NNGH... I DON'T KNOW WHAT TO DO. I'M SO NERVOUS...
AWW, DON'T BE SO PATHETIC.
I MEAN, COME ON! A DANCE MAGAZINE INTERVIEW? IT'S TERRIFYING...!

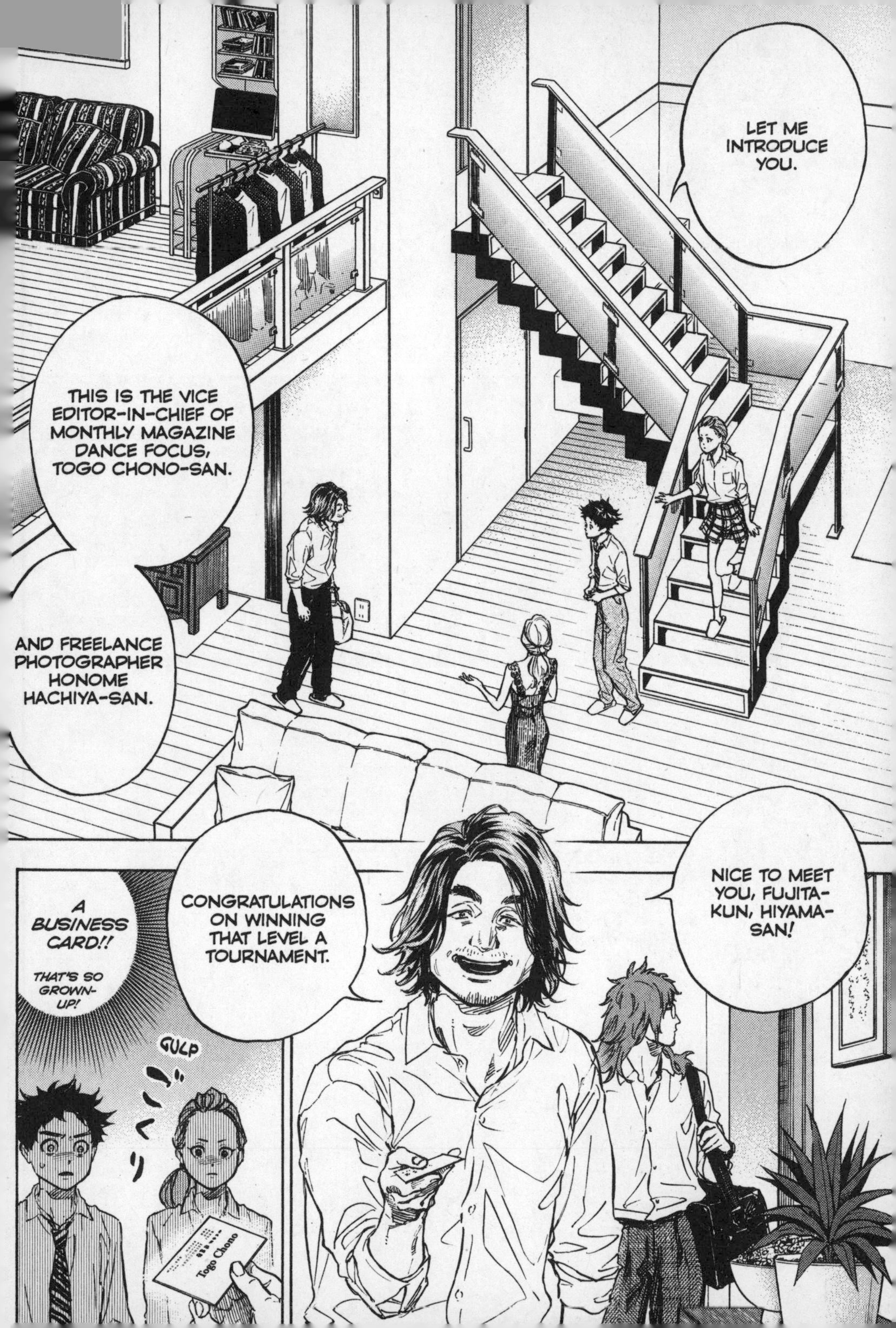
LET ME INTRODUCE YOU.
THIS IS THE VICE EDITOR-IN-CHIEF OF MONTHLY MAGAZINE DANCE FOCUS, TOGO CHONO-SAN.
AND FREELANCE PHOTOGRAPHER HONOME HACHIYA-SAN.
NICE TO MEET YOU, FUJITA-KUN, HIYAMA-SAN!
CONGRATULATIONS ON WINNING THAT LEVEL A TOURNAMENT.
A BUSINESS CARD!!
THAT'S SO GROWN-UP!
GULP
Togo Chono

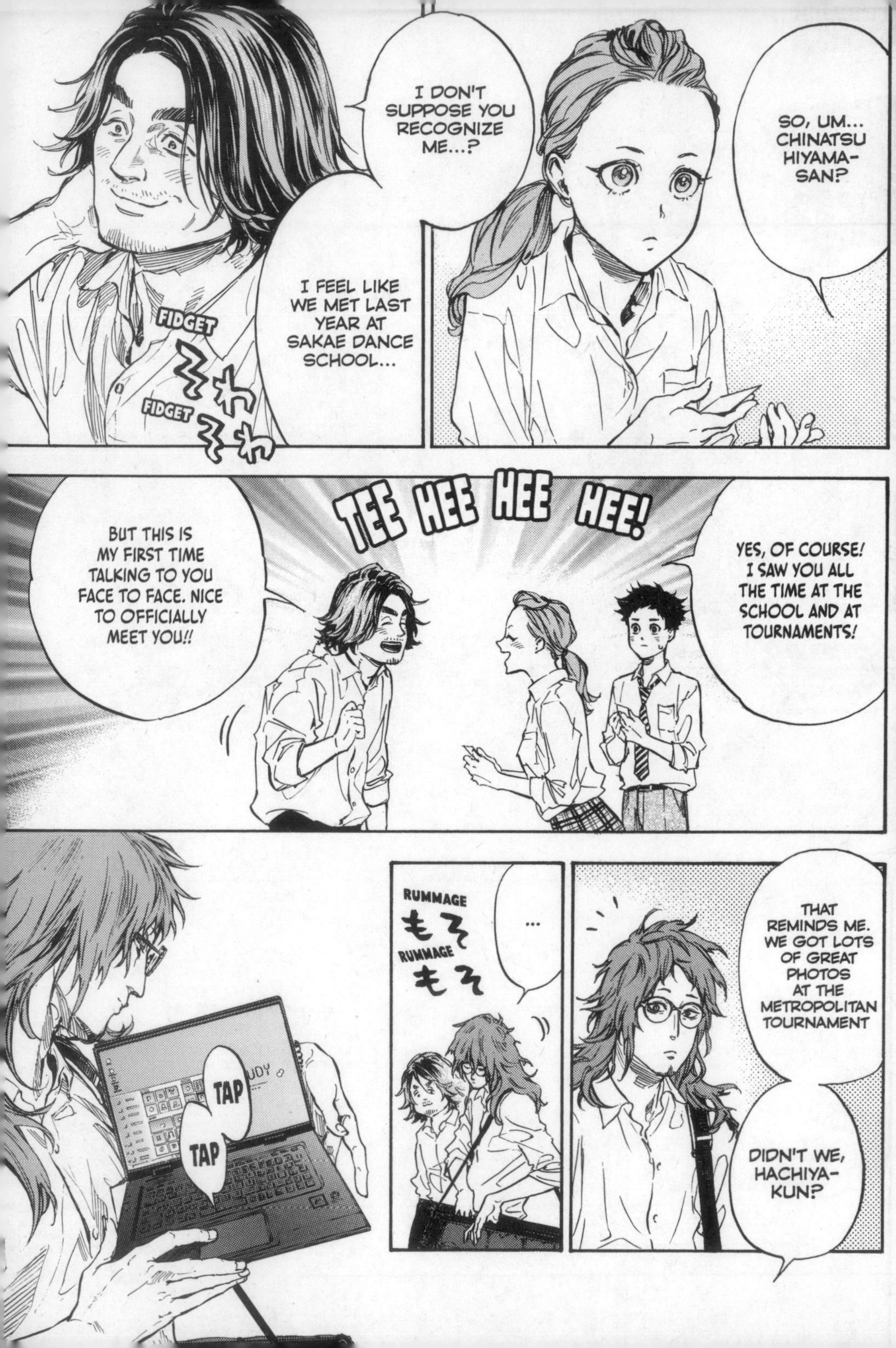
SO, UM... CHINATSU HIYAMA-SAN?
I DON'T SUPPOSE YOU RECOGNIZE ME...?
I FEEL LIKE WE MET LAST YEAR AT SAKAE DANCE SCHOOL...
FIDGET
そわ
FIDGET
そわ
YES, OF COURSE! I SAW YOU ALL THE TIME AT THE SCHOOL AND AT TOURNAMENTS!
TEE HEE HEE HEE!
BUT THIS IS MY FIRST TIME TALKING TO YOU FACE TO FACE. NICE TO OFFICIALLY MEET YOU!!
THAT REMINDS ME. WE GOT LOTS OF GREAT PHOTOS AT THE METROPOLITAN TOURNAMENT
DIDN'T WE, HACHIYA-KUN?
...
RUMMAGE
もそ
RUMMAGE
もそ
TAP
TAP

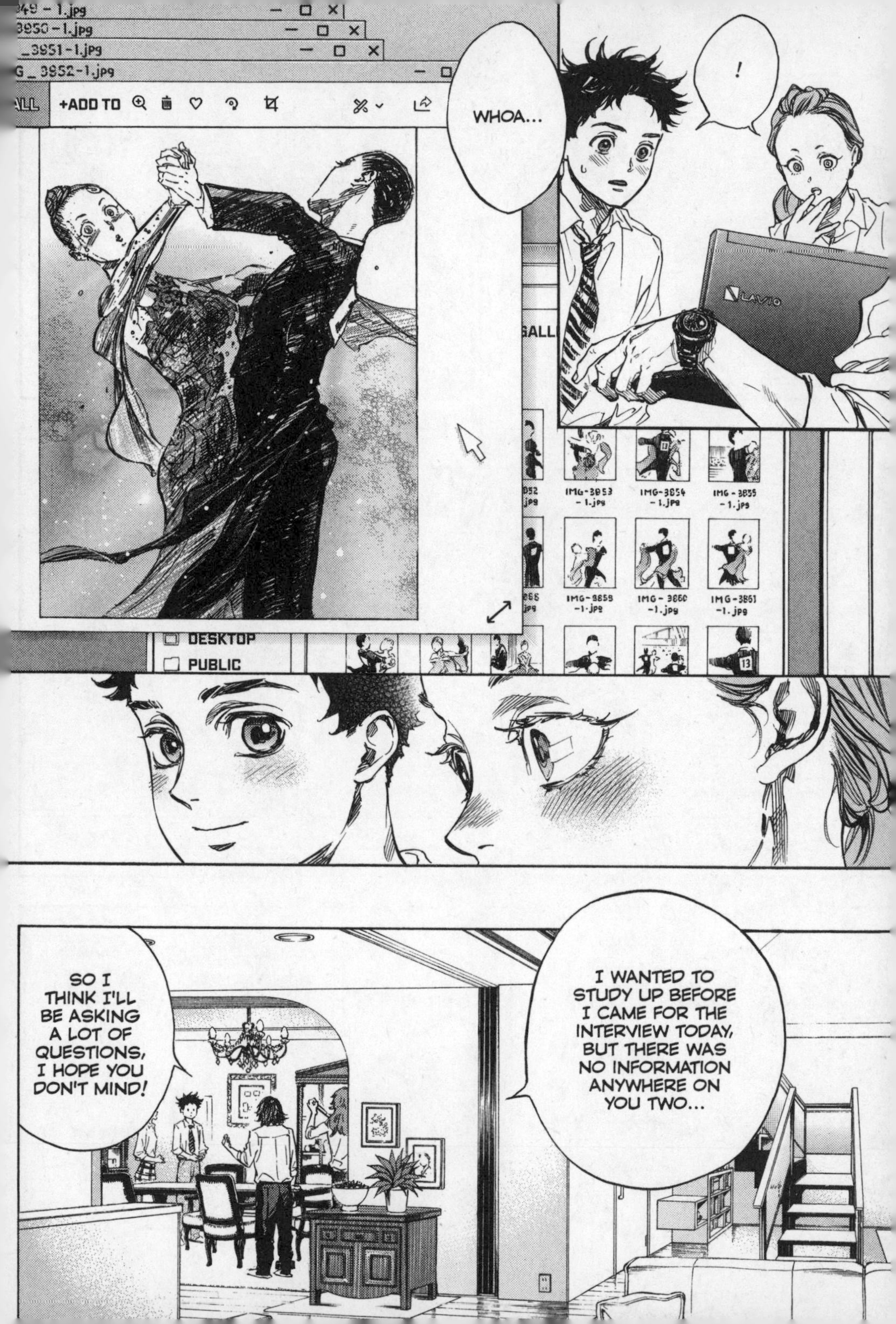
!
WHOA...
LAVIO
+ADD TO
IMG-3853 -1.jpg
IMG-3854 -1.jpg
IMG-3855 -1.jpg
IMG-3859 -1.jpg
IMG-3860 -1.jpg
IMG-3861 -1.jpg
DESKTOP
PUBLIC
I WANTED TO STUDY UP BEFORE I CAME FOR THE INTERVIEW TODAY, BUT THERE WAS NO INFORMATION ANYWHERE ON YOU TWO...
SO I THINK I'LL BE ASKING A LOT OF QUESTIONS, I HOPE YOU DON'T MIND!

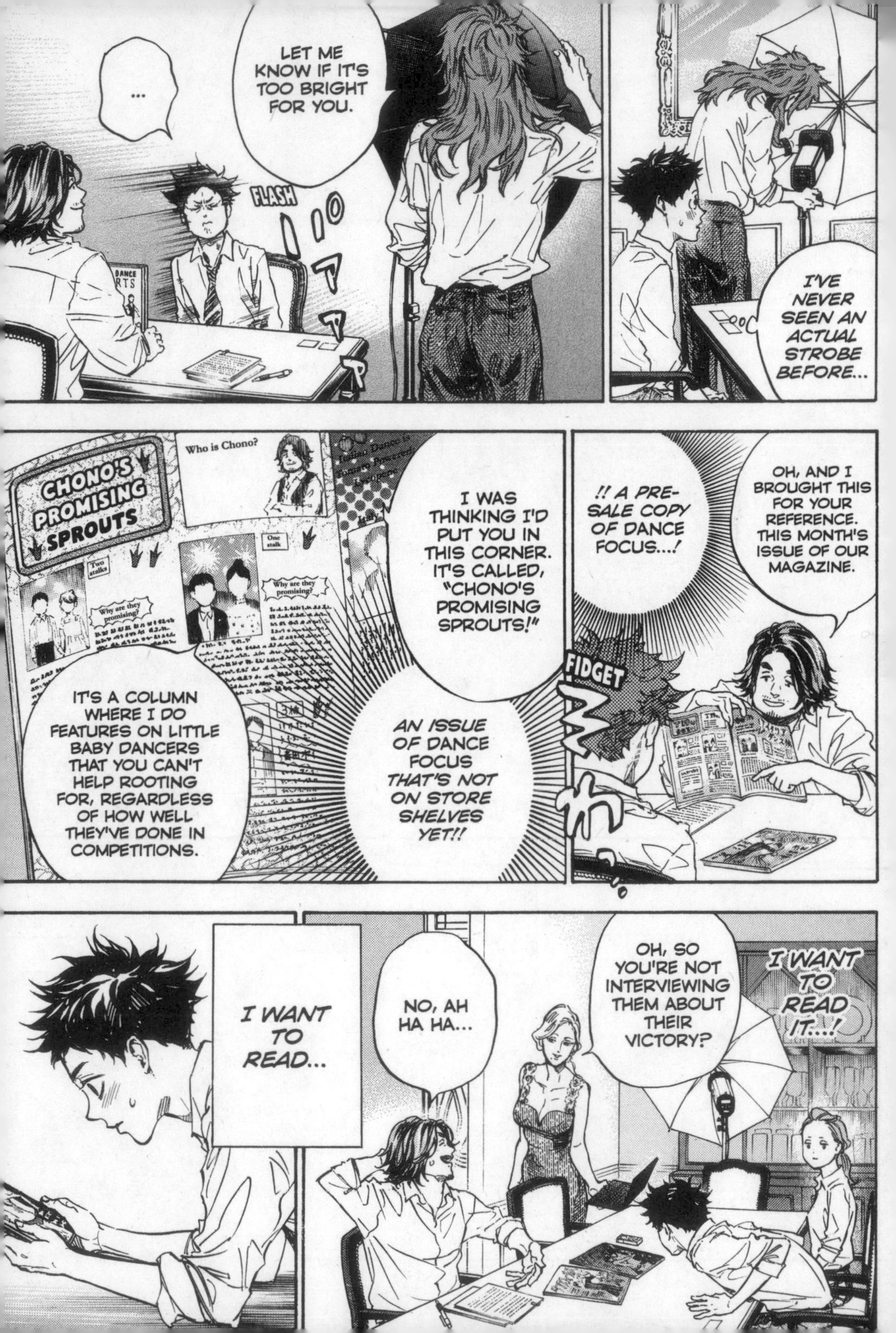
I'VE NEVER SEEN AN ACTUAL STROBE BEFORE...
LET ME KNOW IF IT'S TOO BRIGHT FOR YOU.
FLASH
...
DANCE
RTS
OH, AND I BROUGHT THIS FOR YOUR REFERENCE. THIS MONTH'S ISSUE OF OUR MAGAZINE.
!! A PRE-SALE COPY OF DANCE FOCUS...!
FIDGET
I WAS THINKING I'D PUT YOU IN THIS CORNER. IT'S CALLED, "CHONO'S PROMISING SPROUTS!"
Who is Chono?
CHONO'S PROMISING SPROUTS
One stalk
Two stalks
Why are they promising?
Why are they promising?
AN ISSUE OF DANCE FOCUS THAT'S NOT ON STORE SHELVES YET!!
IT'S A COLUMN WHERE I DO FEATURES ON LITTLE BABY DANCERS THAT YOU CAN'T HELP ROOTING FOR, REGARDLESS OF HOW WELL THEY'VE DONE IN COMPETITIONS.
I WANT TO READ IT...!
OH, SO YOU'RE NOT INTERVIEWING THEM ABOUT THEIR VICTORY?
NO, AH HA HA...
I WANT TO READ...

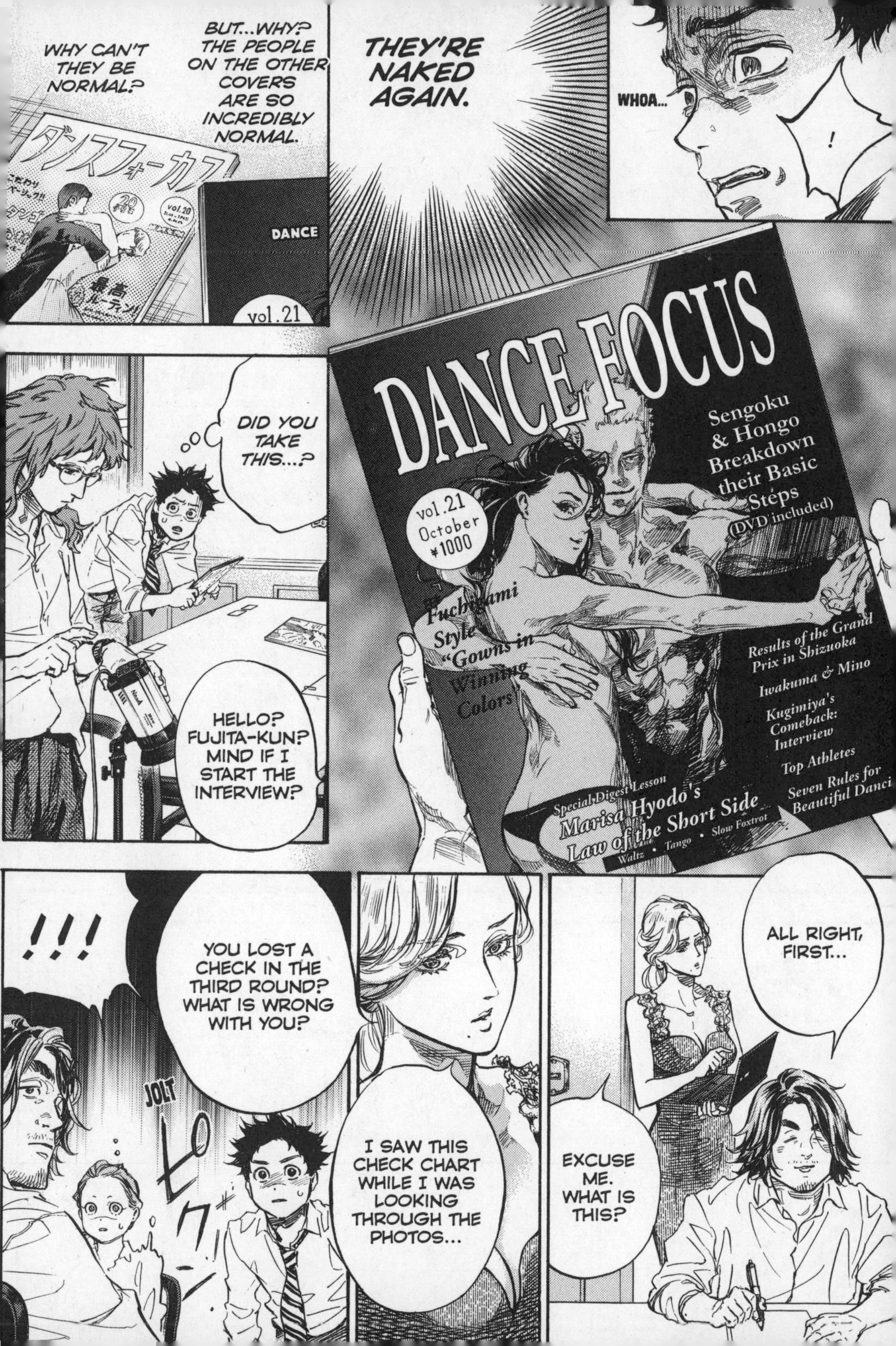
WHOA...
!
THEY'RE NAKED AGAIN.
BUT...WHY? THE PEOPLE ON THE OTHER COVERS ARE SO INCREDIBLY NORMAL.
WHY CAN'T THEY BE NORMAL?
DANCE
vol.21
DANCE FOCUS
Sengoku & Hongo Breakdown their Basic Steps (DVD included)
vol.21 October ¥1000
Fuchigami Style "Gowns in Winning Colors"
Results of the Grand Prix in Shizuoka
Iwakuma & Mino
Kugimiya's Comeback: Interview
Top Athletes
Seven Rules for Beautiful Danci
Special Digest Lesson
Marisa Hyodo's Law of the Short Side
Waltz • Tango • Slow Foxtrot
DID YOU TAKE THIS...?
HELLO? FUJITA-KUN? MIND IF I START THE INTERVIEW?
ALL RIGHT, FIRST...
EXCUSE ME. WHAT IS THIS?
I SAW THIS CHECK CHART WHILE I WAS LOOKING THROUGH THE PHOTOS...
YOU LOST A CHECK IN THE THIRD ROUND? WHAT IS WRONG WITH YOU?
!!!
JOLT

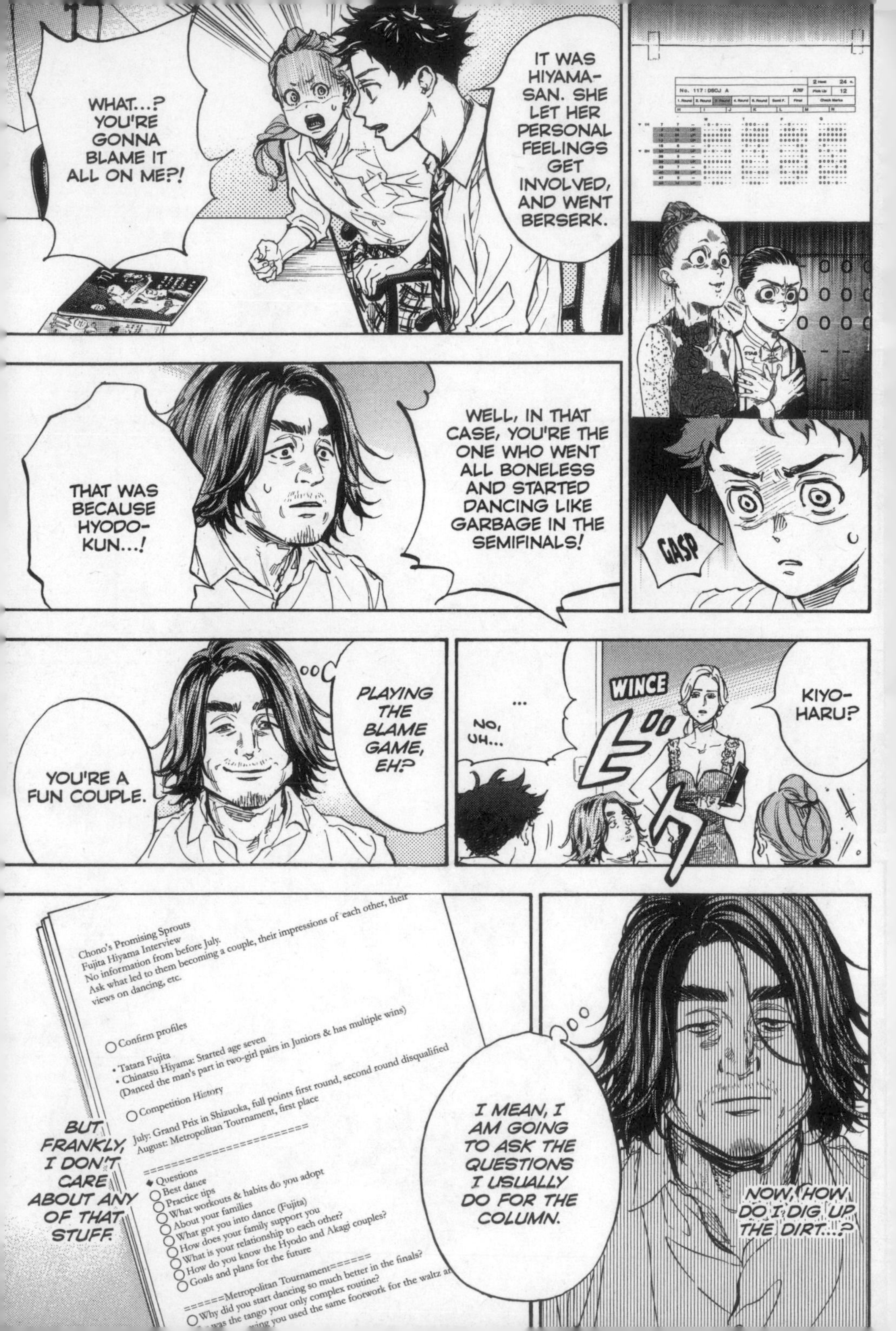
IT WAS HIYAMA-SAN. SHE LET HER PERSONAL FEELINGS GET INVOLVED, AND WENT BERSERK.
WHAT...? YOU'RE GONNA BLAME IT ALL ON ME?!
GASP
WELL, IN THAT CASE, YOU'RE THE ONE WHO WENT ALL BONELESS AND STARTED DANCING LIKE GARBAGE IN THE SEMIFINALS!
THAT WAS BECAUSE HYODO-KUN...!
KIYO-HARU?
WINCE
...
NO, UH...
PLAYING THE BLAME GAME, EH?
YOU'RE A FUN COUPLE.
I MEAN, I AM GOING TO ASK THE QUESTIONS I USUALLY DO FOR THE COLUMN.
NOW, HOW DO I DIG UP THE DIRT...?
Chono's Promising Sprouts
Fujita Hiyama Interview
No information from before July.
Ask what led to them becoming a couple, their impressions of each other, their views on dancing, etc.
○ Confirm profiles
• Tatara Fujita
• Chinatsu Hiyama: Started age seven
(Danced the man's part in two-girl pairs in Juniors & has multiple wins)
○ Competition History
July: Grand Prix in Shizuoka, full points first round, second round disqualified
August: Metropolitan Tournament, first place
=======================
◆ Questions
○ Best dance
○ Practice tips
○ What workouts & habits do you adopt
○ About your families
○ What got you into dance (Fujita)
○ How does your family support you
○ What is your relationship to each other?
○ How do you know the Hyodo and Akagi couples?
○ How do you plan for the future
○ Goals and plans for the future
=====Metropolitan Tournament======
○ Why did you start dancing so much better in the finals?
BUT FRANKLY, I DON'T CARE ABOUT ANY OF THAT STUFF.

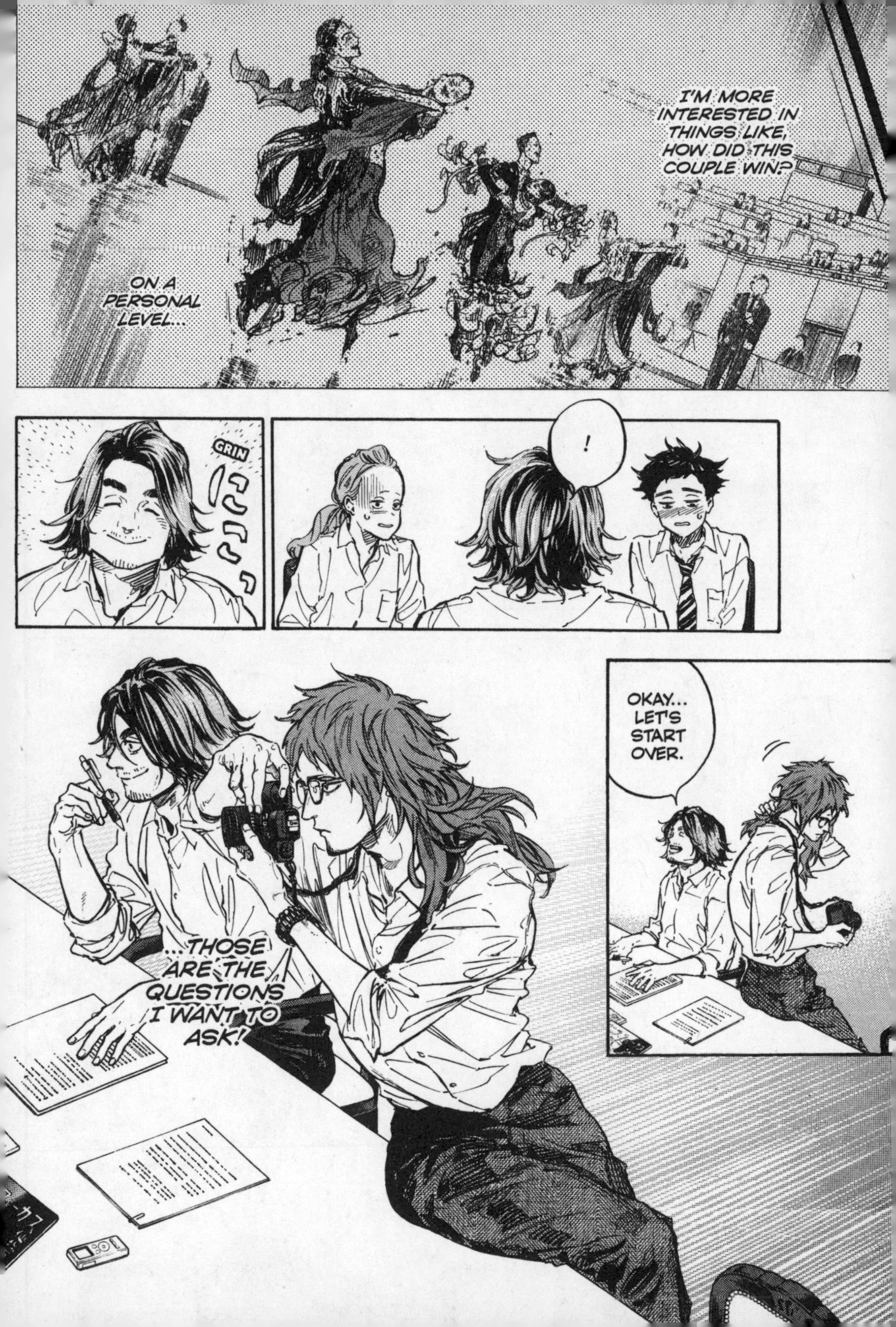

I'M MORE INTERESTED IN THINGS LIKE, HOW DID THIS COUPLE WIN?
ON A PERSONAL LEVEL...
!
GRIN
OKAY... LET'S START OVER.
...THOSE ARE THE QUESTIONS I WANT TO ASK!

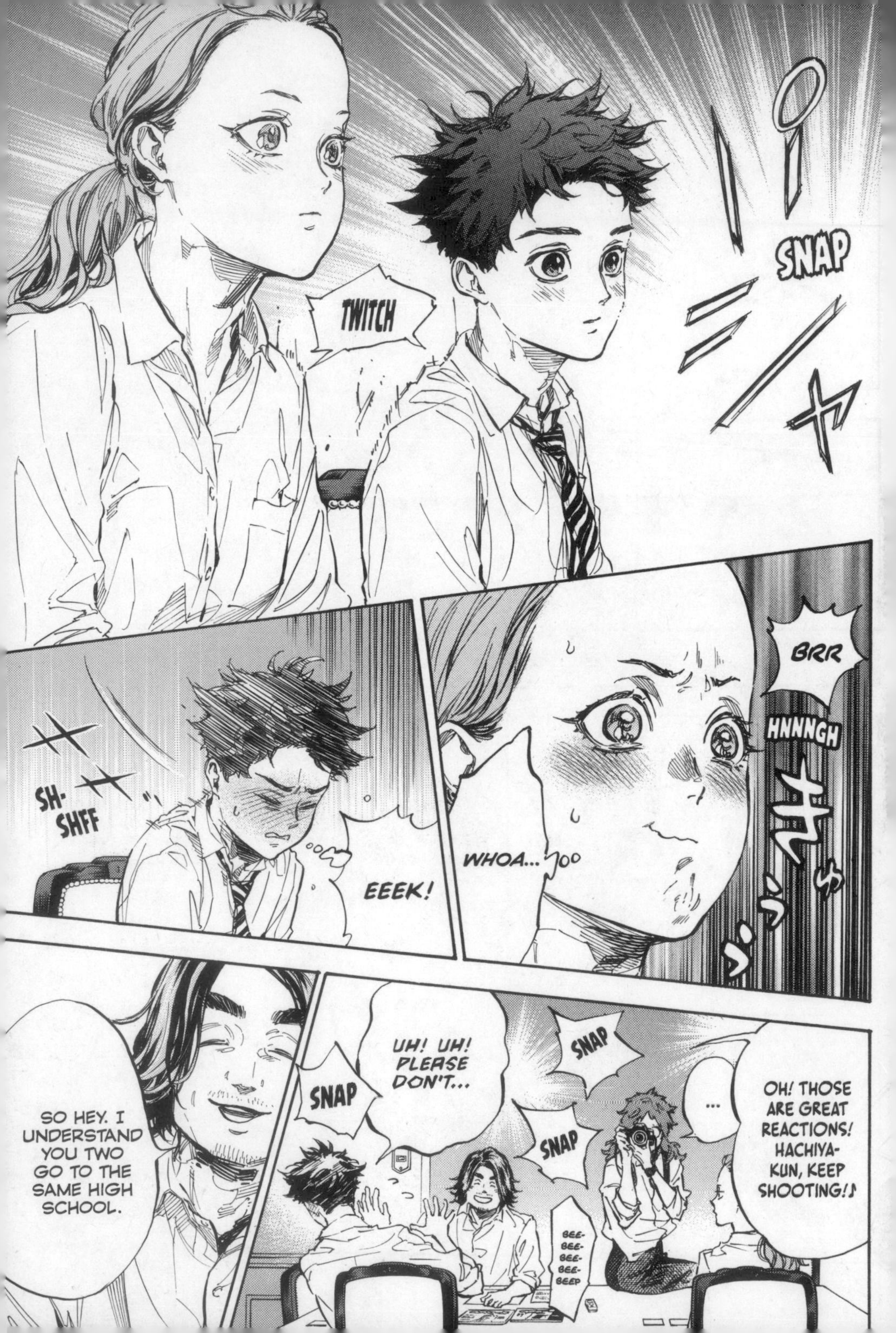
SNAP
TWITCH
BRR
HNNNGH
WHOA...
EEEK!
SH-SHFF
OH! THOSE ARE GREAT REACTIONS! HACHIYA-KUN, KEEP SHOOTING!♪
...
SNAP
UH! UH! PLEASE DON'T...
SNAP
SNAP
BEE-BEE-BEE-BEE-BEEP
SO HEY. I UNDERSTAND YOU TWO GO TO THE SAME HIGH SCHOOL.

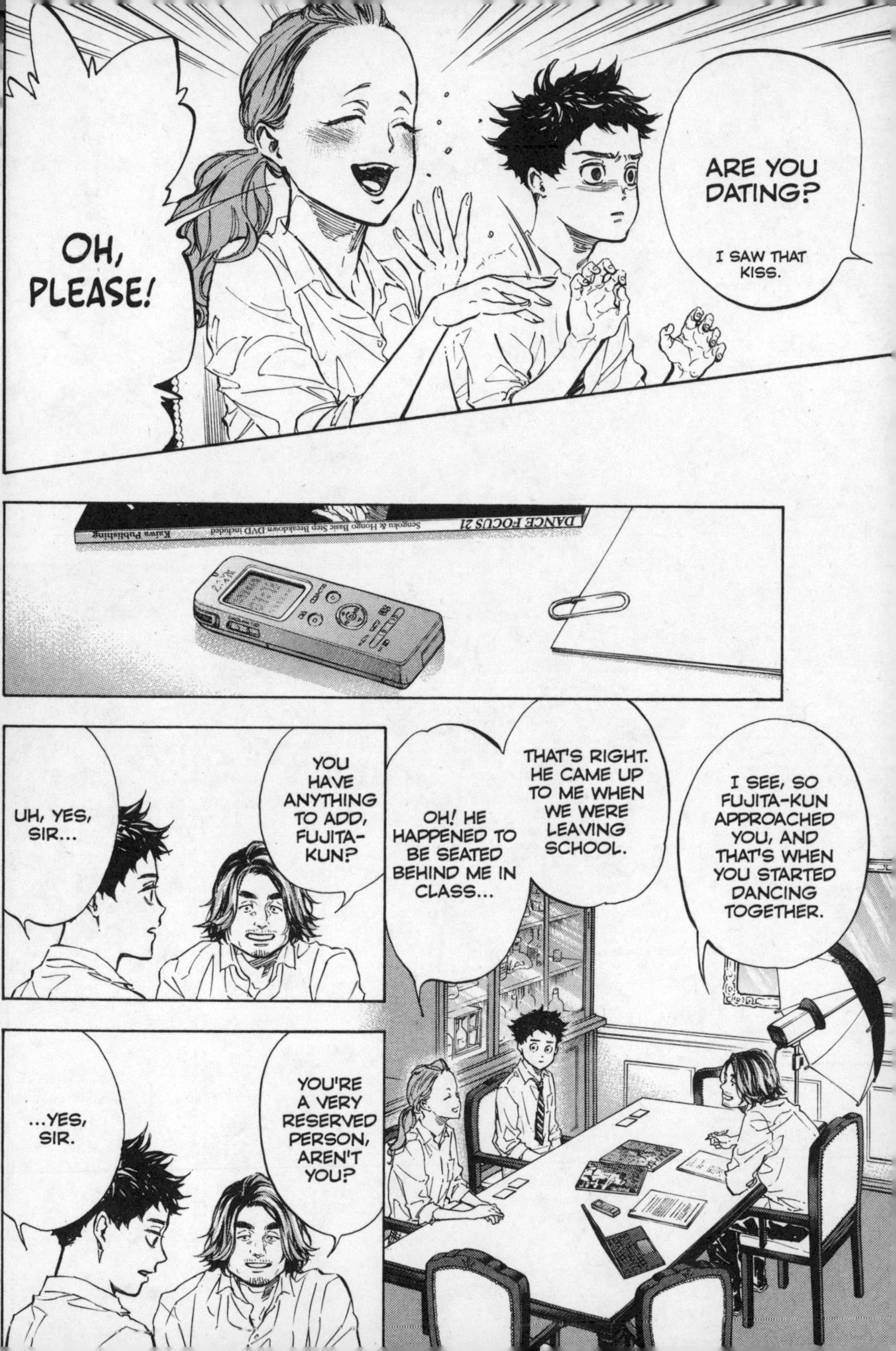
ARE YOU DATING?
I SAW THAT KISS.
OH, PLEASE!
DANCE FOCUS 21
Sengoku & Hongo Basic Step Breakdown DVD included
Kaiwa Publishing
I SEE, SO FUJITA-KUN APPROACHED YOU, AND THAT'S WHEN YOU STARTED DANCING TOGETHER.
THAT'S RIGHT. HE CAME UP TO ME WHEN WE WERE LEAVING SCHOOL.
OH! HE HAPPENED TO BE SEATED BEHIND ME IN CLASS...
YOU HAVE ANYTHING TO ADD, FUJITA-KUN?
UH, YES, SIR...
YOU'RE A VERY RESERVED PERSON, AREN'T YOU?
...YES, SIR.

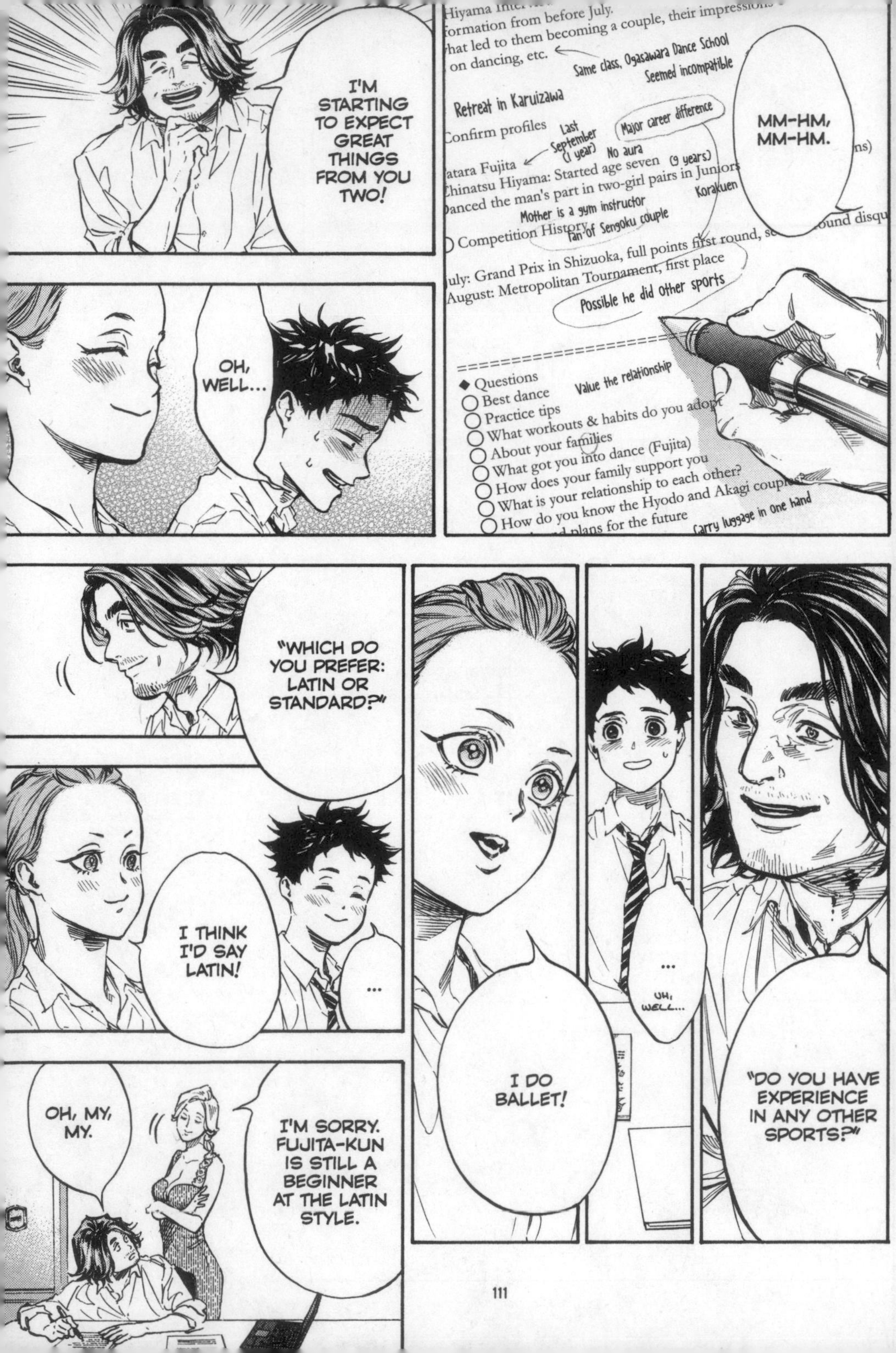
Hiyama Interv
formation from before July.
hat led to them becoming a couple, their impressions
on dancing, etc.
Same class, Ogasawara Dance School
Seemed incompatible
Retreat in Karuizawa
Confirm profiles
Last September (1 year)
Major career difference
No aura
atara Fujita
hinatsu Hiyama: Started age seven (9 years)
anced the man's part in two-girl pairs in Juniors
Korakuen
Mother is a gym instructor
Fan of Sengoku couple
Competition History
July: Grand Prix in Shizuoka, full points first round, se round disqu
August: Metropolitan Tournament, first place
Possible he did other sports
MM-HM, MM-HM.
◆ Questions
Value the relationship
Best dance
Practice tips
What workouts & habits do you adopt
About your families
What got you into dance (Fujita)
How does your family support you
What is your relationship to each other?
How do you know the Hyodo and Akagi couple
Carry luggage in one hand
plans for the future
I'M STARTING TO EXPECT GREAT THINGS FROM YOU TWO!
OH, WELL...
"DO YOU HAVE EXPERIENCE IN ANY OTHER SPORTS?"
...
UH, WELL...
I DO BALLET!
"WHICH DO YOU PREFER: LATIN OR STANDARD?"
I THINK I'D SAY LATIN!
...
I'M SORRY. FUJITA-KUN IS STILL A BEGINNER AT THE LATIN STYLE.
OH, MY, MY.

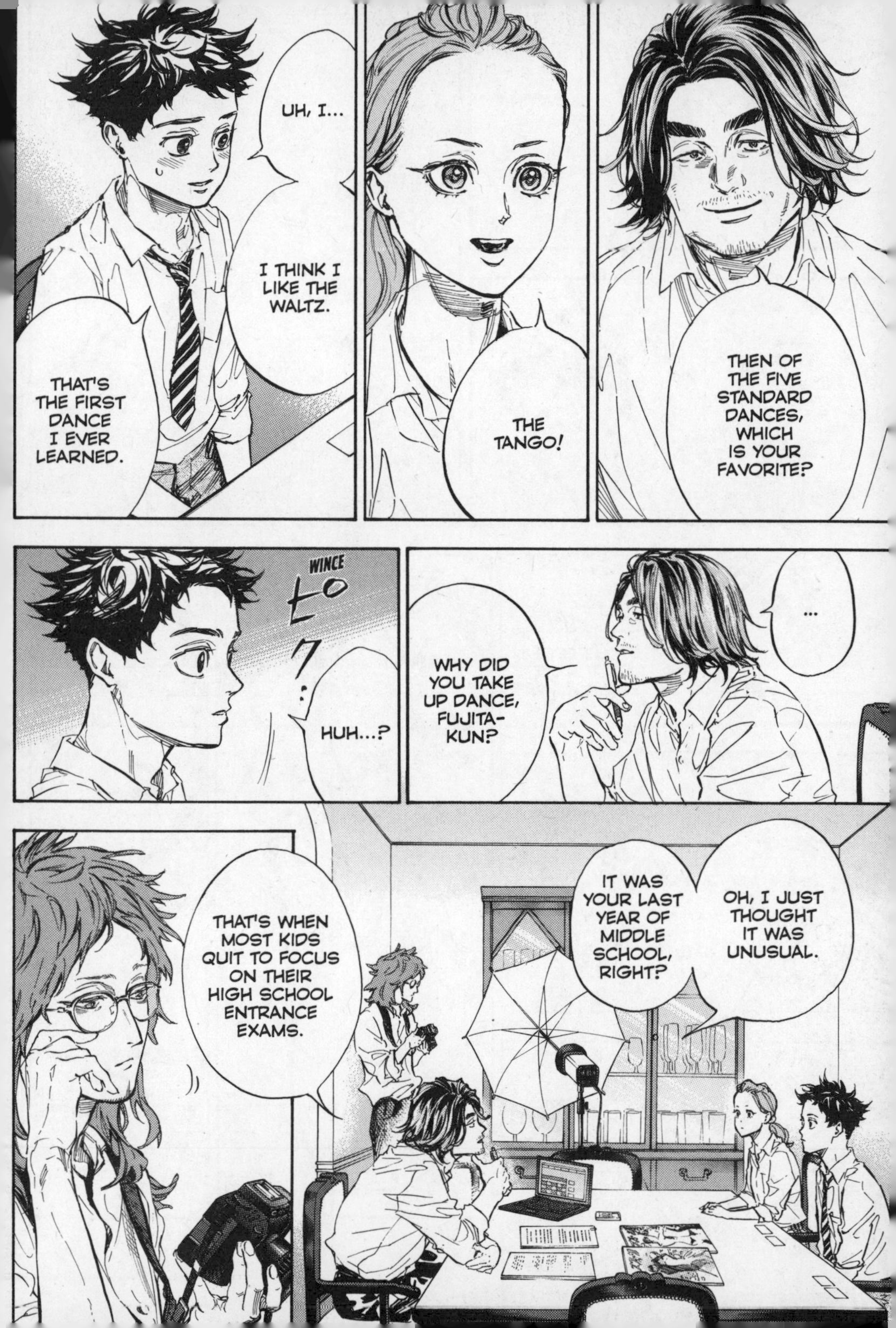
THEN OF THE FIVE STANDARD DANCES, WHICH IS YOUR FAVORITE?
THE TANGO!
UH, I...
I THINK I LIKE THE WALTZ.
THAT'S THE FIRST DANCE I EVER LEARNED.
...
WHY DID YOU TAKE UP DANCE, FUJITA-KUN?
WINCE
HUH...?
OH, I JUST THOUGHT IT WAS UNUSUAL.
IT WAS YOUR LAST YEAR OF MIDDLE SCHOOL, RIGHT?
THAT'S WHEN MOST KIDS QUIT TO FOCUS ON THEIR HIGH SCHOOL ENTRANCE EXAMS.

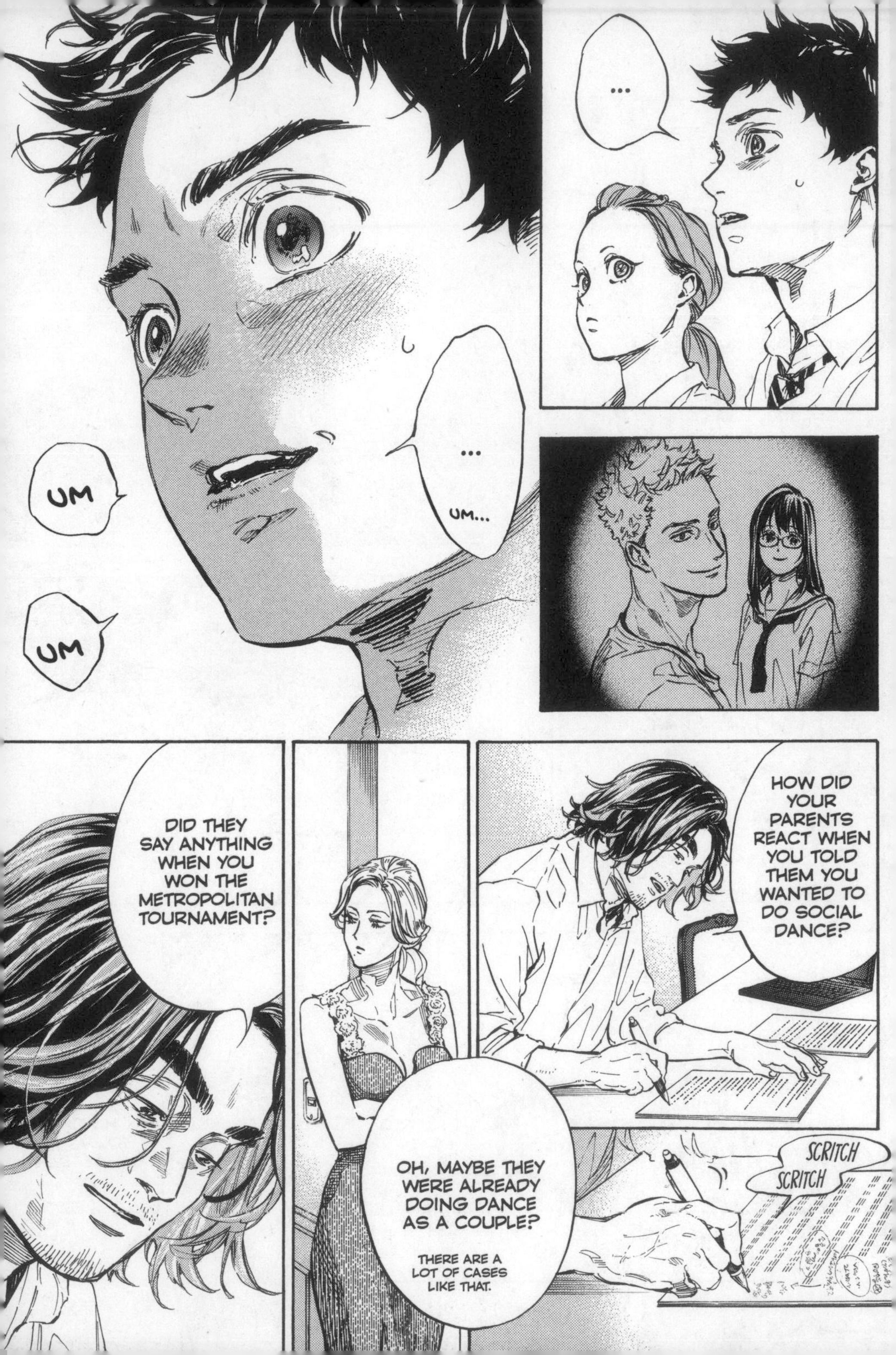
...
...
UM...
UM
UM
HOW DID YOUR PARENTS REACT WHEN YOU TOLD THEM YOU WANTED TO DO SOCIAL DANCE?
SCRITCH
SCRITCH
OH, MAYBE THEY WERE ALREADY DOING DANCE AS A COUPLE?
THERE ARE A LOT OF CASES LIKE THAT.
DID THEY SAY ANYTHING WHEN YOU WON THE METROPOLITAN TOURNAMENT?

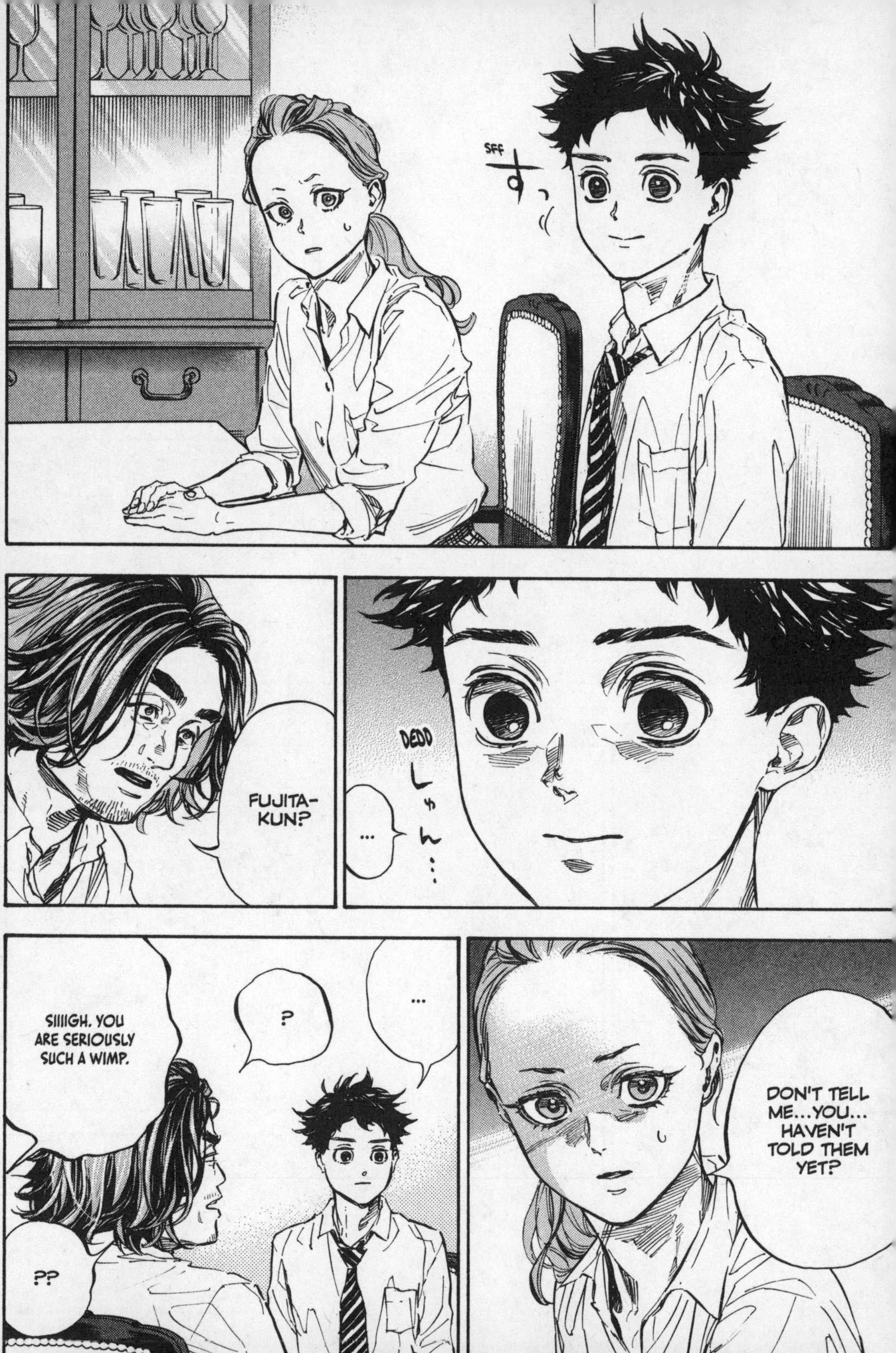
SFF
すっ
DEDD
しゅん…
…
FUJITA-KUN?
DON'T TELL ME…YOU… HAVEN'T TOLD THEM YET?
…
?
SIIIGH. YOU ARE SERIOUSLY SUCH A WIMP.
??

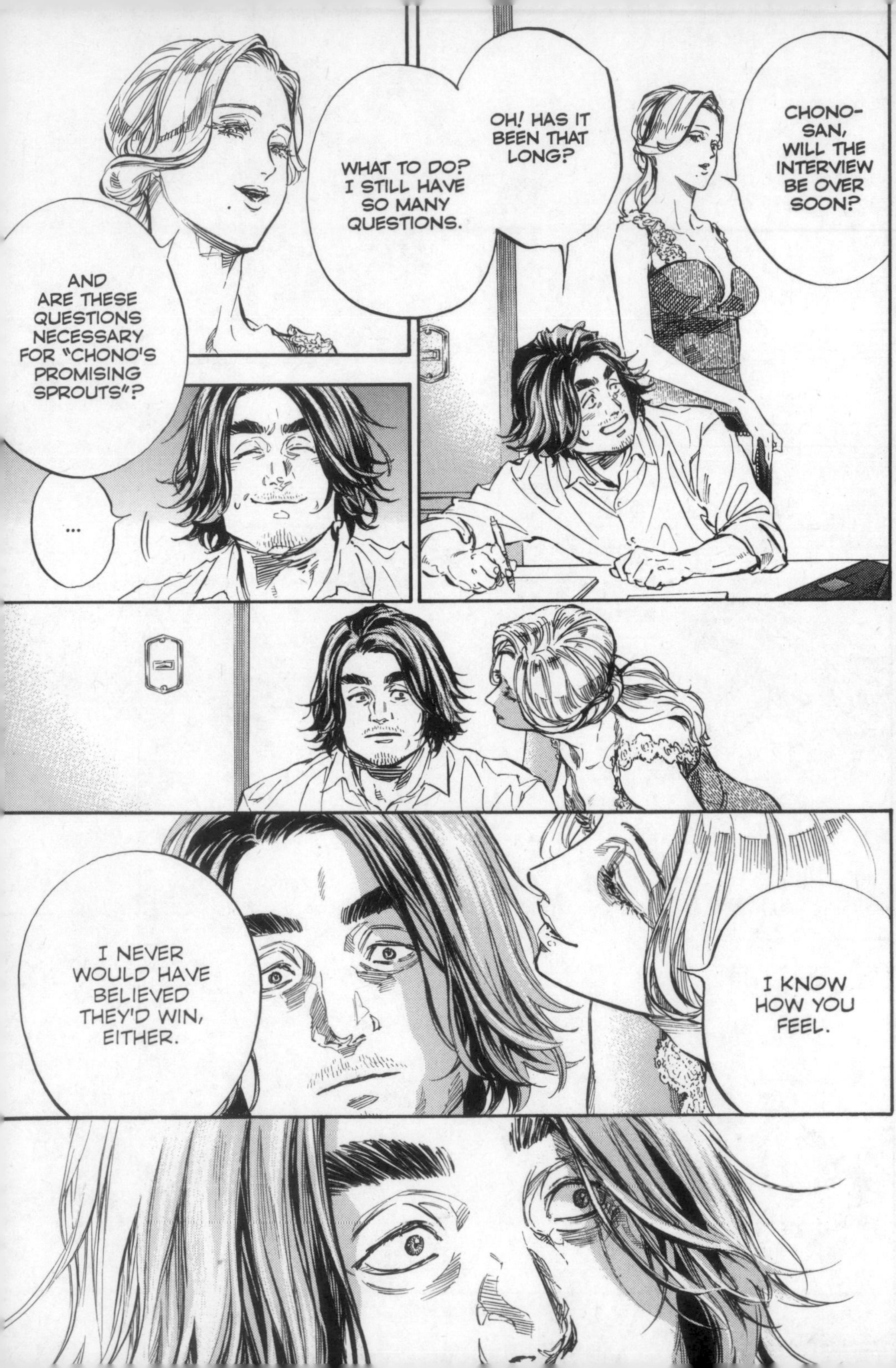
CHONO-SAN, WILL THE INTERVIEW BE OVER SOON?
OH! HAS IT BEEN THAT LONG?
WHAT TO DO? I STILL HAVE SO MANY QUESTIONS.
AND ARE THESE QUESTIONS NECESSARY FOR "CHONO'S PROMISING SPROUTS"?
...
I KNOW HOW YOU FEEL.
I NEVER WOULD HAVE BELIEVED THEY'D WIN, EITHER.

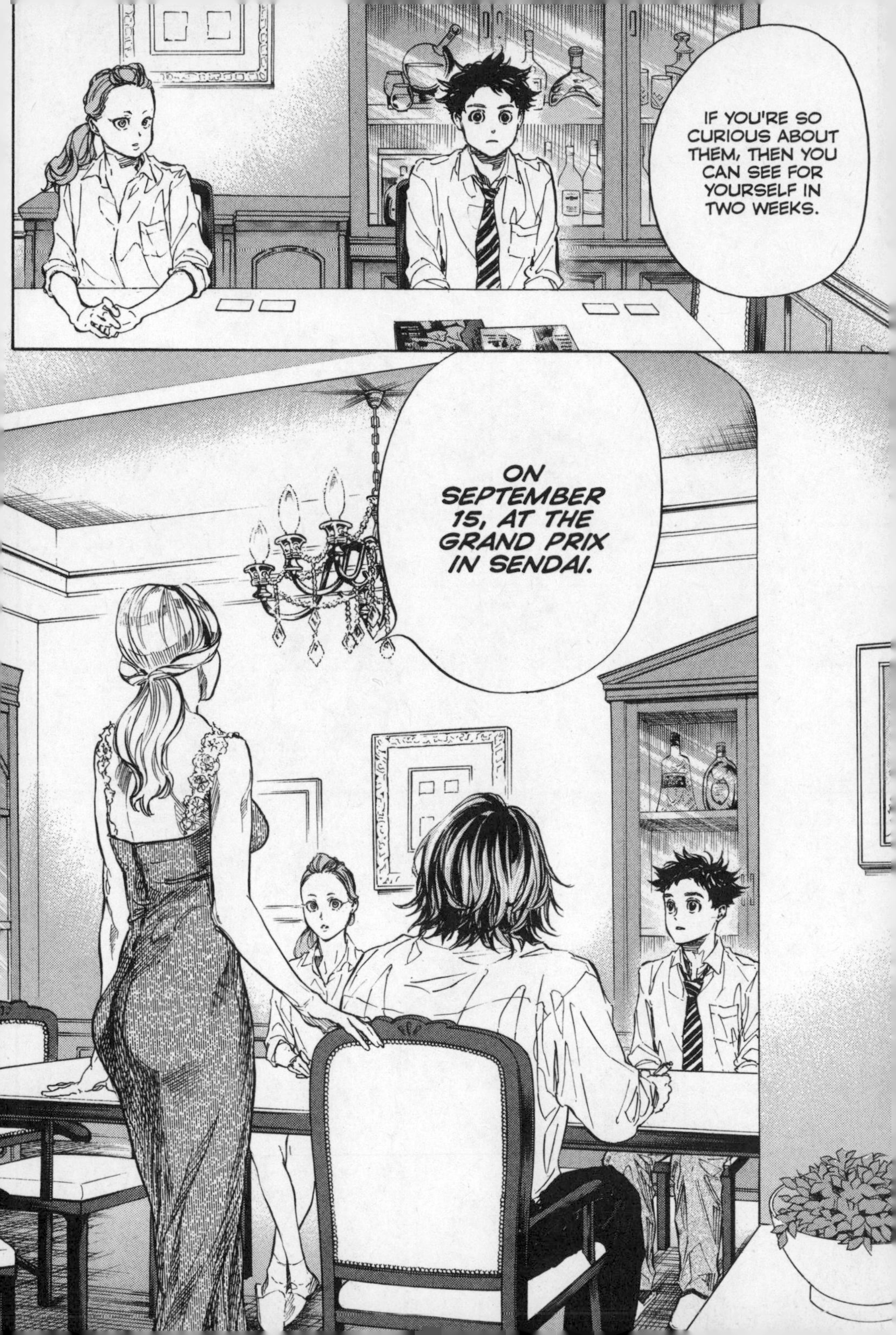
IF YOU'RE SO CURIOUS ABOUT THEM, THEN YOU CAN SEE FOR YOURSELF IN TWO WEEKS.
ON SEPTEMBER 15, AT THE GRAND PRIX IN SENDAI.

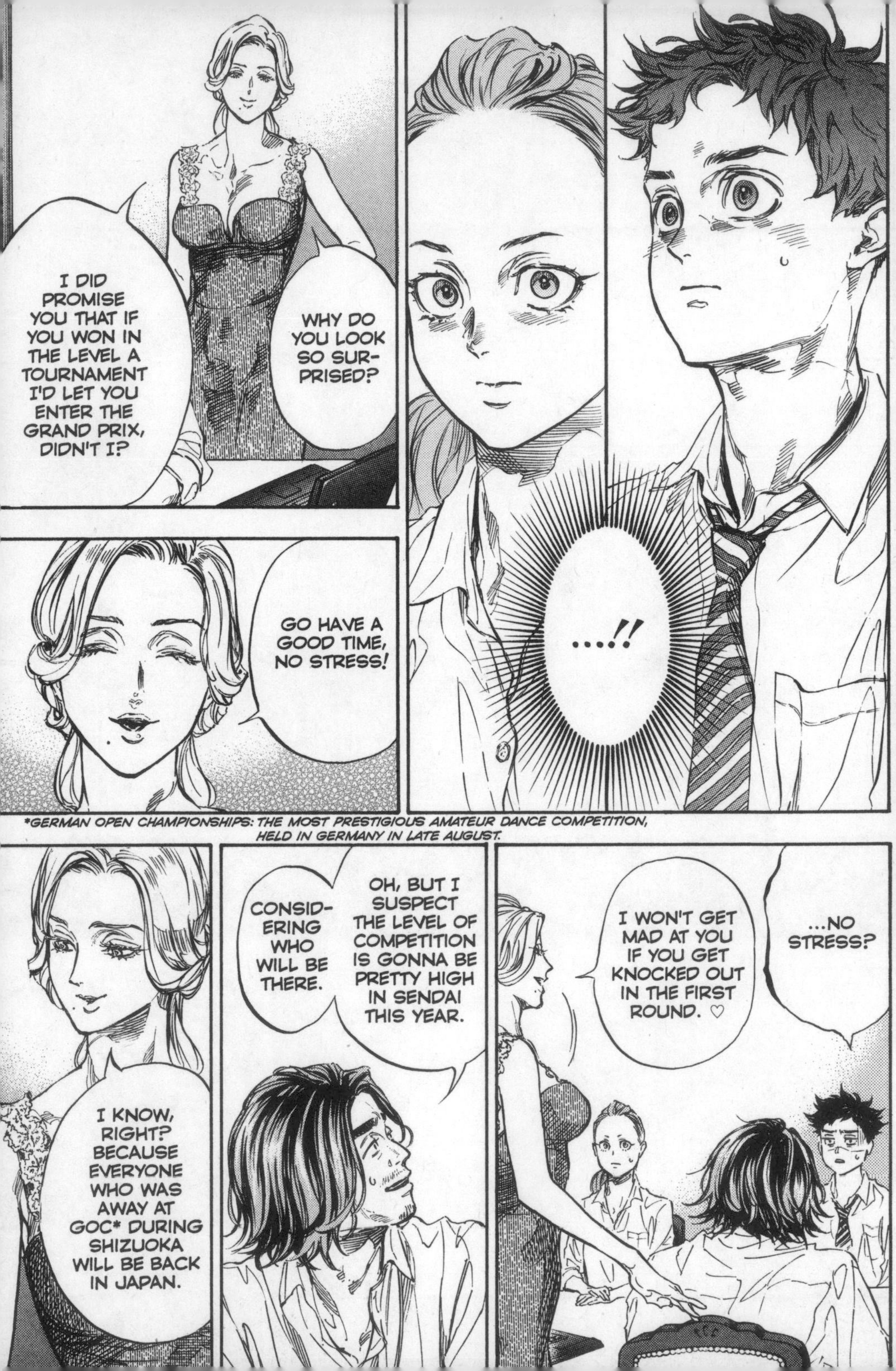
...!!
WHY DO YOU LOOK SO SUR-PRISED?
I DID PROMISE YOU THAT IF YOU WON IN THE LEVEL A TOURNAMENT I'D LET YOU ENTER THE GRAND PRIX, DIDN'T I?
GO HAVE A GOOD TIME, NO STRESS!
...NO STRESS?
I WON'T GET MAD AT YOU IF YOU GET KNOCKED OUT IN THE FIRST ROUND. ♡
OH, BUT I SUSPECT THE LEVEL OF COMPETITION IS GONNA BE PRETTY HIGH IN SENDAI THIS YEAR.
CONSID-ERING WHO WILL BE THERE.
I KNOW, RIGHT? BECAUSE EVERYONE WHO WAS AWAY AT GOC* DURING SHIZUOKA WILL BE BACK IN JAPAN.

*GERMAN OPEN CHAMPIONSHIPS: THE MOST PRESTIGIOUS AMATEUR DANCE COMPETITION, HELD IN GERMANY IN LATE AUGUST.

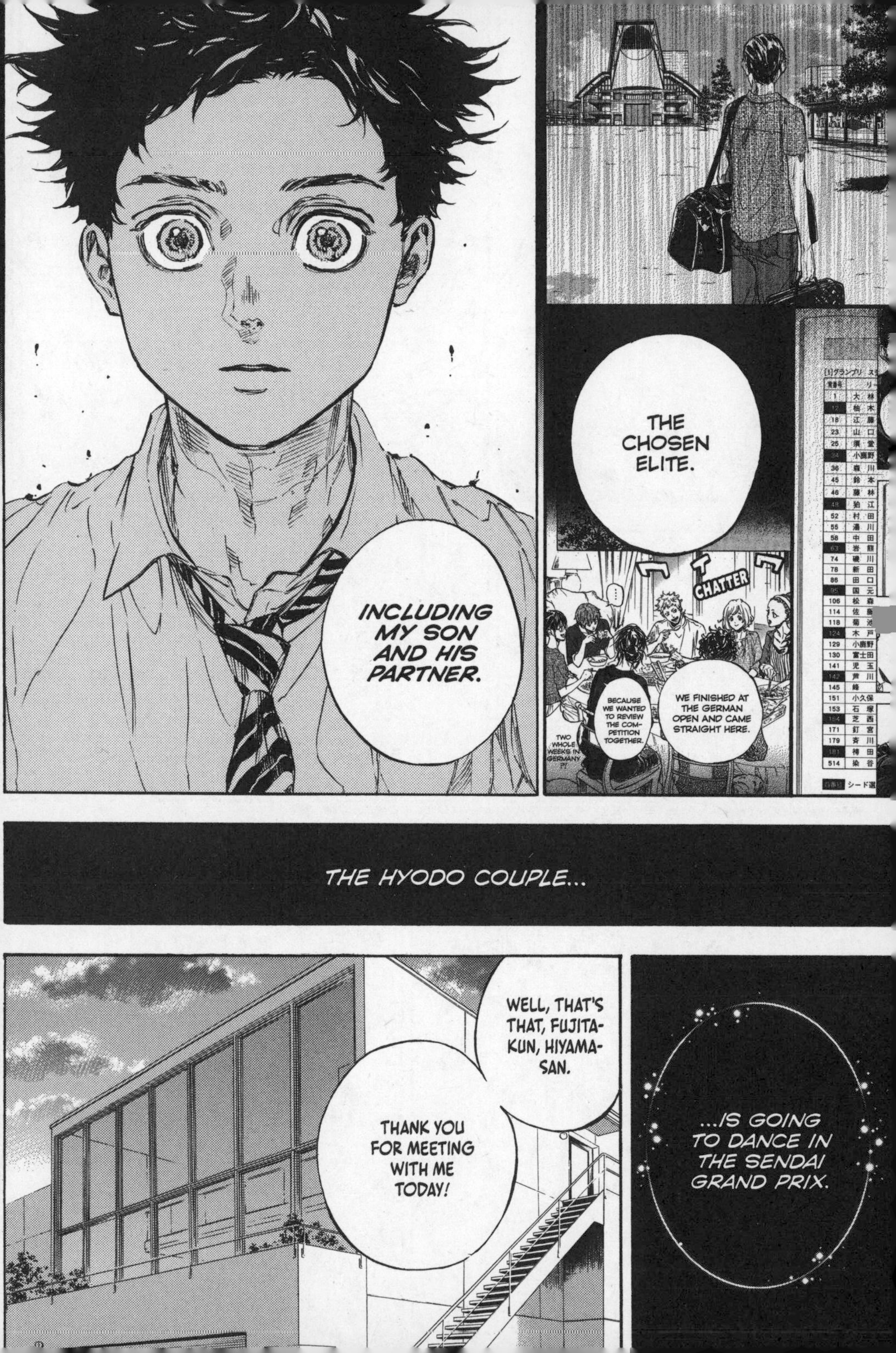

CHATTER
...
WE FINISHED AT THE GERMAN OPEN AND CAME STRAIGHT HERE.
BECAUSE WE WANTED TO REVIEW THE COMPETITION TOGETHER.
TWO WHOLE WEEKS IN GERMANY?!
THE CHOSEN ELITE.
INCLUDING MY SON AND HIS PARTNER.
THE HYODO COUPLE...
...IS GOING TO DANCE IN THE SENDAI GRAND PRIX.
WELL, THAT'S THAT, FUJITA-KUN, HIYAMA-SAN.
THANK YOU FOR MEETING WITH ME TODAY!

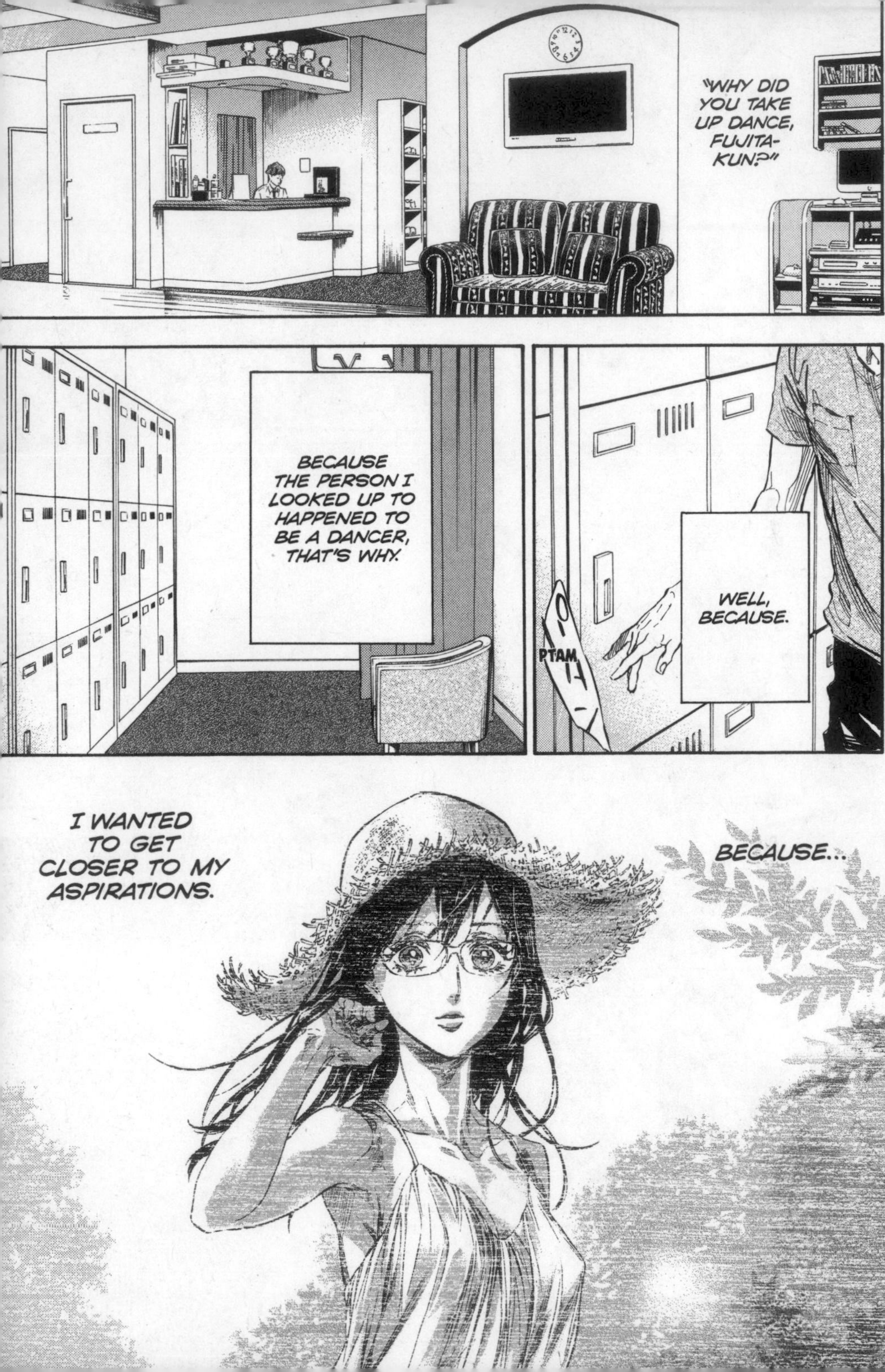
"WHY DID YOU TAKE UP DANCE, FUJITA-KUN?"
PTAM
WELL, BECAUSE.
BECAUSE THE PERSON I LOOKED UP TO HAPPENED TO BE A DANCER, THAT'S WHY.
BECAUSE...
I WANTED TO GET CLOSER TO MY ASPIRATIONS.

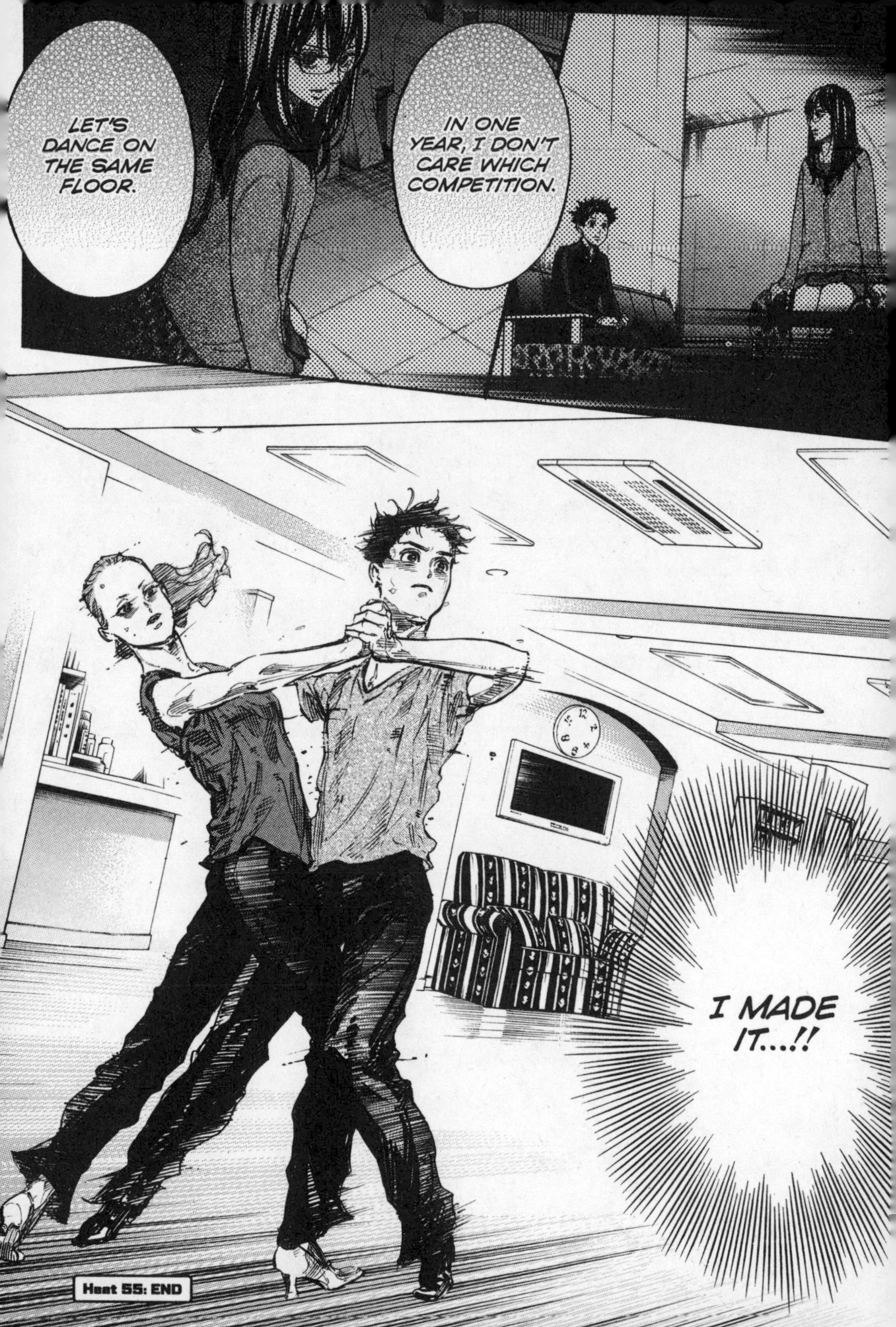
IN ONE YEAR, I DON'T CARE WHICH COMPETITION.
LET'S DANCE ON THE SAME FLOOR.
I MADE IT...!!
Heat 55: END

WELCOME TO THE BALLROOM

WELCOME TO THE BALLROOM

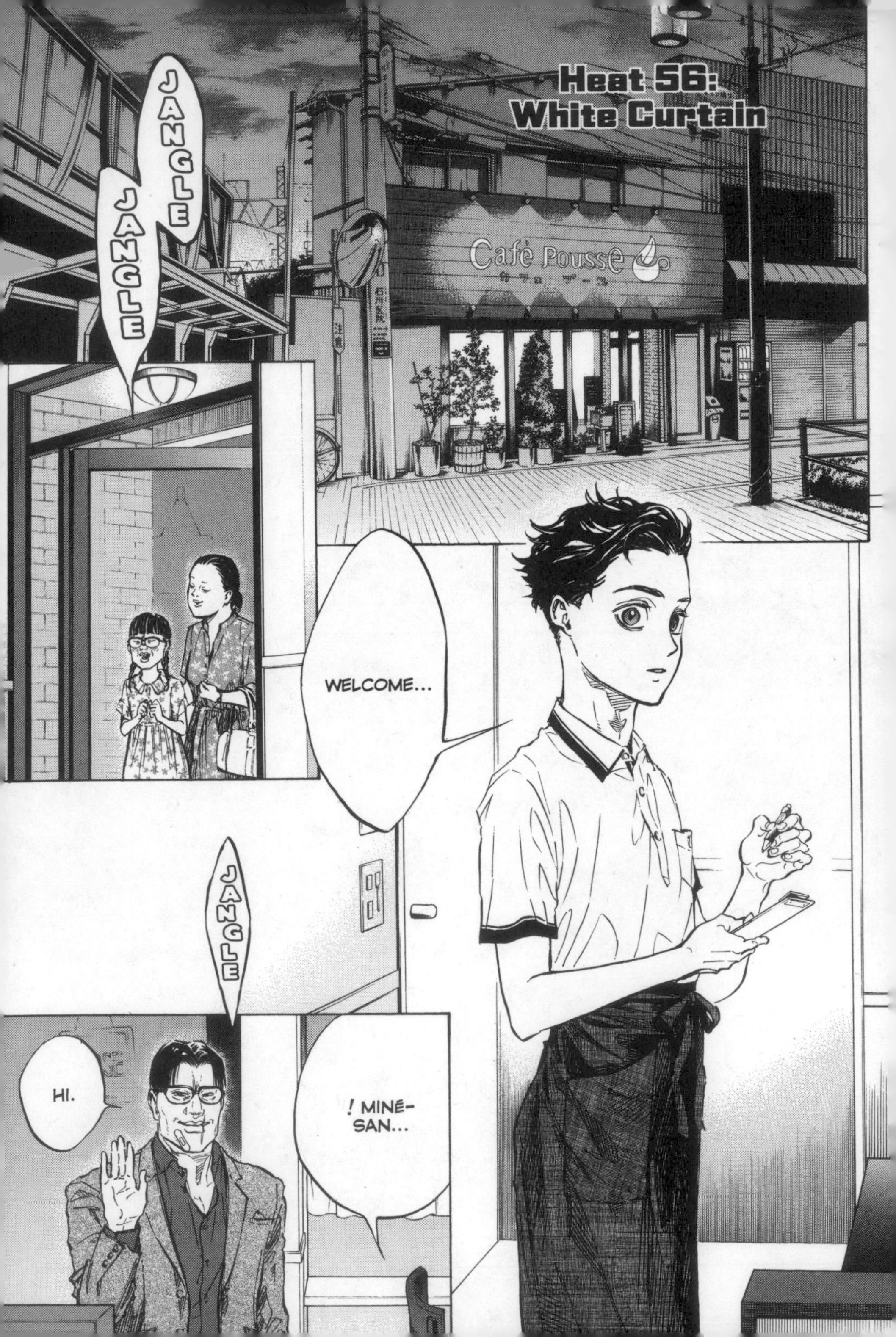
Heat 56:
White Curtain
Café Pousse
JANGLE
JANGLE
WELCOME...
JANGLE
! MINÉ-SAN...
HI.

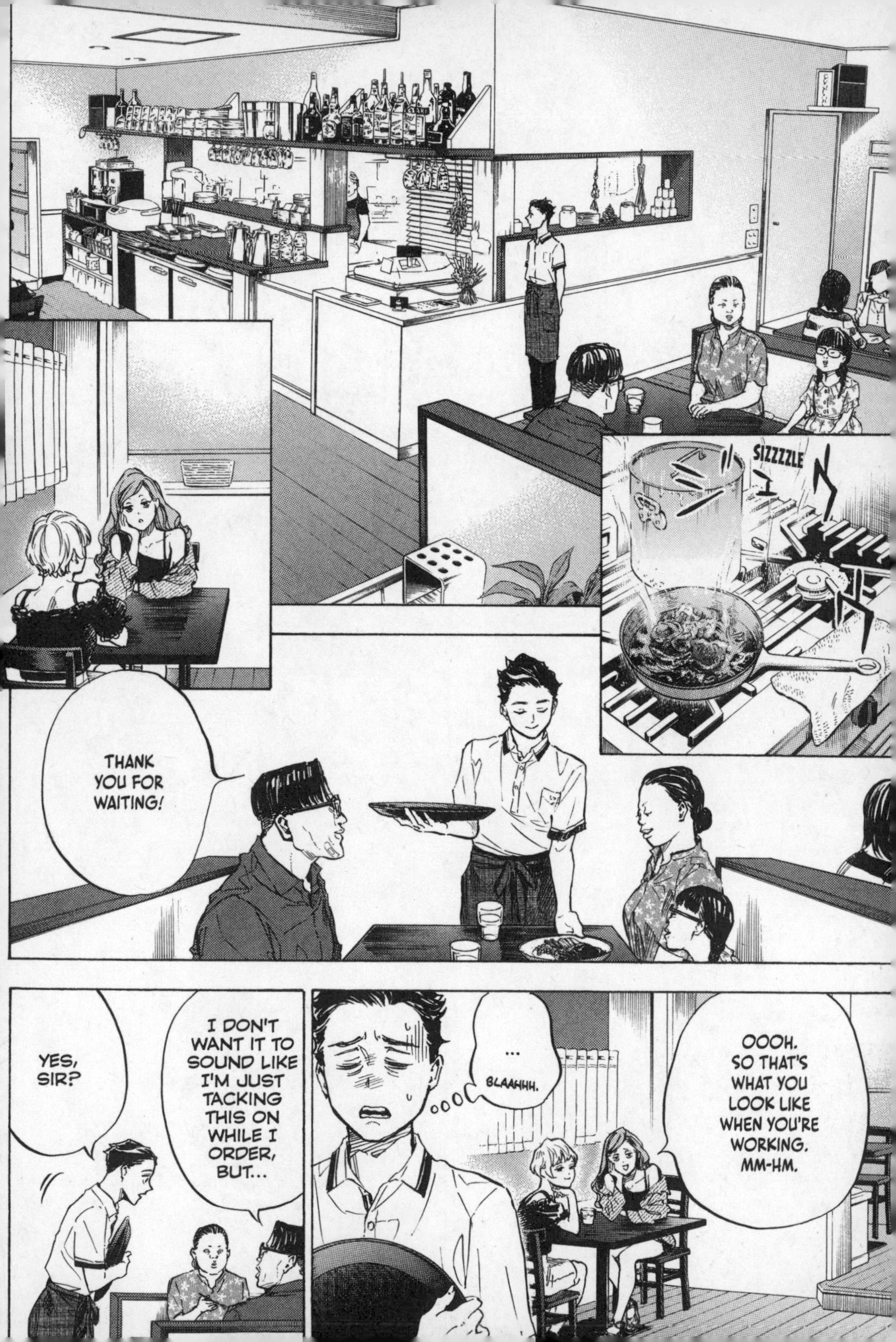
SIZZZZLE
THANK YOU FOR WAITING!
OOOH. SO THAT'S WHAT YOU LOOK LIKE WHEN YOU'RE WORKING. MM-HM.
...
BLAAHHH.
I DON'T WANT IT TO SOUND LIKE I'M JUST TACKING THIS ON WHILE I ORDER, BUT...
YES, SIR?

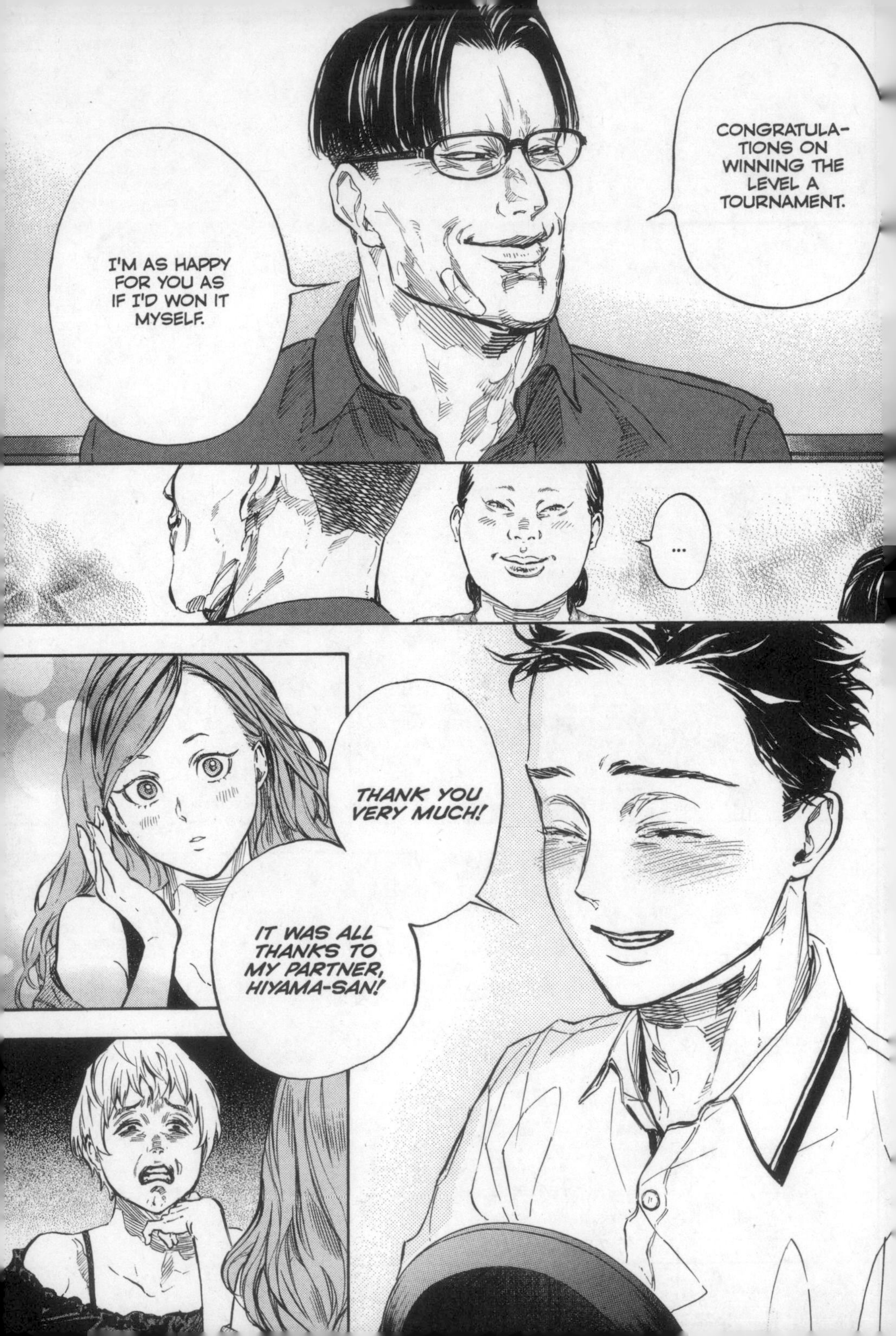
CONGRATULA-TIONS ON WINNING THE LEVEL A TOURNAMENT.
I'M AS HAPPY FOR YOU AS IF I'D WON IT MYSELF.
...
THANK YOU VERY MUCH!
IT WAS ALL THANKS TO MY PARTNER, HIYAMA-SAN!

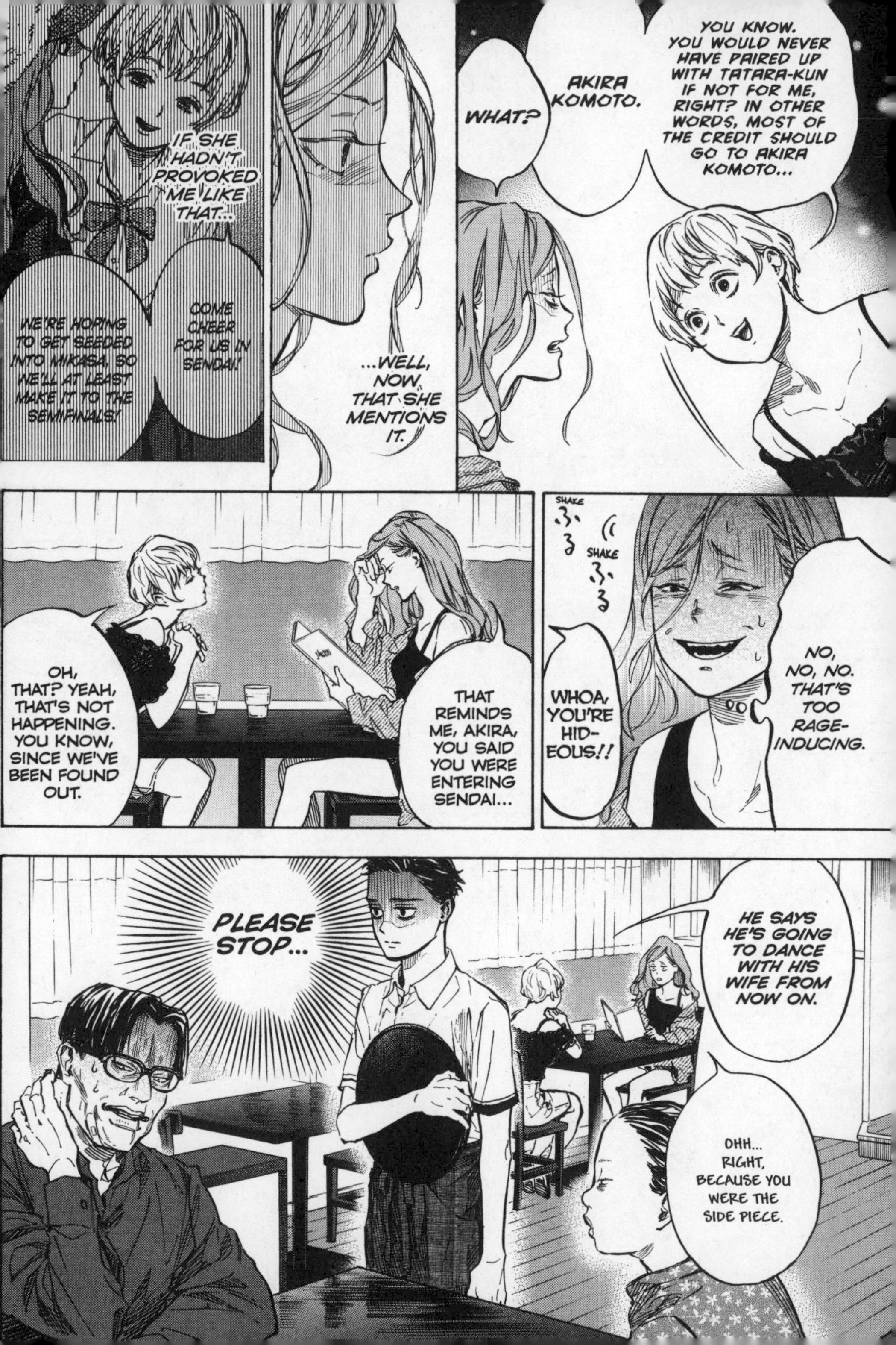
YOU KNOW. YOU WOULD NEVER HAVE PAIRED UP WITH TATARA-KUN IF NOT FOR ME, RIGHT? IN OTHER WORDS, MOST OF THE CREDIT SHOULD GO TO AKIRA KOMOTO...
AKIRA KOMOTO.
WHAT?
...WELL, NOW THAT SHE MENTIONS IT.
IF SHE HADN'T PROVOKED ME LIKE THAT...
COME CHEER FOR US IN SENDAI!
WE'RE HOPING TO GET SEEDED INTO MIKASA, SO WE'LL AT LEAST MAKE IT TO THE SEMIFINALS!
NO, NO, NO. THAT'S TOO RAGE-INDUCING.
SHAKE ふる
SHAKE ふる
WHOA, YOU'RE HIDEOUS!!
THAT REMINDS ME, AKIRA, YOU SAID YOU WERE ENTERING SENDAI...
OH, THAT? YEAH, THAT'S NOT HAPPENING. YOU KNOW, SINCE WE'VE BEEN FOUND OUT.
HE SAYS HE'S GOING TO DANCE WITH HIS WIFE FROM NOW ON.
OHH... RIGHT, BECAUSE YOU WERE THE SIDE PIECE.
PLEASE STOP...

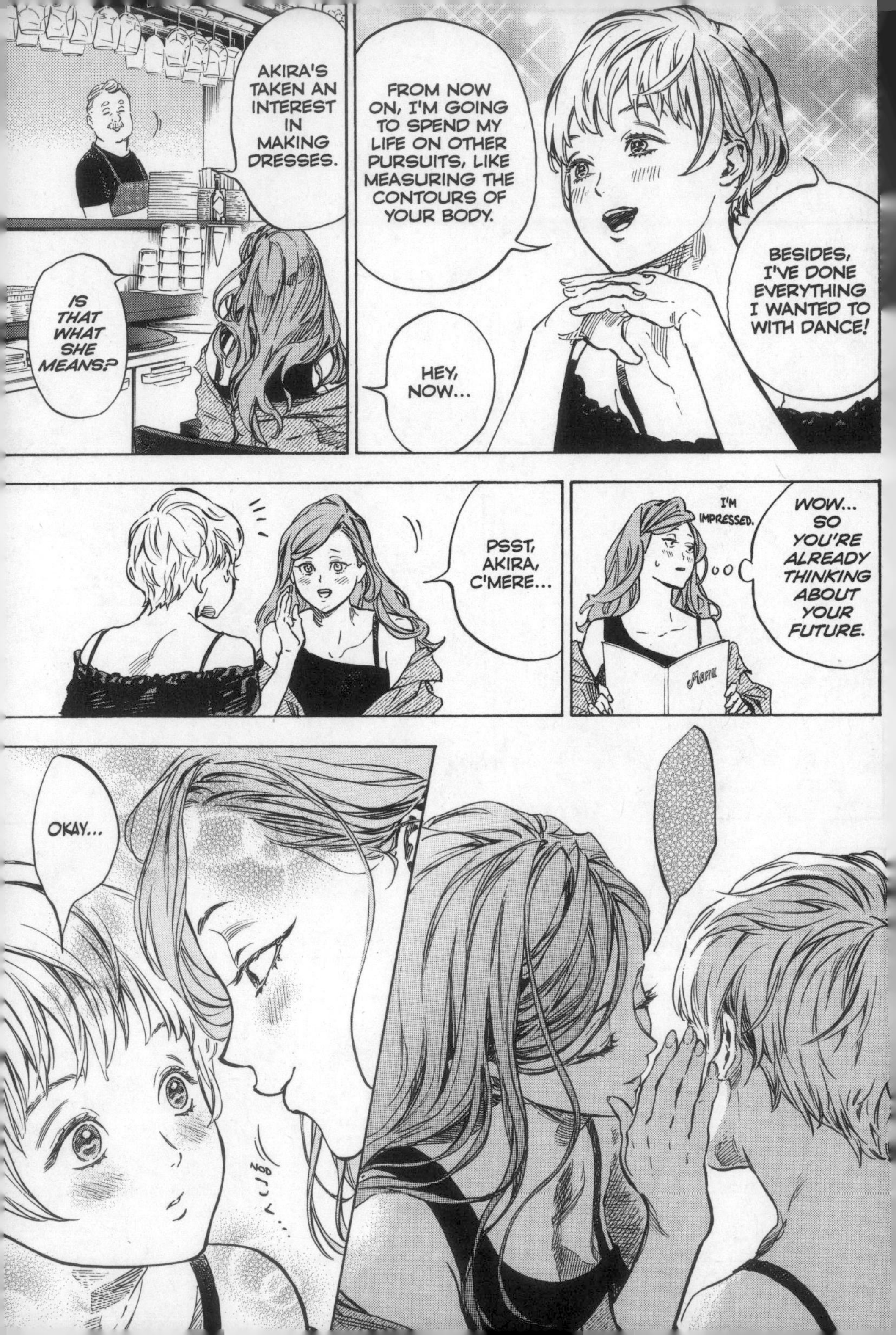
FROM NOW ON, I'M GOING TO SPEND MY LIFE ON OTHER PURSUITS, LIKE MEASURING THE CONTOURS OF YOUR BODY.
BESIDES, I'VE DONE EVERYTHING I WANTED TO WITH DANCE!
HEY, NOW...
AKIRA'S TAKEN AN INTEREST IN MAKING DRESSES.
IS THAT WHAT SHE MEANS?
WOW... SO YOU'RE ALREADY THINKING ABOUT YOUR FUTURE.
I'M IMPRESSED.
PSST, AKIRA, C'MERE...
OKAY...
NOD

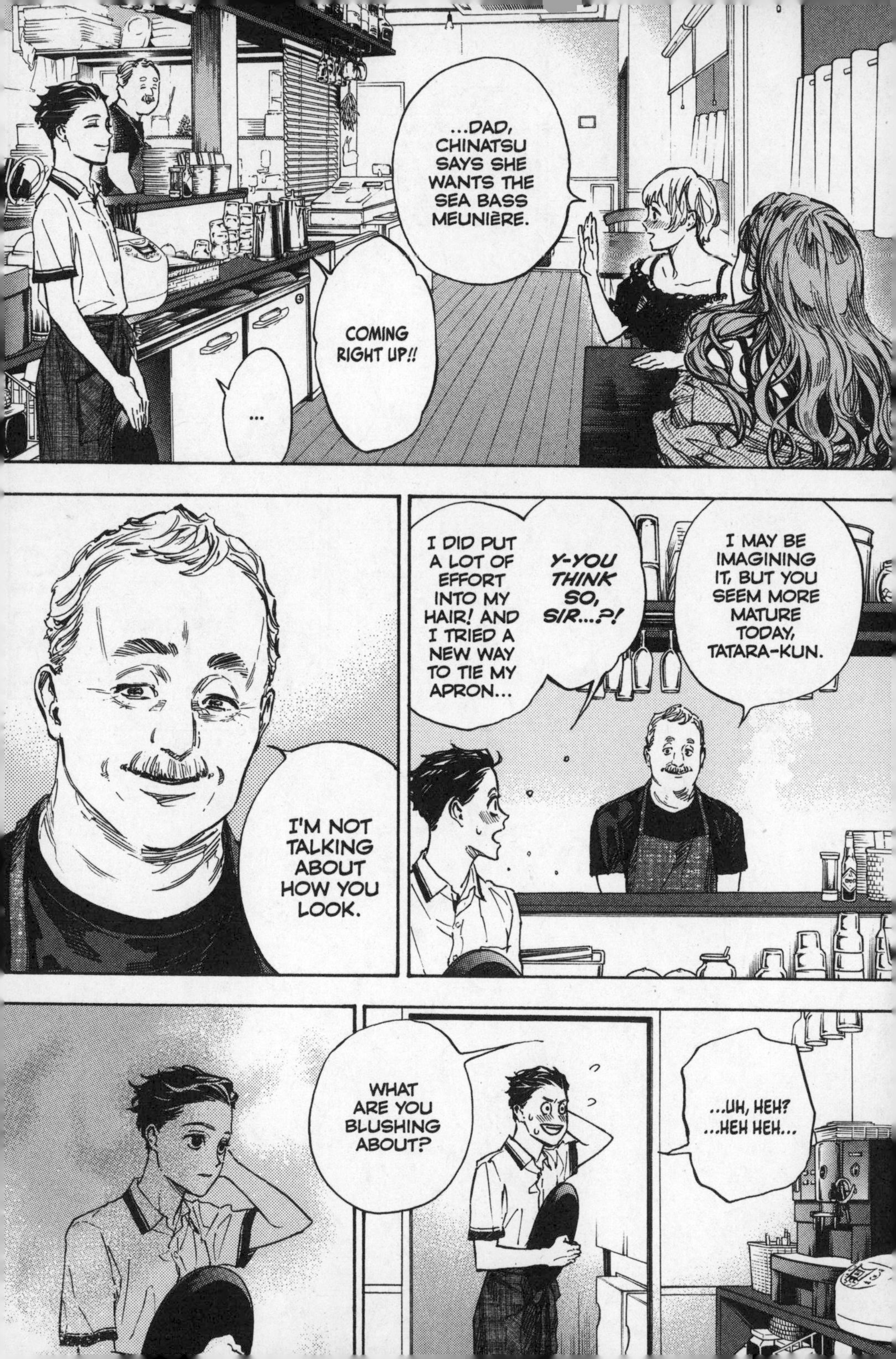
...DAD, CHINATSU SAYS SHE WANTS THE SEA BASS MEUNIÈRE.
COMING RIGHT UP!!
...
I MAY BE IMAGINING IT, BUT YOU SEEM MORE MATURE TODAY, TATARA-KUN.
Y-YOU THINK SO, SIR...?!
I DID PUT A LOT OF EFFORT INTO MY HAIR! AND I TRIED A NEW WAY TO TIE MY APRON...
I'M NOT TALKING ABOUT HOW YOU LOOK.
...UH, HEH? ...HEH HEH...
WHAT ARE YOU BLUSHING ABOUT?

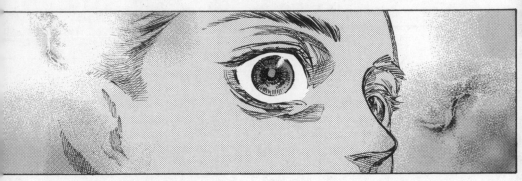

YOU THINK YOU'RE SEEING THINGS ....?

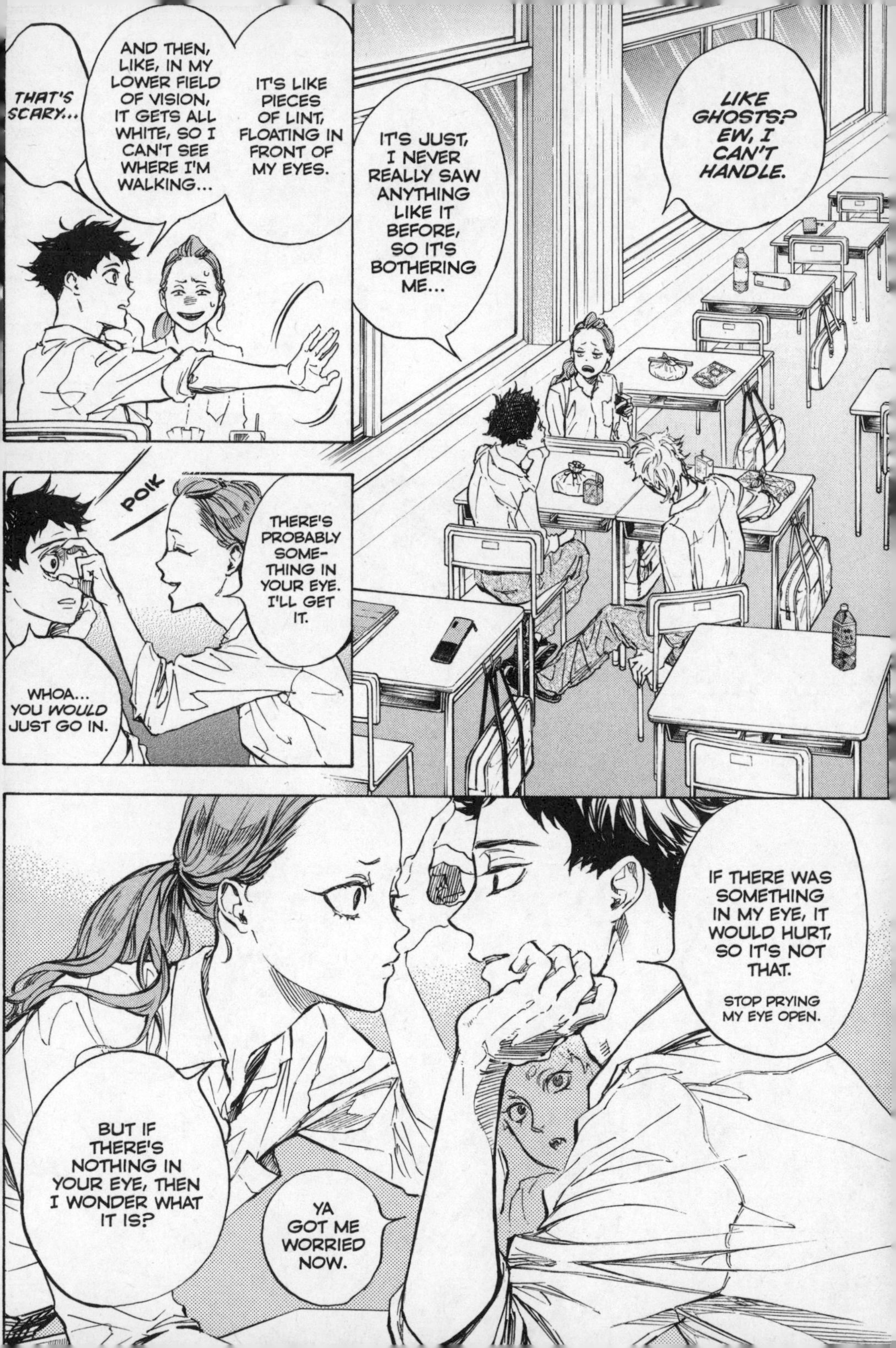
LIKE GHOSTS? EW, I CAN'T HANDLE.
IT'S JUST, I NEVER REALLY SAW ANYTHING LIKE IT BEFORE, SO IT'S BOTHERING ME...
IT'S LIKE PIECES OF LINT, FLOATING IN FRONT OF MY EYES.
AND THEN, LIKE, IN MY LOWER FIELD OF VISION, IT GETS ALL WHITE, SO I CAN'T SEE WHERE I'M WALKING...
THAT'S SCARY...
POIK
THERE'S PROBABLY SOME-THING IN YOUR EYE. I'LL GET IT.
WHOA... YOU WOULD JUST GO IN.
IF THERE WAS SOMETHING IN MY EYE, IT WOULD HURT, SO IT'S NOT THAT.
STOP PRYING MY EYE OPEN.
BUT IF THERE'S NOTHING IN YOUR EYE, THEN I WONDER WHAT IT IS?
YA GOT ME WORRIED NOW.

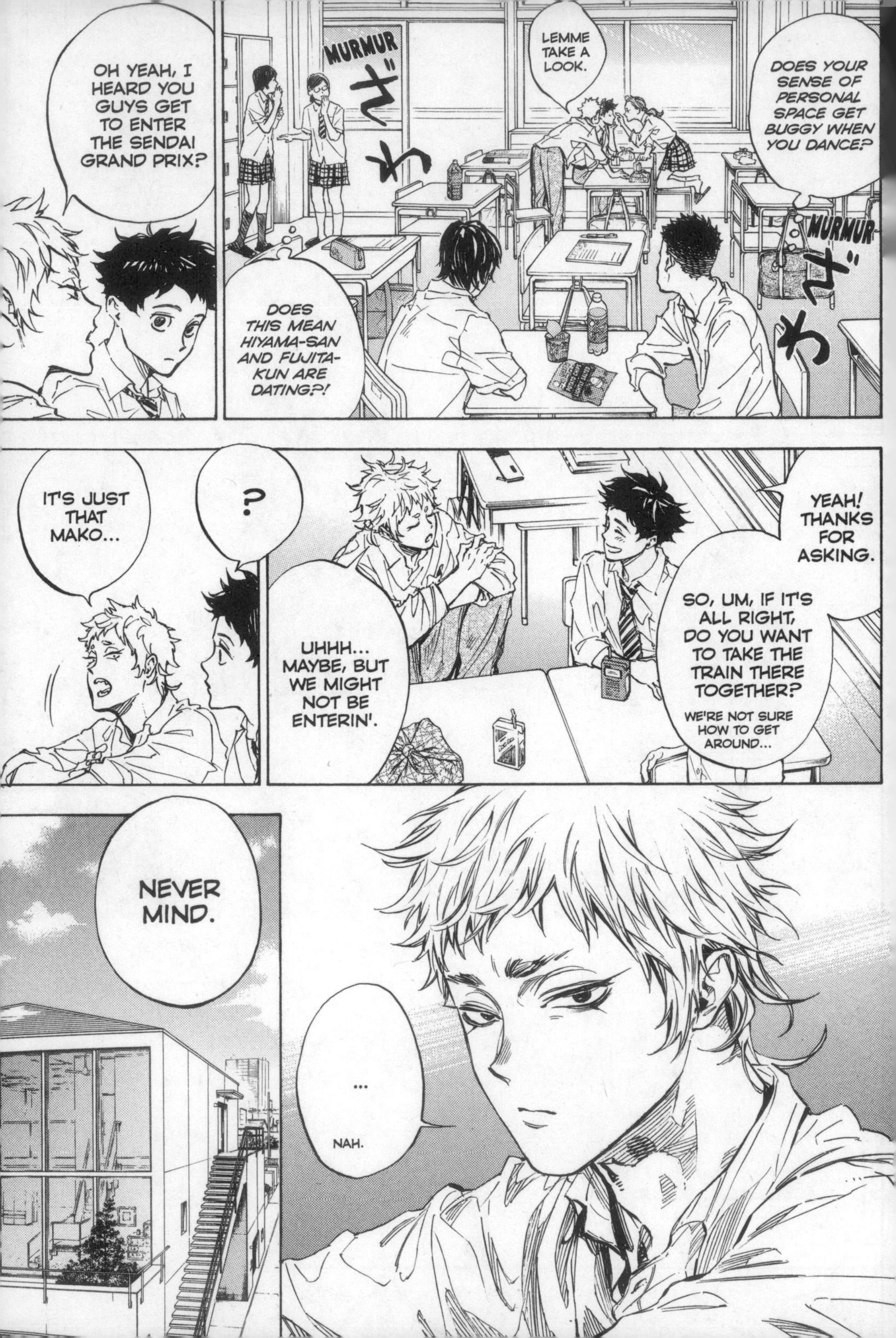
DOES YOUR SENSE OF PERSONAL SPACE GET BUGGY WHEN YOU DANCE?
LEMME TAKE A LOOK.
MURMUR ざわ
MURMUR ざわ
DOES THIS MEAN HIYAMA-SAN AND FUJITA-KUN ARE DATING?!
OH YEAH, I HEARD YOU GUYS GET TO ENTER THE SENDAI GRAND PRIX?
YEAH! THANKS FOR ASKING.
SO, UM, IF IT'S ALL RIGHT, DO YOU WANT TO TAKE THE TRAIN THERE TOGETHER?
WE'RE NOT SURE HOW TO GET AROUND...
UHHH... MAYBE, BUT WE MIGHT NOT BE ENTERIN'.
?
IT'S JUST THAT MAKO...
...
NAH.
NEVER MIND.

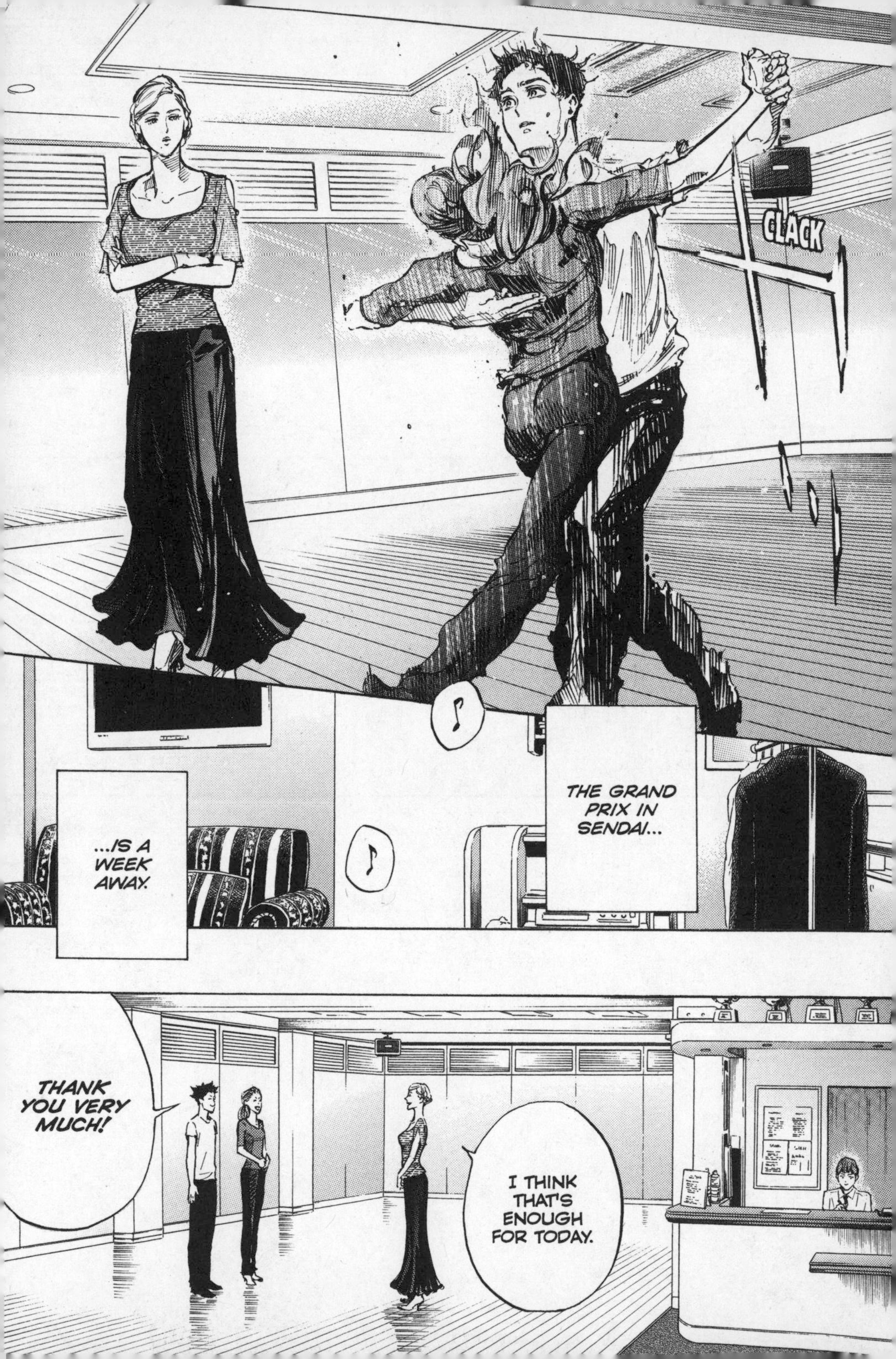
CLACK
THE GRAND PRIX IN SENDAI...
...IS A WEEK AWAY.
I THINK THAT'S ENOUGH FOR TODAY.
THANK YOU VERY MUCH!

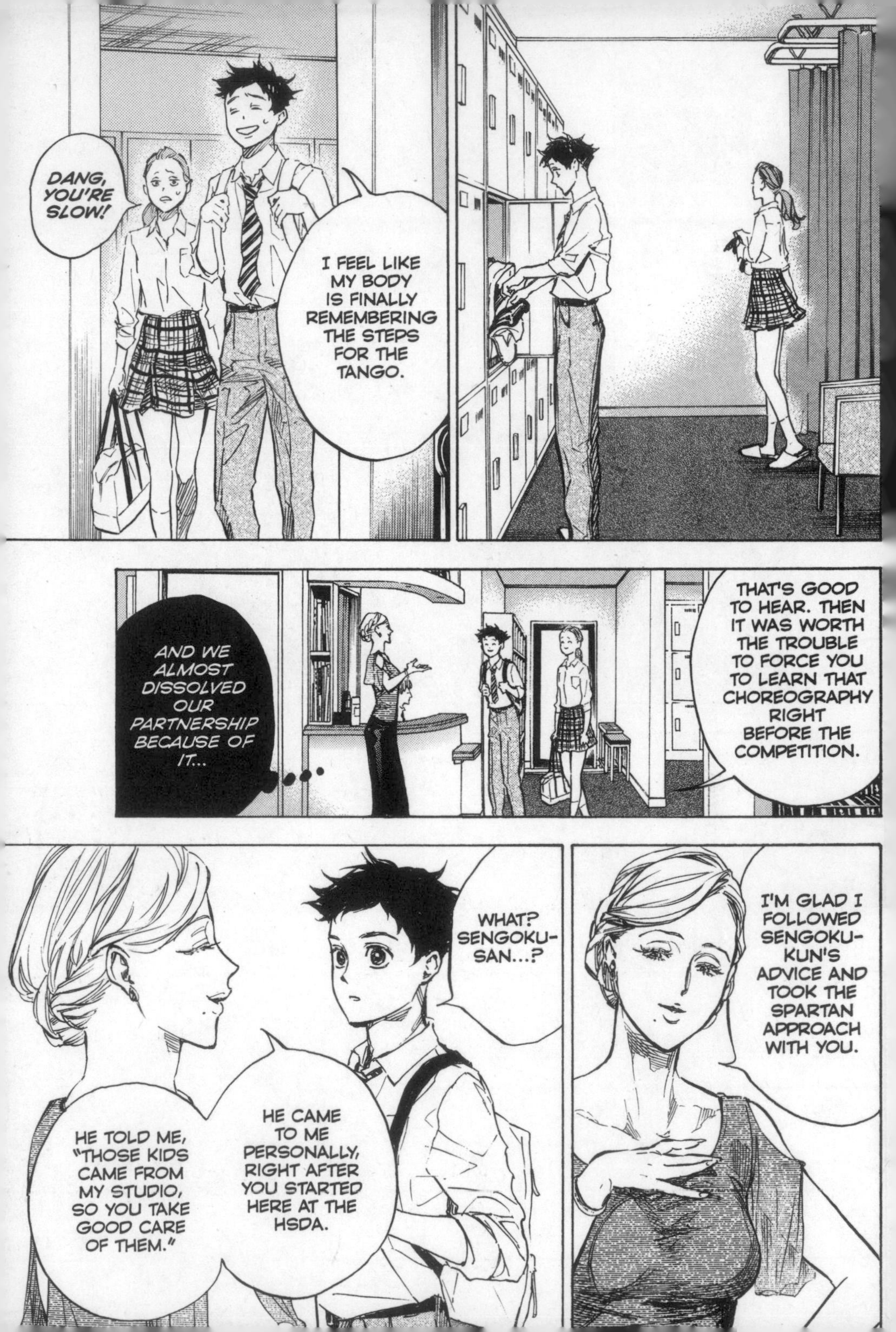
DANG, YOU'RE SLOW!
I FEEL LIKE MY BODY IS FINALLY REMEMBERING THE STEPS FOR THE TANGO.
THAT'S GOOD TO HEAR. THEN IT WAS WORTH THE TROUBLE TO FORCE YOU TO LEARN THAT CHOREOGRAPHY RIGHT BEFORE THE COMPETITION.
AND WE ALMOST DISSOLVED OUR PARTNERSHIP BECAUSE OF IT...
...
I'M GLAD I FOLLOWED SENGOKU-KUN'S ADVICE AND TOOK THE SPARTAN APPROACH WITH YOU.
WHAT? SENGOKU-SAN...?
HE CAME TO ME PERSONALLY, RIGHT AFTER YOU STARTED HERE AT THE HSDA.
HE TOLD ME, "THOSE KIDS CAME FROM MY STUDIO, SO YOU TAKE GOOD CARE OF THEM."

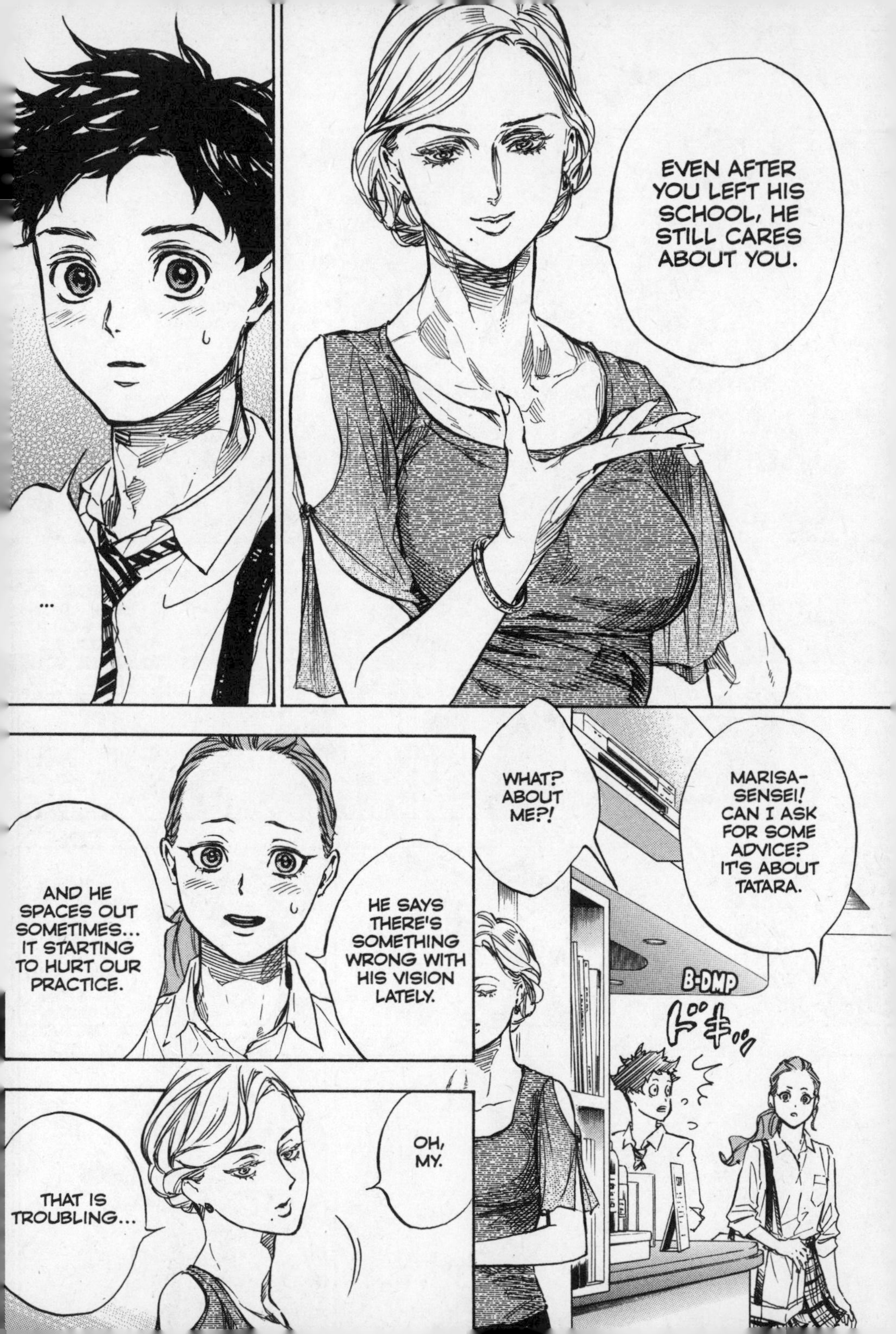
EVEN AFTER YOU LEFT HIS SCHOOL, HE STILL CARES ABOUT YOU.
...
MARISA-SENSEI! CAN I ASK FOR SOME ADVICE? IT'S ABOUT TATARA.
WHAT? ABOUT ME?!
B-DMP
ドキッ
HE SAYS THERE'S SOMETHING WRONG WITH HIS VISION LATELY.
AND HE SPACES OUT SOMETIMES... IT STARTING TO HURT OUR PRACTICE.
OH, MY.
THAT IS TROUBLING...

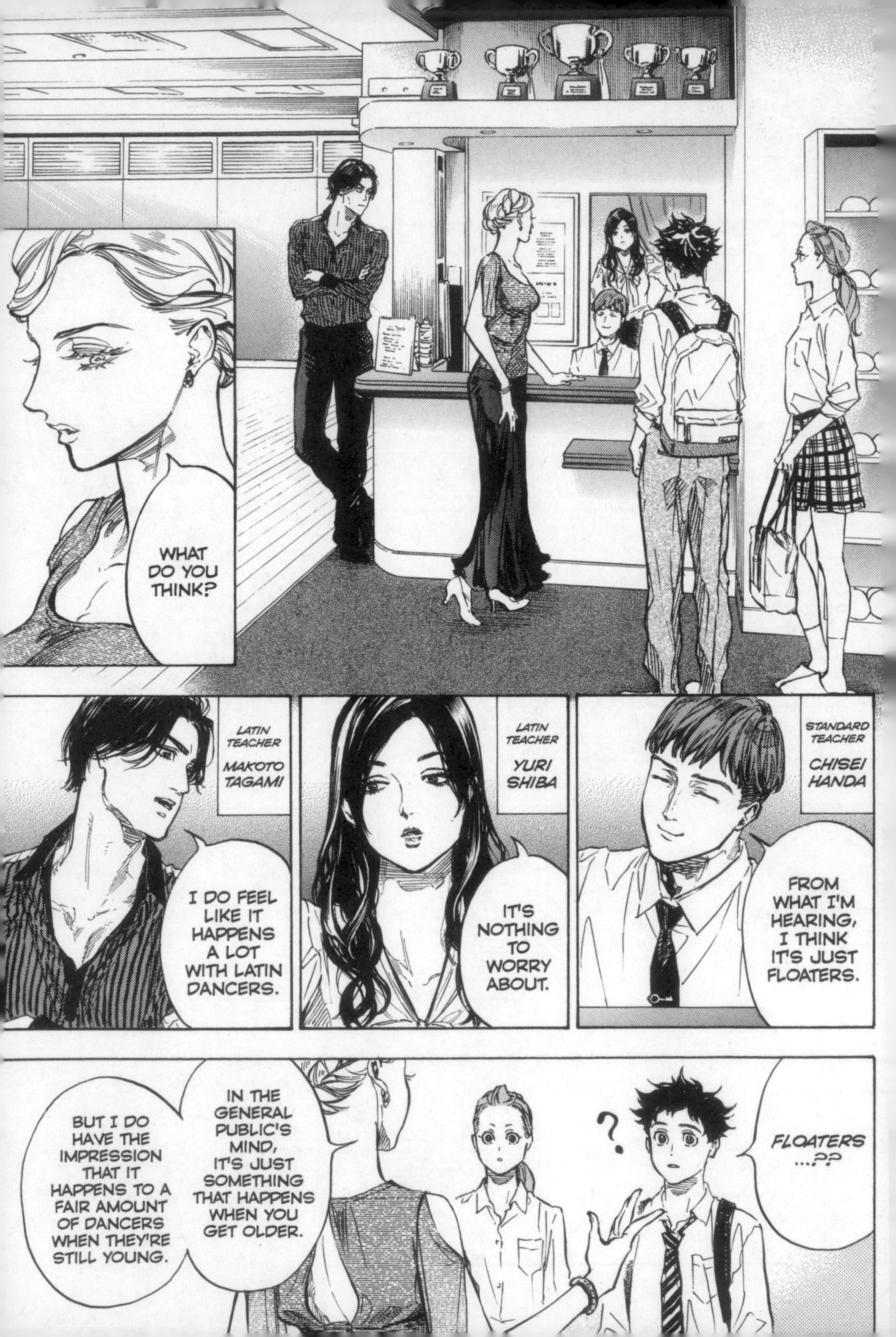
WHAT DO YOU THINK?
STANDARD TEACHER
CHISEI HANDA
FROM WHAT I'M HEARING, I THINK IT'S JUST FLOATERS.
LATIN TEACHER
YURI SHIBA
IT'S NOTHING TO WORRY ABOUT.
LATIN TEACHER
MAKOTO TAGAMI
I DO FEEL LIKE IT HAPPENS A LOT WITH LATIN DANCERS.
FLOATERS ...??
?
IN THE GENERAL PUBLIC'S MIND, IT'S JUST SOMETHING THAT HAPPENS WHEN YOU GET OLDER.
BUT I DO HAVE THE IMPRESSION THAT IT HAPPENS TO A FAIR AMOUNT OF DANCERS WHEN THEY'RE STILL YOUNG.

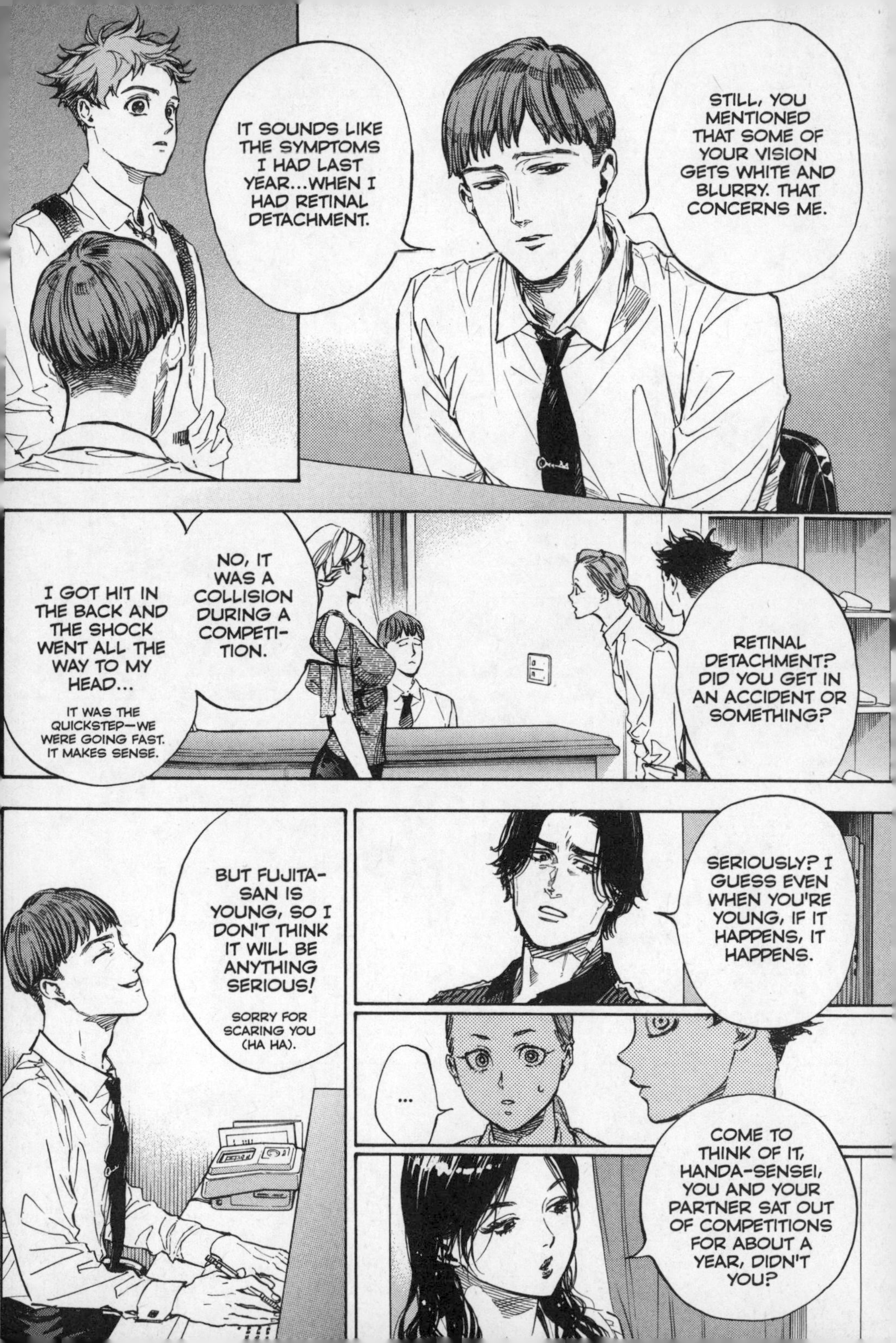
STILL, YOU MENTIONED THAT SOME OF YOUR VISION GETS WHITE AND BLURRY. THAT CONCERNS ME.
IT SOUNDS LIKE THE SYMPTOMS I HAD LAST YEAR...WHEN I HAD RETINAL DETACHMENT.
RETINAL DETACHMENT? DID YOU GET IN AN ACCIDENT OR SOMETHING?
NO, IT WAS A COLLISION DURING A COMPETITION.
I GOT HIT IN THE BACK AND THE SHOCK WENT ALL THE WAY TO MY HEAD...
IT WAS THE QUICKSTEP—WE WERE GOING FAST. IT MAKES SENSE.
SERIOUSLY? I GUESS EVEN WHEN YOU'RE YOUNG, IF IT HAPPENS, IT HAPPENS.
...
COME TO THINK OF IT, HANDA-SENSEI, YOU AND YOUR PARTNER SAT OUT OF COMPETITIONS FOR ABOUT A YEAR, DIDN'T YOU?
BUT FUJITA-SAN IS YOUNG, SO I DON'T THINK IT WILL BE ANYTHING SERIOUS!
SORRY FOR SCARING YOU (HA HA).

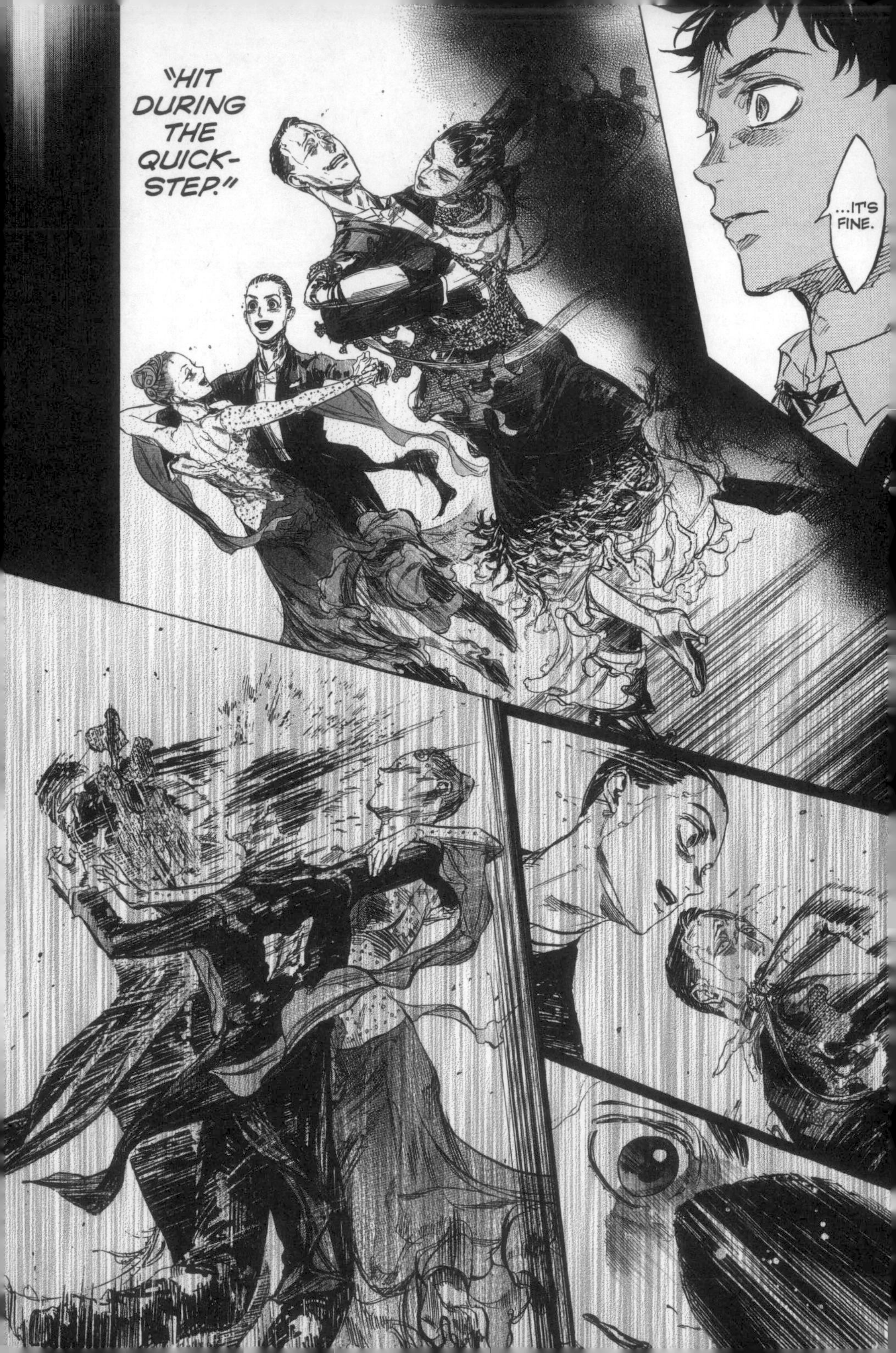
...IT'S FINE.
"HIT DURING THE QUICK-STEP."

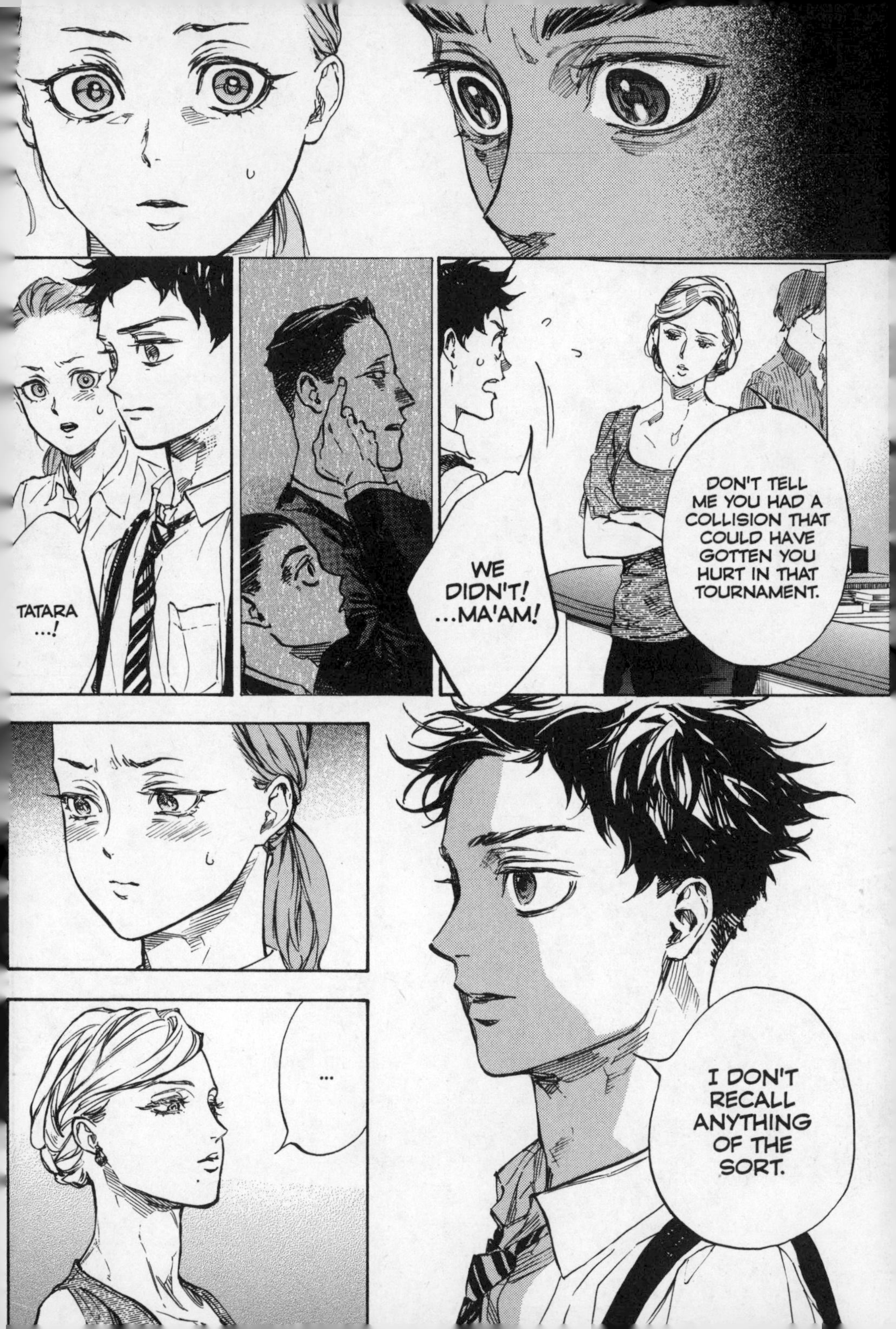

DON'T TELL ME YOU HAD A COLLISION THAT COULD HAVE GOTTEN YOU HURT IN THAT TOURNAMENT.
WE DIDN'T! ...MA'AM!
TATARA ...!
I DON'T RECALL ANYTHING OF THE SORT.
...

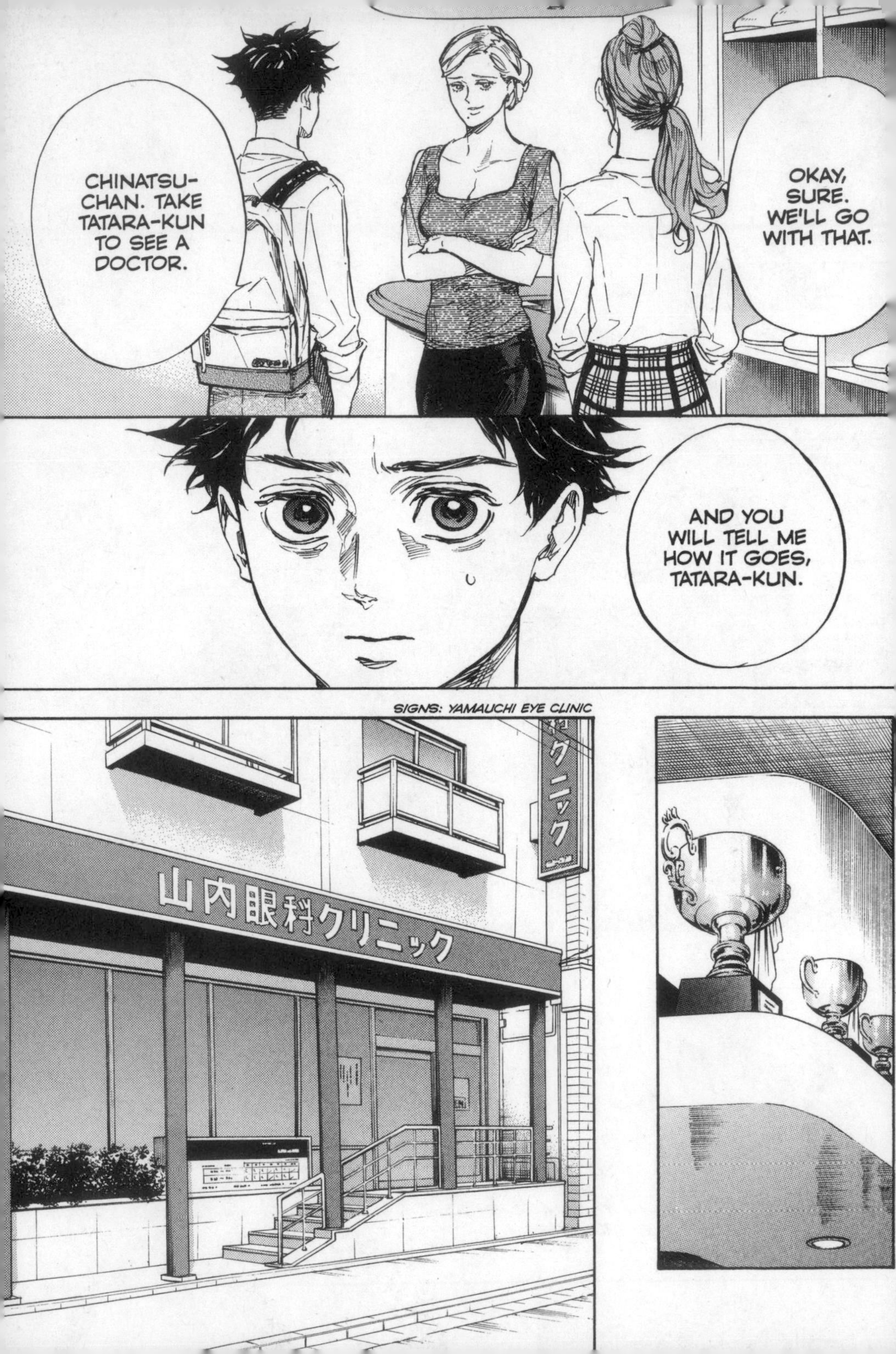
OKAY, SURE. WE'LL GO WITH THAT.
CHINATSU-CHAN. TAKE TATARA-KUN TO SEE A DOCTOR.
AND YOU WILL TELL ME HOW IT GOES, TATARA-KUN.
SIGNS: YAMAUCHI EYE CLINIC
山内眼科クリニック

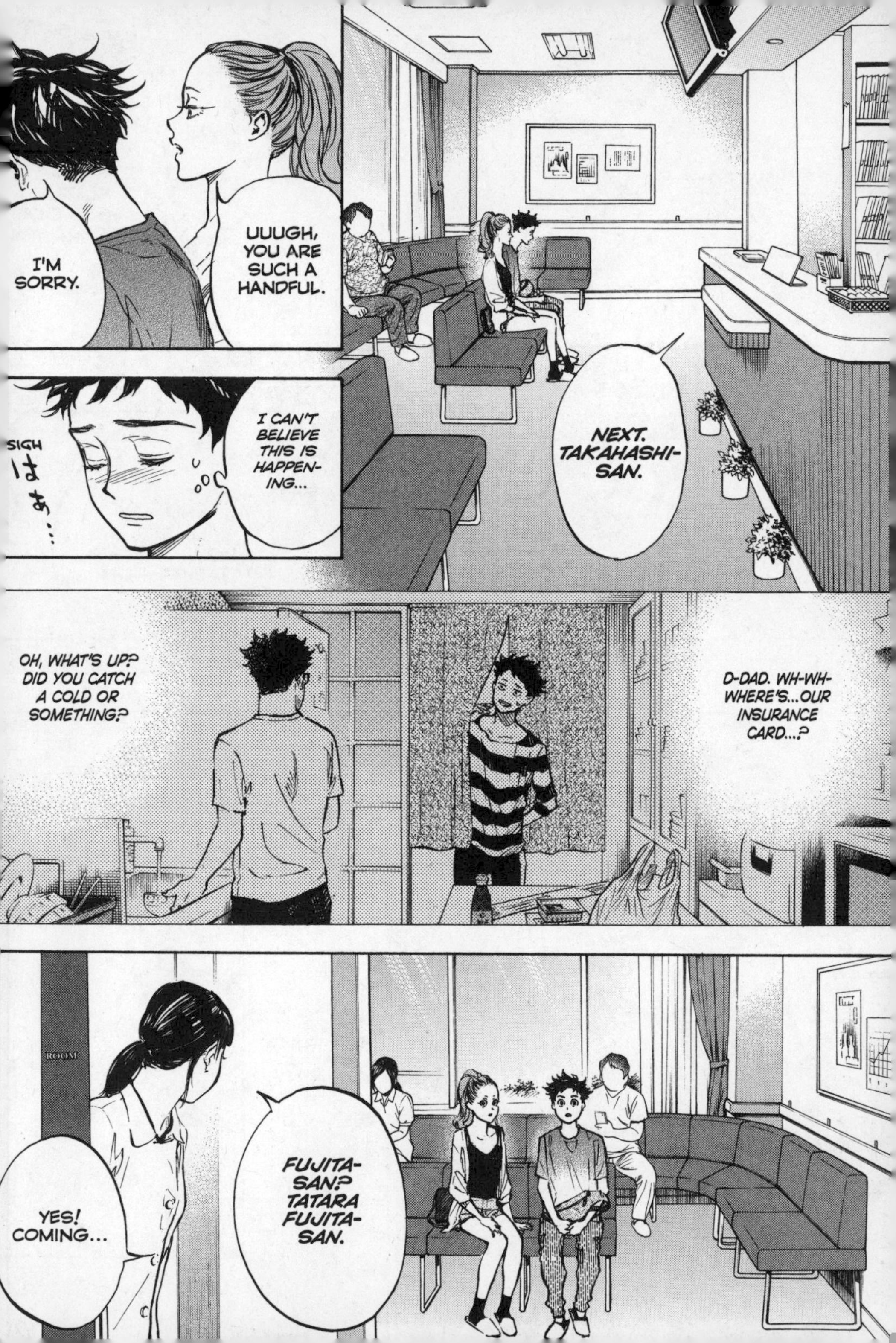
NEXT. TAKAHASHI-SAN.
UUUGH, YOU ARE SUCH A HANDFUL.
I'M SORRY.
I CAN'T BELIEVE THIS IS HAPPEN-ING...
SIGH
はぁ…
D-DAD. WH-WH-WHERE'S...OUR INSURANCE CARD...?
OH, WHAT'S UP? DID YOU CATCH A COLD OR SOMETHING?
ROOM
FUJITA-SAN? TATARA FUJITA-SAN.
YES! COMING...

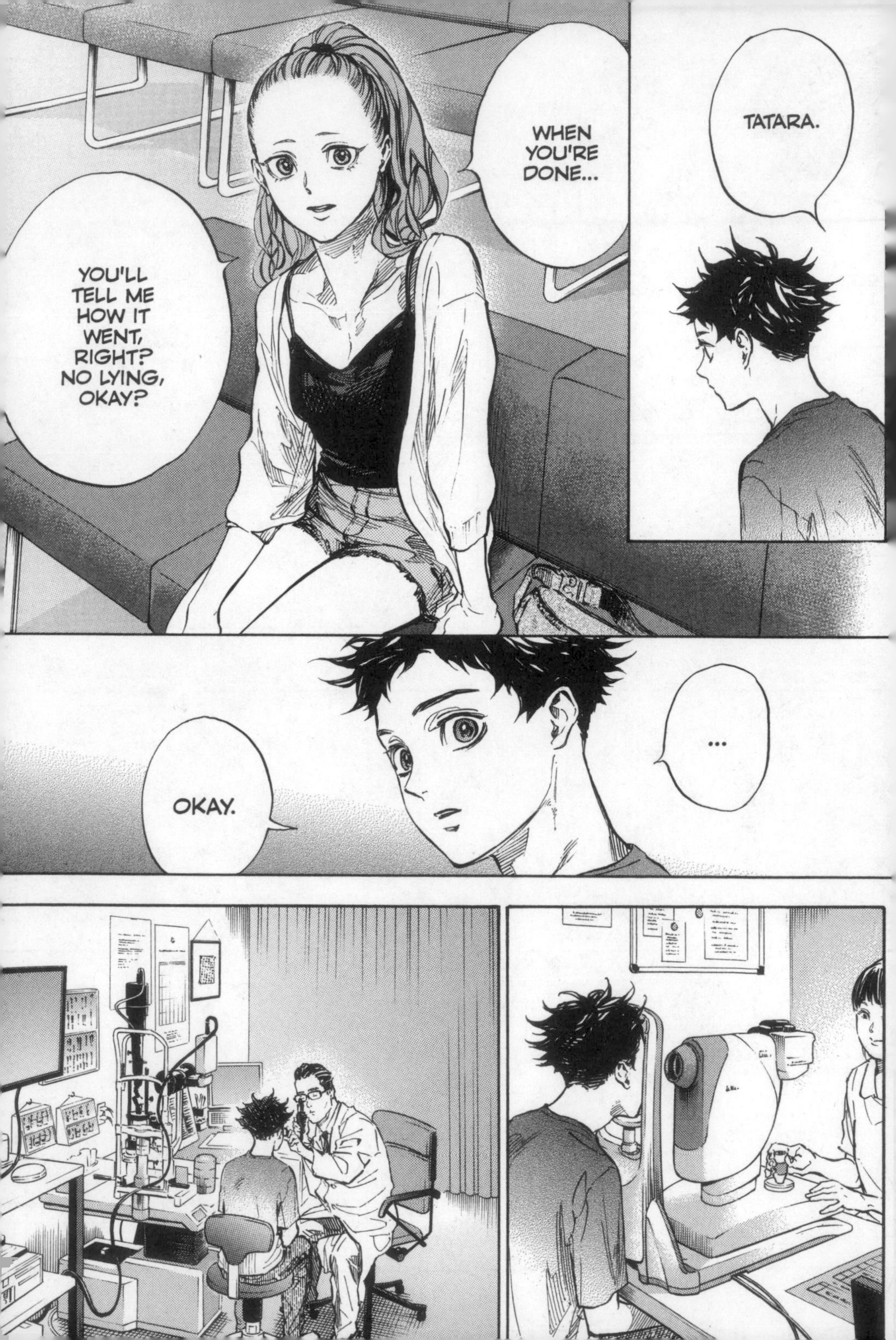
TATARA.
WHEN YOU'RE DONE...
YOU'LL TELL ME HOW IT WENT, RIGHT? NO LYING, OKAY?
...
OKAY.

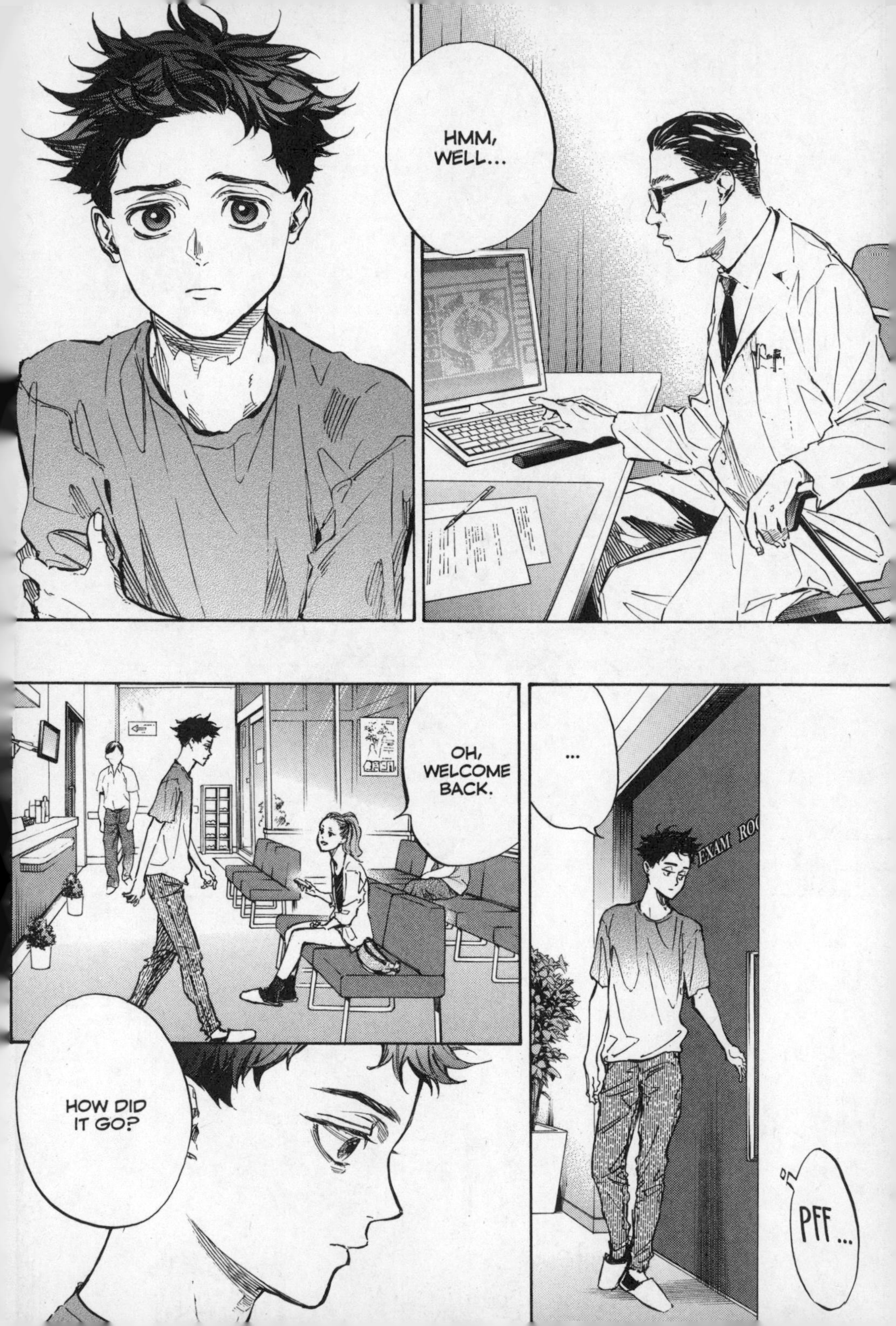
HMM, WELL...
...
PFF...
OH, WELCOME BACK.
HOW DID IT GO?

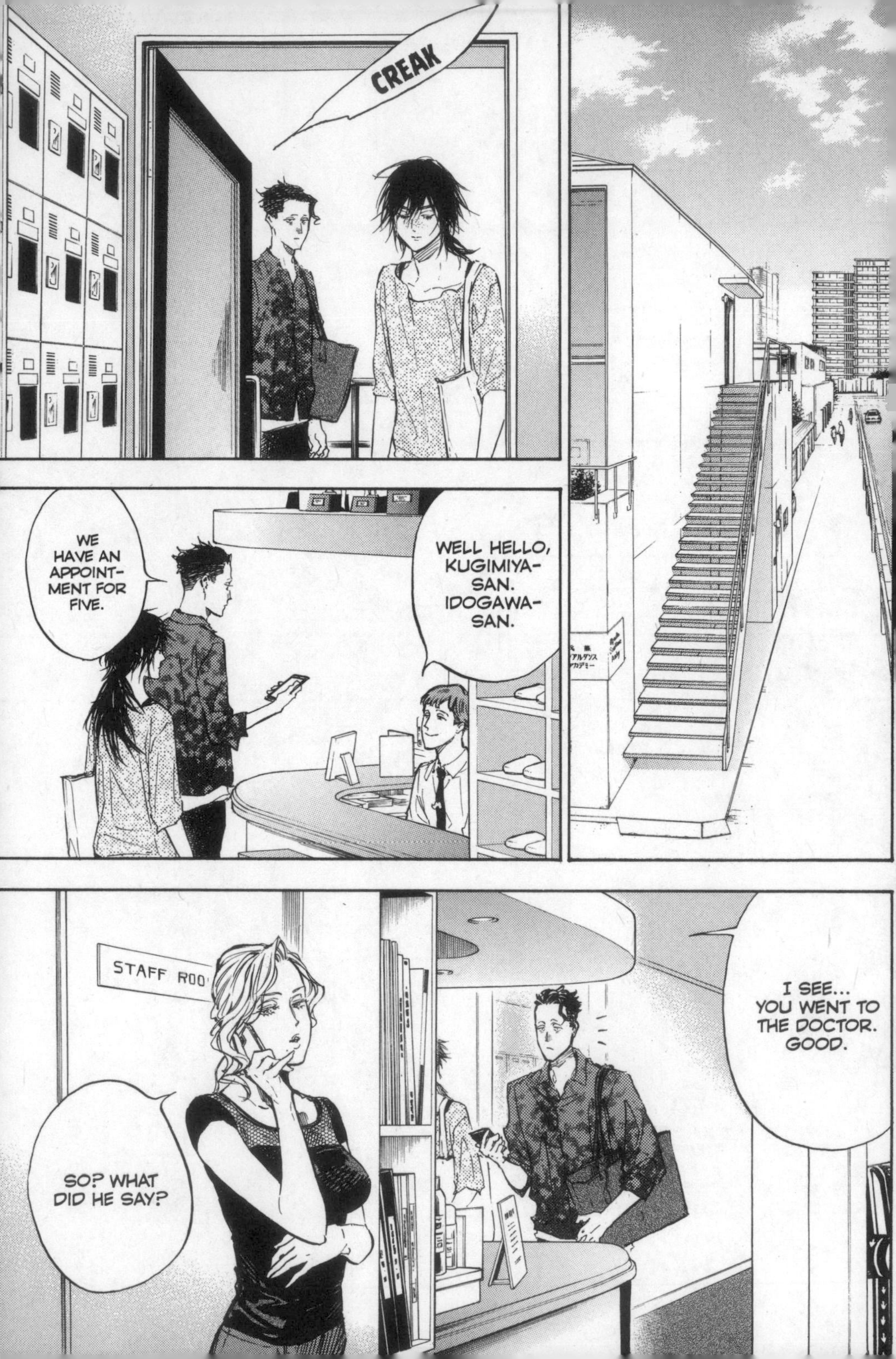
CREAK
WELL HELLO, KUGIMIYA-SAN. IDOGAWA-SAN.
WE HAVE AN APPOINTMENT FOR FIVE.
I SEE... YOU WENT TO THE DOCTOR. GOOD.
STAFF ROO
SO? WHAT DID HE SAY?

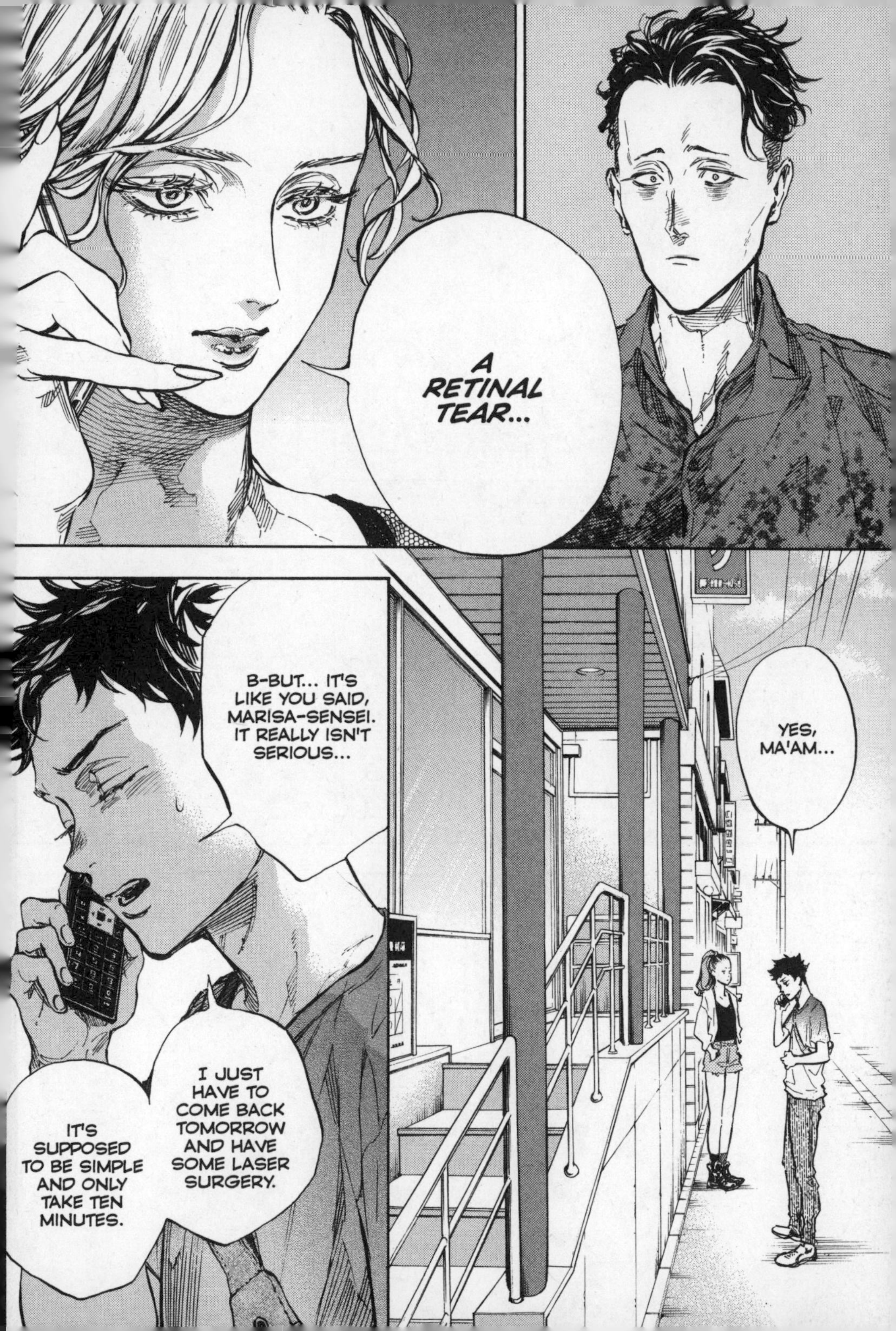
A RETINAL TEAR...
YES, MA'AM...
B-BUT... IT'S LIKE YOU SAID, MARISA-SENSEI. IT REALLY ISN'T SERIOUS...
I JUST HAVE TO COME BACK TOMORROW AND HAVE SOME LASER SURGERY.
IT'S SUPPOSED TO BE SIMPLE AND ONLY TAKE TEN MINUTES.

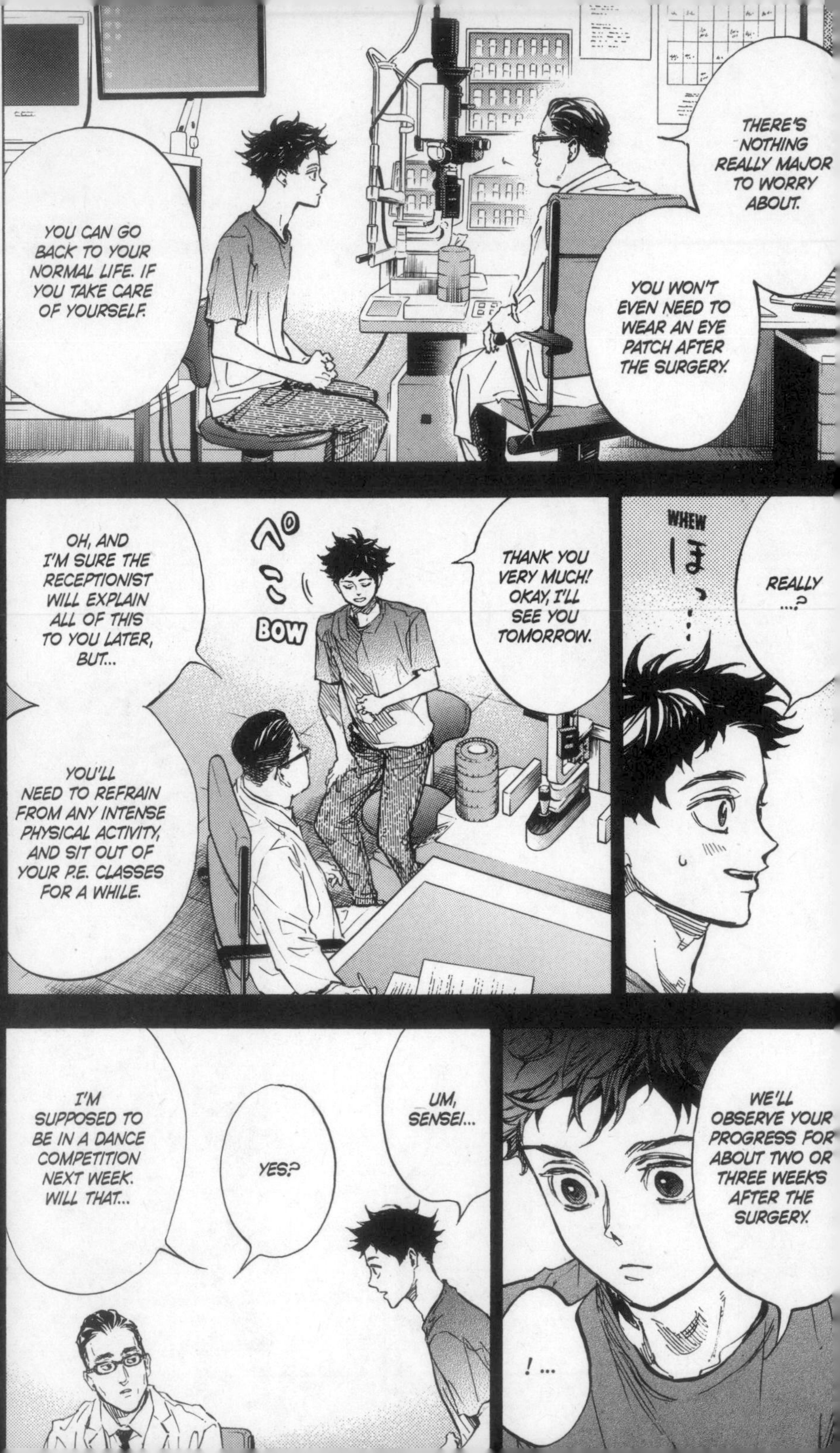
THERE'S NOTHING REALLY MAJOR TO WORRY ABOUT.
YOU WON'T EVEN NEED TO WEAR AN EYE PATCH AFTER THE SURGERY.
YOU CAN GO BACK TO YOUR NORMAL LIFE. IF YOU TAKE CARE OF YOURSELF.
WHEW
ほっ…
REALLY ...?
THANK YOU VERY MUCH! OKAY, I'LL SEE YOU TOMORROW.
ぺこ
BOW
OH, AND I'M SURE THE RECEPTIONIST WILL EXPLAIN ALL OF THIS TO YOU LATER, BUT...
YOU'LL NEED TO REFRAIN FROM ANY INTENSE PHYSICAL ACTIVITY, AND SIT OUT OF YOUR P.E. CLASSES FOR A WHILE.
WE'LL OBSERVE YOUR PROGRESS FOR ABOUT TWO OR THREE WEEKS AFTER THE SURGERY.
! ...
UM, SENSEI...
YES?
I'M SUPPOSED TO BE IN A DANCE COMPETITION NEXT WEEK. WILL THAT...

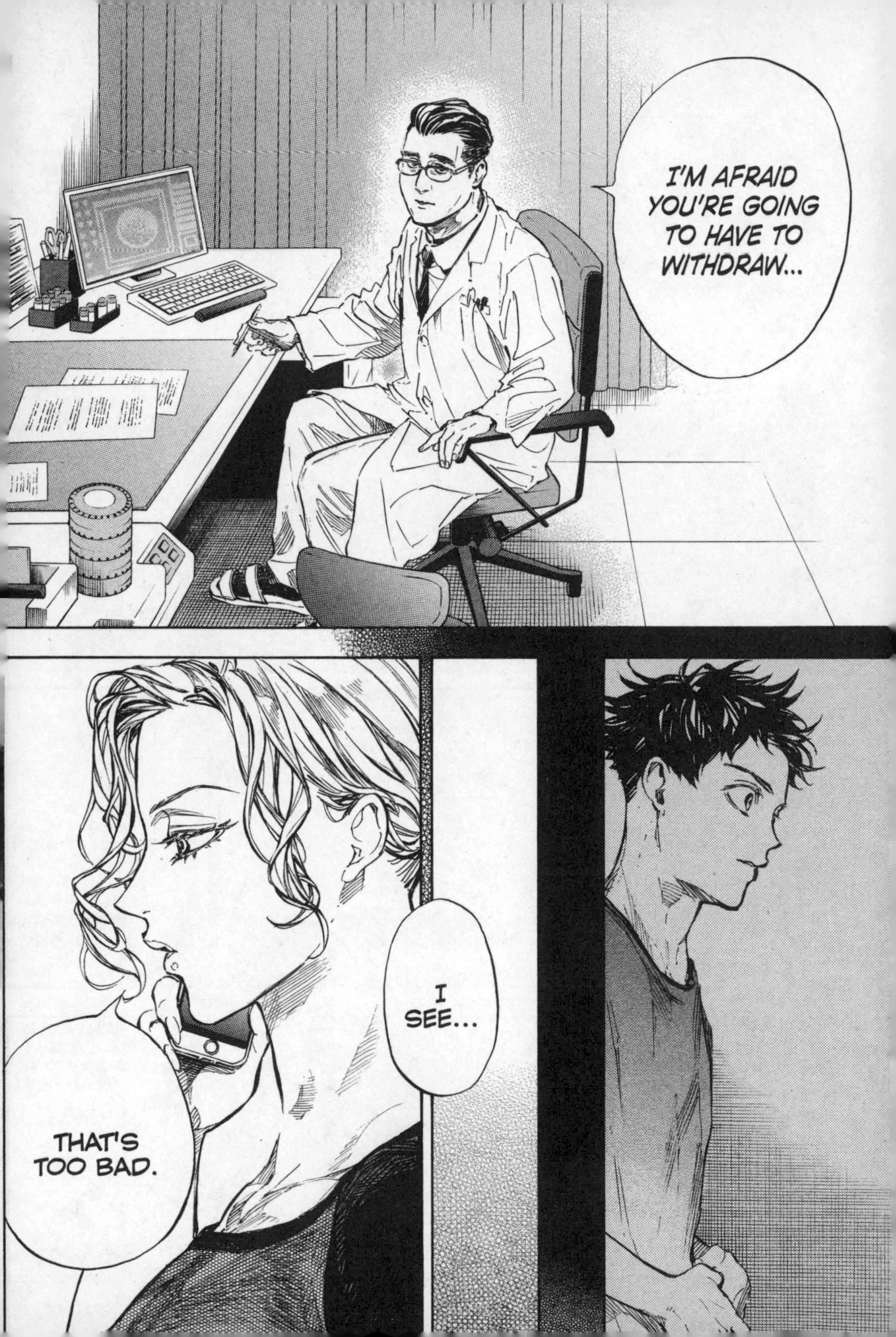
I'M AFRAID YOU'RE GOING TO HAVE TO WITHDRAW...
I SEE...
THAT'S TOO BAD.

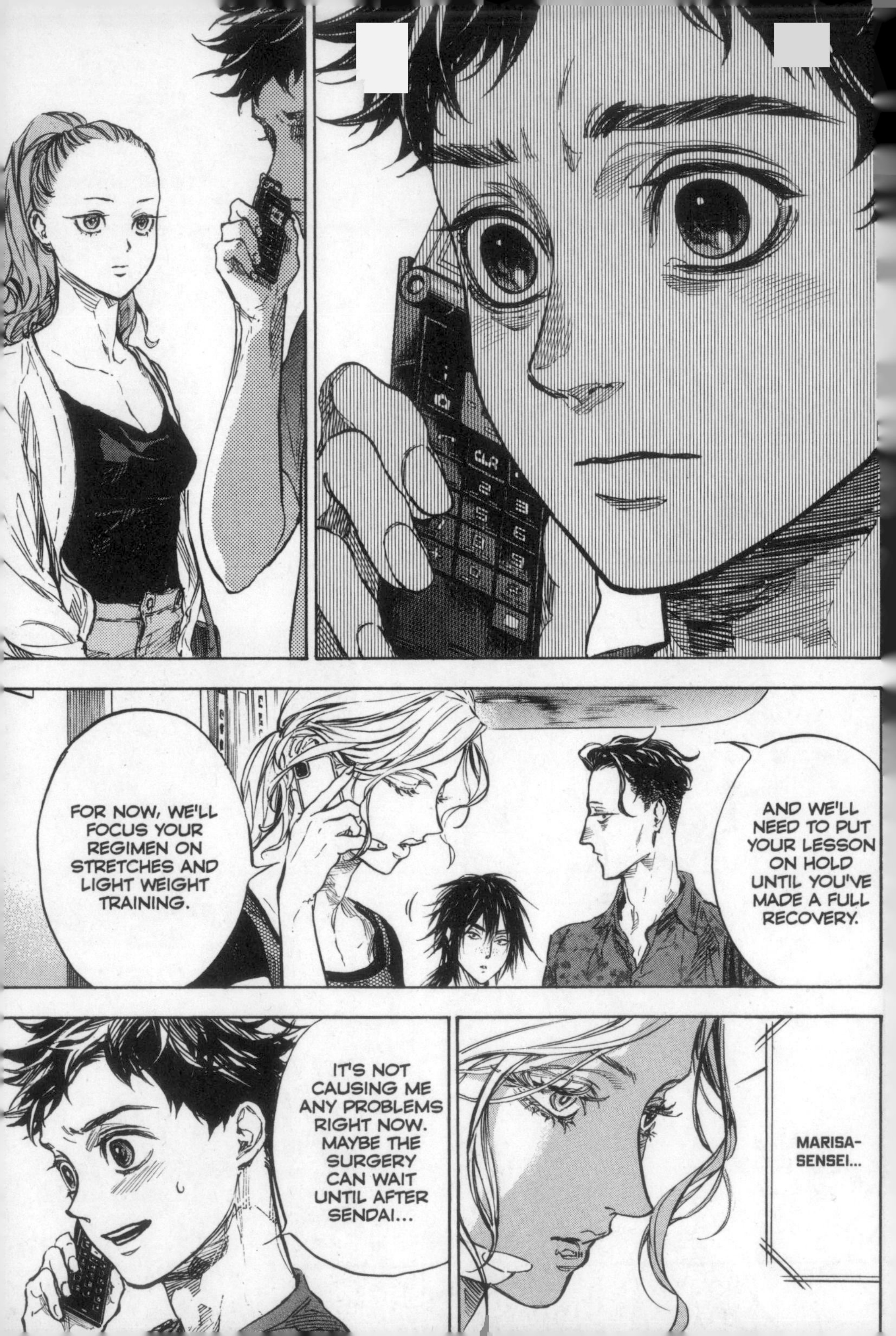
FOR NOW, WE'LL FOCUS YOUR REGIMEN ON STRETCHES AND LIGHT WEIGHT TRAINING.
AND WE'LL NEED TO PUT YOUR LESSON ON HOLD UNTIL YOU'VE MADE A FULL RECOVERY.
MARISA-SENSEI...
IT'S NOT CAUSING ME ANY PROBLEMS RIGHT NOW. MAYBE THE SURGERY CAN WAIT UNTIL AFTER SENDAI...

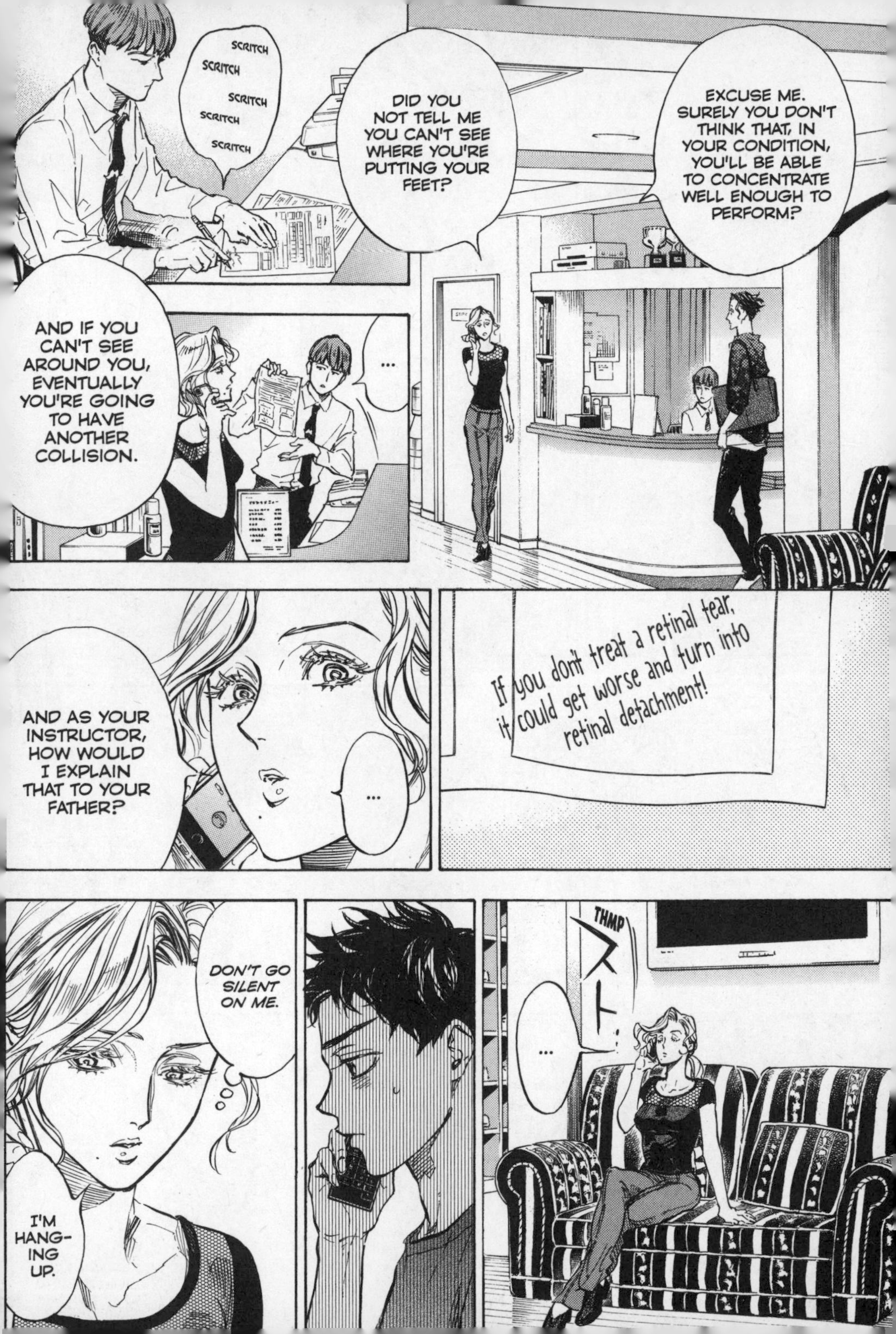

EXCUSE ME. SURELY YOU DON'T THINK THAT, IN YOUR CONDITION, YOU'LL BE ABLE TO CONCENTRATE WELL ENOUGH TO PERFORM?
DID YOU NOT TELL ME YOU CAN'T SEE WHERE YOU'RE PUTTING YOUR FEET?
SCRITCH SCRITCH SCRITCH SCRITCH SCRITCH
...
AND IF YOU CAN'T SEE AROUND YOU, EVENTUALLY YOU'RE GOING TO HAVE ANOTHER COLLISION.
If you don't treat a retinal tear, it could get worse and turn into retinal detachment!
AND AS YOUR INSTRUCTOR, HOW WOULD I EXPLAIN THAT TO YOUR FATHER?
...
THMP
...
DON'T GO SILENT ON ME.
I'M HANG-ING UP.

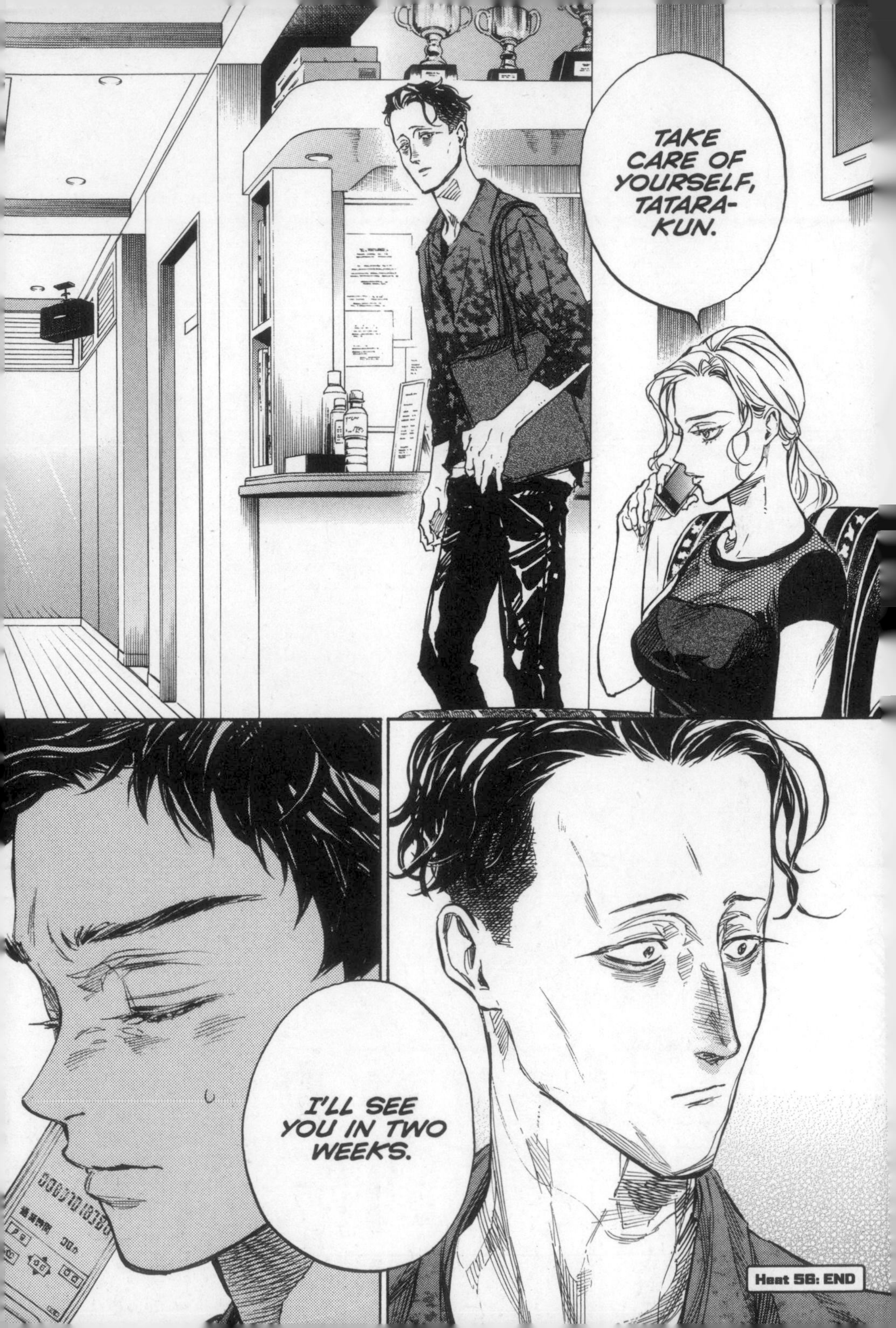
TAKE CARE OF YOURSELF, TATARA-KUN.
I'LL SEE YOU IN TWO WEEKS.
Heat 56: END

WELCOME TO THE BALLROOM

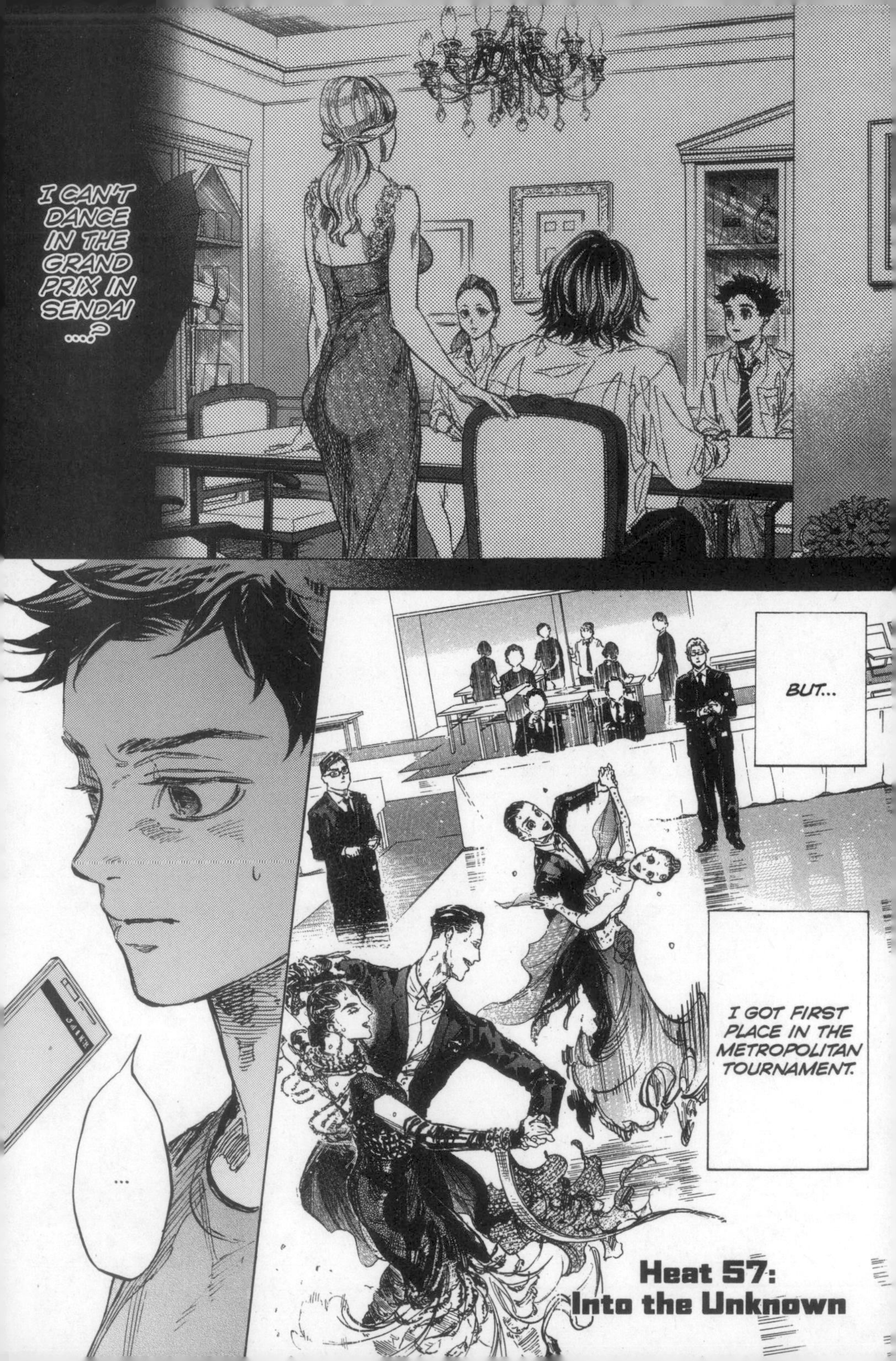
I CAN'T DANCE IN THE GRAND PRIX IN SENDAI ...?
BUT...
I GOT FIRST PLACE IN THE METROPOLITAN TOURNAMENT.
...

Heat 57: Into the Unknown

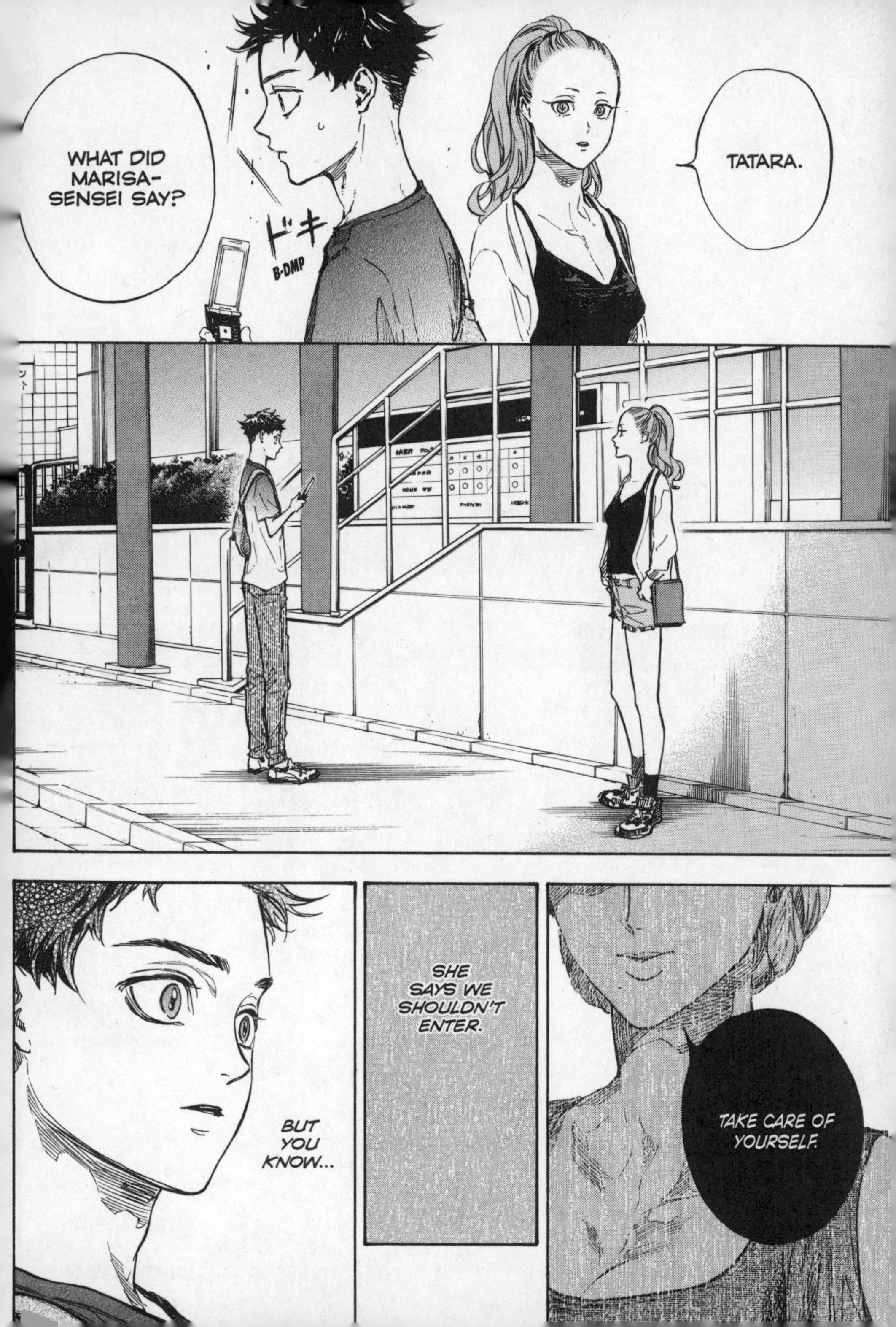
TATARA.
WHAT DID MARISA-SENSEI SAY?
ドキ
B-DMP
TAKE CARE OF YOURSELF.
SHE SAYS WE SHOULDN'T ENTER.
BUT YOU KNOW...

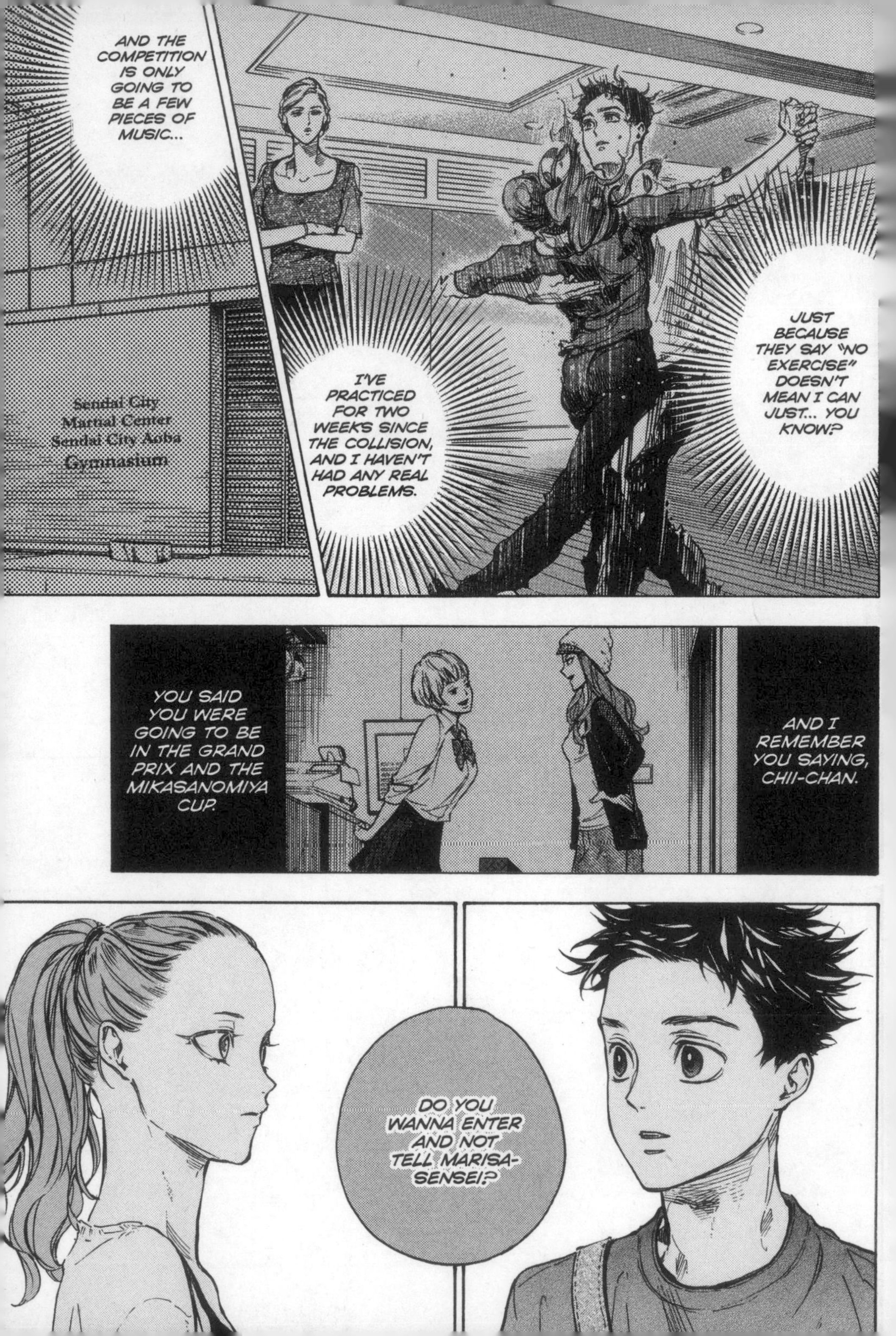
JUST BECAUSE THEY SAY "NO EXERCISE" DOESN'T MEAN I CAN JUST... YOU KNOW?
I'VE PRACTICED FOR TWO WEEKS SINCE THE COLLISION, AND I HAVEN'T HAD ANY REAL PROBLEMS.
AND THE COMPETITION IS ONLY GOING TO BE A FEW PIECES OF MUSIC...
Sendai City Martial Center Sendai City Aoba Gymnasium
AND I REMEMBER YOU SAYING, CHII-CHAN.
YOU SAID YOU WERE GOING TO BE IN THE GRAND PRIX AND THE MIKASANOMIYA CUP.
DO YOU WANNA ENTER AND NOT TELL MARISA-SENSEI?

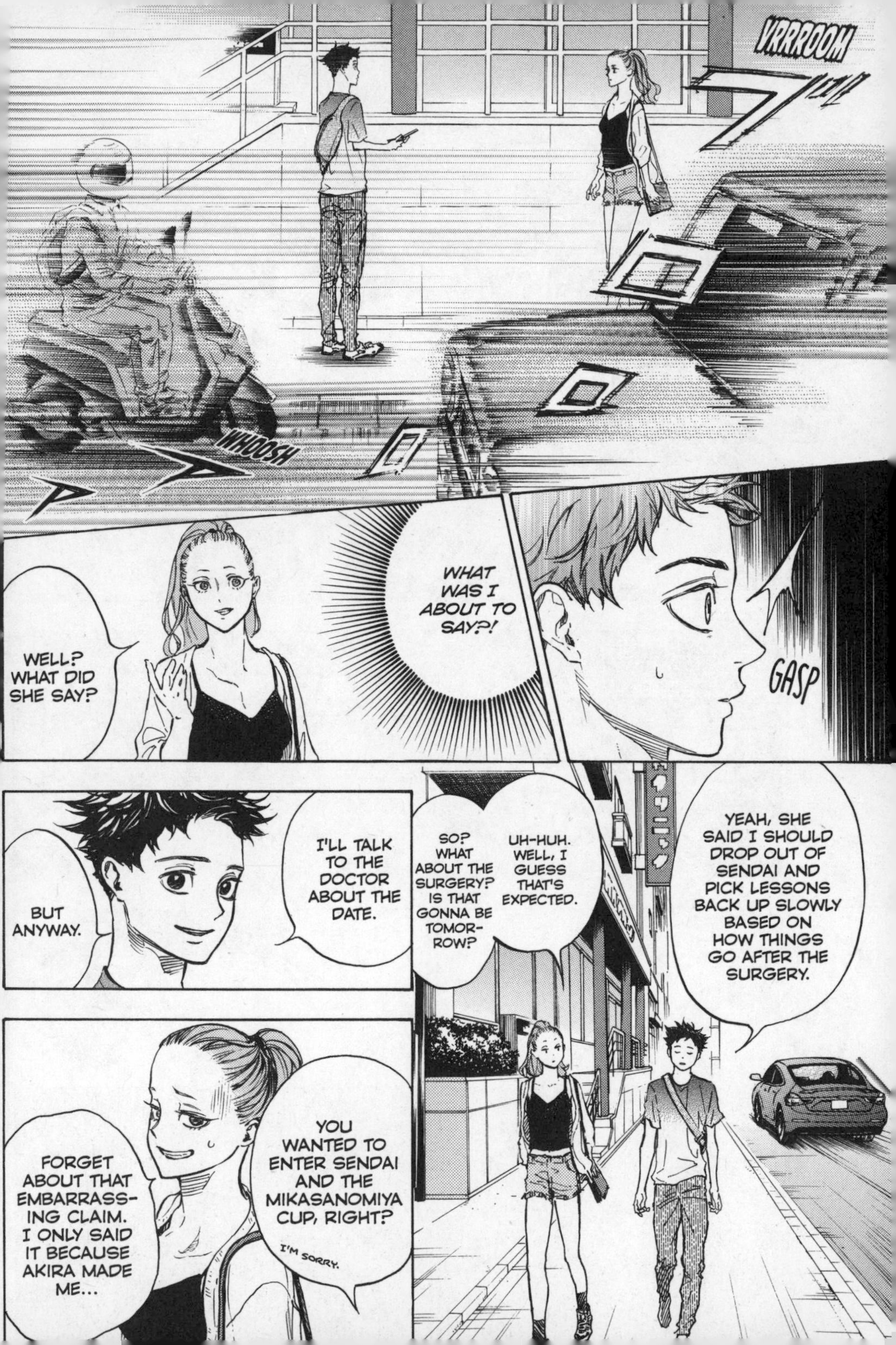
VRRROOM
WHOOSH
GASP
WHAT WAS I ABOUT TO SAY?!
WELL? WHAT DID SHE SAY?
YEAH, SHE SAID I SHOULD DROP OUT OF SENDAI AND PICK LESSONS BACK UP SLOWLY BASED ON HOW THINGS GO AFTER THE SURGERY.
UH-HUH. WELL, I GUESS THAT'S EXPECTED.
SO? WHAT ABOUT THE SURGERY? IS THAT GONNA BE TOMOR-ROW?
I'LL TALK TO THE DOCTOR ABOUT THE DATE.
BUT ANYWAY.
YOU WANTED TO ENTER SENDAI AND THE MIKASANOMIYA CUP, RIGHT?
I'M SORRY.
FORGET ABOUT THAT EMBARRASS-ING CLAIM. I ONLY SAID IT BECAUSE AKIRA MADE ME...

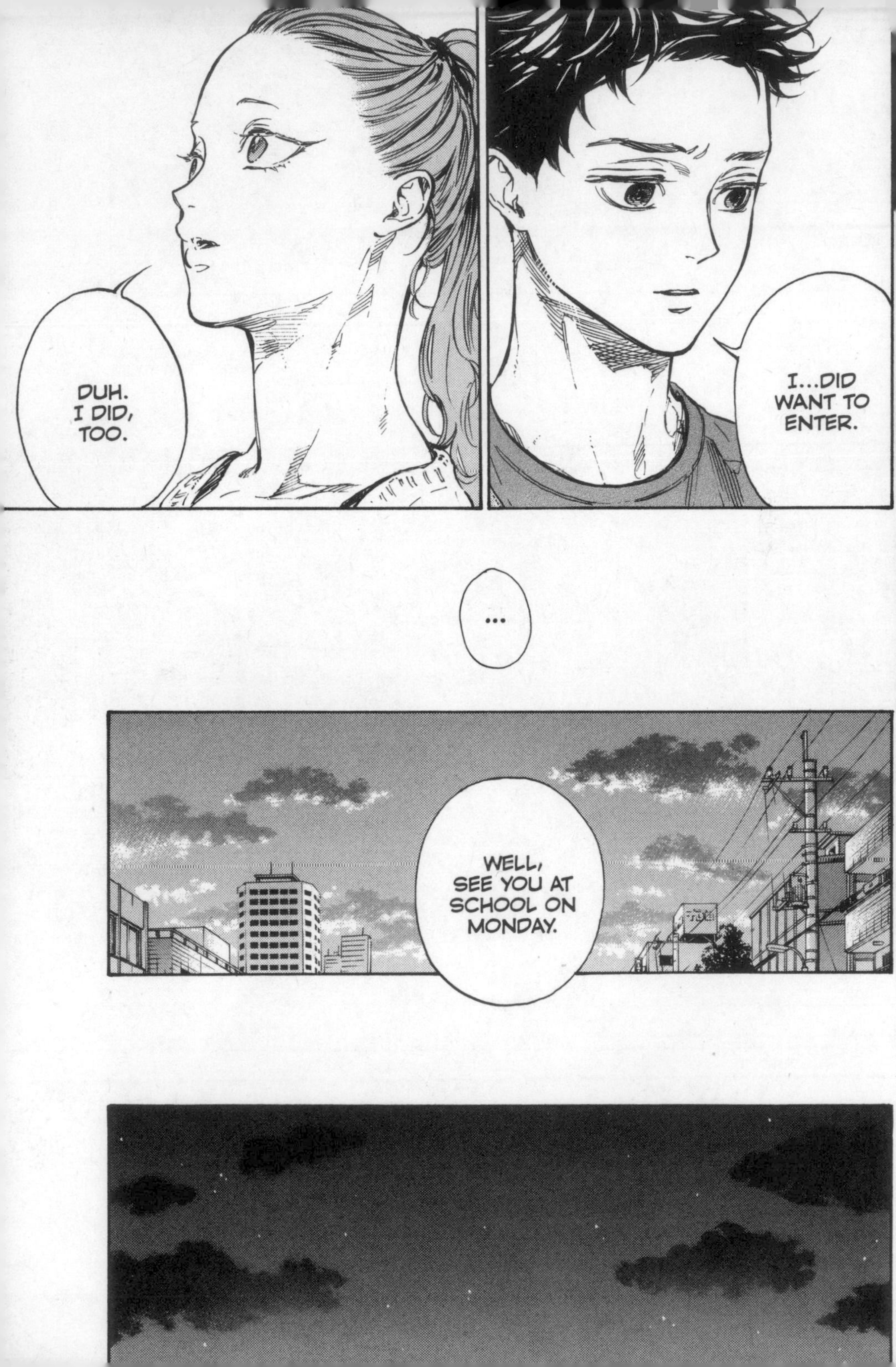
I...DID WANT TO ENTER.
DUH. I DID, TOO.
...
WELL, SEE YOU AT SCHOOL ON MONDAY.

SIGN: OGASAWARA DANCE STUDIO

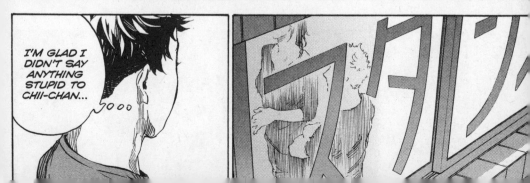

I'M GLAD I DIDN'T SAY ANYTHING STUPID TO CHII-CHAN...

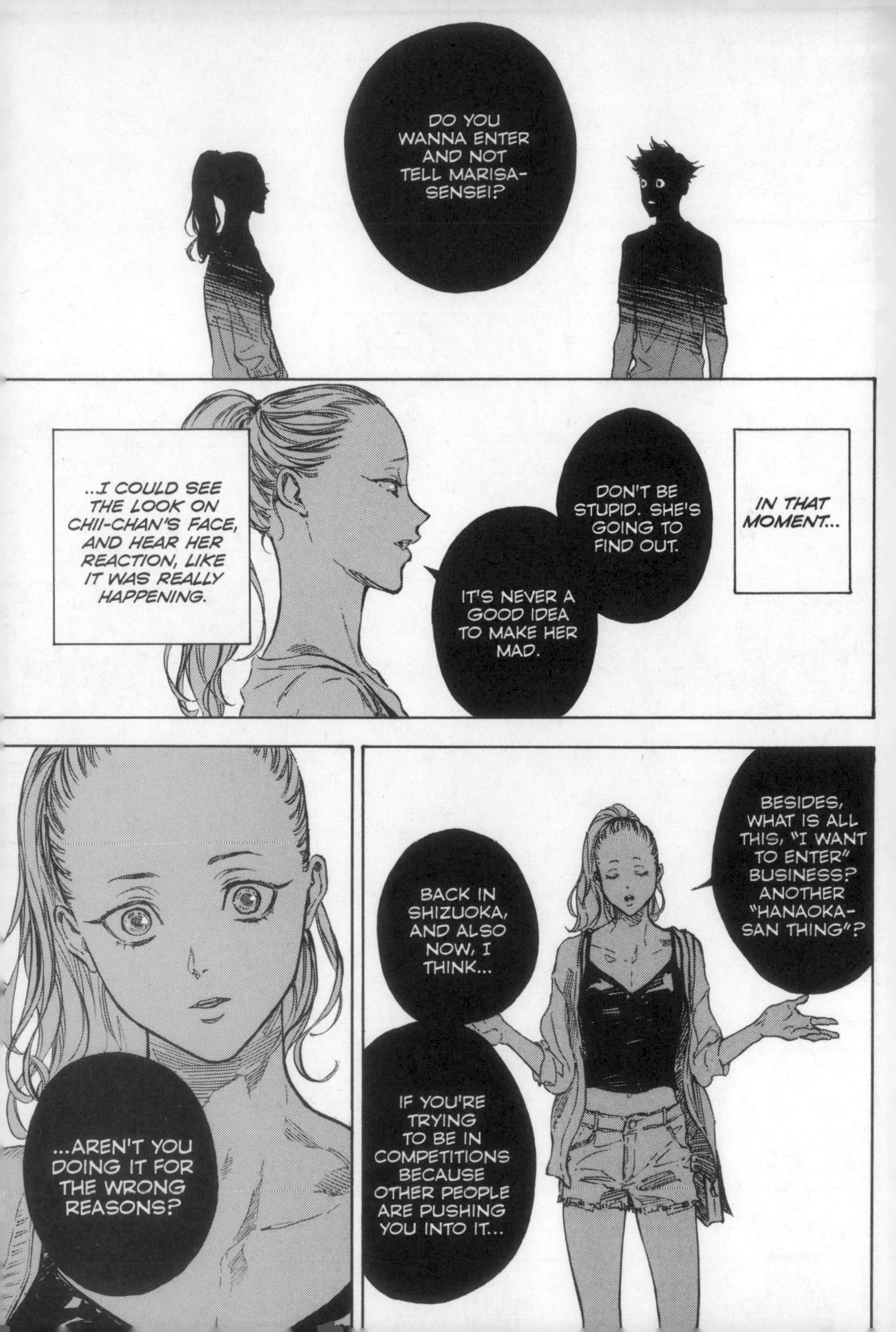
DO YOU WANNA ENTER AND NOT TELL MARISA-SENSEI?
IN THAT MOMENT...
DON'T BE STUPID. SHE'S GOING TO FIND OUT.
IT'S NEVER A GOOD IDEA TO MAKE HER MAD.
...I COULD SEE THE LOOK ON CHII-CHAN'S FACE, AND HEAR HER REACTION, LIKE IT WAS REALLY HAPPENING.
BESIDES, WHAT IS ALL THIS, "I WANT TO ENTER" BUSINESS? ANOTHER "HANAOKA-SAN THING"?
BACK IN SHIZUOKA, AND ALSO NOW, I THINK...
IF YOU'RE TRYING TO BE IN COMPETITIONS BECAUSE OTHER PEOPLE ARE PUSHING YOU INTO IT...
...AREN'T YOU DOING IT FOR THE WRONG REASONS?

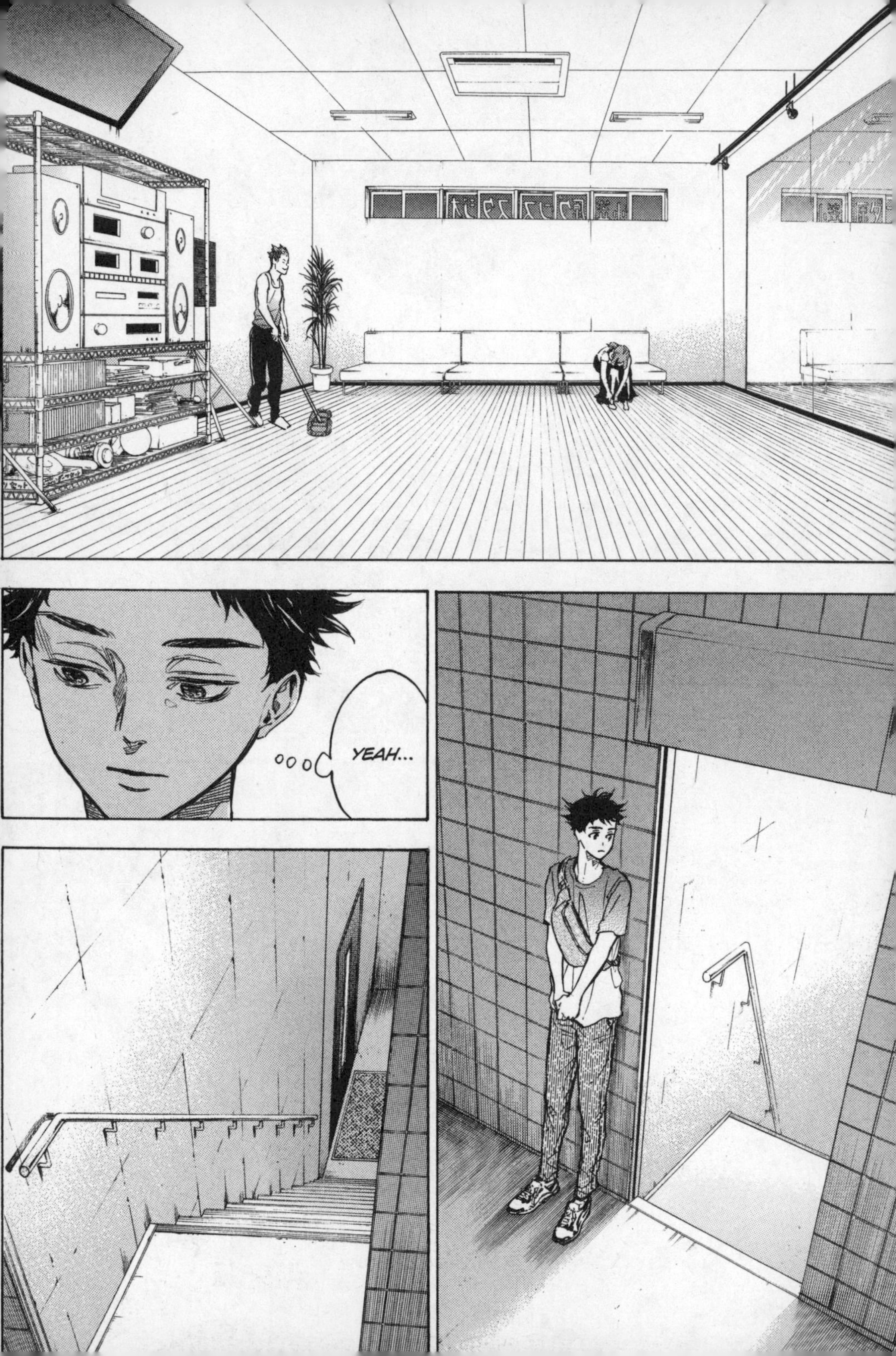
○○○ YEAH...

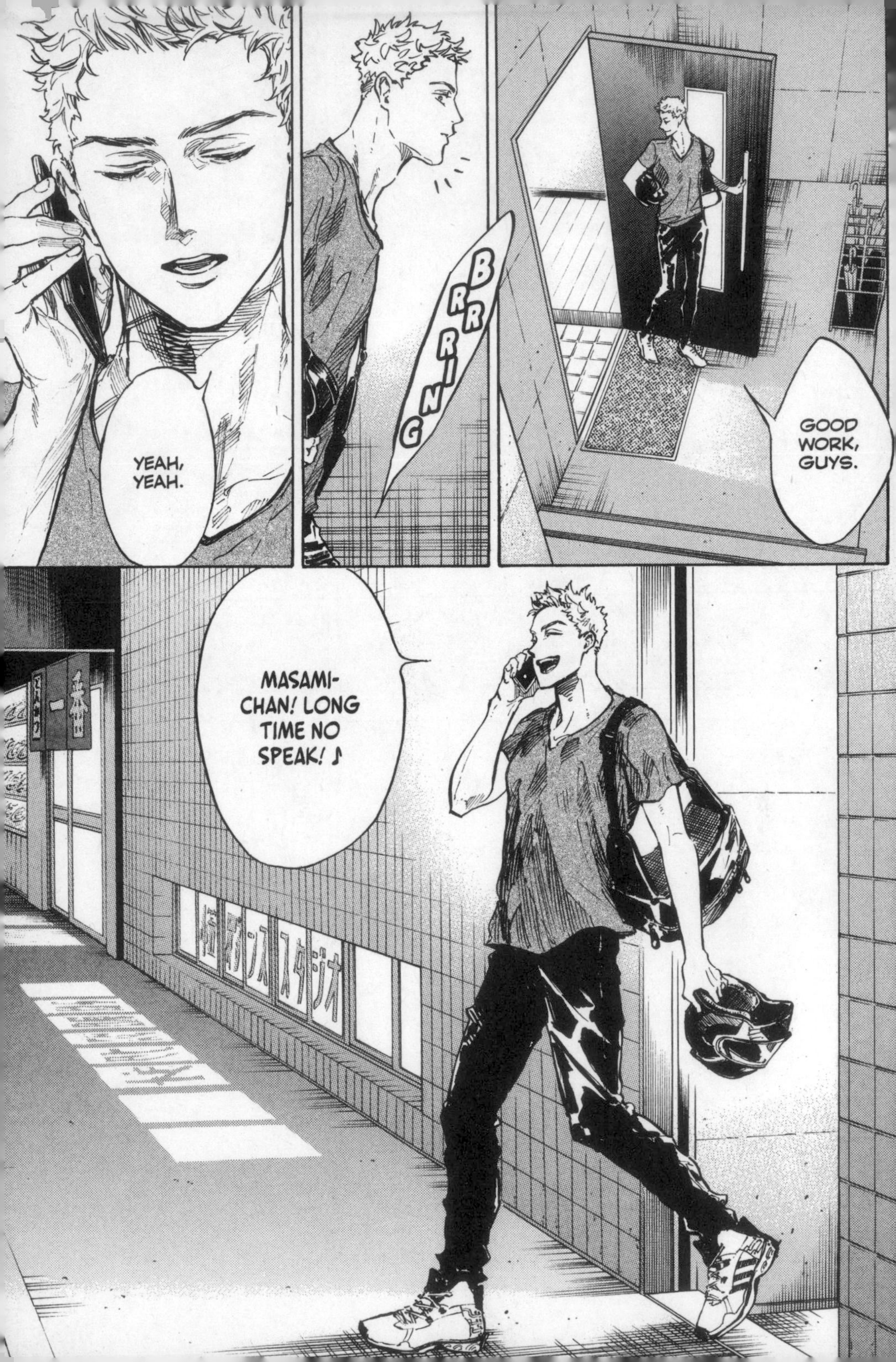
GOOD WORK, GUYS.
BRRRRING
YEAH, YEAH.
MASAMI-CHAN! LONG TIME NO SPEAK! ♪

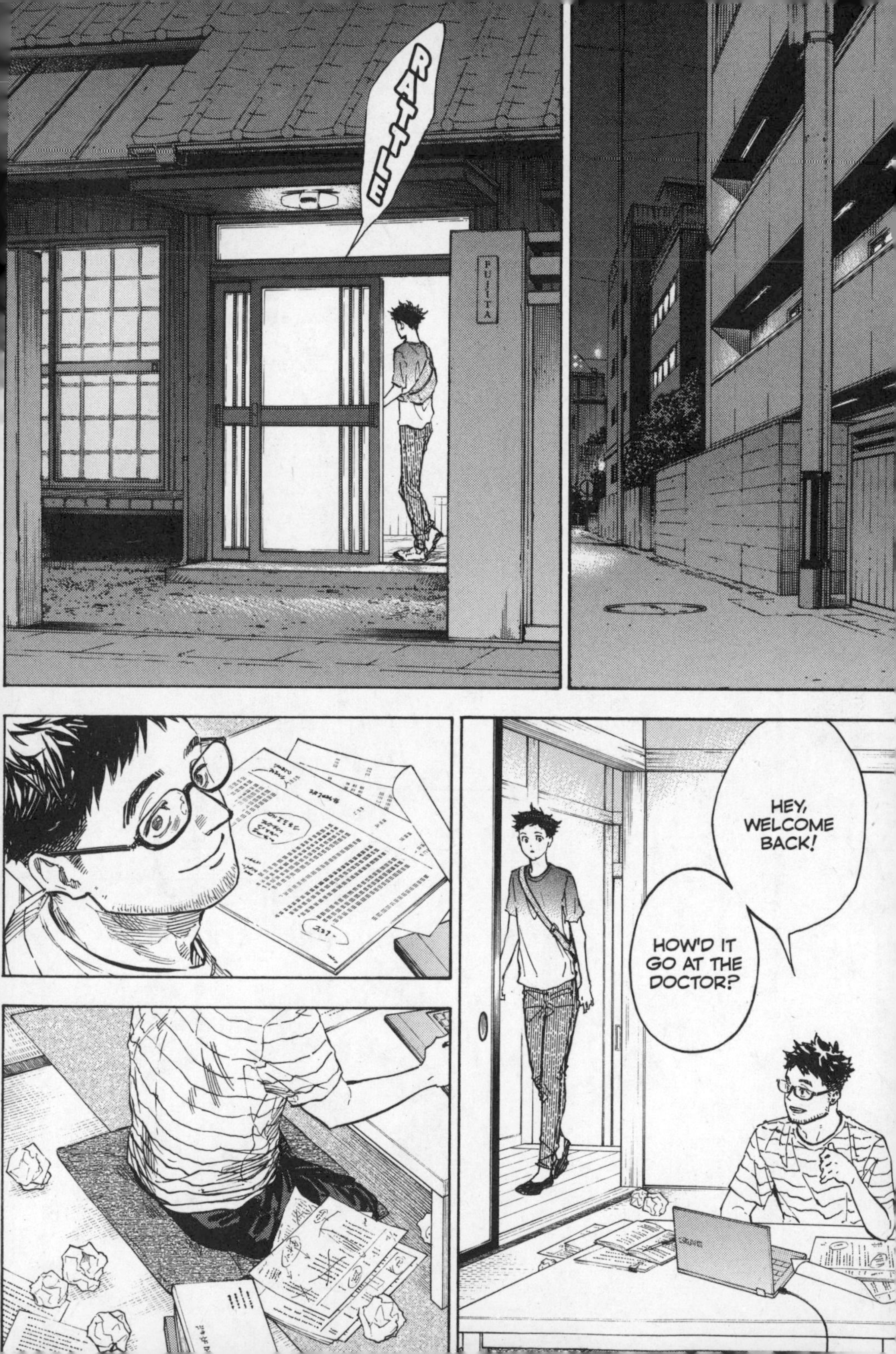
RATTLE
FUJITA
HEY, WELCOME BACK!
HOW'D IT GO AT THE DOCTOR?

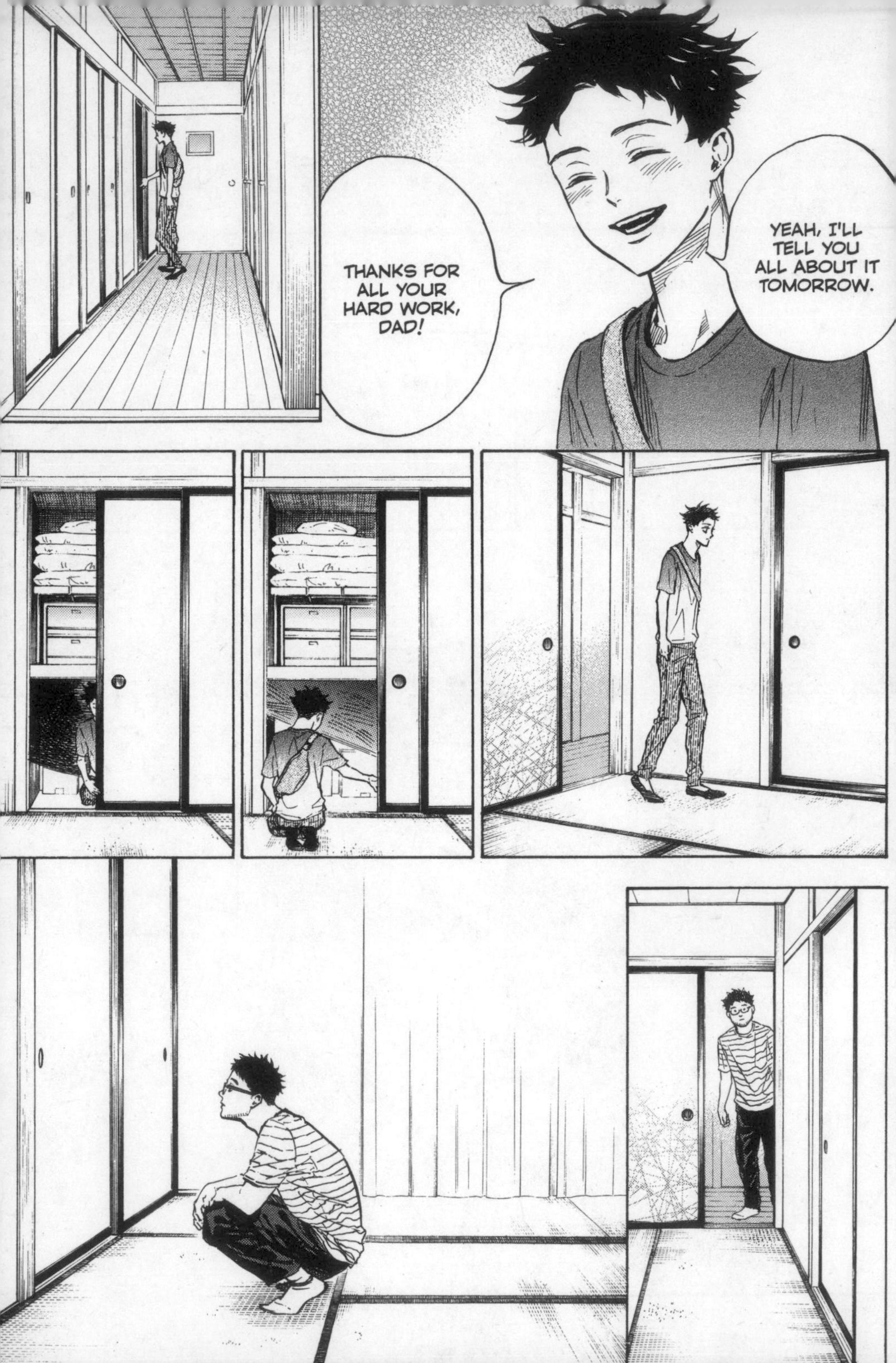
YEAH, I'LL TELL YOU ALL ABOUT IT TOMORROW.
THANKS FOR ALL YOUR HARD WORK, DAD!

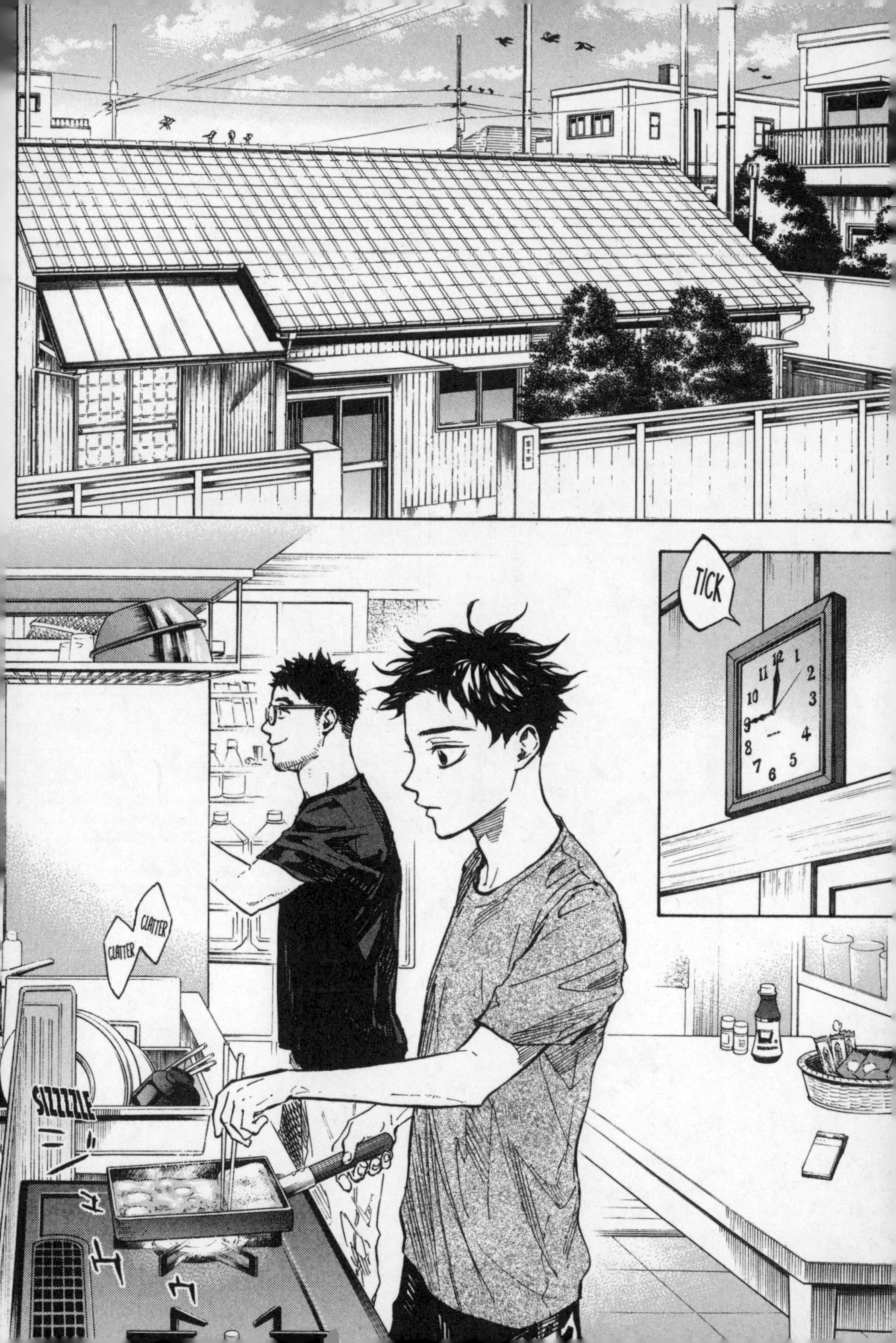
TICK
CLATTER
CLATTER
SIZZZZLE

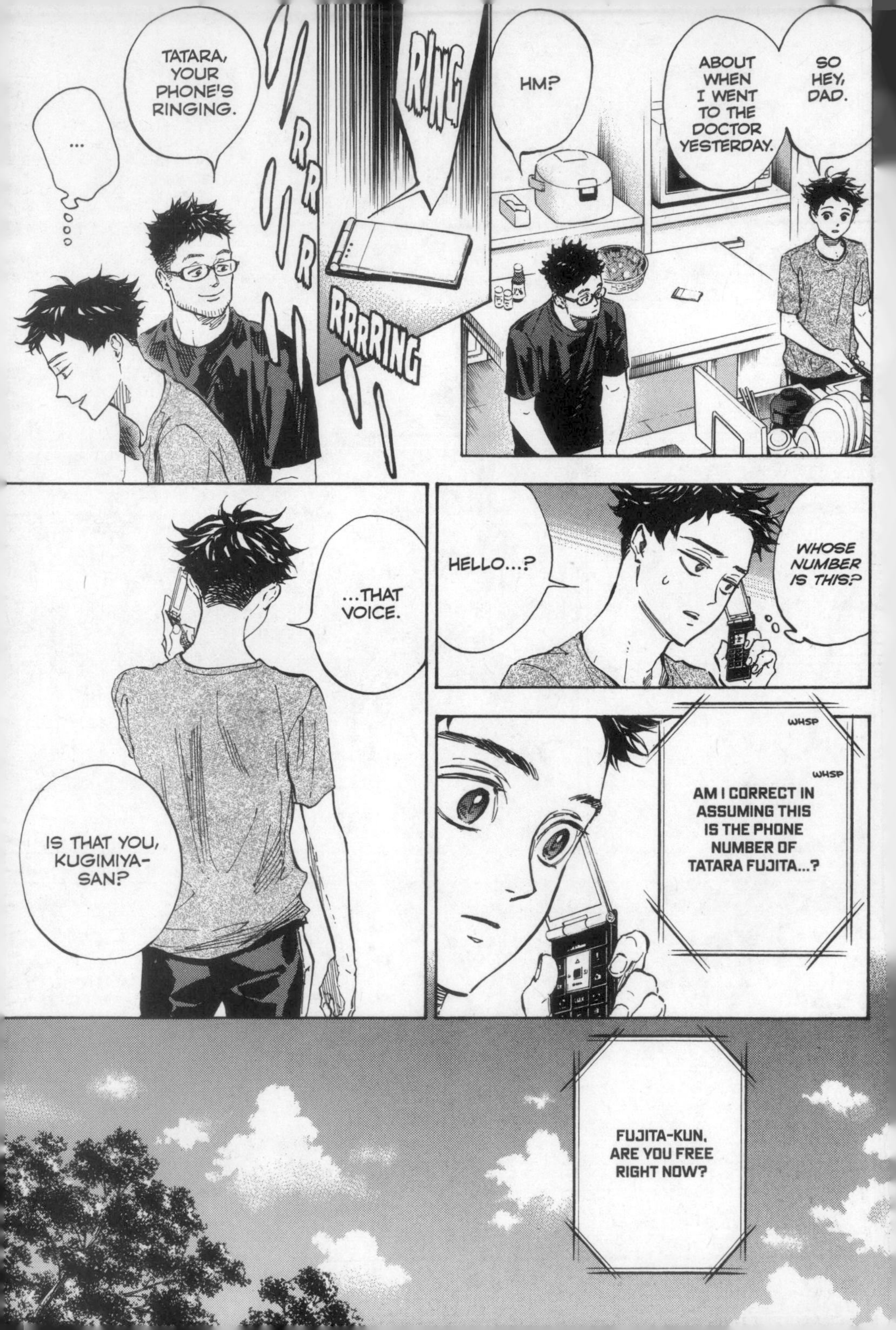
SO HEY, DAD.
ABOUT WHEN I WENT TO THE DOCTOR YESTERDAY.
HM?
RING
RRR
RRRRING
TATARA, YOUR PHONE'S RINGING.
...
WHOSE NUMBER IS THIS?
HELLO...?
WHSP
WHSP
AM I CORRECT IN ASSUMING THIS IS THE PHONE NUMBER OF TATARA FUJITA...?
...THAT VOICE.
IS THAT YOU, KUGIMIYA-SAN?
FUJITA-KUN, ARE YOU FREE RIGHT NOW?

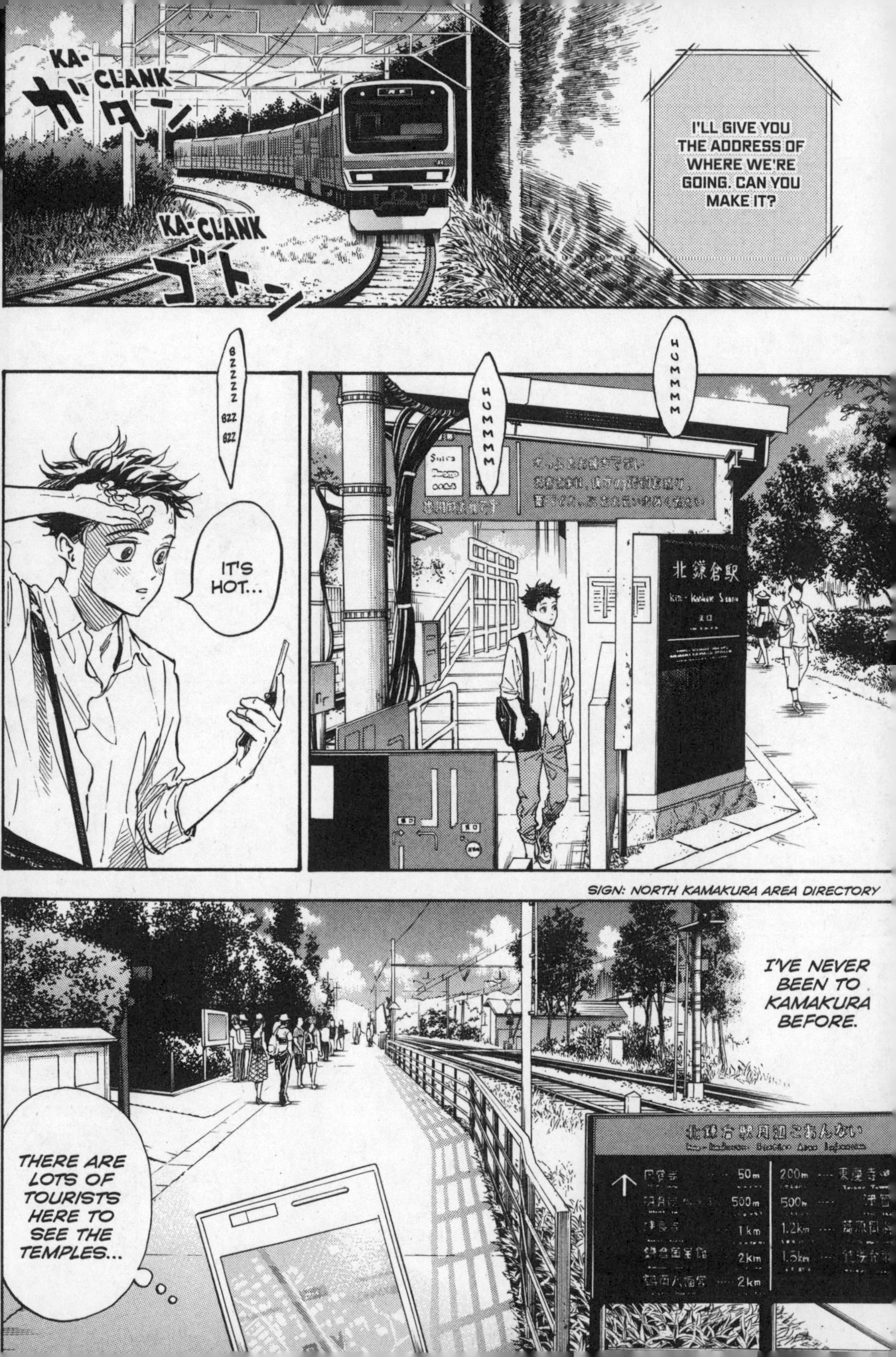
I'LL GIVE YOU THE ADDRESS OF WHERE WE'RE GOING. CAN YOU MAKE IT?
KA-CLANK
ガターン
KA-CLANK
ゴトーン
HUMMMM
HUMMMM
北鎌倉駅
BZZZZ BZZ BZZ
IT'S HOT...
SIGN: NORTH KAMAKURA AREA DIRECTORY
I'VE NEVER BEEN TO KAMAKURA BEFORE.
北鎌倉駅周辺ごあんない
THERE ARE LOTS OF TOURISTS HERE TO SEE THE TEMPLES...

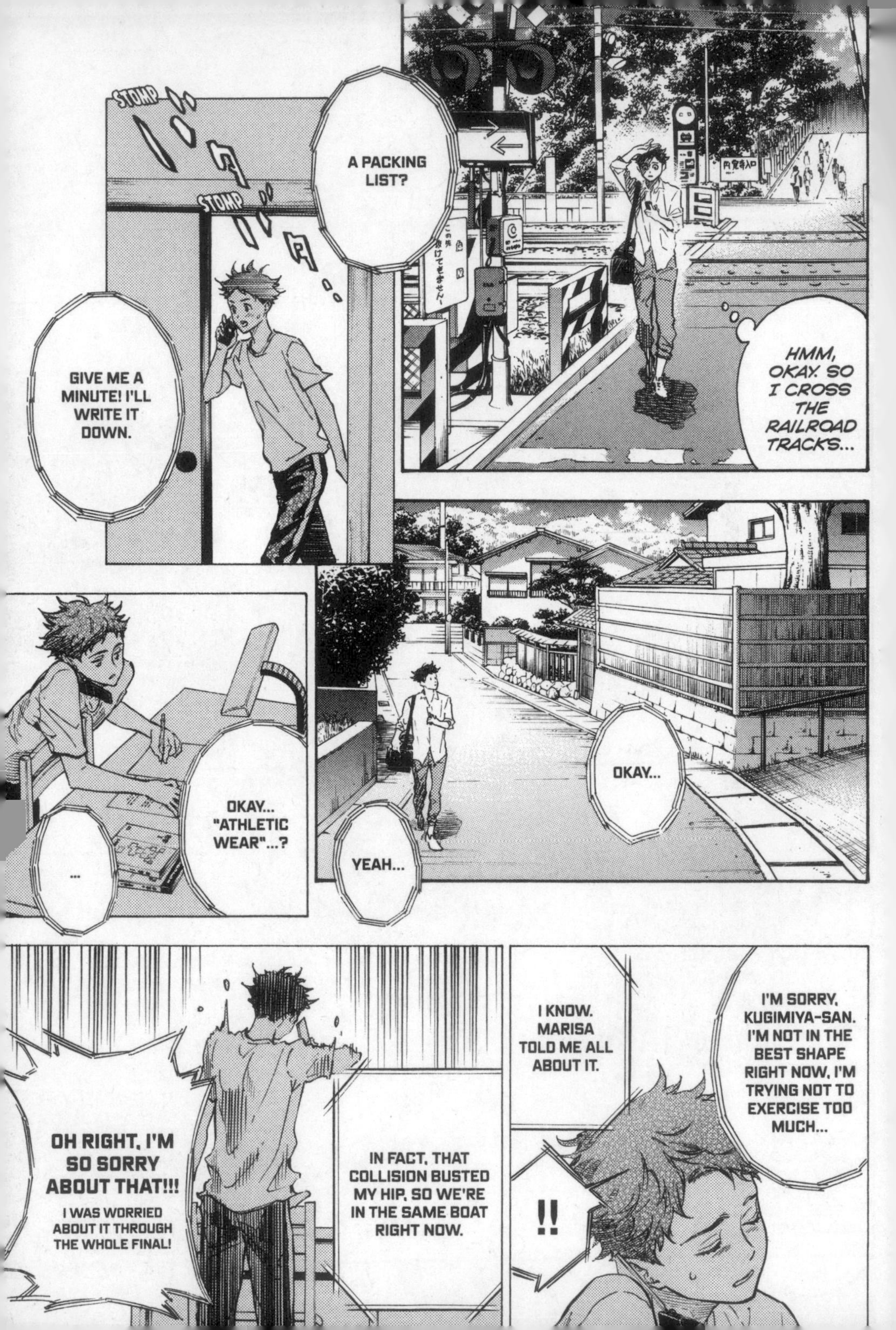

HMM, OKAY. SO I CROSS THE RAILROAD TRACKS...
A PACKING LIST?
STOMP
STOMP
GIVE ME A MINUTE! I'LL WRITE IT DOWN.
OKAY...
YEAH...
OKAY... "ATHLETIC WEAR"...?
...
I'M SORRY, KUGIMIYA-SAN. I'M NOT IN THE BEST SHAPE RIGHT NOW, I'M TRYING NOT TO EXERCISE TOO MUCH...
I KNOW. MARISA TOLD ME ALL ABOUT IT.
!!
IN FACT, THAT COLLISION BUSTED MY HIP, SO WE'RE IN THE SAME BOAT RIGHT NOW.
OH RIGHT, I'M SO SORRY ABOUT THAT!!!
I WAS WORRIED ABOUT IT THROUGH THE WHOLE FINAL!

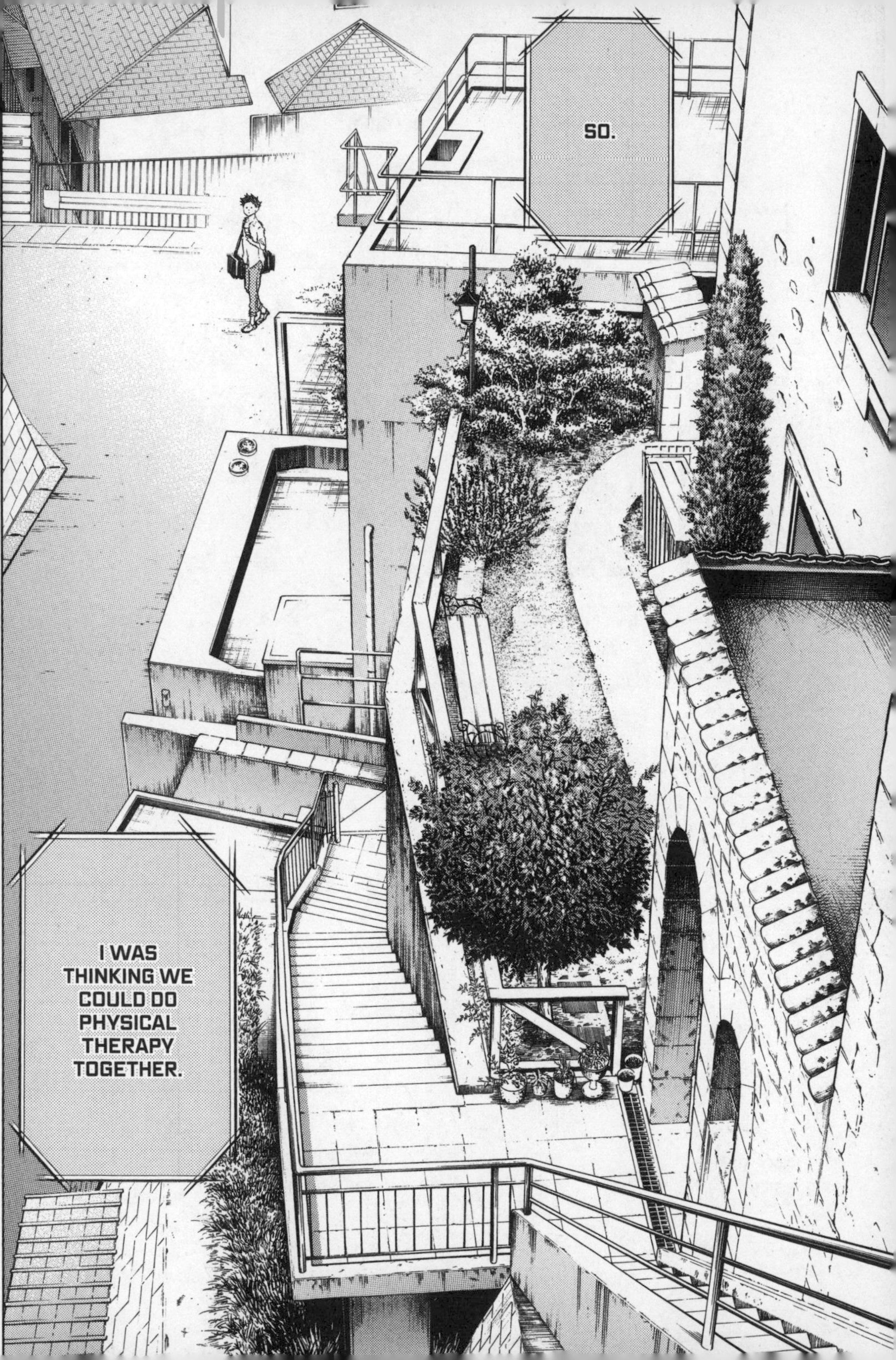
SO.
I WAS THINKING WE COULD DO PHYSICAL THERAPY TOGETHER.

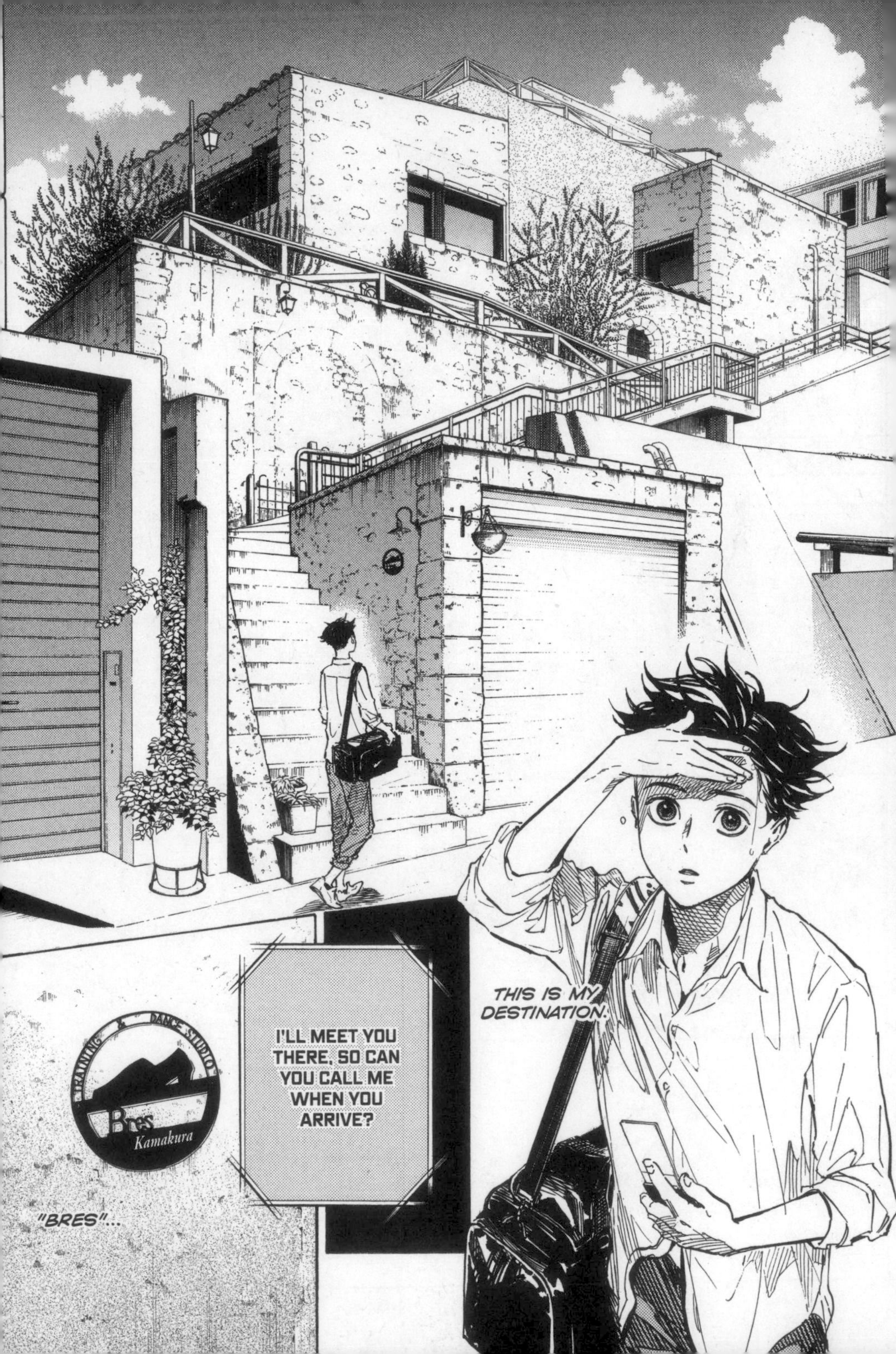
THIS IS MY DESTINATION.
I'LL MEET YOU THERE, SO CAN YOU CALL ME WHEN YOU ARRIVE?
TRAINING & DANCE STUDIO
Bres
Kamakura
"BRES"...

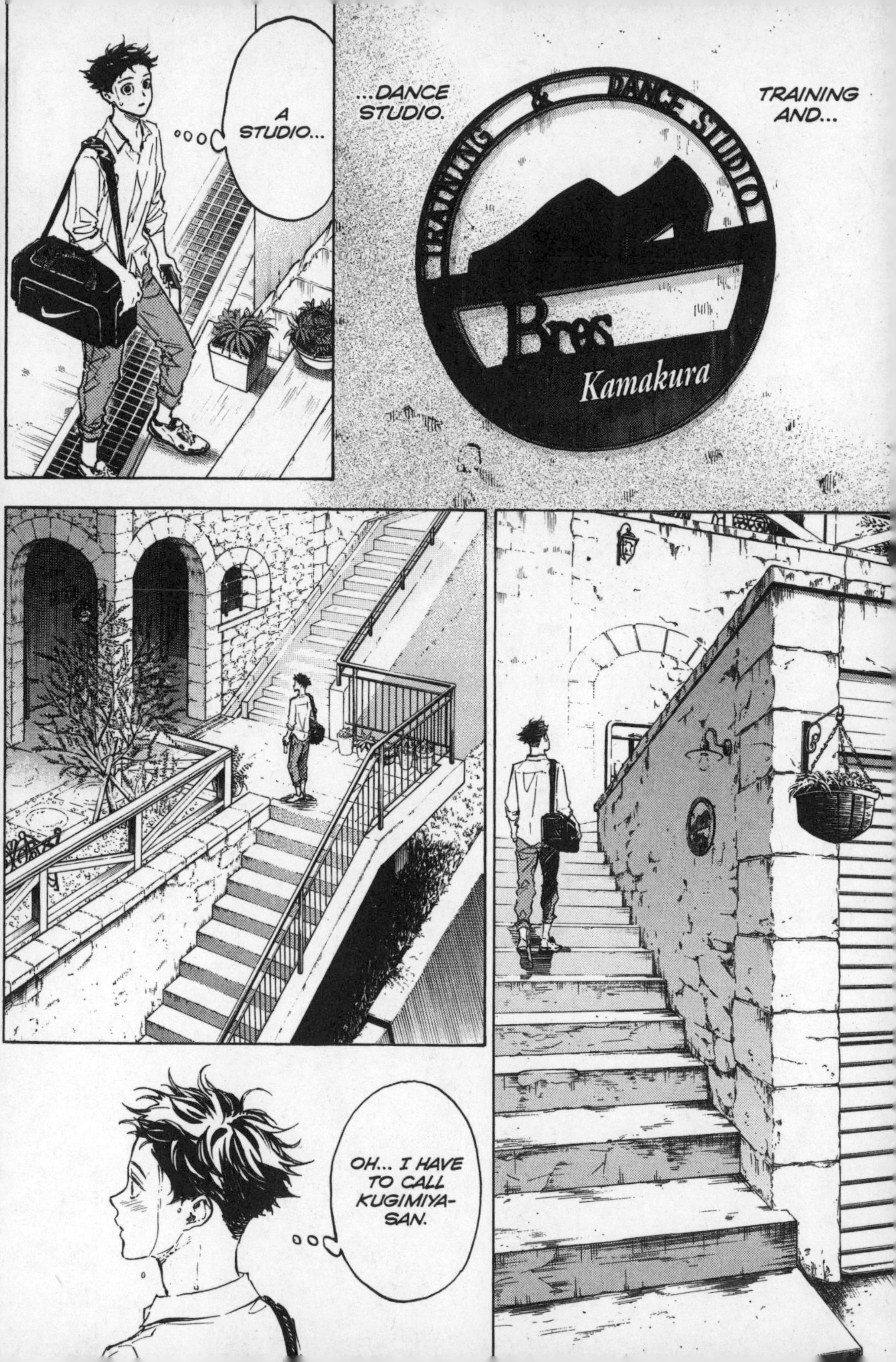
TRAINING AND...
TRAINING & DANCE STUDIO
Bres
Kamakura
...DANCE STUDIO.
A STUDIO...
OH... I HAVE TO CALL KUGIMIYA-SAN.

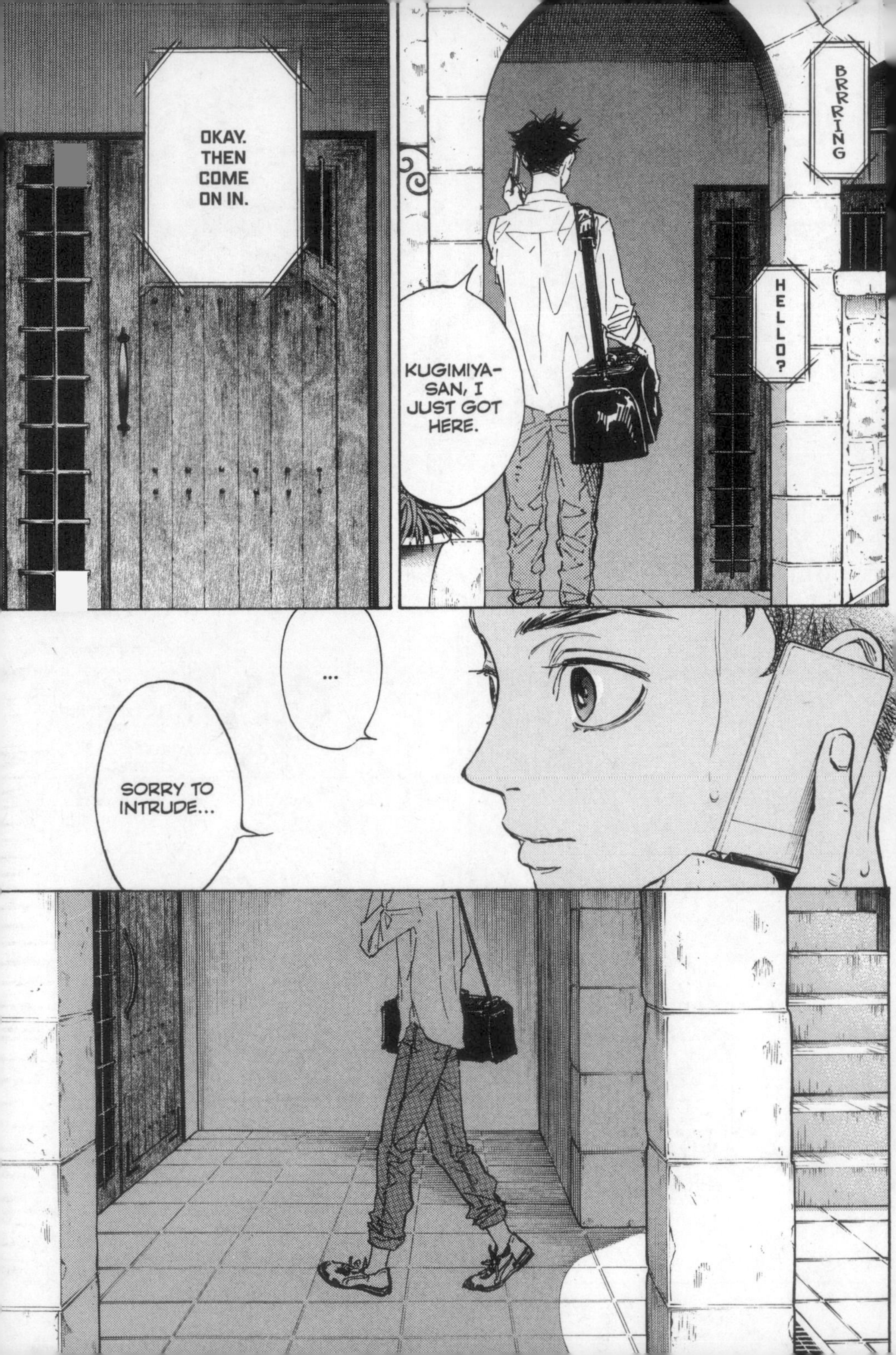
BRRRING
HELLO?
KUGIMIYA-SAN, I JUST GOT HERE.
OKAY. THEN COME ON IN.
...
SORRY TO INTRUDE...

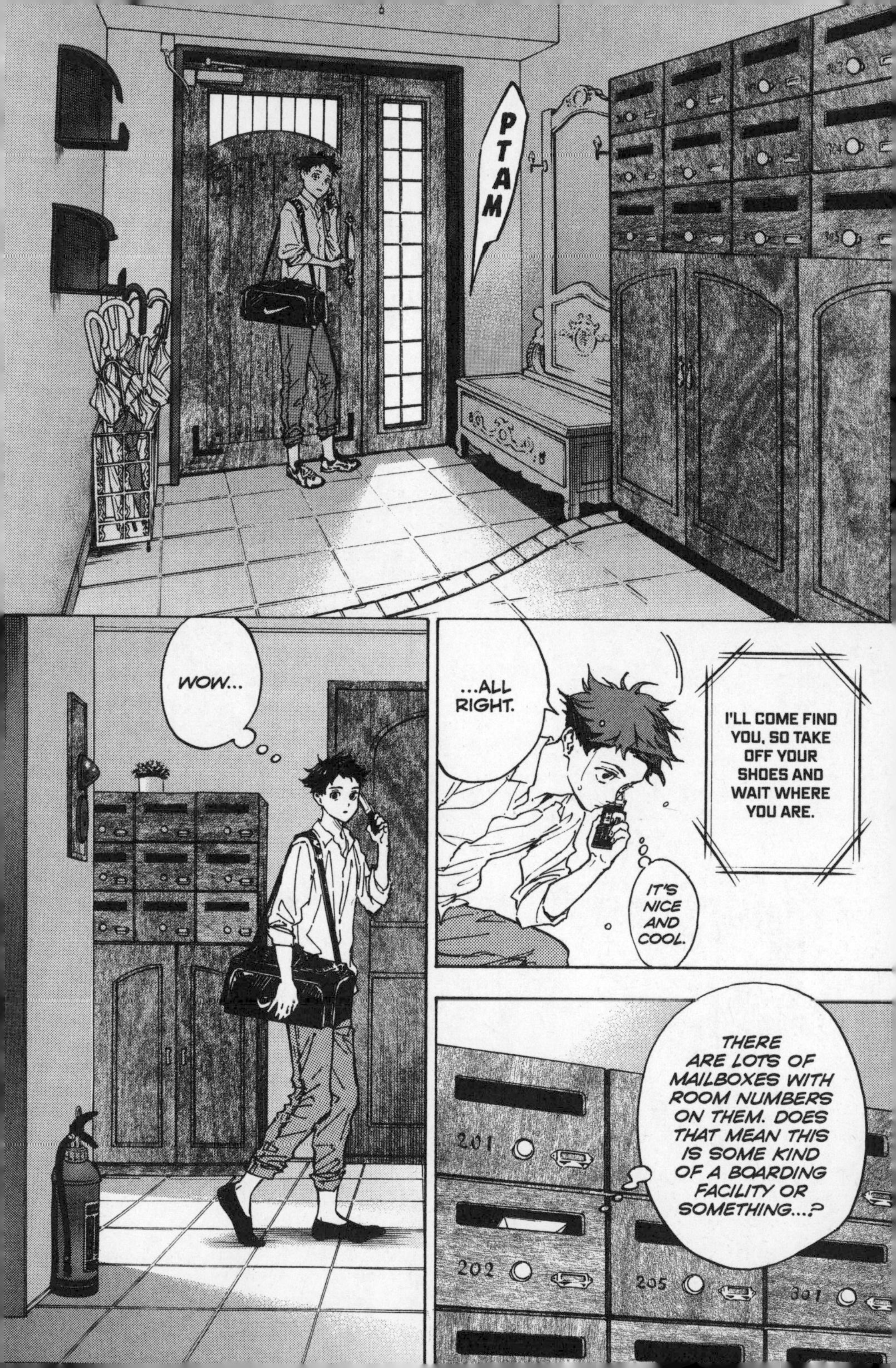
PTAM
I'LL COME FIND YOU, SO TAKE OFF YOUR SHOES AND WAIT WHERE YOU ARE.
...ALL RIGHT.
IT'S NICE AND COOL.
THERE ARE LOTS OF MAILBOXES WITH ROOM NUMBERS ON THEM. DOES THAT MEAN THIS IS SOME KIND OF A BOARDING FACILITY OR SOMETHING...?
201
202
205
301
WOW...

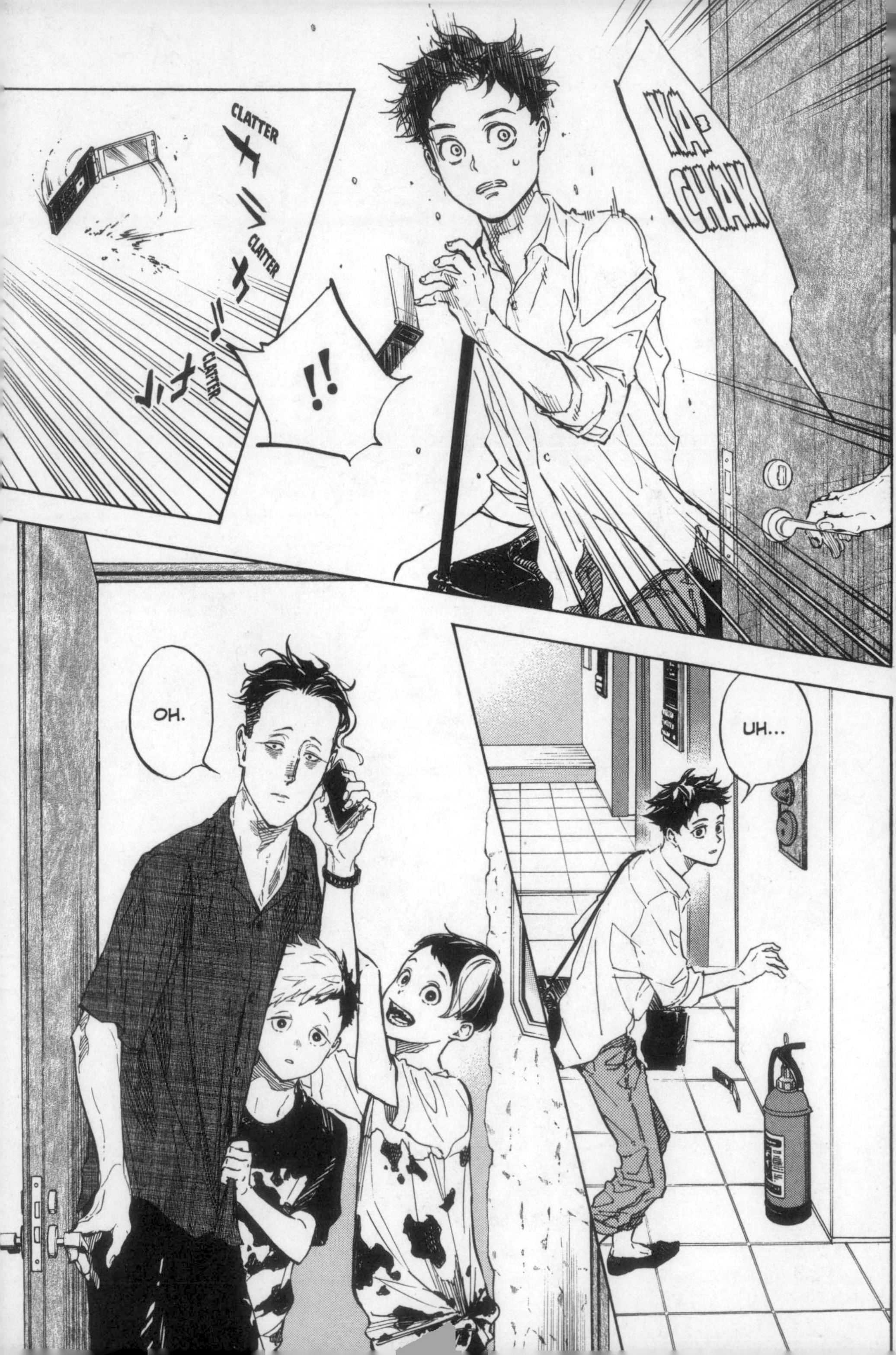
KA-CHAK
!!
CLATTER
CLATTER
CLATTER
CLATTER
UH...
OH.

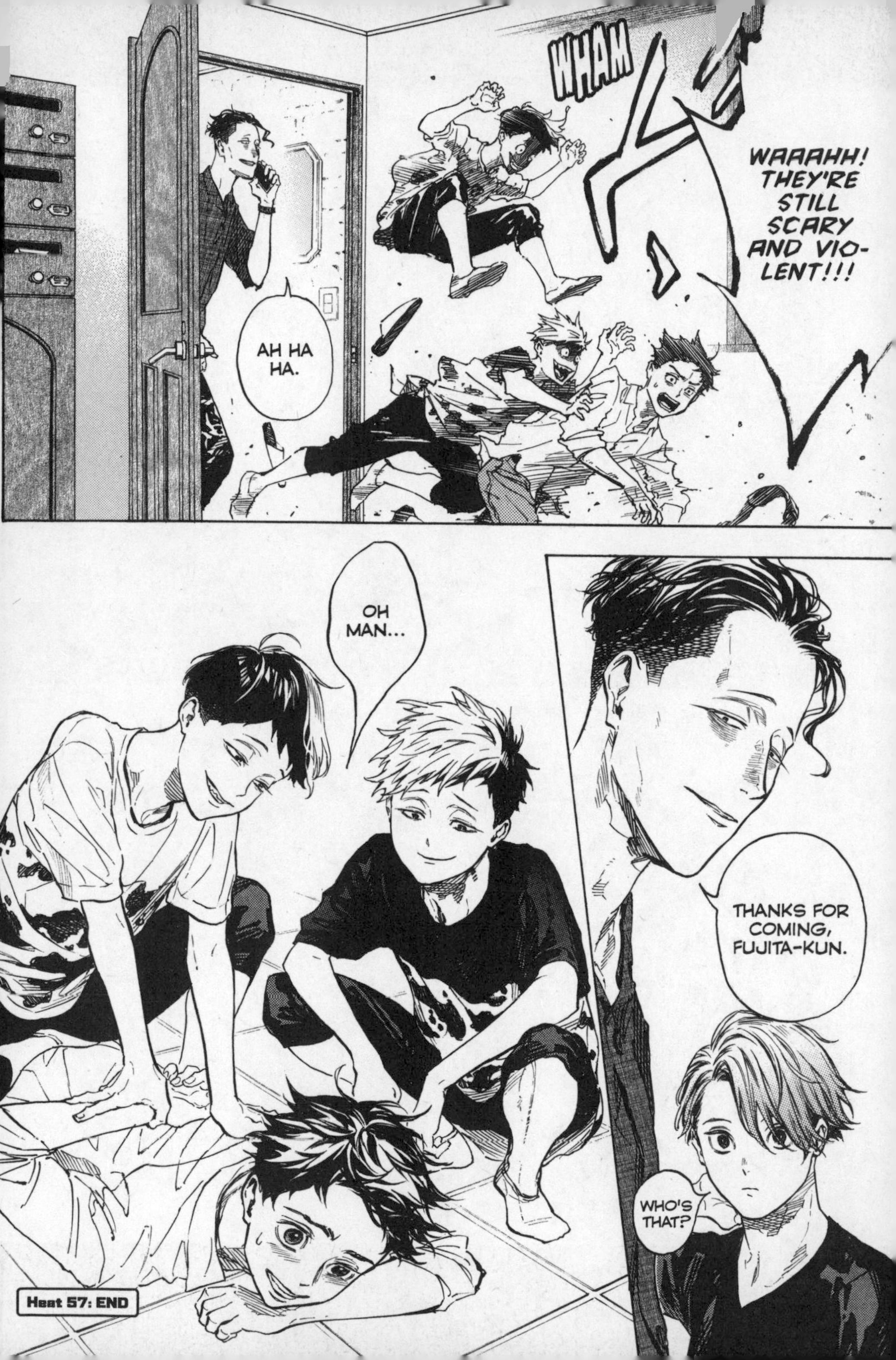
WHAM
WAAAHH! THEY'RE STILL SCARY AND VIO-LENT!!!
AH HA HA.
THANKS FOR COMING, FUJITA-KUN.
WHO'S THAT?
OH MAN...
Heat 57: END

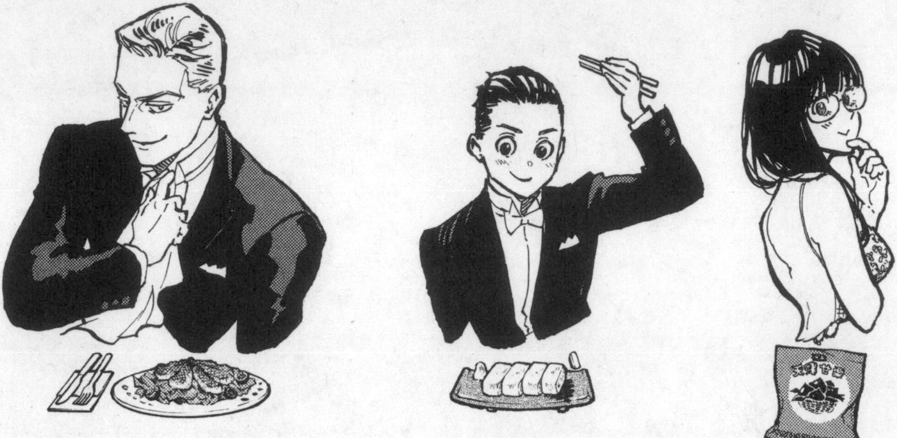

Extra Heat
Anime Blu-ray & DVD Bonus Features Short Stories

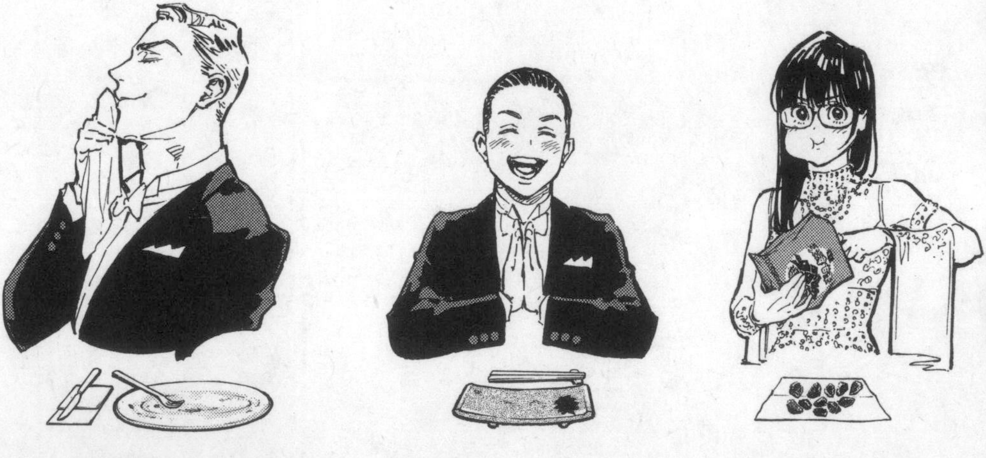

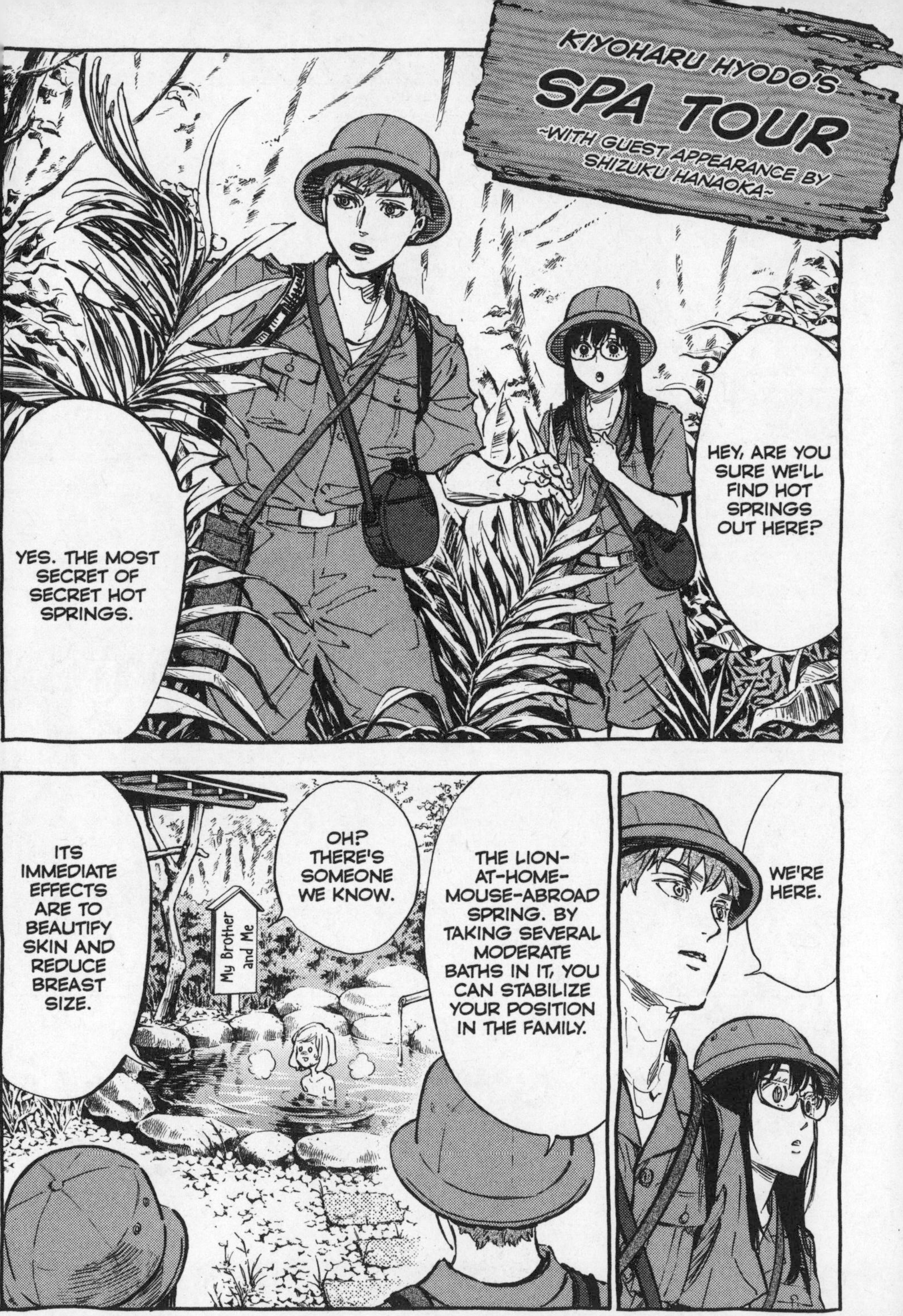
KIYOHARU HYODO'S
SPA TOUR
~WITH GUEST APPEARANCE BY SHIZUKU HANAOKA~
HEY, ARE YOU SURE WE'LL FIND HOT SPRINGS OUT HERE?
YES. THE MOST SECRET OF SECRET HOT SPRINGS.
WE'RE HERE.
THE LION-AT-HOME-MOUSE-ABROAD SPRING. BY TAKING SEVERAL MODERATE BATHS IN IT, YOU CAN STABILIZE YOUR POSITION IN THE FAMILY.
OH? THERE'S SOMEONE WE KNOW.
My Brother and Me
ITS IMMEDIATE EFFECTS ARE TO BEAUTIFY SKIN AND REDUCE BREAST SIZE.

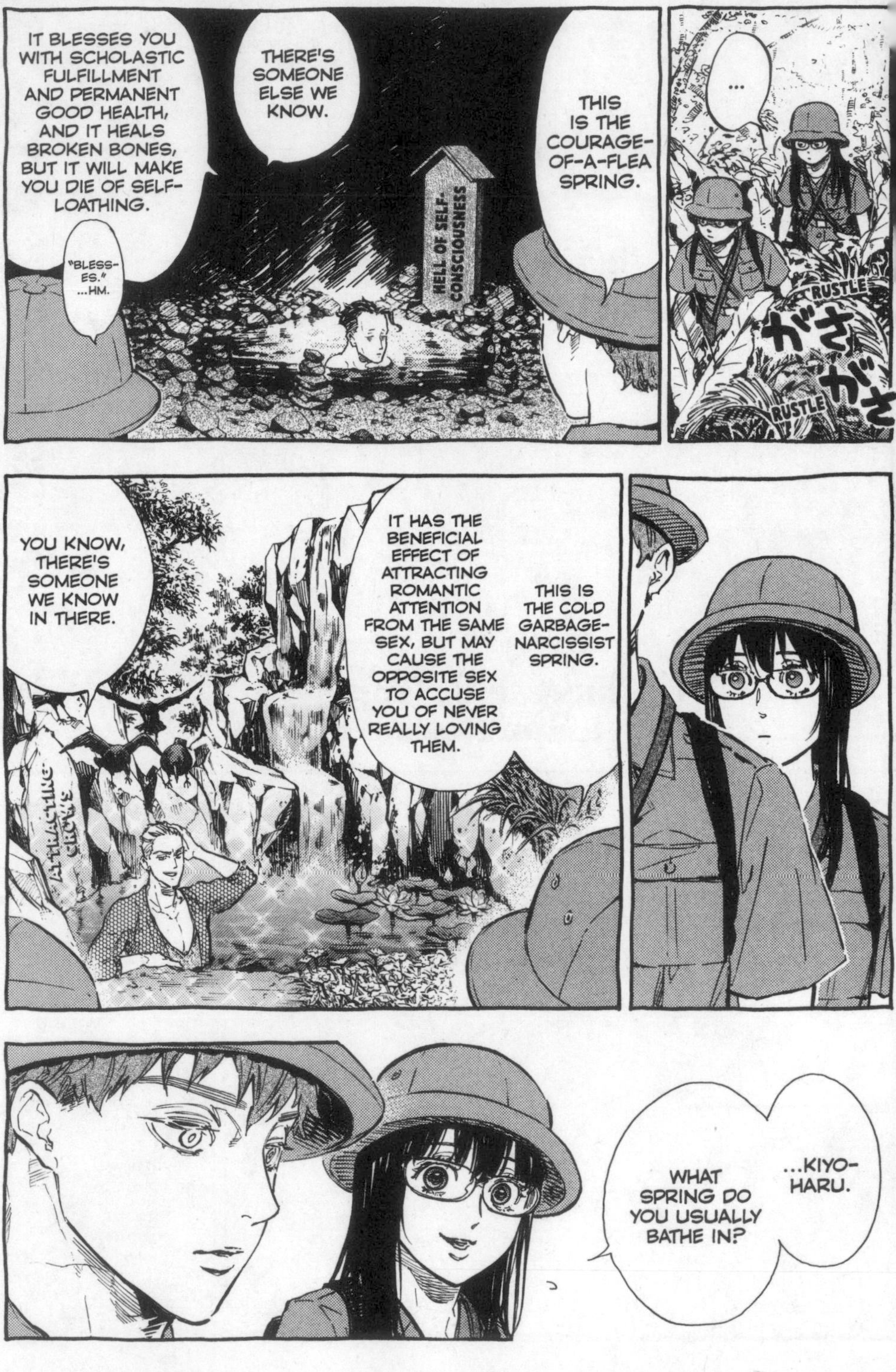
...
RUSTLE
がさ
RUSTLE
がさ
THIS IS THE COURAGE-OF-A-FLEA SPRING.
THERE'S SOMEONE ELSE WE KNOW.
HELL OF SELF-CONSCIOUSNESS
IT BLESSES YOU WITH SCHOLASTIC FULFILLMENT AND PERMANENT GOOD HEALTH, AND IT HEALS BROKEN BONES, BUT IT WILL MAKE YOU DIE OF SELF-LOATHING.
"BLESS-ES." ...HM.
THIS IS THE COLD GARBAGE-NARCISSIST SPRING.
IT HAS THE BENEFICIAL EFFECT OF ATTRACTING ROMANTIC ATTENTION FROM THE SAME SEX, BUT MAY CAUSE THE OPPOSITE SEX TO ACCUSE YOU OF NEVER REALLY LOVING THEM.
YOU KNOW, THERE'S SOMEONE WE KNOW IN THERE.
ATTRACTING CROWS
...KIYO-HARU.
WHAT SPRING DO YOU USUALLY BATHE IN?

I DON'T WANT THE MANGA LIKE THIS I DON'T WANT THE MANGA LIKE THIS I DON'T WANT THE MANGA LIKE THIS I DON'T WANT THE MANGA LIKE THIS NOPE CAN'T DO IT

THE STORY SO FAR:
THERE IS A CERTAIN FAMOUS PRIVATE SCHOOL IN THE CITY, WHICH IS FAMOUS FOR BEING SUPER MERITOCRATIC, WITH A POLICY OF "SKILL IN COMPETITIVE DANCE IS EVERYTHING"! IN AN ATTEMPT TO GET CLOSER TO THE APPLE OF HER EYE, TRANSFER STUDENT AND 16-YEAR-OLD HIGH SCHOOL GIRL YOSHINORI IWAKUMA (AGE 33), APPROACHES THE BESPECTACLED PRETTY BOY REI MINO. BUT SHE IS STOPPED BY THE STUDENT COUNCIL'S MERCILESS BAG INSPECTION...! MEANWHILE, IN THE NEIGHBORING CLASSROOM, TATARA, KIYOHARU, AND GAJU ARE HAVING A DEBATE ON THE PROPER WAY FOR A BOY AND GIRL TO HAVE A WHOLESOME RELATIONSHIP.

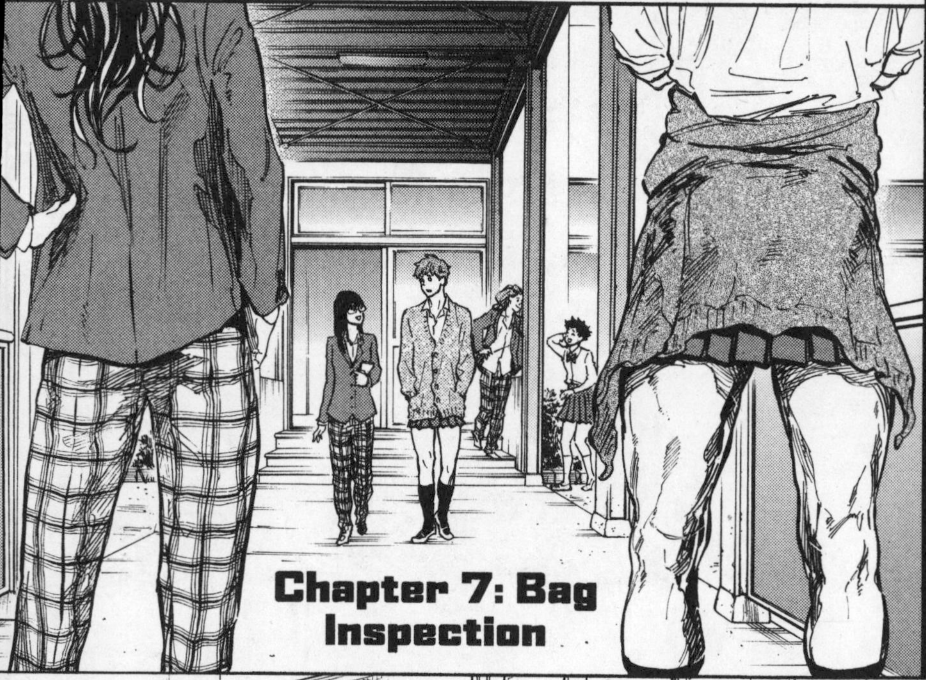
Chapter 7: Bag Inspection

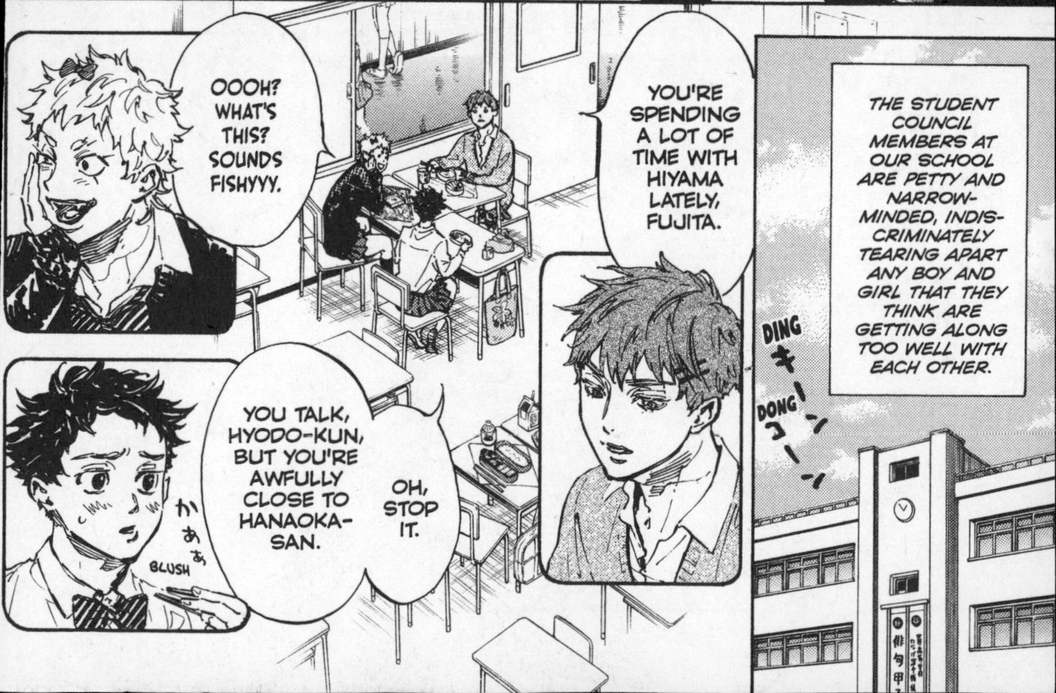
THE STUDENT COUNCIL MEMBERS AT OUR SCHOOL ARE PETTY AND NARROW-MINDED, INDIS-CRIMINATELY TEARING APART ANY BOY AND GIRL THAT THEY THINK ARE GETTING ALONG TOO WELL WITH EACH OTHER.
DING
DONG
YOU'RE SPENDING A LOT OF TIME WITH HIYAMA LATELY, FUJITA.
OOOH? WHAT'S THIS? SOUNDS FISHYYY.
OH, STOP IT.
YOU TALK, HYODO-KUN, BUT YOU'RE AWFULLY CLOSE TO HANAOKA-SAN.
BLUSH

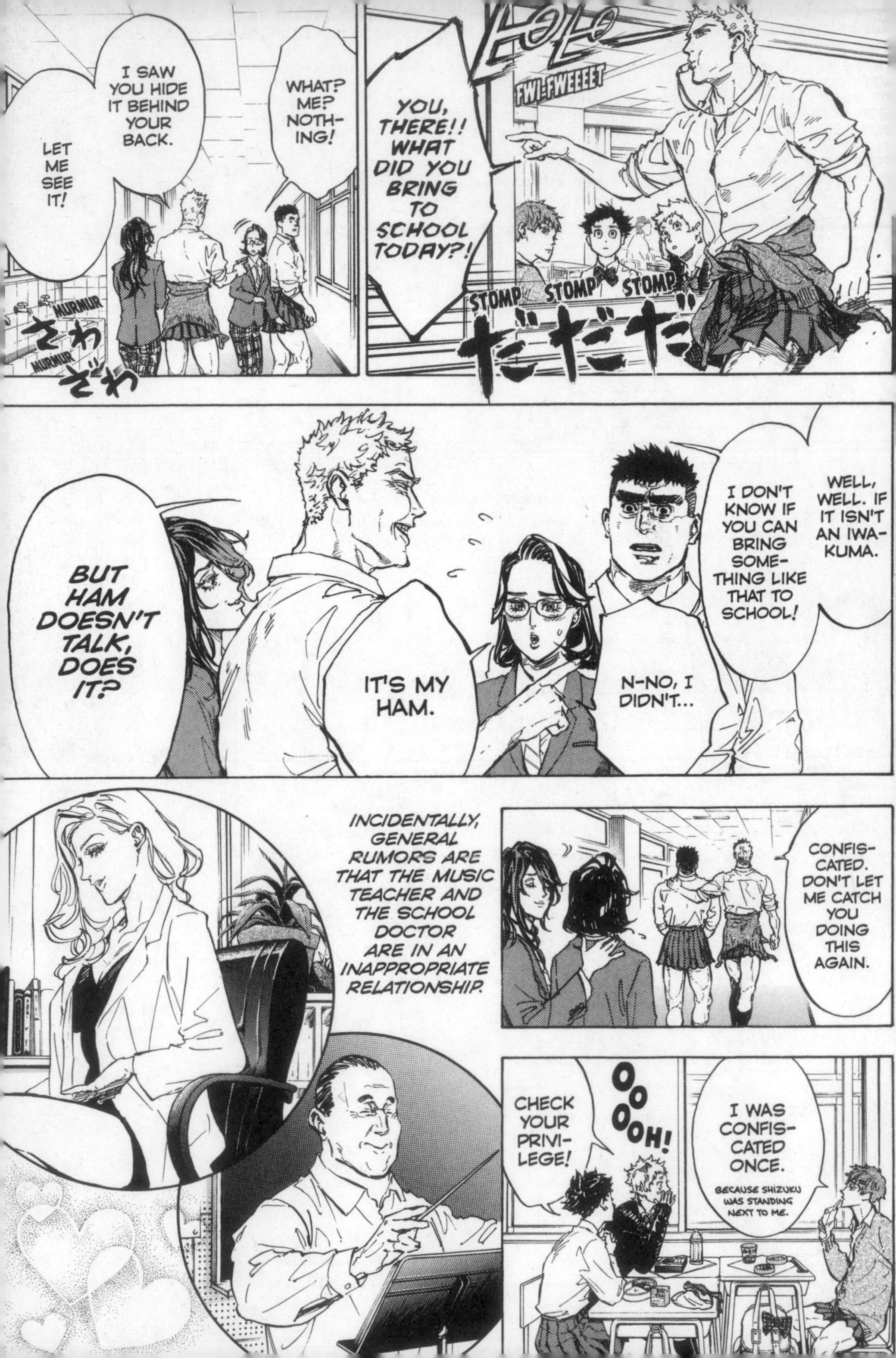
FWI-FWEEEET
YOU, THERE!! WHAT DID YOU BRING TO SCHOOL TODAY?!
STOMP STOMP STOMP
だだだ
WHAT? ME? NOTHING!
I SAW YOU HIDE IT BEHIND YOUR BACK.
LET ME SEE IT!
MURMUR
さわ
MURMUR
ざわ
WELL, WELL. IF IT ISN'T AN IWAKUMA.
I DON'T KNOW IF YOU CAN BRING SOMETHING LIKE THAT TO SCHOOL!
N-NO, I DIDN'T...
IT'S MY HAM.
BUT HAM DOESN'T TALK, DOES IT?
CONFISCATED. DON'T LET ME CATCH YOU DOING THIS AGAIN.
I WAS CONFISCATED ONCE.
BECAUSE SHIZUKU WAS STANDING NEXT TO ME.
OOOOH!
CHECK YOUR PRIVILEGE!
INCIDENTALLY, GENERAL RUMORS ARE THAT THE MUSIC TEACHER AND THE SCHOOL DOCTOR ARE IN AN INAPPROPRIATE RELATIONSHIP.

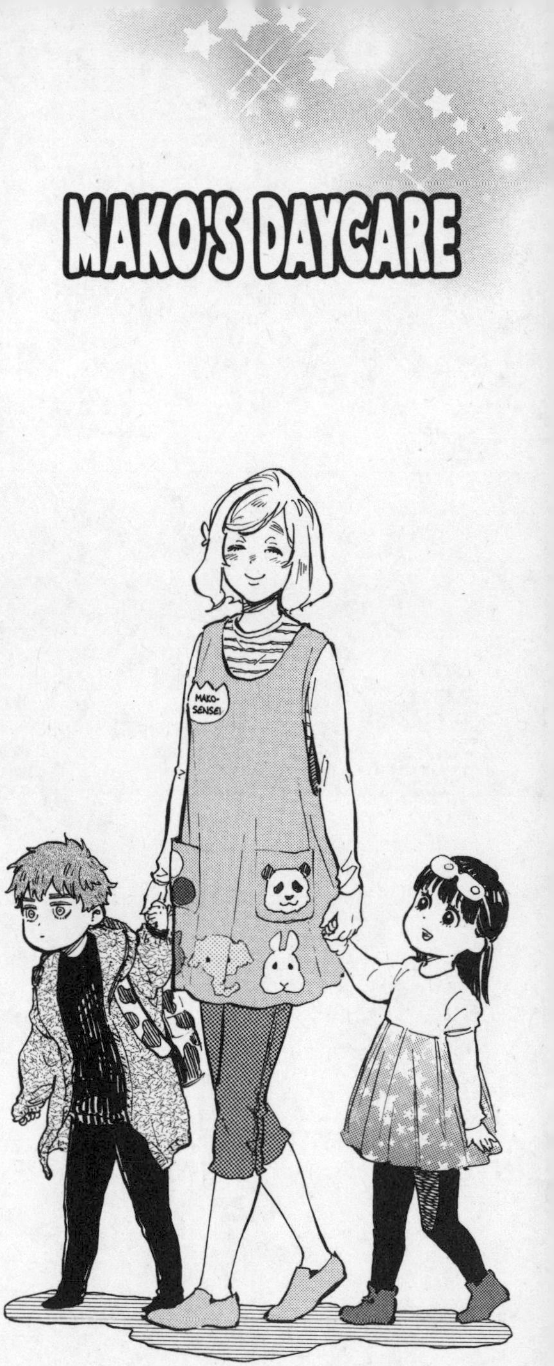
MAKO'S DAYCARE
MAKO-SENSEI
BASED ON INFORMATION IN THE FANBOOK:
"MAKO'S DREAM PROFESSION: DAYCARE TEACHER"

MARRIAGE

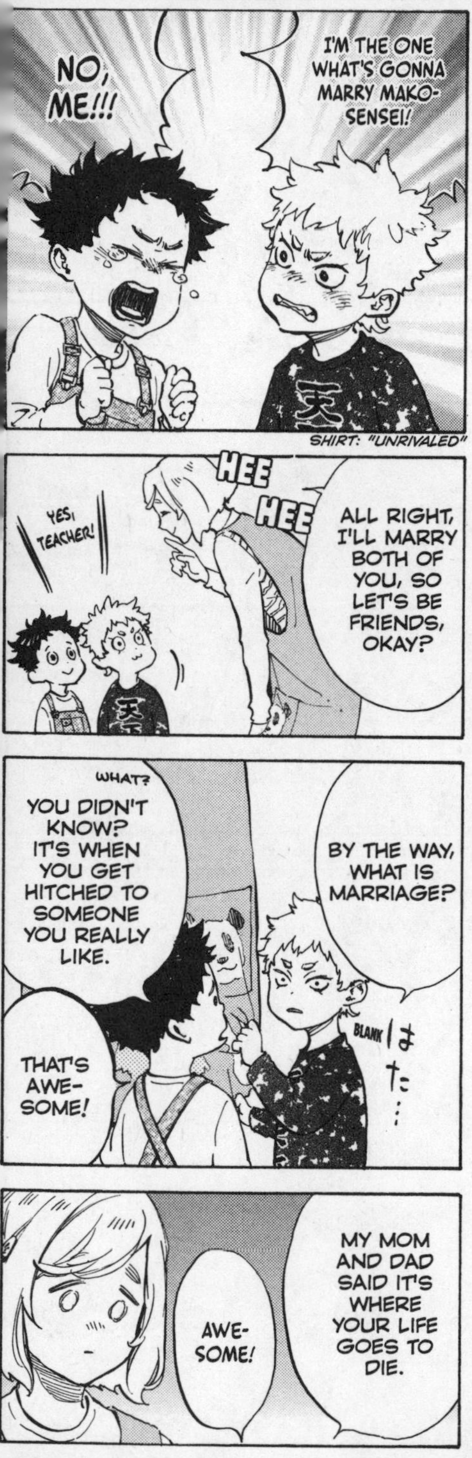
I'M THE ONE WHAT'S GONNA MARRY MAKO-SENSEI!
NO, ME!!!
SHIRT: "UNRIVALED"
ALL RIGHT, I'LL MARRY BOTH OF YOU, SO LET'S BE FRIENDS, OKAY?
HEE HEE
YES, TEACHER!
BY THE WAY, WHAT IS MARRIAGE?
BLANK
WHAT?
YOU DIDN'T KNOW? IT'S WHEN YOU GET HITCHED TO SOMEONE YOU REALLY LIKE.
THAT'S AWESOME!
MY MOM AND DAD SAID IT'S WHERE YOUR LIFE GOES TO DIE.
AWE-SOME!

TRAIN

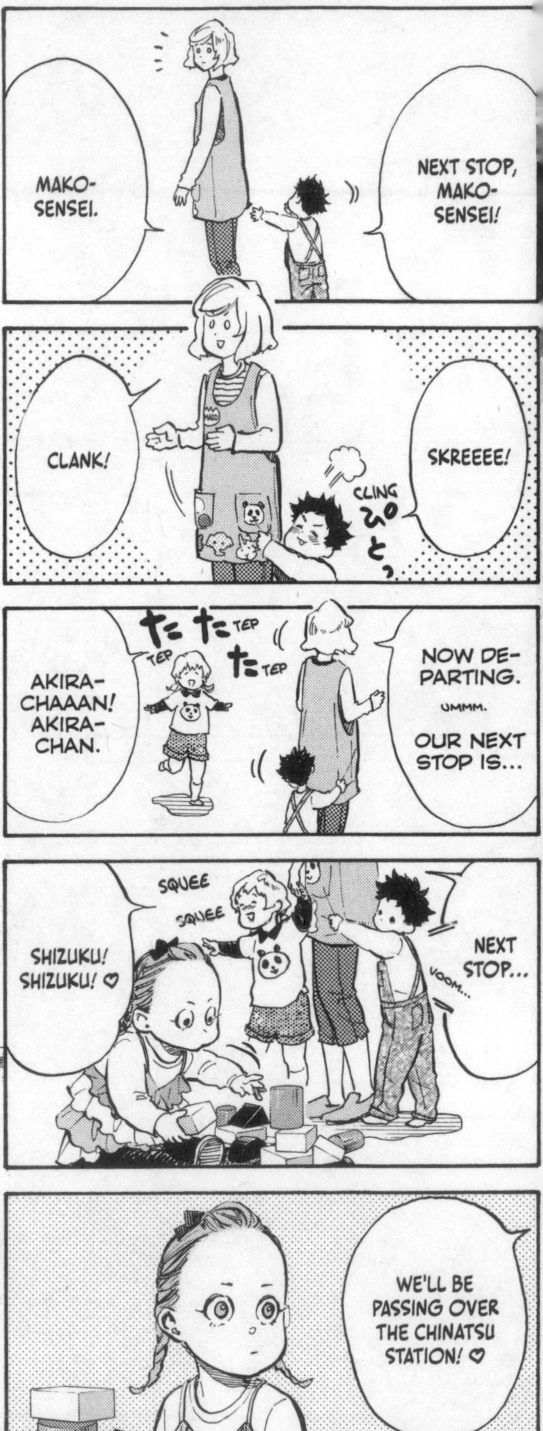
NEXT STOP, MAKO-SENSEI!
MAKO-SENSEI.
SKREEEE!
CLING
CLANK!
NOW DEPARTING.
UMMM.
OUR NEXT STOP IS...
TEP
TEP
TEP
TEP
AKIRA-CHAAAN! AKIRA-CHAN.
NEXT STOP...
VOOM...
SQUEE
SQUEE
SHIZUKU! SHIZUKU! ♡
WE'LL BE PASSING OVER THE CHINATSU STATION! ♡

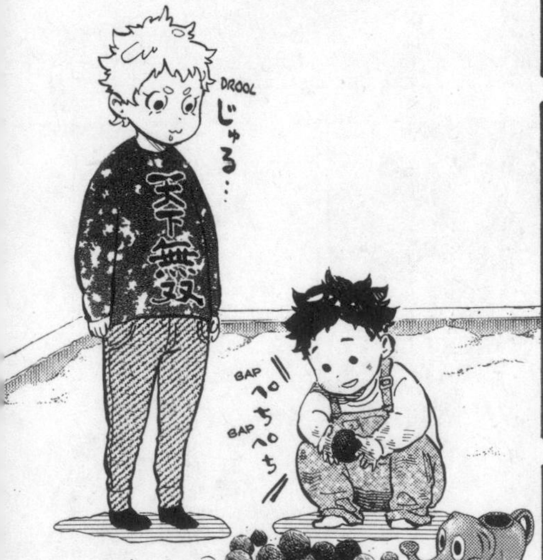
DROOL
じゅる…
BAP
BAP

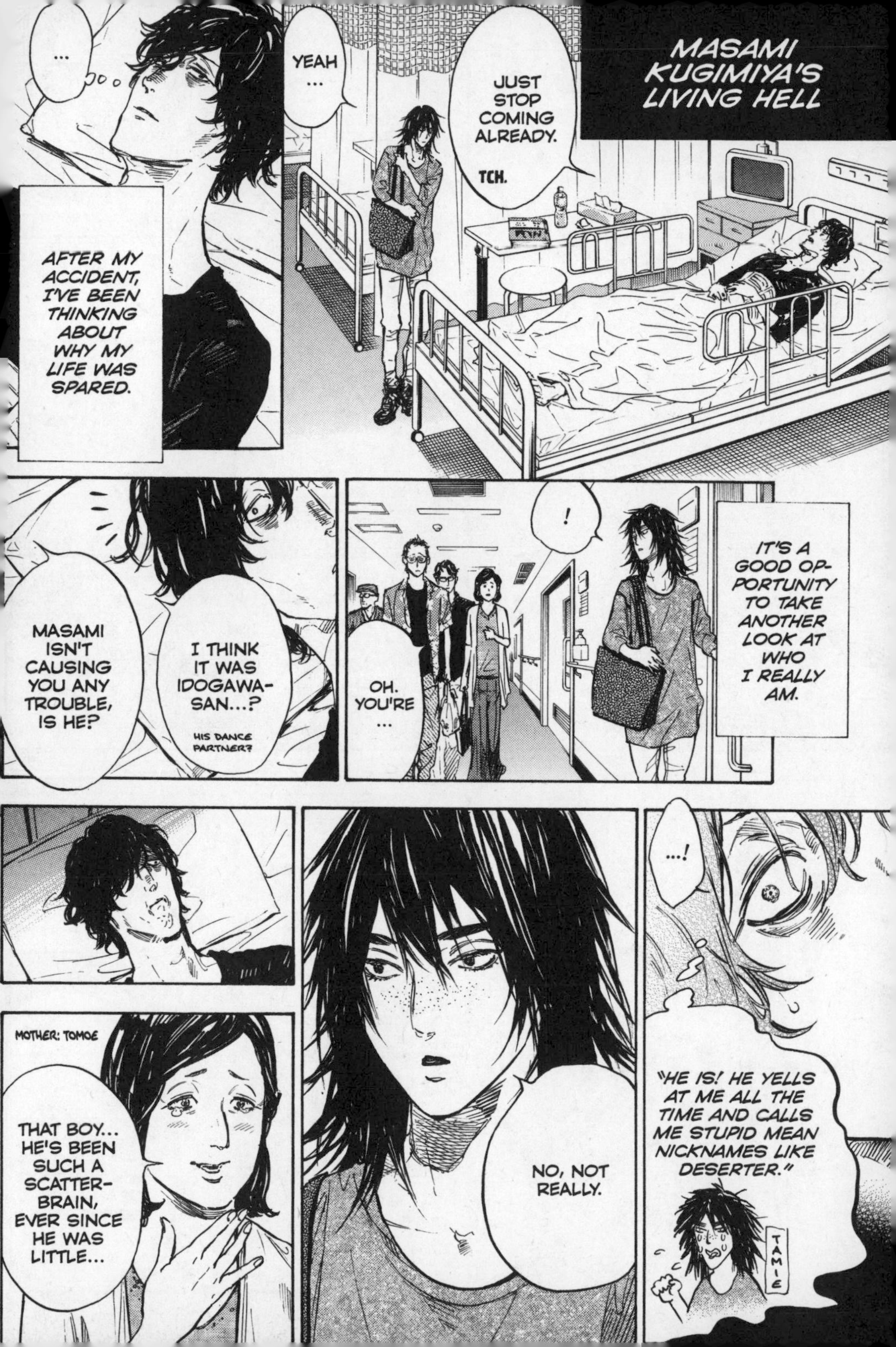
MASAMI KUGIMIYA'S LIVING HELL
JUST STOP COMING ALREADY.
TCH.
YEAH ...
...
AFTER MY ACCIDENT, I'VE BEEN THINKING ABOUT WHY MY LIFE WAS SPARED.
IT'S A GOOD OP-PORTUNITY TO TAKE ANOTHER LOOK AT WHO I REALLY AM.
!
OH. YOU'RE ...
I THINK IT WAS IDOGAWA-SAN...?
HIS DANCE PARTNER?
MASAMI ISN'T CAUSING YOU ANY TROUBLE, IS HE?
...!
"HE IS! HE YELLS AT ME ALL THE TIME AND CALLS ME STUPID MEAN NICKNAMES LIKE DESERTER."
TAMIE
NO, NOT REALLY.
MOTHER: TOMOE
THAT BOY... HE'S BEEN SUCH A SCATTER-BRAIN, EVER SINCE HE WAS LITTLE...

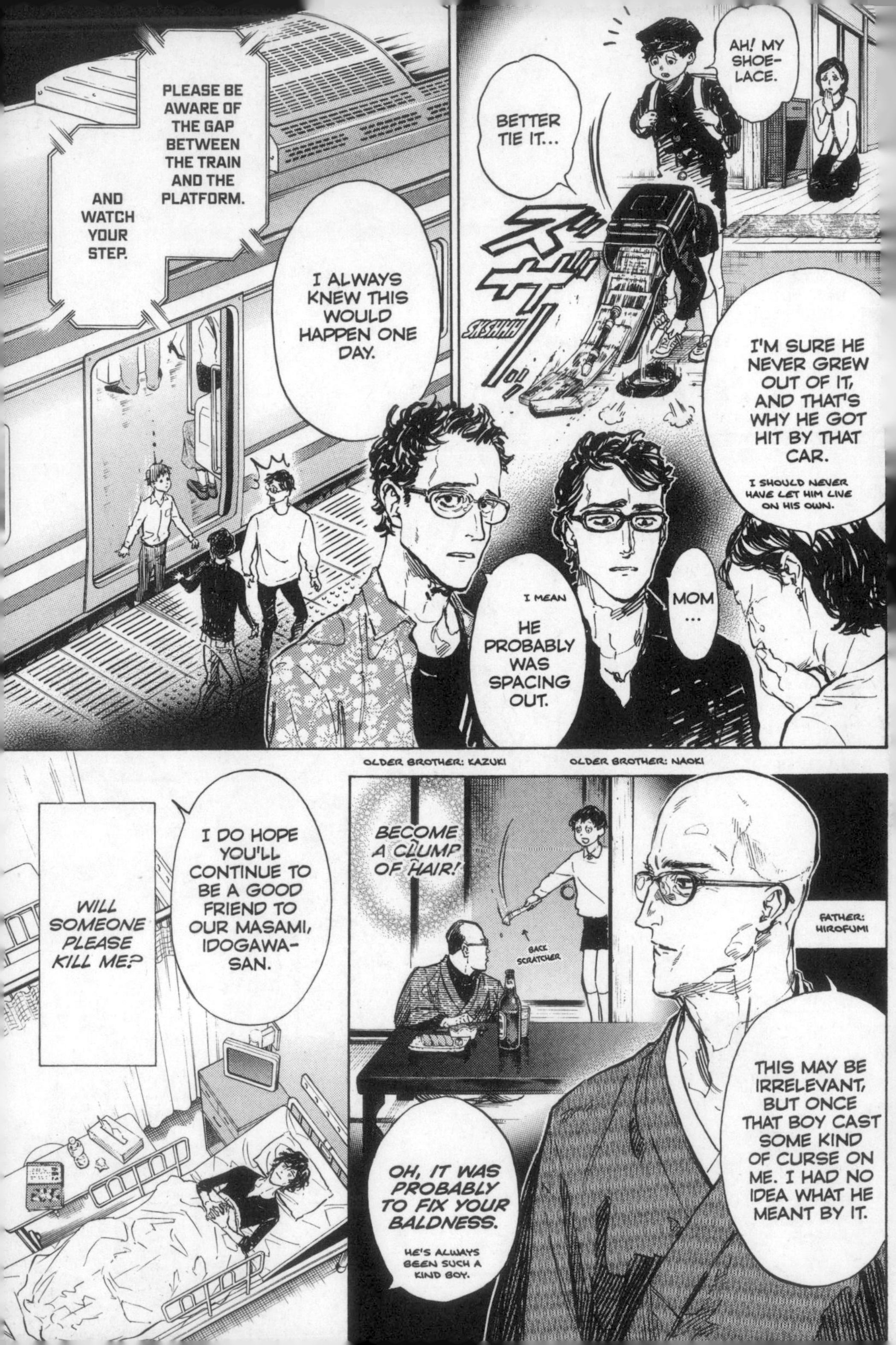
AH! MY SHOE-LACE.
BETTER TIE IT...
SKSHHH
I'M SURE HE NEVER GREW OUT OF IT, AND THAT'S WHY HE GOT HIT BY THAT CAR.
I SHOULD NEVER HAVE LET HIM LIVE ON HIS OWN.
MOM...
I MEAN
HE PROBABLY WAS SPACING OUT.
I ALWAYS KNEW THIS WOULD HAPPEN ONE DAY.
PLEASE BE AWARE OF THE GAP BETWEEN THE TRAIN AND THE PLATFORM.
AND WATCH YOUR STEP.
OLDER BROTHER: NAOKI
OLDER BROTHER: KAZUKI
FATHER: HIROFUMI
THIS MAY BE IRRELEVANT, BUT ONCE THAT BOY CAST SOME KIND OF CURSE ON ME. I HAD NO IDEA WHAT HE MEANT BY IT.
BECOME A CLUMP OF HAIR!
BACK SCRATCHER
OH, IT WAS PROBABLY TO FIX YOUR BALDNESS.
HE'S ALWAYS BEEN SUCH A KIND BOY.
I DO HOPE YOU'LL CONTINUE TO BE A GOOD FRIEND TO OUR MASAMI, IDOGAWA-SAN.
WILL SOMEONE PLEASE KILL ME?

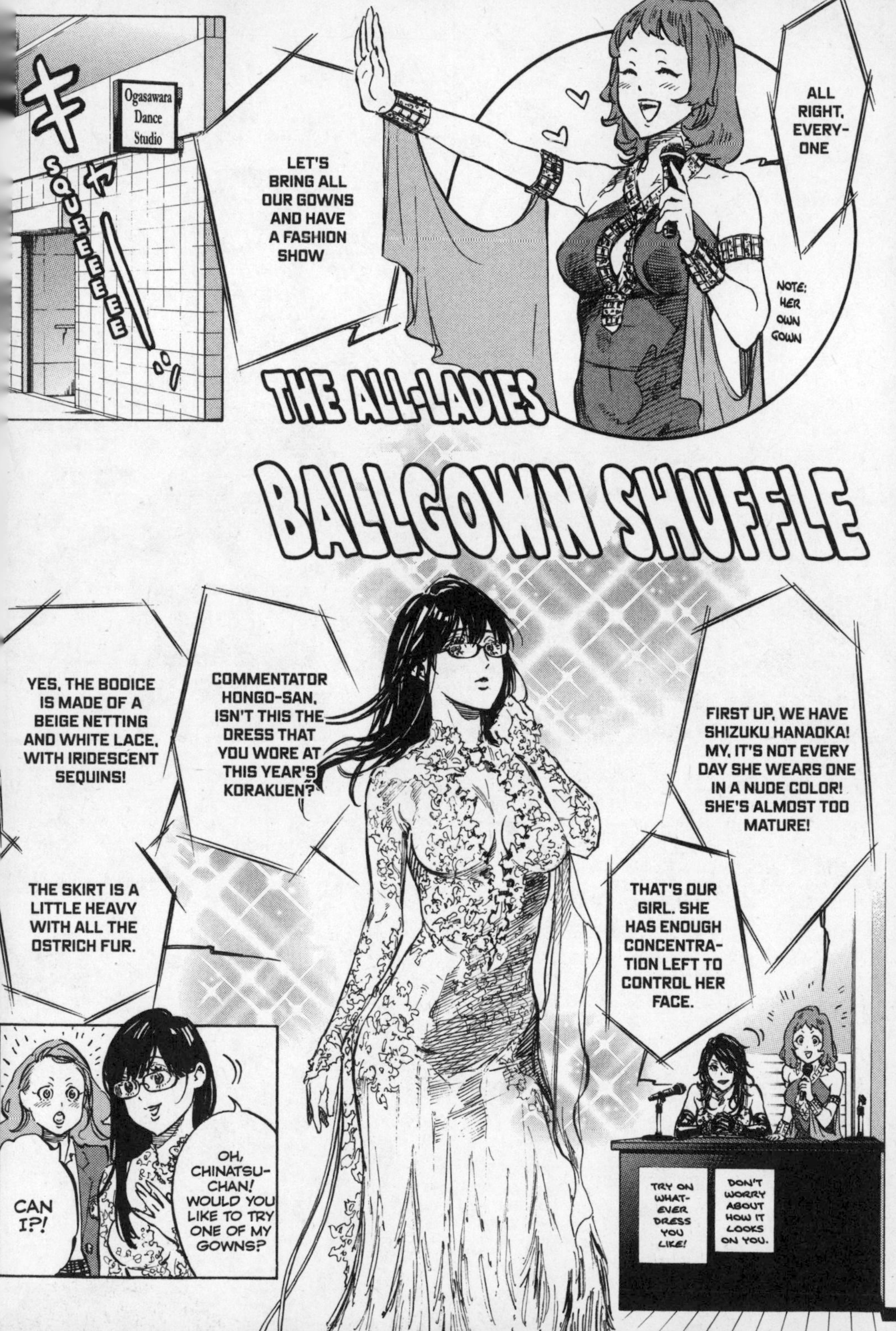
ALL RIGHT, EVERY-ONE
LET'S BRING ALL OUR GOWNS AND HAVE A FASHION SHOW
NOTE: HER OWN GOWN
THE ALL-LADIES
BALLGOWN SHUFFLE
Ogasawara Dance Studio
キャ
SQUEEEEEEE
FIRST UP, WE HAVE SHIZUKU HANAOKA! MY, IT'S NOT EVERY DAY SHE WEARS ONE IN A NUDE COLOR! SHE'S ALMOST TOO MATURE!
COMMENTATOR HONGO-SAN, ISN'T THIS THE DRESS THAT YOU WORE AT THIS YEAR'S KORAKUEN?
YES, THE BODICE IS MADE OF A BEIGE NETTING AND WHITE LACE, WITH IRIDESCENT SEQUINS!
THAT'S OUR GIRL. SHE HAS ENOUGH CONCENTRA-TION LEFT TO CONTROL HER FACE.
THE SKIRT IS A LITTLE HEAVY WITH ALL THE OSTRICH FUR.
DON'T WORRY ABOUT HOW IT LOOKS ON YOU.
TRY ON WHAT-EVER DRESS YOU LIKE!
OH, CHINATSU-CHAN! WOULD YOU LIKE TO TRY ONE OF MY GOWNS?
CAN I?!

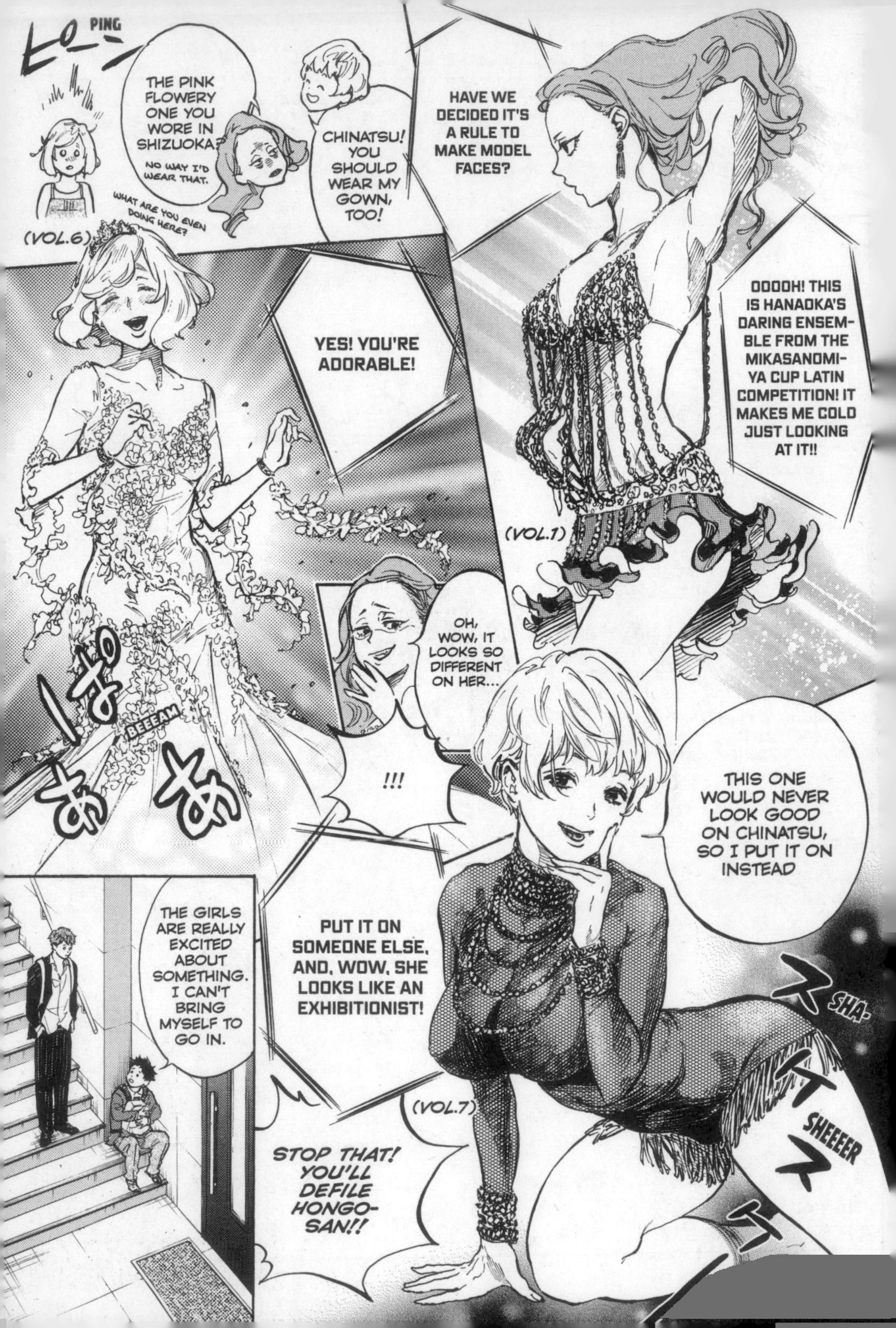
HAVE WE DECIDED IT'S A RULE TO MAKE MODEL FACES?
OOOOH! THIS IS HANAOKA'S DARING ENSEMBLE FROM THE MIKASANOMIYA CUP LATIN COMPETITION! IT MAKES ME COLD JUST LOOKING AT IT!!
(VOL.1)
CHINATSU! YOU SHOULD WEAR MY GOWN, TOO!
PING
THE PINK FLOWERY ONE YOU WORE IN SHIZUOKA?
NO WAY I'D WEAR THAT.
WHAT ARE YOU EVEN DOING HERE?
(VOL.6)
YES! YOU'RE ADORABLE!
OH, WOW, IT LOOKS SO DIFFERENT ON HER...
!!!
BEEEAM
THIS ONE WOULD NEVER LOOK GOOD ON CHINATSU, SO I PUT IT ON INSTEAD
SHA-
SHEEEER
(VOL.7)
PUT IT ON SOMEONE ELSE, AND, WOW, SHE LOOKS LIKE AN EXHIBITIONIST!
STOP THAT! YOU'LL DEFILE HONGO-SAN!!
THE GIRLS ARE REALLY EXCITED ABOUT SOMETHING. I CAN'T BRING MYSELF TO GO IN.

The Dancer Species

THEY HAVE A HABIT OF ARBITRARILY DECIDING IF SOMEONE WOULD DANCE LATIN OR STANDARD BASED ON PHYSIQUE AND FIRST IMPRESSION. (YES, EVEN IF THE OTHER PERSON IS NOT A DANCER.)

THEY THINK OF THE SWAYING OF A TRAIN AS "CORE TRAINING," AND REFUSE TO HOLD ON TO THE HAND STRAPS, ABSORBING ALL THE MOTION WITH THEIR BODIES. THEY SOMETIMES MOVE THEIR HEELS, TOO.

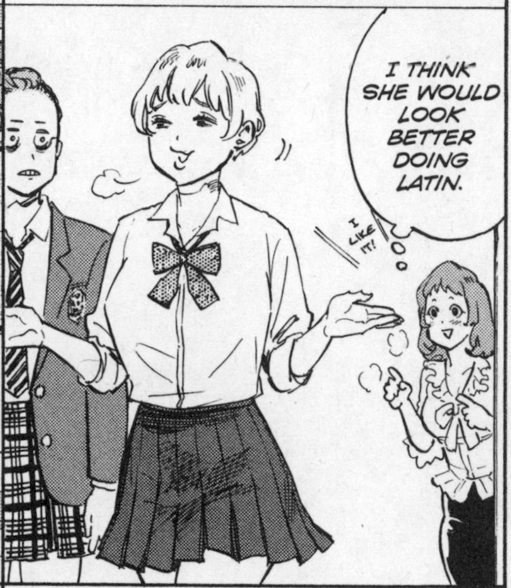
I THINK SHE WOULD LOOK BETTER DOING LATIN.
I LIKE IT!

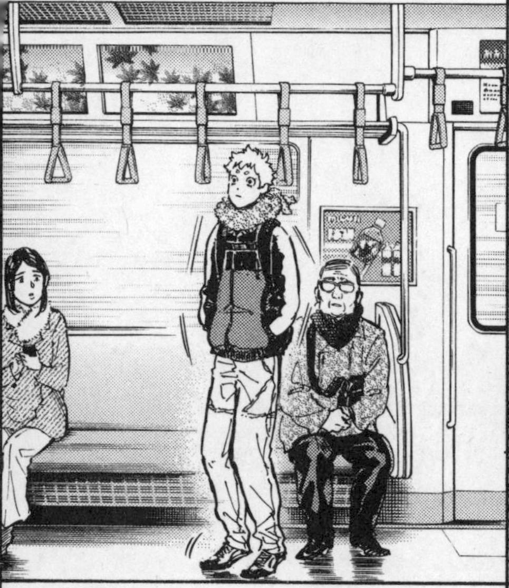

THEY SUBCONSCIOUSLY CATEGORIZE EVERY SONG THEY HEAR INTO A TYPE OF DANCE, AND SOMETIMES START DANCING IN THEIR HEADS.

WHEN THEY PUT THEIR HAIR UP, EVEN CLOSE ACQUAINTANCES DON'T KNOW WHO THEY ARE.

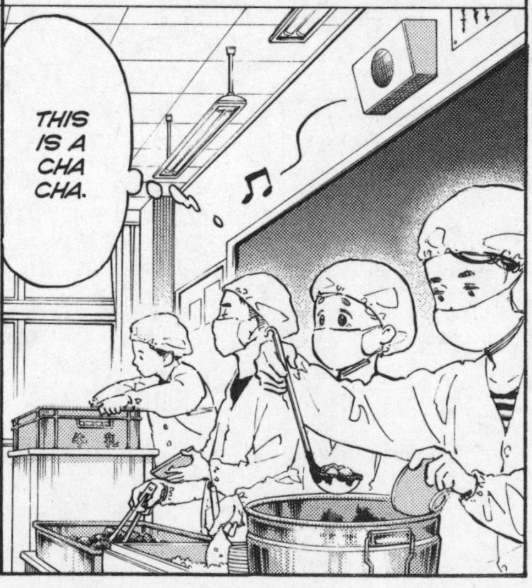
THIS IS A CHA CHA.

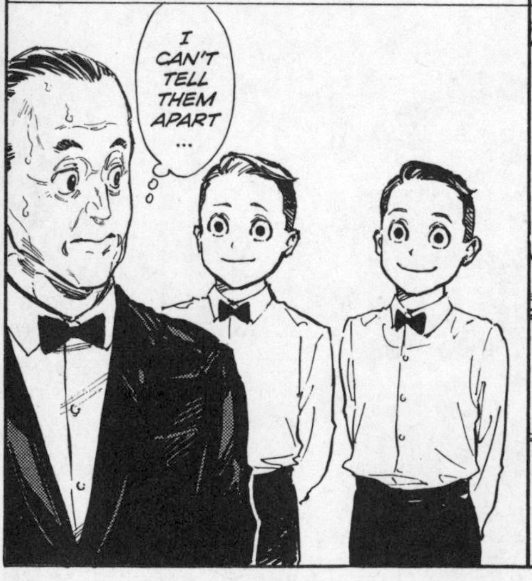
I CAN'T TELL THEM APART ...

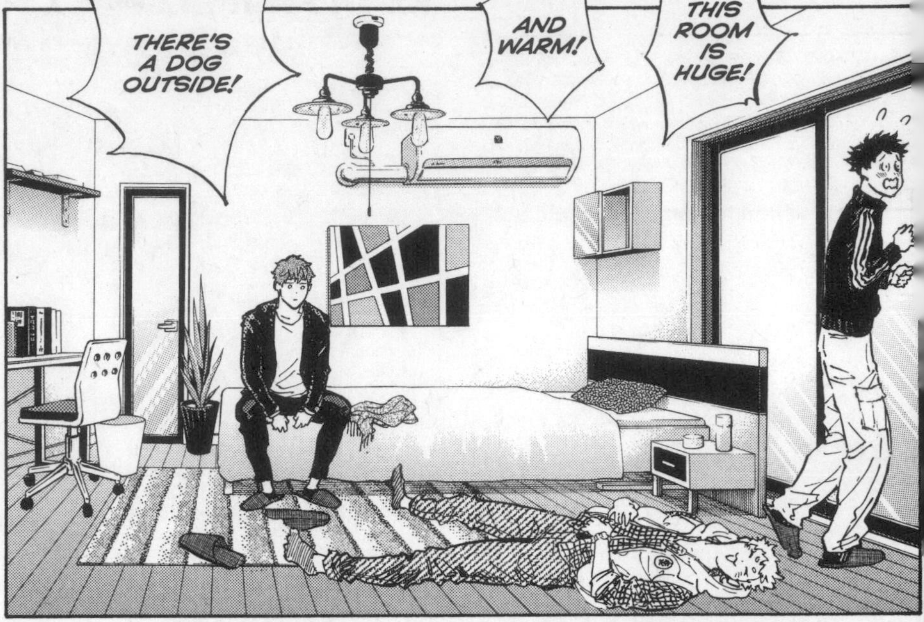
THIS ROOM IS HUGE!
AND WARM!
THERE'S A DOG OUTSIDE!

Visit to Kiyoharu's Room Gaju's Room

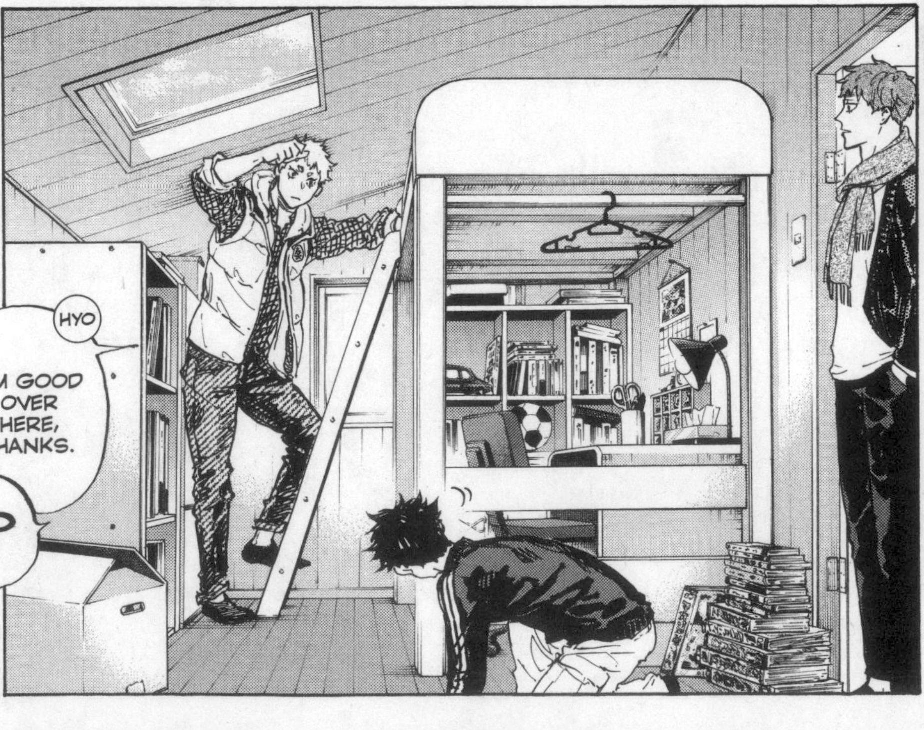
HYO
I'M GOOD OVER HERE, THANKS.
?

At the Karuizawa Camp ~Video Viewing~

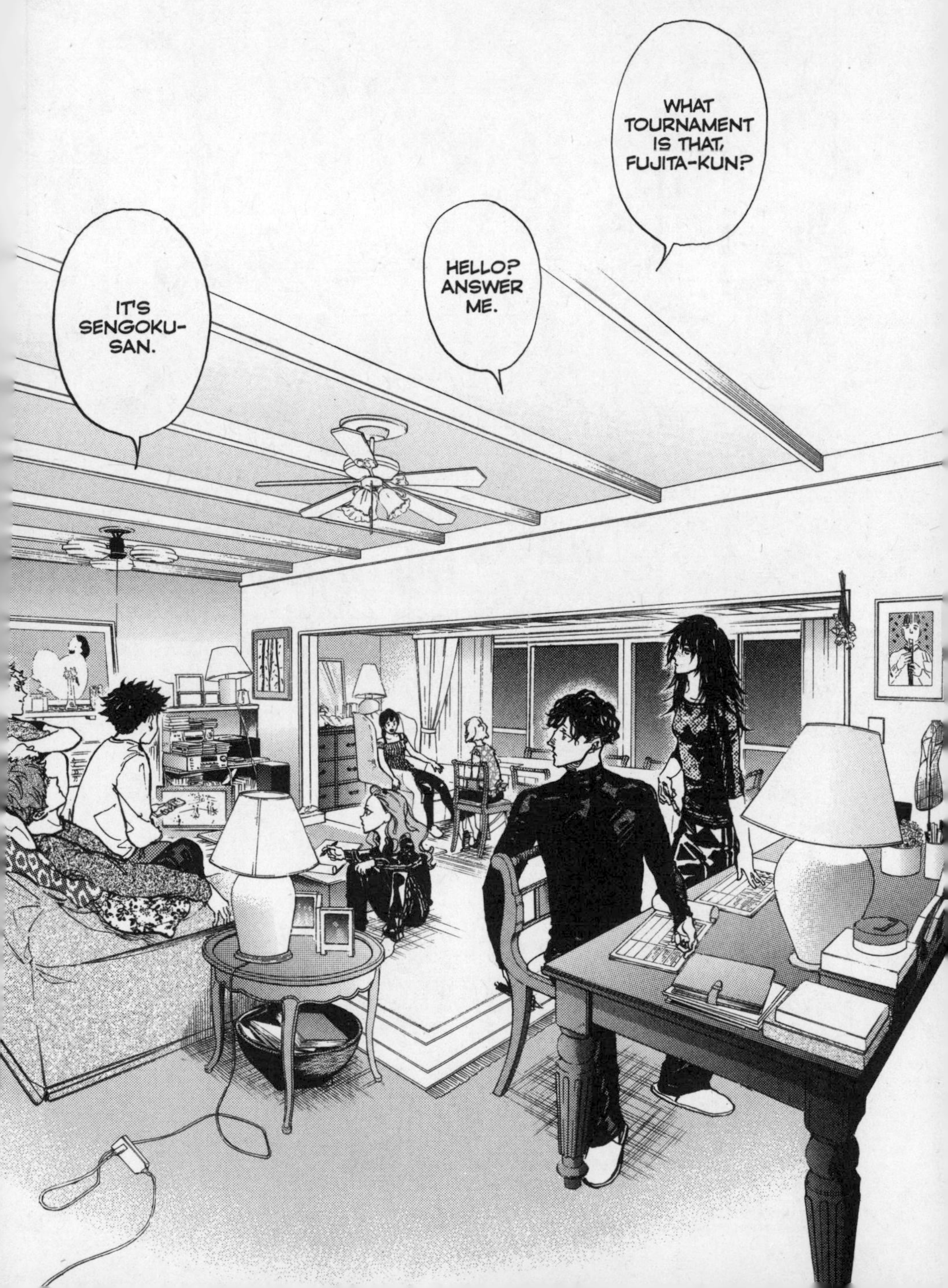
WHAT TOURNAMENT IS THAT, FUJITA-KUN?
HELLO? ANSWER ME.
IT'S SENGOKU-SAN.

ASSEMBLED

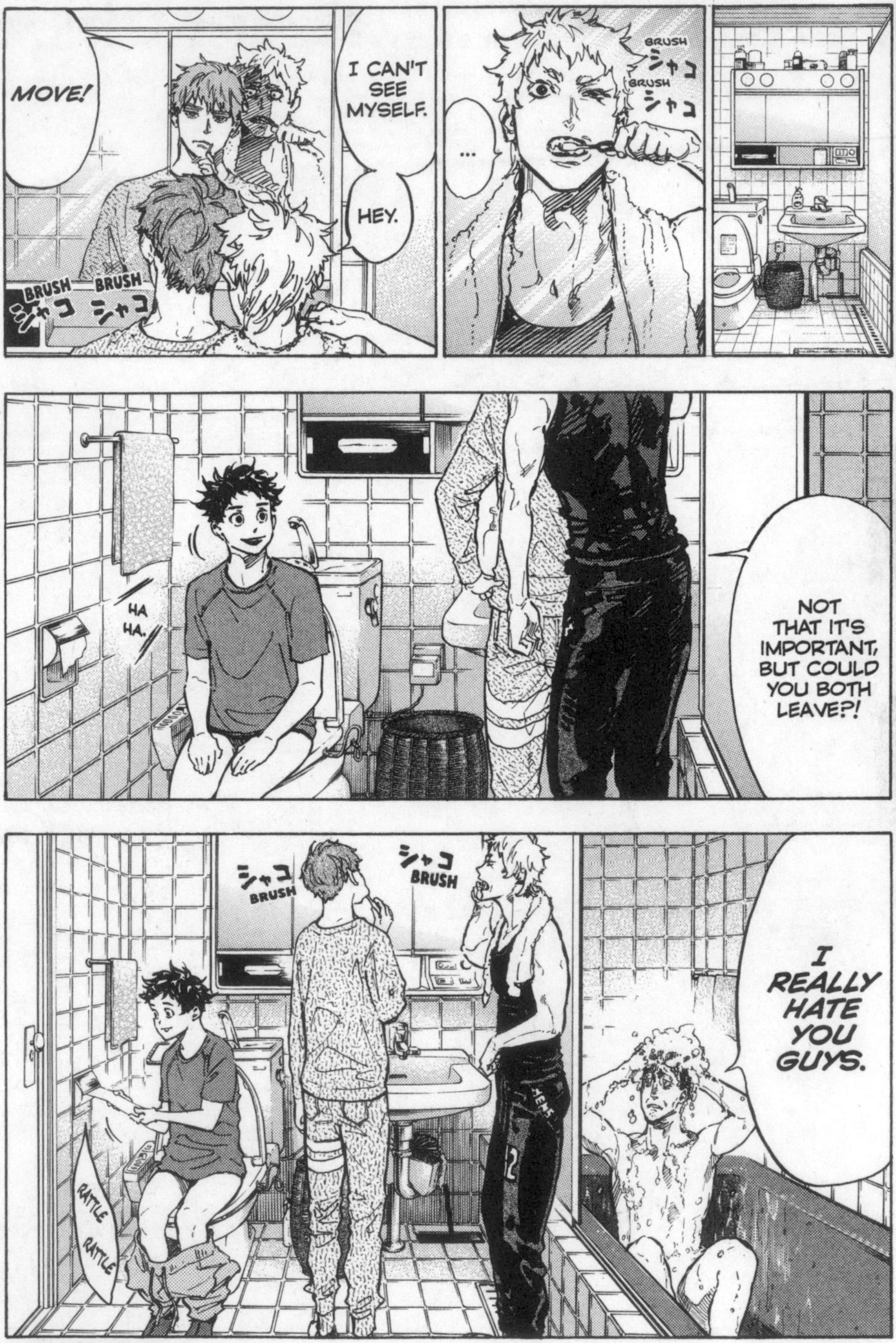
BRUSH シャコ
BRUSH シャコ
...
I CAN'T SEE MYSELF.
HEY.
MOVE!
BRUSH シャコ
BRUSH シャコ
NOT THAT IT'S IMPORTANT, BUT COULD YOU BOTH LEAVE?!
HA HA.
I REALLY HATE YOU GUYS.
シャコ BRUSH
シャコ BRUSH
RATTLE RATTLE

Extra Heat: END

Tokyo Metropolitan Tournament Level A Competition (Governor's Cup) Score Charts

Tatara and Chinatsu pulled a stunning victory in a competition with 55 total couples. Let's take look back at the score charts from Round 2 through the Finals, with some comments from each of the seven judges!

Judges

Currently, there are approximately 400 people in Japan with the credentials to act as judge. They come from a wide range of experience levels, and are assigned to competitions accordingly based on the level of the competition. (Refer to the JDSF Judge Authorization System.)

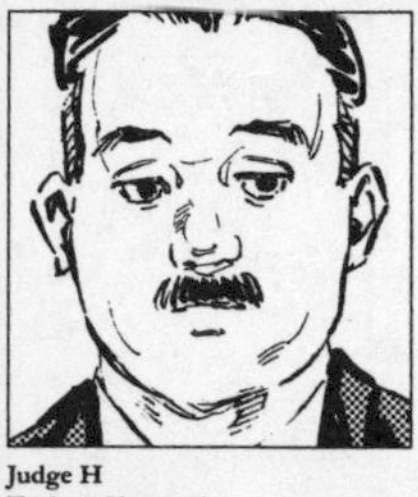

Judge H
Tsukasa Yamanobe
A former All-Japan Championship finalist. Currently runs a dance school.

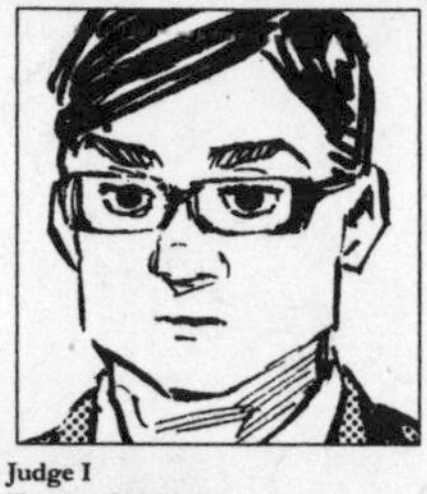

Judge I
Tetsuya Onishi
Gakuren Summer All Champion. Former semifinalist for the Mikasanomiya Cup. Works sales at a brokerage firm.

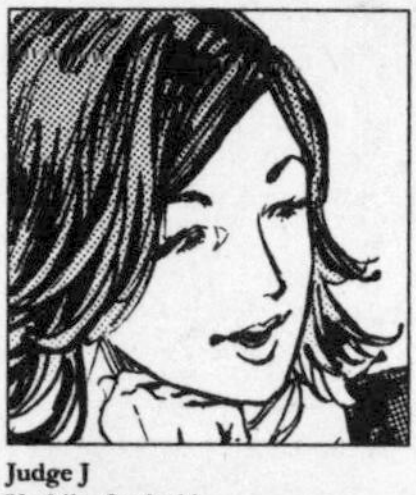

Judge J
Yoshiko Sugisaki
Former Mikasanomiya Cup finalist. Teaches at a dance studio, with a focus on group lessons.

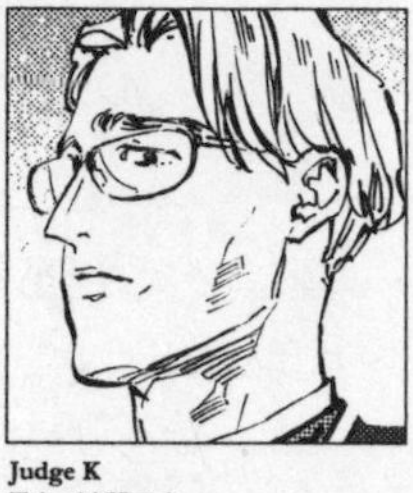

Judge K
Takashi Honda
Form JBDF Championship finalist. Practicing dentist.

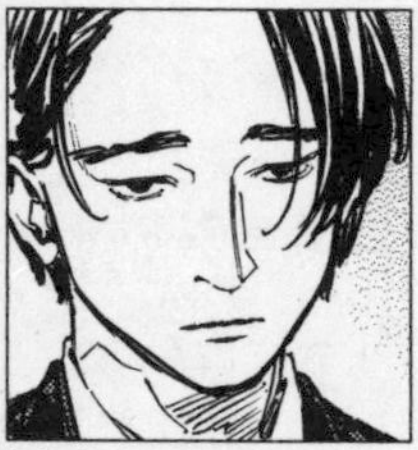

Judge L
Naoto Terashima
Former All-Japan 10-Dance champion. After retiring from competition, he works to train young athletes.

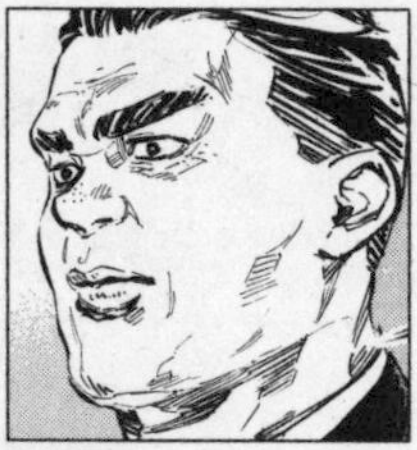

Judge M
Takeshi Ando
Former JBDF Championship finalist. Executive at an electronics manufacturer.

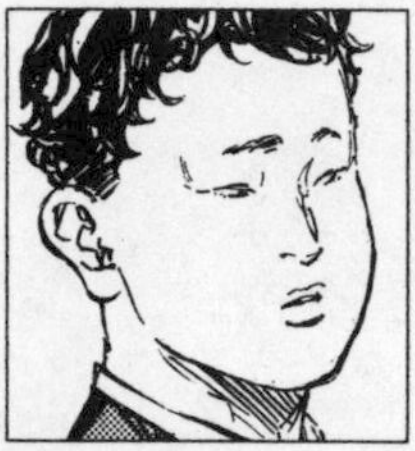

Judge N
Keiji Hayashi
Former Mikasanomiya Cup finalist. Civil servant.

< How to read the chart >

From left to right, each check represents a passing mark from each of the judges H through N.

H I J K L M N
0 0 0 - 0 0 -

Check for Tatara & Chinatsu, No.13, and Kugimiya & Idogawa, no. 42, starting in the semifinals!

《 Round 2 》

	Entry Number	Totals	Result	W	T	F	Q
1H	8	21	UP	- 0 - 0 - - -	0 0 0 0 0 0 0	0 0 0 0 0 0 0	0 0 0 - 0 0 -
	10	8	—	- - 0 - 0 0 0	- - 0 - 0 - -	- - - - 0 - -	- - - 0 - - -
	12	28	UP	0 0 0 0 0 0 0	0 0 0 0 0 0 0	0 0 0 0 0 0 0	0 0 0 0 0 0 0
	13	28	UP	0 0 0 0 0 0 0	0 0 0 0 0 0 0	0 0 0 0 0 0 0	0 0 0 0 0 0 0
	16	20	UP	- 0 0 0 0 0 0	- 0 0 0 0 - 0	- 0 0 0 0 - 0	- - 0 0 0 - 0
	20	27	UP	0 0 0 0 0 0 0	0 0 0 0 0 0 0	0 0 0 0 0 0 -	0 0 0 0 0 0 0
2H	24	14	—	0 - 0 - - - 0	0 0 - - - 0 0	0 - 0 - - 0 0	0 0 - - - 0 -
	29	4	—	- 0 - - - - -	- - - - - - -	- - - - - - 0	- - - - - 0 0
	39	28	UP	0 0 0 0 0 0 0	0 0 0 0 0 0 0	0 0 0 0 0 0 0	0 0 0 0 0 0 0
3H	45	28	UP	0 0 0 0 0 0 0	0 0 0 0 0 0 0	0 0 0 0 0 0 0	0 0 0 0 0 0 0
	48	7	—	- - - - 0 0 -	- - - - - - -	- 0 - - - 0 -	- 0 0 - - - 0
	52	4	—	0 - - - - - -	0 - - - - - -	0 - - - - - -	- - - - 0 - -

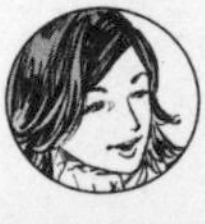

It felt like the Kugimiya pair was dominating the Standard competition today. I don't find the Fujita pair to be appealing at all. I don't like disconnected dancing.

《 Quarter Final 》

	Entry Number	Totals	Result	W	T	F	Q
1H	7	7	—	- 0 - 0 - - -	- 0 0 0 - - 0	- - 0 - - - -	- - - - - - -
	9	16	UP	- - - - 0 0 0	- 0 - 0 0 0 0	- 0 0 0 - 0 -	- - 0 0 0 0 -
	12	28	UP	0 0 0 0 0 0 0	0 0 0 0 0 0 0	0 0 0 0 0 0 0	0 0 0 0 0 0 0
	13	27	UP	0 0 0 0 0 0 0	0 0 0 0 0 0 0	0 0 0 0 0 - 0	0 0 0 0 0 0 0
	15	6	—	- 0 - - - - -	- 0 - - 0 - -	- - - - 0 0 -	- 0 - - - - -
2H	30	14	UP	0 - 0 - - 0 0	0 - - 0 - 0 -	0 - - - - 0 0	0 - 0 - - 0 0
	36	3	—	- - - - - - -	- - - - - 0 -	- - - - - 0 -	- - - 0 - - -
	39	23	UP	0 0 0 0 0 0 0	0 0 0 - - - 0	0 0 0 0 0 - 0	0 0 0 0 - 0 0
	43	7	—	0 - - - - - -	0 - - - - - -	0 - - - - - 0	0 - - - 0 - 0
	46	26	UP	0 0 0 0 0 0 0	0 0 0 - 0 0 0	0 0 - 0 0 0 0	0 0 0 0 0 0 0
	47	5	—	0 - - - - - -	0 - - - - - -	- - - - 0 - -	0 0 - - - - -
	49	14	UP	- - 0 0 0 - -	- - 0 0 0 - -	0 0 0 0 - - -	0 0 0 - 0 - -

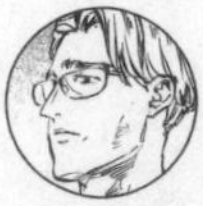

I like the elegant and artistic feel of the Kugimiya pair's dancing. I heard that their old teacher Kunieda-kun closed his dance school. I wonder how he's doing...

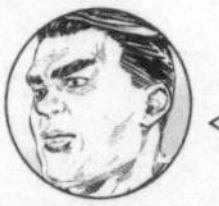

Hmm, I'm seeing more and more sports-like elements in competitive dance (it's too different from how it was in my day; honestly I can't keep up).

《 Semifinals 》

	Entry Number	Totals	Result	W	T	V	F	Q
1H	9	13	—	- - - 0 - - 0	0 - - 0 0 - -	- - - - - 0 0	- - - 0 0 0 -	- - - 0 0 0 -
	12	29	UP	0 0 - 0 0 0 0	0 0 0 0 0 0 0	- 0 0 0 0 - 0	- 0 - 0 0 0 0	- 0 0 0 0 0 0
	13	27	UP	- 0 - - - - 0	0 0 0 0 0 - 0	0 0 0 0 0 - 0	0 0 0 0 0 - 0	0 0 0 0 0 0 0
	26	4	—	- - - - - - -	- - - - - - -	- - - - - 0 -	- - - 0 - - 0	- - - 0 - - -
	30	8	—	0 - 0 - - 0 -	- - - - - 0 0	- - - - - - -	0 - 0 - - - 0	- - - - - - -
	32	21	UP	0 0 0 - 0 - 0	- 0 0 - - - 0	- 0 0 - 0 0 0	0 0 0 - 0 0 0	- - 0 - - - 0
	39	26	UP	0 0 0 0 0 0 0	0 0 0 - - 0 0	0 0 - 0 0 0 0	0 0 0 - - 0 -	0 0 0 - - 0 -
	41	9	—	- - 0 0 - - -	- - - - 0 - -	0 - 0 0 - - -	- - - - - - -	0 - - - 0 - 0
	42	35	UP	0 0 0 0 0 0 0	0 0 0 0 0 0 0	0 0 0 0 0 0 0	0 0 0 0 0 0 0	0 0 0 0 0 0 0
	45	8	—	- - - - 0 0 -	- - - - - 0 -	0 - - - - - -	- 0 0 - - - -	0 0 - - - - -
	46	28	UP	0 0 0 0 0 0 -	0 0 0 0 0 0 -	0 0 - 0 0 0 -	0 - - 0 0 0 -	0 0 0 0 0 0 0
	49	2	—	- - - - - - -	- - - 0 - - -	- - 0 - - - -	- - - - - - -	- - - - - - -

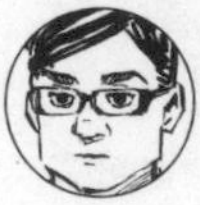

I was watching Fujita's team since Round 2! Whenever I see a shorter couple giving it their all, I can't help rooting for them...!!

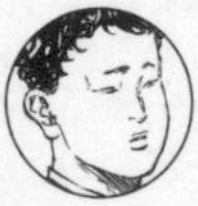

This is my first judging; I'm so nervous. Anyway, I'm sure the Kugimiya pair will win—they were well-liked before.

《 Finals 》

In the finals, the judges rank the six remaining couples from best to worst. Tatara and Chinatsu had the lowest total score, and three first-place checks, so they won.

No.	W								T							
	H	I	J	K	L	M	N	順	H	I	J	K	L	M	N	順
12	4	4	3	4	4	4	2	4	3	2	4	3	2	4	3	3
13	3	2	4	3	2	3	4	3	1	1	2	2	1	2	1	1
32	6	6	6	6	6	6	5	6	6	6	5	6	6	6	5	6
39	5	5	5	5	5	5	6	5	5	5	6	5	5	5	6	5
42	1	1	1	1	1	1	1	1	2	3	1	1	3	1	2	2
46	2	3	2	2	3	2	3	2	4	4	3	4	4	3	4	4

No.	V								F								Q							
	H	I	J	K	L	M	N	順	H	I	J	K	L	M	N	順	H	I	J	K	L	M	N	順
12	4	2	3	3	2	5	3	3	5	4	4	3	3	3	3	3	5	3	4	4	4	5	3	4
13	1	1	2	2	1	1	1	1	2	1	2	2	2	2	2	2	1	1	2	1	1	2	2	1
32	6	6	4	6	6	6	5	6	3	3	3	5	4	4	4	4	6	6	5	6	6	6	5	6
39	3	4	5	4	4	3	4	4	4	5	5	6	6	6	5	5	4	5	6	5	5	4	6	5
42	2	3	1	1	3	2	2	2	1	2	1	1	1	1	1	1	2	2	1	2	2	1	1	2
46	5	5	6	5	5	4	6	5	6	6	6	4	5	5	6	6	3	4	3	3	3	3	4	3

No.	W	T	V	F	Q	Result	Totals	Verdict
12	4	3	3	3	4	3	17.0	
13	3	1	1	2	1	1	8.0	Majority
32	6	6	6	4	6	6	28.0	
39	5	5	4	5	5	5	24.0	
42	1	2	2	1	2	2	8.0	Majority
46	2	4	5	6	3	4	20.0	

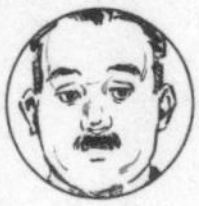

I generally judge on instinct. That does mean it's based on my tastes, but I like to think I have a good eye for talent.

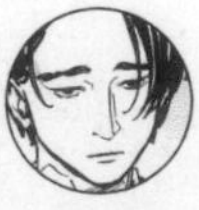

Number 13. They transformed since the semifinals. In the finals, I think Kugimiya's pair was best at WF, but Fujita's pair excelled in TQ.

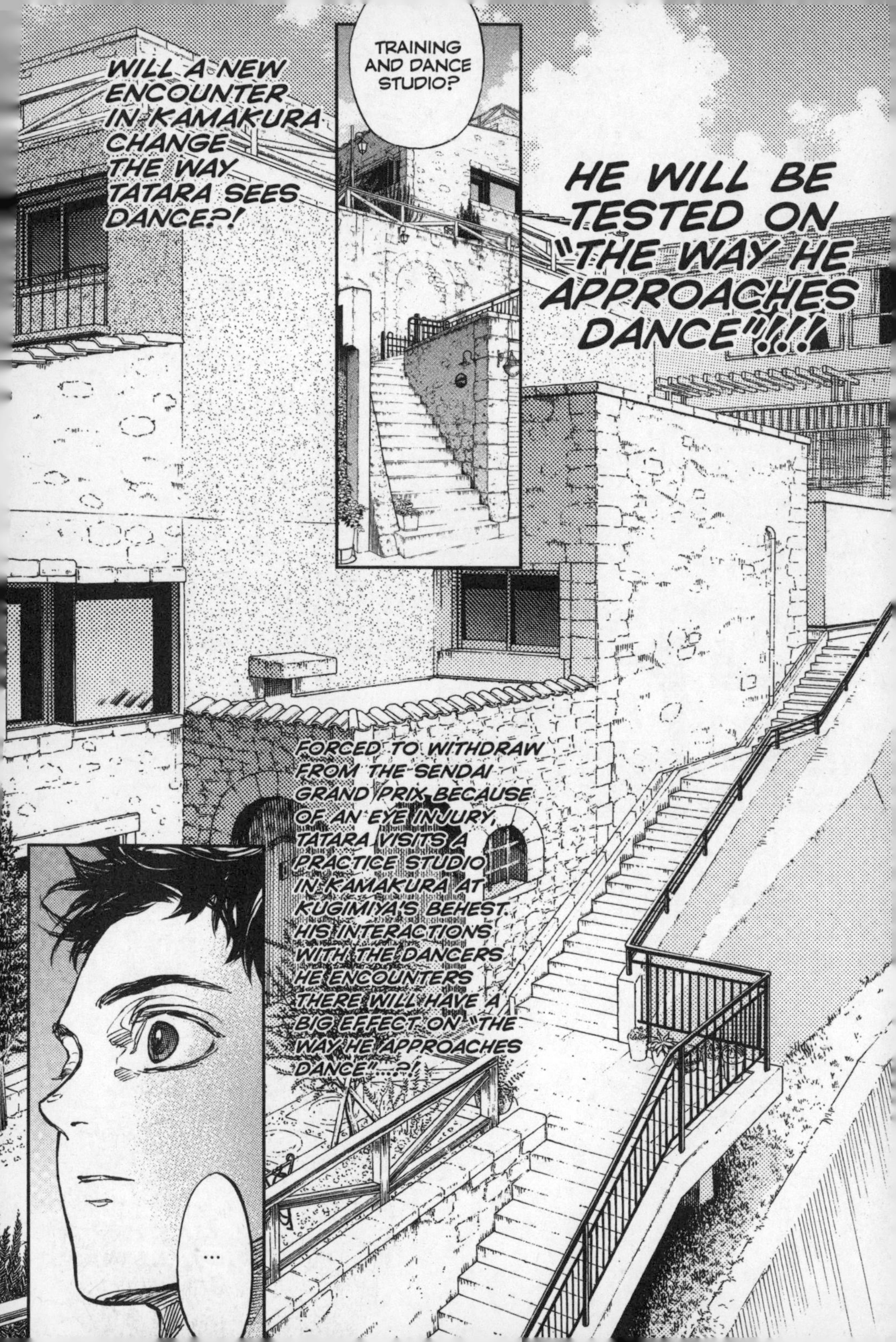
HE WILL BE TESTED ON "THE WAY HE APPROACHES DANCE"!!!
TRAINING AND DANCE STUDIO?
WILL A NEW ENCOUNTER IN KAMAKURA CHANGE THE WAY TATARA SEES DANCE?!
FORCED TO WITHDRAW FROM THE SENDAI GRAND PRIX BECAUSE OF AN EYE INJURY, TATARA VISITS A PRACTICE STUDIO IN KAMAKURA AT KUGIMIYA'S BEHEST. HIS INTERACTIONS WITH THE DANCERS HE ENCOUNTERS THERE WILL HAVE A BIG EFFECT ON "THE WAY HE APPROACHES DANCE"...?!
...

WELCOME TO THE BALLROOM

TOMO
TAKEUCHI

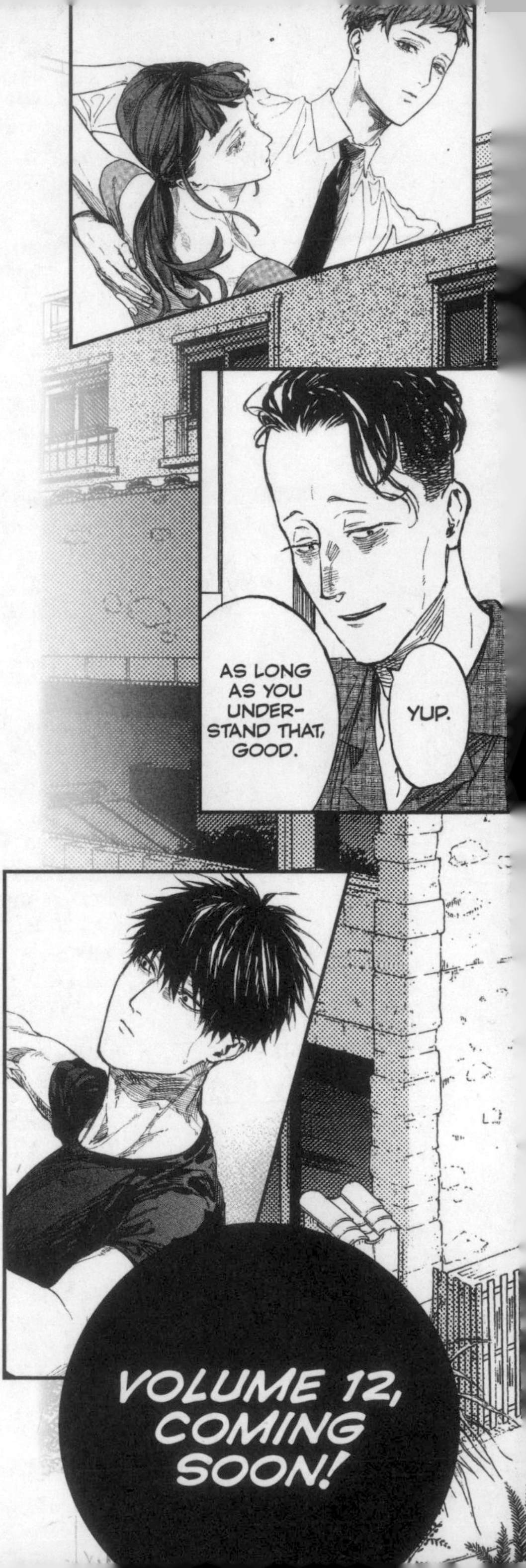
YUP.
AS LONG AS YOU UNDER-STAND THAT, GOOD.
VOLUME 12, COMING SOON!

A Kodansha Comics Trade Paperback Original
Welcome to the Ballroom 11 copyright © 2021 Tomo Takeuchi
English translation copyright © 2022 Tomo Takeuchi

All rights reserved.

Published in the United States by Kodansha Comics, an imprint of Kodansha USA Publishing, LLC, New York.

Publication rights for this English edition arranged through Kodansha Ltd., Tokyo.

First published in Japan in 2021 by Kodansha Ltd., Tokyo as *Booruruumu e Youkoso*, volume 11.

ISBN 978-1-63236-582-8

Printed in the United States of America.

www.kodansha.us

9 8 7 6 5 4 3 2 1
Translation: Alethea Nibley & Athena Nibley
Lettering: Brndn Blakeslee
Editing: David Yoo
Kodansha Comics edition cover design by My Truong
Kodansha Comics edition logo deisgn by Phil Balsman

Publisher: Kiichiro Sugawara

Director of publishing services: Ben Applegate
Director of publishing operations: Dave Barrett
Associate director of publishing operations: Stephen Pakula
Publishing services managing editors: Madison Salters, Alanna Ruse, with Grace Chen
Production manager: Jocelyn O'Dowd